Making

Democracy

Work

Better

Richard A. Couto

with Catherine S. Guthrie

Making Democracy Work Better

Mediating Structures, Social Capital, and the Democratic Prospect

The University of North Carolina Press

© 1999 The University of North Carolina Press
All rights reserved
This book was set in Aldus by G & S Typesetters, Inc.

Library of Congress Cataloging-in-Publication Data
Couto, Richard A., 1941–
Making democracy work better : mediating structures,
social capital, and the democratic prospect / by Richard A.
Couto with Catherine S. Guthrie.
p.   cm.   Includes bibliographical references and index.
ISBN 978-0-8078-2488-7 (cloth).
ISBN 978-0-8078-4824-1 (pbk.)
1. Social participation—United States.   2. Democracy—
United States.   I. Guthrie, Catherine S.   II. Title.
HN59.2.C68 1999   302'.14—dc21   98-53439 CIP

They say in Harlan County,
There are no neutrals there.
You'll either be a union man
Or a thug for J. H. Blair.

Which side are you on?
Which side are you on?
—Florence Reece,
  "Which Side Are You On?"

CONTENTS

Preface xiii

Acknowledgments xvii

Introduction 1

PART I Social Capital and Democratic Theory 7

CHAPTER 1 Social Capital and Appalachia 9

CHAPTER 2 Mediating Structures and the Democratic
  Prospect 37

PART II The Democratic Prospect of Mediating Structures 71

CHAPTER 3 Social Dimensions 75

CHAPTER 4 Political Dimensions 113

CHAPTER 5 Economic Dimensions I: Mitigating the Market 147

CHAPTER 6 Economic Dimensions II: Providing Social Capital 173

PART III Mediating Structures and Social Capital 205

CHAPTER 7 Creating and Maintaining Community 207

CHAPTER 8 Management Matters 239

CHAPTER 9 Community Change 271

Conclusion 295

APPENDIX A Community-based Mediating Structures by Area
of Focus 303
APPENDIX B Methodology 307
References 313
Index 323

MAPS
AND TABLES

Maps   1. The Spatial Distribution of Appalachian
           Poverty, 1990 13
        2. Changes in Poverty in Appalachia, 1980–1990 14
        3. Labor Force Participation in Appalachia, 1990 26
        4. Percentage of Appalachian Working-Age Population
           with a Work Disability, 1990 158
        5. Substandard Housing in Appalachia, 1990 166
        6. Children in Poverty in Appalachia, 1990 179

Tables 1. Changes in Percentage Share of Aggregate
           American Family Income, by Income Groups,
           1980–1995 20
        2. Social Capital Measures of Population 28
        3. Social Capital Measures of Income 29
        4. Social Capital Measures of Family 30
        5. Social Capital Measures of Education 31
        6. Social Capital Measures of Housing 32
        7. Social Capital Measures of Health 33
        8. Percentage of Children in Poverty in
           Appalachia, 1970–1990 178

ILLUSTRATIONS

pages 131–34   Opening celebration of This and That Laundromat,
                        Dungannon, Virginia
                Nancy Robinson, Barbara Green, and Kitty Cole,
                        Dungannon, Virginia
                Virginia Madge Lilly, Brumley Gap, Virginia
                View of Brumley Gap
                Greg Morrell and Jeannette Seitz of the Appalachian
                        Independence Center
                Linda Walls, Gail Story Sams, and Roxy Wilson of
                        Bumpass Cove Citizens Group
                Members of the Appalachian Peoples Action Coalition
                        (APAC)
                APAC member explains a community analysis
                APAC monthly potluck supper
                Roadside Theater improvises at the Appalachian
                        Identity Center, Cincinnati, Ohio
pages 182–86   Marilyn Carroll, Calvin Dunford, and Sister Carolyn
                        Brink of the Virginia Black Lung Association,
                        Richlands, Virginia
                House built by a member group of the Federation of
                        Appalachian Housing Enterprises (FAHE)
                Directors of the member groups of FAHE

The West Virginia Education Association makes its
case for higher teacher salaries

West Virginia Education Association celebrates the pay
increase it won

Adrinka cloth produced in workshop hosted by
Appalachian Communities for Children (ACC)

Participants in ACC's Community in the Classroom
workshop

When I began this work in 1992, *social capital* was an uncommon term. Briefly, I even thought I had invented the concept. In 1986, I heard a presentation at the annual meeting of Llafur, the Welsh labor history association, about the initiation of services for victims of domestic violence in Swansea, Wales. The speaker explained how recent economic decline and cutbacks at the large steel plant had increased unemployment, had strained family resources, and had expressed themselves in increases in the incidence and severity of violence toward women and children within families. These women and children had nowhere to go—domestic violence was not on the agenda of public or social services. She recounted finding an unused parsonage to shelter women and children. After securing this space, she and her colleagues found beds, furniture, and volunteers to repair and paint the shelter. They found other volunteers to staff the shelter and provide counseling and referrals to the women and children who found refuge there.

Somewhere in the middle of this account, the speaker observed, "We didn't go about this in a very businesslike way." I used the question-and-answer period to challenge her assertion. I suggested that contrary to her assessment, she and her colleagues had been very businesslike. She had found a market in which a new demand for services had an inadequate supply of providers. She had accumulated resources to meet that demand and instituted services. Only its lack of profit distinguished her effort from "business." The domestic violence shelter had little chance to make a profit and to provide a financial reward to those who instituted it. The efforts to risk the time and effort to recruit resources and invest them in people without money to pay for the shelter's services was what distinguished the shelter from "business."

The distinction was particularly sharp at the time. It was the 1980s, the "Greed is good" era, the time when we celebrated the risk capitalists of profit and justified a growing inequality of wealth in terms of the virtues of risk and entrepreneurship. In the case of the domestic violence shelter, however, the virtues of risk and entrepreneurship did not have individual financial reward. That was un-"businesslike," but the rest of her effort suggested, in general terms, the entrepreneurship and risk capital so celebrated at the time on both sides of the Atlantic Ocean.

As I searched for a term to distinguish her work from other forms of capital enterprise, I came up with social capital. It seemed to me that her work expressed a willingness to invest resources in people that others had not, the willingness to value people despite their decreased value in a declining labor force. That conceptualization brought together huge fragments of work that I had underway. I had just concluded, I thought, a study on the creation and conduct of community health centers in African American communities of the rural South and their ties with the local civil rights movement (Couto 1991). I was working with a set of community organizations in the Appalachian region that regularly did the kind of social capital entrepreneurship that I heard described in the Llafur conference.

As part of my work on the rural health clinics and after the idea of social capital occurred to me, I searched for others' use of the term social capital. I was already familiar with James O'Connor's use of the term (1973) and recognized it as the origin of my own thinking. I learned that James Coleman also used the term. His work, up until that time, 1990, was limited to family influence on high school success (Coleman 1988). Though narrow, this focus helped distinguish social capital from the far more popular term *human capital*. Human capital refers to the investment in and of people in terms of the economy and their role in the labor force. Social capital incorporated this but also more. It referred to the resources that we invest to reproduce people as members of a community with value apart from their economic role and place in the labor force.

By 1996, social capital had become a much more familiar term than it had been just a few years previously. James Coleman had thought and written more about it. Robert Putnam had produced *Making Democracy Work*, a book that placed social capital at the center of successful civil society and at the center of scholarly and policy discussions about it. Their works drew upon a rich literature that provided a history and deeper theory of social capital. I am obviously indebted to their scholarship and that of others. The title of this book builds directly upon Putnam's work (1993).

Nonetheless, I am glad I came to a conceptualization of social capital earlier and separate from this work. I owe my view of social capital to what Clifford Geertz (1983) calls the "local knowledge" of people who provide social capital rather than the social scientists who study it. Thanks to my unique sources, I depart from the current scholarship on social capital. I present social capital as the moral resources and public goods that we invest to produce and reproduce ourselves in community. My sources of local knowledge taught me that public programs were part of the cause of poverty in places like Central Appalachia and were responsible for the poor provision and lack of social capital. These insights lead me to dig further into the concept of social capital. The deeper I went the firmer a foundation I found on which to ground an analysis of community-based organizations as agents of the democratic prospect of increased communal bonds and social and economic equality. Thus, although this work will be read within the framework that Putnam's work has created, it is distinct because of its origins.

Likewise, *Making Democracy Work Better* is distinct in its intended audience. Naturally, I expect social scientists and policy analysts and their students to read and use this work. I am also interested in reaching decision makers in philanthropic foundations and government policy makers to help them understand that their resources provide important streams of social capital. I write also for the people, such as those described in this book, who get up every day and work intentionally and deliberately, despite obstacles and the frustration of slow progress, to make democracy work better. Finally, I write for the young people, of age and heart, who would aspire to be like them in their pursuit of the democratic prospect of decreased disparity and increased communal bonds.

The rapid dissemination of the concept of social capital represents something of a social phenomenon. In less than a decade, it was transformed from an arcane, academic term to a phrase in common usage, a reference in a presidential State of the Union address, and a social science paradigm— the 1998 annual meeting of the American Political Science Association had scores of papers testing a range of hypotheses about social capital and civic society in different parts of the world and different organizational settings. This book is not part of that phenomenon. Its purpose is to bring us back to the local knowledge of people in the civic associations that provide democratic societies the social capital they require, not separate and apart from public policy but more often than not as an agent of current policy or a purveyor of needed policies.

ACKNOWLEDGMENTS

Putting the pieces of a manuscript together, however complex, is always simpler than figuring out the puzzle of who helped me. I mean those who helped in a fundamental way, the people who planted ideas in my mind, challenged me, and somehow provided me—the son of loving, working-class parents who themselves had little formal education (a sixth-grade education and a night school diploma)—with the ambition to write a book.

I thought a lot of Brother Michael Kiernan, F.M.S., who taught me English in high school. Those who helped me in countless revisions of this text will testify that I still cannot do justice to the grammar that he tried to teach me. But I think of him still, every day, carrying his books in a pile under his arm, resting on a narrow ledge that he made with his hip. He set those books down on the teacher's desk in the front of the room and in the next forty-five minutes, each and every class, day after day, he evoked and demanded the attentive collaboration of myself and my classmates in developing a level of potential that he insisted we had but that we protested. He tempered his determination to challenge us to realize our own importance with a gentleness and humor that I have found in exactly the same combination in no human being since. He checked our increased sense of competence with his own firm belief, which he exemplified, that the ability to laugh at ourselves made the serious business of life manageable and success at it possible. To all my teachers I am grateful, and to them I dedicate this book.

I am also grateful for those who bring the spirit of the muse into my life and encourage me to try to tell stories well, creatively, and attentively. The examples of Charlie King and Guy and Candy Carawan come to mind. Obviously, I found inspiration in the words of Florence Reece, words I think will prove to be as immemorial as any human expression can be. Tom Paxton and John Prine were my frequent musical companions when the tasks of research and writing became tedious. At perilous moments of agonizing over hairsplitting accuracy in anticipation of careful and critical academic readers, Prine's lyrics reminded me, as "Mike" Kiernan had, to keep in mind that in some ways it always remains "a big old goofy world."

There are more proximate contributions to my work on this book that are much easier to identify. Most of all, I am grateful to Cathy Guthrie and all the staff and board members of the organizations that she and I pestered. I have made clear that the democratic prospect requires sweat equity, and Cathy provided it. She brought an unusual combination of intelligence, talent, idealism, common sense, and energy to the tasks of researching and traveling to more than two dozen organizations in Central Appalachia. My gratitude extends to notice of her name on the title page for the entire world to see the debt that I owe her. Thanks also to Julia Scatliff for bringing Cathy to my attention.

Successful management also requires opportunity costs, as I also explain. The participation of the many people who run the organizations on which this book reports gave generously of time that they could have used for other matters. I hope this description and analysis of their work provides some compensation for the costs they incurred in helping us. I hope also that it provides them the satisfaction of knowing that at least one person understands the importance of their work to the region, the nation, and to democracy at every time and in every place. Obviously, there would be nothing to report without their extraordinary hard work and dedication. I am grateful for their willingness to share time and information with us and, of course, for the inspiration of their personal and programmatic efforts. Dick Austin provided thoughtful criticism and additional information on Brumley Gap and Dungannon. I hope this book brings funders and others to their "side" of making democracy work better. I want to thank also Helen Lewis, Jim Sessions, and Tena Willemsma for helping us select which community groups to include in the study.

Next, I am grateful to the funders. The Aspen Nonprofit Sector Research Fund provided generous financial support. The Fund also brought me into a network of scholars and practitioners that renewed old acquaintances and made new ones for me. I am grateful for the opportunity to participate in the 1994 conference on the Eastern Shore and the encouragement to join professional associations such as Independent Sector and the International Society for Third Sector Research. In addition, Elizabeth Boris and Alan Abrams provided me with time. The grant period expired without the book product, only progress. They patiently waited as paper after paper dribbled forth long after one promised deadline after another expired. They were quite extraordinary in the patience and understanding that they showed me and the confidence that they showed in this work. My colleagues also provided significant endorsement and financial support through the research committees of the University of Richmond and the Jepson School of Leadership Studies. Although the Commission on Religion in Appalachia (CORA) did not fund this work, they provided support to each of the community groups we studied and administered the grant funds. Gaye Evans and Linda Selfridge helped with documents and records of each of the groups. In this task, as in so many others in the past, CORA has been a wonderful organization with which to work.

Finally, there are the numerous people who helped along the way in one small part or another. Students in my course "Leadership in Community Organizations" provided me evaluative feedback on earlier versions of this book. I continued with the work, nonetheless. Kathryn J. Brownlee, Darden H. Copeland, and Ben E. Wallerstein provided fresh eyes for proofreading and suggestions for revisions. Charlotte Chandler, Teresa Hudson, Judy Mable, and Caroline Mabry typed numerous drafts, found missing files, followed the circuitous paths of barely decipherable revisions, and dealt with my frustrations and their own with patience and good humor. Amy Keown provided the prompt, accurate help of a model research assistant, which she is. Joe Szakos read the manuscript in draft form and made important comments. Likewise, I presented several portions of the book as papers at professional conferences, and I am grateful for the comments that I received from readers, discussants, and panelists on this work in progress. Dwight Billings and James Morone gave the manuscript a careful reading and provided me with comments that improved the book greatly. Lewis Bateman set the bar of expectation for this work high, and Kathy Malin, another editor at the University of North Carolina Press, did her best to get me and this book over that bar. As always, my wife Took provided me with space, time, and the right combination of criticism and encouragement.

I am happy to share the strengths and successful elements of this book with all of the above and the many others who helped me. Nothing gives me more pleasure in writing a book than to say thank you to the people who helped me and to entertain the possibility that I may have served them in their efforts in a manner befitting their wonderful generosity. Nothing gives me more dread than the realization that, despite my very best efforts, there may be errors of commission and omission. If any errors remain, I regret them and wish the reader to hold the message innocent of the mistakes of the messenger.

Making

Democracy

Work

Better

Some people, ordinary people like Florence Reece, step forward to make democracy work better for the rest of us. Their efforts require hard work and creativity, as these pages attest. Sometimes their efforts bring dangerous reprisals. One evening, for example, armed men ransacked Florence Reece's home looking for her husband. After their unsuccessful search, they stepped into the dark night to wait in ambush with hope of killing her husband when he returned home. Sam Reece organized coal miners into a labor union, the United Mine Workers of America. This organizing effort, in Harlan County, Kentucky, in the 1930s, added violent reprisal to the dangers that poverty and coal mining already placed on Reece, her husband, and their seven children. Fortunately, her husband did not come home, and no further harm came to him and his family that night. Days later, Reece transformed her fears from that frightening night into the lyrics of a song, *Which Side Are You On?* This book is about other groups and people who, like the Reeces, extend the democratic prospect of increased communal bonds and decreased gaps between wealth and want in our society.

Reece's lyrics described a two-part society: the company and the miners, the affluent and the working people. J. H. Blair was the Harlan County sheriff. He and a set of "deputies," provided from the security forces of the coal companies, enforced the wishes of the companies as law. These were the armed men who terrorized Reece. The question "Which side are you on?" gave miners and their families a stark choice: side with the union or side with the company and sheriff; take collective action for improvement or resign yourselves to intolerable conditions and the repressive actions of company and local authorities that enforce them.

The words of this ordinary woman in a seldom noticed part of the world have touched the hearts and minds of millions of people. They have traveled around the world to provide determination in the face of fear and inspiration at times of doubt to those fighting for social change and social justice in this and other nations. More than a half century later, Reece remained convinced that people have to take sides: "Some people say, 'I don't take sides— I'm neutral.' There's no such thing. In your own mind you're one side or the other. In Harlan County there wasn't no neutral. If you wasn't a gun thug, you was a union man. You *had* to be" (Carawan and Carawan 1982: 119).

Reece's lyrics and this book reach deep into the notion of standing up against social and economic injustice. Harlan County in the 1930s measured some of what was wrong with America, including obstacles to the democratic prospect of improved social and economic equality. The democratic promise of financial reward and security for hard work seemed preeminently applicable to coal miners. Who could work harder and in more difficult and dangerous conditions than they did? Yet the promise of economic sufficiency and security, never mind prosperity, by and large eluded them.

Reece's song lamented the shortcomings of market capitalism. It made clear that some forms of capitalism are savage, placing workers in dangerous conditions and paying them as little as possible, wages even below subsistence for a family. Enshrined in law, these savage forms of capital repressed resistance to them. Reece portrayed the United Mine Workers as a vessel of hope, hope for social improvement through collective action to end a debilitating combination of state and economic power. That hope remains alive in the lyrics of Reece's song, in the voices that sing them, and in the organized actions of people in new vessels of collective action, like those that this book presents.

Americans often make the relationship of democracy and organized action axiomatic. Hope becomes hubris, however, when taken for granted. So this book makes their relationship a problem. It portrays the need for community-based organizations in terms of the social and economic inequality in American life. It describes community-based organizations as mediating structures. It uses Central Appalachia as the context of social and economic inequality. It depicts the specific political, social, and economic functions of community-based mediating structures and enumerates the conditions necessary for their success. Readers can find new but tempered hope in "how" as well as "when" and "why" organized action promotes the democratic prospect of increased social and political equality.

The book's three parts examine the relationship of democracy and organized action through different lenses. Part I explains the theoretical relationship of community-based mediating structures and democracy. Chapter 1 explains Appalachian poverty as the consequence of public policies that tie education, health care, housing, and other forms of human welfare to labor force participation. Chapter 2 examines democratic theories about the social, political, and economic roles of mediating structures in redressing social and economic inequality. Part II illustrates the social, political, and economic roles of community-based mediating structures in achieving the democratic prospect. It conveys specific elements of the experience of twenty-three community-based mediating structures in Central Appalachia and adjoining areas. The wellspring and practices of successful community-based mediating structures are the materials of Part III, which examines the questions: what are the characteristics of successful community-based mediating structures and how do effective community-based mediating structures illustrate them?

There are still sides to take since Reece wrote her song. The sides may not be as stark as Reece's song depicts, but there are still sides: market capital and social capital. There is of course plenty of middle ground between these sides. It seems everyone sings the praises of mediating structures, even if we call them by different names, such as the nonprofit sector, intermediate associations, civic associations, or voluntary associations. Within this chorus of praise, however, there are two sometimes discordant parts. Some see mediating structures as alternatives to and protection from government intrusion in individual liberty. Others see mediating structures as protection from the savage side of market capitalism and as partners with government in protecting consumers, workers, and others from the market's excesses and failings. I want to restore attention to this latter side, which is an older and richer tradition of thought about community and capital. What side you start from to approach the middle makes considerable difference in where you arrive and why. I focus on community-based mediating structures because of their clear capacity to address and redress the excesses of market economics. I focus on Appalachia because of the obvious failure of market capitalism there.

It may seem strange to some readers to suggest that market capitalism has excesses and shortcomings. The 1980s heralded a decade of triumph for market capitalism. The world of the 1990s seemed to celebrate it, embrace it, and reject alternative economic systems. The Reagan and Thatcher administrations certainly extolled the market. They took radical measures to restrict government and to place it squarely in the service of capital. Rejecting recent democratic practice, they pursued an ideological version of the democratic promise of limited government and individual liberty: market democracy. In the 1990s, local, state, and federal officials, Democrats and Republicans alike, sought to reinvent government into the image and likeness of private enterprise, the market. Conservative Republicans in America went even further. They sought to restore the government-market relationship of the early 1930s, indeed even of the late nineteenth century, the grand era of savage capitalism. Strangely then, Americans seriously discussed moving forward by returning to the past; entering the twenty-first century by restoring the debilitatingly undemocratic political and economic relations that inspired Reece's lyrics.

This book is short on the critique of capitalism, which is in sufficient supply, and longer on what to do about its shortcomings. It explains that community-based mediating structures adapt capitalism to serve families, communities, and their broad social purposes. They do this by increasing the amounts of and improving the forms of social capital—public goods and moral resources by which we produce and reproduce ourselves in community. Taken together, this book's "side" maintains that mediating structures make democracy work better when they promote the democratic prospect. They do so when they provide and advocate for the public provision of new forms and increased amounts of social capital, which increase social and economic equality and communal bonds.

This "side" differs from the social science of the 1990s. Beginning in the late 1970s, conservative policy analysts promoted the public policy role of mediating structures. The social science of mediating structures helped policy makers to justify dismantling social welfare policies and programs in the 1990s. Conservative policy makers who diminished the forms and amounts of publicly provided social capital celebrated mediating structures for their capacity to fill in for government programs. In particular, Robert Putnam's work on social capital and civic organizations, *Making Democracy Work* (1993), seemed to lift from the shoulders of government the responsibility to do anything about poverty or the excesses of capital. Unequal conditions, Putnam explained, flowed from the characteristics of prosperous and poor regions, that is, *from* their social capital. In his study of the Italian democracy, he found that the prosperous regions had abundant civic organizations, with histories dating back centuries, and the poor regions had a paucity of civic organizations. Without civic organizations, the poor lacked social capital, which in turn undermined political and economic activity. Government policies, he argued, are better directed at encouraging local self-help efforts than at redistributing social and economic resources more equally.

This book does not rebut Putnam's work on democracy, civic associations, and social capital so much as it seeks to move beyond it. There is not an automatic link among mediating structures (civic associations, in Putnam's terms) and social capital and democracy. Mediating structures are a necessary but not sufficient condition for some kinds of democratic values and practices. Civic associations, as Putnam recognizes, may also deter some forms of democracy. The task of this book is to better explain when and how mediating structures make democracy work better.

For those most interested in the relationship of this book to Putnam's work, here is a an outline of comparative features. Part I begins by setting the stage and introducing the characters. Chapter 1 describes Central Appalachia, a region of chronic poverty, in terms of its social capital and offers an analysis of the public forms of social capital, which are limited primarily to investments to create a labor force. Chapter 2 explains the relationship of civic associations (community-based mediating structures, in my terms) to different forms of democracy. Part II then grounds the factors that relate civic associations to social capital and the democratic prospect in a discussion of the work and experience of more than a score of community-based mediating structures. Part III then discusses the deliberate practices required of mediating structures if they are to increase or protect social capital. No one organization exemplifies all of these practices, but taken as a whole, these examples make clearer some of the necessary and sufficient conditions for civic associations to make democracy work better.

Mediating structures and social capital will be an important part of public policy in the twenty-first century. The excesses of the 1980s and 1990s will eventually undo themselves. For the sake of the democratic prospect of the next century, it will be useful to understand the mistaken policies and conceptual notions of the recent past about mediating structures and social capital. Mediating structures do not have mystery-shrouded, centuries-old traditions. They can be explained in terms of local leadership and deliberate policies of local leaders supported by philanthropic organizations and government agencies. Social capital means more than merely the moral resources of groups and individuals. It extends to the public and social provision of economic goods and human services, such as housing, education, cultural expression, environmental quality, children's services, and other policies so unpopular in the 1990s. This book revisits the 1980s to explain the political, social, and economic challenges that social science and public policy distorted and exacerbated into market democracy in the 1990s.

Like Reece's lyrics, this book protests market democracy and delineates a more genuine democracy premised on organized action for social and economic equality. Like those lyrics, this book applies to many situations. For example, Appalachian community-based mediating structures relate directly to current efforts to democratize the politics and economics of other parts of America, Eastern Europe, Latin America, South Africa, and other parts of the world. These Appalachian structures and their counterparts around the world resist efforts to reduce labor and people to cash value and then to reach the lowest possible price for them. The context, functions, and experiences of these organizations provide a firm foundation for civil discourse about the remaining work to be done at home and abroad to achieve the democratic prospect of increased social and economic equality and of improved communal bonds.

Florence Reece gained some peace of mind and new resolve from the lyrics of her song. They expressed a determined hope to improve the conditions and opportunities of ordinary working people through their efforts to organize. This book extends the lyrics and simple message of Florence Reece's song: organized, collective efforts of ordinary people offer hope for correcting the consequences of inequality. Our times are times such as Reece described. Social and economic inequality has increased to a point that threatens the communal bonds upon which we build democratic practice. Something needs to be done about it. Fortunately, we still have within the American political tradition the means to redress social and economic inequality: the organized, collective efforts of ordinary people.

PART I

Social Capital and
Democratic Theory

American public leaders blinked in the face of the challenges of the economic changes of the 1970s. The conservative resurgence of the 1980s led a retreat to some mythical past, extolled the virtues of the market and limited government, and placed new emphasis on personal and private paths to social problem solving. Republicans and Democrats alike suggested a policy role for mediating structures that dodged the challenges of new economic times. Policy makers invoked mediating structures as if the tasks of addressing social and individual needs flowed naturally from a divine endowment of voluntary associations—first revealed by the prophet Alexis de Tocqueville—and from the market—as revealed by its prophet, Adam Smith. This reverential consensus obfuscates the challenges of recent economic changes. This section clears them up.

Chapter 1 explains that the democratic prospect of increased social and political equality has been elusive since the American economy changed in the early 1970s. A quarter century of expanding economic activity and prosperity ended. The real income of most Americans began to decline. The middle income groups expected a lower standard of living and had less economic security. Differences between the very rich and the very poor increased. Fifty years after Florence Reece's lyrics were written, the entire nation began to notice the dissonance between market democracy and the democratic prospect—Wall Street and Main Street.

These changes meant new hardships for the Appalachian region in the

1980s. In addition to providing some background on the Appalachian region, Chapter 1 interprets Appalachian poverty and human needs in terms of the post-1970s economic changes and social capital policies. Specifically, American public policy provides social capital to produce and reproduce people in a labor force. In places where work has declined or diminished, we invest less social capital. Chapter 1 provides the context for the serious challenge of community-based mediating structures' work on the democratic prospect. The new economic challenges highlight the economic roles of mediating structures in mitigating market failures.

Conservative Republicans, first in the Reagan administration and then in the congressional Republican majorities after 1994, guided much of the search for answers to the challenges posed by the economic changes of the 1970s. Their policies continued the tension between individualism and community, which as James Morone (1990) explains, prevails in American political history. Morone describes that history as an unceasing effort to fashion the democratic wish from the promise of liberty and individualism and the prospect of equality and community.

Chapter 2 explains social capital and mediating structures in terms of democratic theory, including Morone's. The policy changes of the 1980s marked a triumph of the democratic promise of limited government over the democratic prospect of community. This triumph expressed the preference for the market and economics, rather than government and politics, to solve social problems. Eventually, in the 1990s, this conservative reaction reached back to the 1930s to undo programs of the New Deal. Changes in social policies—reductions in the forms and amounts of social capital—followed the changes in the American economy in the 1970s. Advocates of market democracy exaggerated the capacity of mediating structures to solve increasingly difficult social problems with fewer public resources. Market democrats invoked mediating structures to mitigate the adverse consequences of the growth of government and organizational bureaucracy. However, they ignored the other role of mediating structures: to mitigate the adverse consequences of market economics.

This part of the book explains the challenge of social capital in postindustrial economies. It argues that the democratic prospect requires mediating structures to advocate for or provide new forms and increased amounts of social capital. The importance of this role increases when policy makers rely too much on market mechanisms to address human needs. Ironically, however, this overemphasis on the market overstates the capacity of mediating structures to redress social problems and at the same time diminishes their chances for success.

CHAPTER 1

Social Capital and Appalachia

The end of the post–World War II economic boom presented new challenges for the democratic prospect of increased equality and expanded communal bonds. After 1972, growth in output, real wages, profit rates, and investment rates in the American manufacturing economy declined (Bowles, Gordon, and Weisskopf 1990: 6). This meant that working-class and middle-class Americans lost opportunities for steady employment at wages that permitted a middle-class lifestyle, one that included home ownership, health care, and educational opportunities for children.

Appalachia illustrates especially well the dimmed democratic prospect that accompanied the economic decline. Despite a long history of being popularly conceived as a region outside of the American mainstream, Appalachia is very much part and product of American economics and public policy. What distinguish the region are the shortcomings of market economics and public policy, which are more apparent there. Rather than being behind the rest of the nation, Appalachia in fact typically heralds the challenges of the American economy (Couto 1994). It heralded industrial relations at the time when Florence Reece asked workers to take a stand. It heralds class relations now in postindustrial economies (Fisher 1990).

The past, present, and future challenges of Appalachia and postindustrial economics involve social capital. This chapter explains that American policies of social capital create and maintain a labor force. In places where there is little work in general and much low-wage, low-skill work, we find little social capital. Some places in and near Central Appalachia had declining work prospects in the 1980s and consequently new problems of poverty. Other places, especially metropolitan areas in Southern Appalachia, had improved prospects in work, and these areas showed considerable increases in prosperity. This chapter first explains the problem of social capital in American public policy generally and then presents its impact in Appalachia.

The Space of Appalachia

The Appalachian Mountains form one part of the logic of the current, broad geographic definition of Appalachia. Other parts of that logic include economic similarities, contiguity, measures of low income, and pork barrel politics. Early sociologists, such as John C. Campbell (1921) and Horace Kephart (1913), used regional boundaries to separate a group of people with some common cultural characteristics in a region they referred to as the Southern Highlands. Kephart's study incorporated an uncertain number of counties in the Smoky Mountain region of three states: Tennessee, North Carolina, and Georgia. Campbell's study offered a much broader definition, which extended north of Kephart's region and included 210 counties in nine states. A 1960 study by the Maryland Department of Economic Development expanded the boundaries of Appalachia to eleven states, from New York through Alabama. The 1962 survey of Thomas Ford, another sociologist, included 205 counties in just six states (Ford 1962: 1–9). By the mid-1960s, a half century of analysis had provided several different geographic boundaries for Appalachia.

In 1965, the Appalachian Regional Development Act, which created the Appalachian Regional Commission (ARC), drew the boundaries of the region once again. These boundaries, the most expansive to date, are now widely accepted. They follow the spine and vertebrae of the Appalachian Mountains from the southern tier of New York counties to a tier of counties in northeast Mississippi. In 1993, the region encompassed 399 counties in thirteen states. All of West Virginia falls into the region, as do portions of New York, Pennsylvania, Ohio, Maryland, Virginia, Kentucky, Tennessee, North Carolina, South Carolina, Georgia, Alabama, and Mississippi. The ARC definition assumed acute human need as a common factor within this region. More than twenty-five years of ARC's programs and reports create additional reasons to accept the ARC's broad geographic boundaries. In addition, local political and business elites in 400 counties and thirteen states are now organized into area development districts, giving regional identity an additional impetus. ARC recognized differences within in the region and organized three subregions within Appalachia: North, Central, and South.

Other definitions of Appalachia contrast the culture and economics of Appalachia and other regions. Scholars trace the origins of the popular concepts of Appalachia back to national trends in the late nineteenth century in markets for literature and social interventions. Literary magazines seeking local color and short stories found them in descriptions of parts of Appalachia. Social workers in settlement schools seeking contributions for their work found them in responses to their descriptions of the needs of the region and its residents whom they served and the many more whom they did not serve (Shapiro 1978). Later, political and social activists looking for conditions of poverty that needed change found them in Appalachia (Batteau 1990: 144–67). Consequently, definitions of Appalachian involve the commercial, financial, social, or political needs of people outside as well as inside the region.

These observations suggest a political dimension to the cultural boundaries of Appalachia. Misleading depictions of local people are disseminated to people who have influence and gain wealth as part of the interaction of disparate cultural systems. Representatives from distant cultural systems—for example, financial capitals of late-nineteenth-century America—distort local culture and separate it from the broader social, political, and economic history that explains it. Lost also are the political implications of efforts of outside capital to "improve" Appalachia by introducing elements of the culture of capital (Whisnant 1983: 6–16). In doing so, representatives of outside capital interests assume the superiority of their own cultural forms and establish the justification for their social, political, and economic interventions and their consequences. Economic and political power have shaped the boundaries of Appalachia, including some aspects of its cultural identity.

Much of the recent scholarship on Appalachia focuses on power and counters the "inferior culture" explanations of Appalachia. For example, Harry Caudill (1962) explained the poverty of Eastern Kentucky by contrasting its political economy with that of other regions. Others have built upon or exceeded this interpretation to place Appalachian events and conditions into the mainstream of American life and the processes of industrialization and economic development. In these studies, Appalachian conditions of poverty and human need are the consequence of economic decision making by coal companies, textile companies, the timber industry, and absentee landowners. The region's extractive industries send mineral and timber to centers of power, for which the region receives as little in return as possible. Legislation to benefit the companies developing the raw materials of the region has left local and state governments with little tax base to provide essential services such as education, medical care, and public health. The political corruption that has gone into forming this legislative inequity has left reformers few avenues to justice (Appalachian Land Ownership Task Force 1983; Eller 1982; Gaventa 1980; Gaventa, Smith, and Willingham 1990; Gaventa, Lewis, and Williams 1992; Lewis, Johnson, and Askins 1978; Walls 1978). One study reinterprets the feud of the Hatfields and McCoys, which has stimulated so many stereotypes of "hillbillies," in terms of these economic transformations and responses to them (Waller 1988). Unlike the cultural interpretations of Appalachia, these socioeconomic and sociopolitical studies emphasize what was done to the region by national economic and political forces. Rather than finding a subculture that incapacitated citizens to resist negative influences, these studies suggest how Appalachian people fought back against what they had to deal with (Fisher 1993; Hinsdale, Lewis, and Waller 1995). The studies generally focus on a particular set of counties, most often in Central Appalachia; a particular time; or a particular industry, such as coal, textiles, or steel.

However it is defined, the poverty of portions of Appalachia is a frequently cited benchmark of human need, much like the inner city or barrio or reservation. A map of poverty in Appalachia explains why it serves as a benchmark. At its center is a set of very poor counties. But there is another benchmark in Appalachia. In the 1980s, the poor regions of the area fell farther behind the rest of the nation. Maps 1 and 2 portray poverty in Appalachia in 1990 and its changes during the previous decade.

In his groundbreaking book, *The Affluent Society* (1958), John Kenneth Galbraith combined cultural and economic analysis in distinguishing Appalachia from more prosperous regions of the country. His later reflection on American life, *The Culture of Contentment* (1992), offers a cultural interpretation of America to explain the poverty of the Appalachian region. America's "culture of contentment" entails a majority made up of those who are fortunate and favored and those who hope to be, all of whom act on behalf of their own immediate, short-term benefit. They accept the need for increased and improved social welfare policies in places such as Appalachia without doing much to meet those needs or to achieve those policies (Galbraith 1992). Because poverty, unemployment, and related conditions in Appalachia may disrupt the contentment of American life, Galbraith finds that Americans use frames of reference to interpret them in a way that alleviates the need to address such problems by public policies.

Thomas Sowell illustrates one such frame of reference that is grounded

Map 1. The Spatial Distribution of Appalachian Poverty, 1990

Percentage of population with below-poverty-level incomes, by county, 1990

Less than 10.0 percent

Comparable figures:
U.S. = 13.1 percent
Appalachia = 14.9 percent

FPO

10.0–14.9 percent

15.0–19.9 percent

20.0–29.9 percent

More than 30.0 percent

Source: U.S. Bureau of the Census.
Poverty in the United States, 1991.

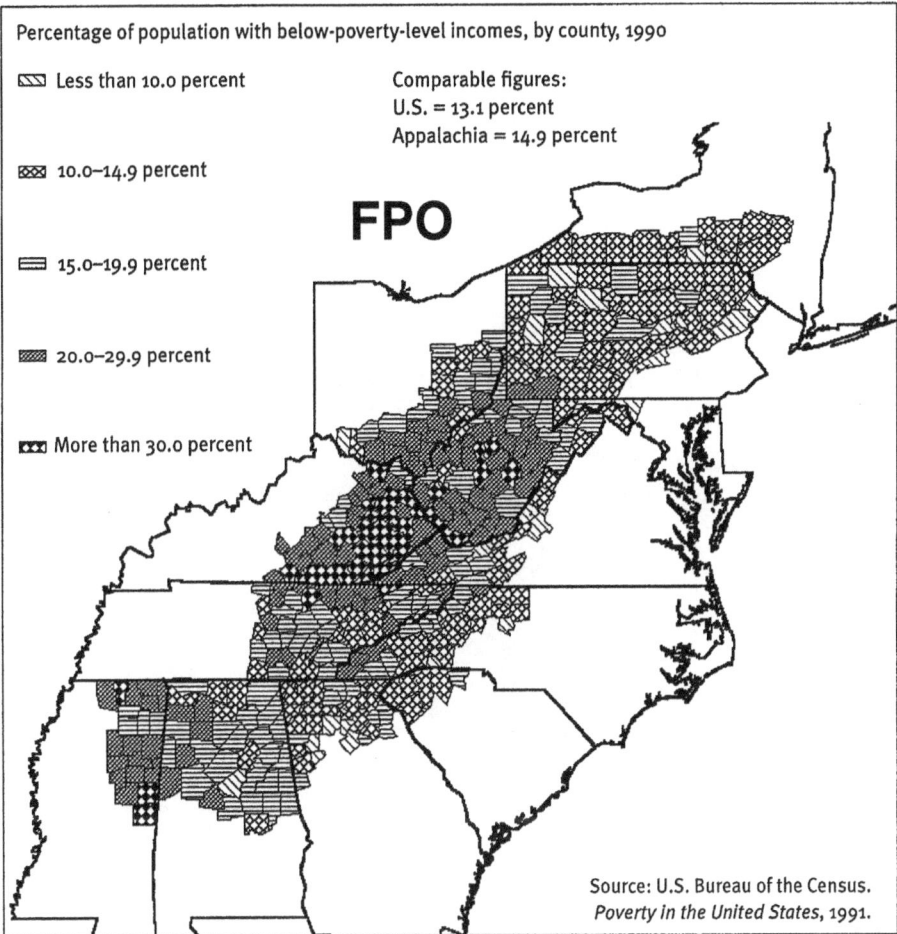

in cultural differences between prosperous and poor groups. Sowell is among the social theorists who provide an intellectual underpinning for the advancement of market democracy and society's consequent withdrawal from the democratic prospect. As others did before him, Sowell looks to Appalachia for data for his theory. He brushes aside the last twenty years of political economic analysis of the region and focuses on culture and space. Sowell explains Appalachian poverty through the culture of the Ulster Scots who settled it.

He argues that as long as we confine our view to American society, as Sowell criticizes others for doing, it may be plausible to believe that "objective conditions" in Appalachia, or the ways in which people were "treated"

Map 2. *Changes in Poverty in Appalachia, 1980–1990*

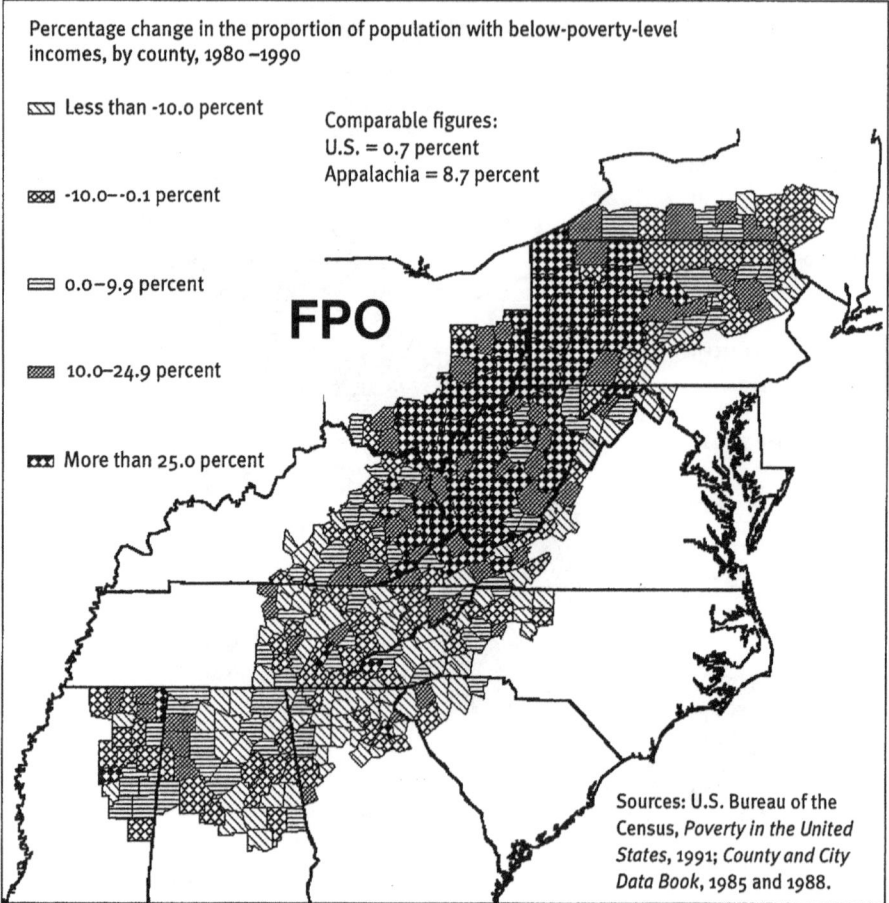

Percentage change in the proportion of population with below-poverty-level incomes, by county, 1980 –1990

▨ Less than -10.0 percent

▨ -10.0--0.1 percent

▤ 0.0–9.9 percent

▨ 10.0–24.9 percent

▨ More than 25.0 percent

Comparable figures:
U.S. = 0.7 percent
Appalachia = 8.7 percent

FPO

Sources: U.S. Bureau of the Census, *Poverty in the United States*, 1991; *County and City Data Book*, 1985 and 1988.

there, accounts for the poverty we find in the region. Yet, if the history of the Scots is viewed internationally, as he does, then the evidence, he concludes, suggests that the subgroup that settled in Appalachia differed culturally from other Scots before its members boarded the ships to cross the Atlantic and subsequently manifested its differences in Appalachian poverty (Sowell 1994: 3, 230, 261 n. 15).

In general, discussions of Appalachia such as Sowell's, which use the region as a benchmark of poverty and human need, actually refer to Central Appalachia and the immediately adjoining areas of Northern and Southern Appalachia. One is hard pressed to imagine Sowell applying his argument about the cultural shortcomings of Ulster Scots to the "Appalachian" affluent suburbs of Atlanta, Winston-Salem, or Pittsburgh. Culturally pejorative interpreters like Sowell explain the chronic poverty in parts of Appalachia by the traits of the people living there.

Other studies, such as this one, focus on the political economic interpretations of Appalachia, not the cultural ones. This study looks outside the region for the political, economic, cultural, and social factors that shape conditions of poverty and human need inside the region. It goes beyond previous studies to explain Appalachia in terms of American social capital.

The Recent Political Economy of Appalachia

By the late 1960s and even more clearly by the early 1970s, America and the world had changed, and Appalachia, naturally, changed with them. The economies of Japan and Germany, shattered by World War II, were restored. American political and military interventions in the affairs of other nations, such as oil-rich Iran in the 1950s, were stymied by the national revulsion with the Vietnam War and by increased cooperation among other nations, seen, for example, in the Organization of Petroleum Exporting Countries (OPEC), formed in 1973. Peaceful industrial relations, which accords between workers and managers and among managers had brought after World War II, began to unravel in the late 1960s. Labor costs reentered the calculation of profit and competition (Bowles, Gordon, and Weisskopf 1990: 47–79; Dionne 1996).

Barry Bluestone and Benjamin Harrison (1982; 1988) examined responses of corporate America to increased international competition for their impact on the American economy. They found that corporations attempted to reward and expand management to supervise and profit from global activity while "downsizing" their American workforce and demanding decreases in labor costs as the condition for continued employment. Second, they found that corporations had shifted investment away from productive capacity, which creates jobs and income, into speculative ventures, which create profits and wealth. The 1990s with its unprecedented bull market and continuing stream of layoffs and plant closings testified to the success and sadness of this corporate response.

Appalachian industries certainly changed with this U-turn in corporate action (Couto 1994). New capital managers in the coal industry enthroned "return on investment" (ROI), an acronym of the French word for king, as ruler of Appalachian economics, where coal had once been "king," in plain English. Compared to their predecessors, new coal companies had less stake in a high-wage, stable, coal industry and greater concern for return on investment in any field. Amoco's coal operations, for example, were profitable, but they fell below the company's goal of 13 to 15 percent of return on investment. Consequently, the operations were put up for sale in 1985. Under the rule of ROI, coal companies had to compete with other investment opportunities of their parent companies, not only with other mining ventures. This new competition placed new downward pressure on wages and benefits of miners. New managers proposed to reintroduce labor costs into the calculation of competition. Their proposed action repeated the historic tendency of management to create surplus capacity and then to cut costs by paying less to fewer miners. The accord of the United Mine Workers of America (UMWA) and the Bituminous Coal Operators of America (BCOA) coincided with the postwar prosperity. The accord's end, in the 1970s, heralded the coming changes in the American economy and labor relations that were not yet evident (Couto 1987; Dionne 1996). Since then, employment and income have declined, production remains high, and Appalachia supplies coal markets around the world. The Appalachian coal industry shows how increased mechanization leads to increased productivity, corporate profits, and dislocated workers with declining incomes and prospects for satisfactory employment.

Managers in the American steel industry also searched beyond Appalachia for new places for profits. Between 1972 and 1977, U.S. companies reinvested less money in the steel industry than did Japan, West Germany, and Great Britain and reaped higher net incomes as a percent of fixed assets (Metzgar 1983: 35). Predictably, these actions hastened the obsolescence of existing production sites, disbanded an industrial workforce, and increased the steep slope of decline of the industry.

Ironically, a declining industry is not an unprofitable one. What initiates decline is not necessarily a lack of profits but a rate of profit that corporate managers consider insufficiently high to hold or attract investors and stockholders. For example, between 1974 and 1982, when primary metal employment was cut almost in half in Appalachia, the companies in the steel industry recorded average profit rates of 8 percent. In particular, 1974 and 1981 were record years for steel profits; from 1974 to 1981, steel production fluctuated from a high of 145 million tons to a low of 110 million tons (Metzgar 1983). Companies were not making *enough* profits to keep up with investors' demands and reinvestment requirements. While the steel industry averaged 8 percent profit annually from 1974 to 1981, manufacturing industries as a whole averaged 15 percent, and the general economy averaged 18 percent. Consequently, as the *Wall Street Journal* reported, "Retirement of aging and technologically obsolete capacity has emerged as a prime element of domestic steel makers' strategy to firm up prices when a recovery does come" (DuBois 1983: 13).

Appalachia was a center of early industrial growth. Consequently, its aging and technologically obsolete production capacity has been a center of early postindustrial "growth" as well. "Run down costs" hasten the decline of older industrial centers. E. F. Schumacher (1973) used the term to describe the costs of doing business in an established setting rather than a pristine one. Older industrial areas—such as the coal, steel, and textile centers of Appalachia—have high run down factors, including environmental degradation, higher costs of pensions and benefits for former workers, and declining production facilities. Areas without a run down factor have a comparative advantage. An economy based on seizing the comparative advantage in every instance, such as a profit-maximizing capital market, avoids run down costs. In so doing, the market leaves people in communities to meet the costs of the run down factor and the social capital deficits on their own. This is true immediately of the communities left behind by capital relocation and eventually of those communities where capital relocates. American steel companies diversified to avoid the run down factor in their own industry and to find new profits. This prompted the often-cited comment of U.S. Steel chairman David Roderick: "U.S. Steel is not in the business of making steel. It is in the business of making money" (Metzgar 1983: 26). To prove the point, U.S. Steel used record 1981 profits, which were acquired through tax cuts and generous depletion allowances as well as labor concessions, to purchase Marathon Oil in 1982. To further distance itself from its own industrial history, U.S. Steel changed its name to USX. Only two of the top seven steel companies increased their investments in steel in 1982 (Metzgar 1983: 32). The rate of profit of the steel industry was not high enough to hold or attract the capital of even the steel companies.

Songwriter Charlie King summed up the new corporate mentality in the satirical lyrics of "U.S. $teal":

We are changing our name to money,
We are toppling the oven stacks and towers.
And with every mill that closes,
We come out smelling like roses.
Yes sir, we got ours.

If you're a corporate chameleon,
With a heart that's Machiavellian,

You'll clean up with every shut down.
You'll say "Yes sir, we got ours."

King tempered his humor with a sober assessment of the social consequences of corporate actions and the need to do something about them.

Something's dying,
Makes me crazy.
A life goes down,
You don't stand and watch.

Despite King's alarm, the run down of one area and the shift to another characterizes capitalism's routine. Adam Smith foresaw that economic development would bring a general increase in well being initially but that after a time, "the full complement of riches" based on an area's resources and geographic location would be reached. At that point, accumulation of capital stops and so does growth. The working class of an area where growth has stopped enters a decline in living standards that can drop below subsistence. Smith, the apostle of the gospel of "progress" through economic transitions and dislocations, offered a deeply pessimistic prognosis for a market economy left on its own. The working class, he wrote, was subject to social decay and economic decline: "All the nobler parts of the human character [what we are calling social capital] may be in great measure obliterated and extinguished in the great body of the people" (Smith, in Heilbroner 1993: 124).

Smith was not sanguine about market capitalism and understood, as Reece explained, that market democracy means that the sheriff works for the company. The state would deal with protests of new social inequality, according to Smith. Indeed, this was its purpose: "Civil government, in which the political authority is linked with wealth and equality, so far as it is instituted for the security of property, is in reality instituted for the defense of the rich against the poor, or of all those who have some property against those who have none at all" (Smith 1937 [1776]: 674). Smith is much clearer about the "strong arm of the magistrate" that enforces social differences than about the "invisible hand" that reduces them.

In contrast to his latter-day followers, Smith had no illusions about the market's capacity to redress human need. Citing the poverty of the Scottish Highlands, Smith noted that those "who by the products of their labor feed, clothe, and lodge the whole body of people" did not have "such a share of the product of their own labour as to be themselves tolerably well fed, clothed, and lodged" (Smith 1937 [1776]: 79). "Civilized society," in his

view, marked the progress of a market economy that was still characterized by the destruction of a great part of the children of "inferior ranks of
people" (Smith 1937 [1776]: 79).

New Class Fissures of the Postindustrial Economy

Changes in corporate practice brought new hardship to Appalachia, and related changes in the nature and amount of work have left all American
workers with less income. In particular, the economic recovery of the 1980s
shifted incomes from lower income groups to higher income groups. In
1990, the income share of the wealthiest five percent of American households equaled that of the lowest 40 percent. Similarly, in 1980 the third
and fourth quintiles of households, the 41st to 80th percentiles, had a larger
share of the national income than did the top 20 percent of households. In
1990, they had less. By 1995, the top 20 percent of households had income
shares much larger than these two quintiles and about equal to that of the
other 80 percent of households combined. By 1995, the poor had less income and the rich more. The top 5 percent had a share of household income
equal to that of the bottom 47 percent. Table 1 provides figures on the division of national income by households.

Analysts differ about what portions of the redistribution of wealth have
occurred since 1972 and to what degree the policies of the Republican administrations since 1980 are responsible. Incomes of households and individuals can vary widely from year to year. By 1992, for example, the reces-
sion affected the income distribution once again. Comparing different years
produces very different gaps between income groups, but all comparisons
show gaps and increased gaps over any five-year period of the 1980s. Whatever years one may choose, however, beginning in the 1970s, income has
trickled up rather than down. That trickle became a steady stream in the
1980s under the tax reform measures of the Reagan administration. Kevin
Phillips, a Republican political commentator, has described the 1980s as "a
Republican conservative-capitalist overdrive period, sharing ten common
characteristics [with the 1870s and 1920s] that ranged from tax cuts and
deregulation to surges in debt and speculation" (Phillips 1990: x).

The result, according to Phillips, is that "among major Western nations,
the United States has displayed one of the sharpest cleavages between the
rich and the poor." Phillips's figures show that the low-income households
of the United States have a smaller portion of national income and the high-
income households have a larger portion of national income than is the case
in Germany and Japan, America's most often cited industrial competitors.

Table 1. Changes in Percentage Share of Aggregate American Family Income, by Income Groups, 1980–1995

Income Group	1980	1990	1995	% Change	
				1980–90	1990–95
Poorest fifth	5.3	4.6	4.4	−13.2	−4.3
2nd quintile	11.6	10.8	10.1	−6.9	−6.5
Middle quintile	17.6	16.6	15.8	−5.7	−4.8
4th quintile	24.4	23.8	23.2	−2.5	−2.5
Middle three-fifths	53.6	51.2	49.1	−4.5	−4.1
Wealthiest fifth	41.1	44.3	46.5	7.8	5.0
Top 5%	14.6	17.4	20.0	19.2	14.9

Source: Center on Budget and Policy Priorities 1996: 53.

While the top-income households in America generally enjoyed twelve times the share of wealth of the low-income households, the ratio in Germany was 5:1 and in Japan only 4:1 (Phillips 1990: 9). Our competitors among advanced industrialized nations in the global economy seem capable of competing with far less economic disparity and polarization.

Phillips offers other equally instructive comparisons. According to the World Bank, in 1985 the share of income among the lowest 40 percent of American households placed the United States behind every one of the twenty-five nations with high-income economies except for Australia and Singapore. Of the twenty-one low-income and moderate-income nations that reported their income distribution, the United States fell behind nine of them, including Bangladesh, Ghana, India, and Pakistan. In the 1980s, the income distribution in the United States was more "equitable" than only seven Central and Latin American states: Guatemala, Peru, Colombia, Jamaica, Costa Rica, Venezuela, and Brazil (World Bank 1991: Table 30).

Obviously, the changes in income among groups of Americans have meant that the rich have gotten richer and the poor poorer. The working and professional middle class may not have fallen to poverty, but most middle-income earners and families have "fallen from grace," in the phrase of Katherine S. Newman (1988). Newman, an anthropologist, has chronicled and documented the downward mobility of the American middle class and its consequences for American communities and the social networks of Americans. Examining the impact on the middle-class community of mass employment layoffs—like the closing of the Singer sewing machine factory in Elizabeth, New Jersey, and the nationwide firing of air traffic controllers—she found that "fellowship is an inexplicable source of comfort in the midst of economic dislocation" (Newman 1988: 235). The air traffic controllers, she discovered, had a community of experience, and the Singer workers a community of proximity. Newman drew a direct parallel to Appalachia. "For the better part of a century, the Singer Company was to Elizabeth, New Jersey, what coal mining is to Appalachia" (Newman 1988: 235).

Companies and communities went together, hand in hand, very closely in Appalachia. Not just coal mining but steel making and textile and apparel making companies created "communities of proximity" throughout Appalachia. The unions of these industries created "communities of experience" as well. Such communities grew up around economic activity and changed when the economic activity changed.

The lyrics of Tom Paxton's 1985 song "Factory Whistle's Blowing" succinctly summarized this economic change and its social consequences for working people everywhere.

> Factory whistle's blowing, other side of town.
> Everybody's knowing, factories closing down.
> They can make them cheaper over in Japan.
> That's the way it goes,
> Now, everybody knows, they don't need the working man.

> They can take their money, move it anywhere.
> Here today and gone, they can set up in Taiwan
> Or the moon for all they care.
> Leaving us the factory, all it grows is weeds.
> Leaving us the families, they're the same as ever, hungry mouths
>   to feed.

Paxton used very little poetic license, according to the statements of capital managers. On December 27, 1983, U.S. Steel announced cutbacks that eliminated 15,400 high-paying, union jobs. On the same day its stock rose five-eighths of a point to 29⅞ in active trading on the New York Stock Exchange. Investors anticipated increased profits as the company diminished its payroll. Corporate profitability no longer implied secure employment for large numbers of workers. Corporations had found and would pursue new avenues to profit that would satisfy investors but cost workers their jobs. Corporate managers correctly assessed the response of investors to layoffs. The experience of U.S. Steel indicated the conflict between profit and employment in the economy. "Everybody knows" that corporations can make short-term profits with fewer workers or even without any workers. Good news on Wall Street brought bad news on Main Street.

The Reagan administration indicated clearly that it would brook no dissent from workers about the imposed social costs of changes in the nature and amount of work. Government stood behind corporations in a demand that workers go quietly into the night of declining wages and benefits, higher expectations for productivity, and lower levels of social guarantees. As the nation celebrated the courage of Polish workers' solidarity organization for its strike actions, President Reagan personally intervened to fire and replace 12,000 striking air traffic controllers at the beginning of his administration. Hiring replacement workers for striking workers soon became common practice. The National Football League's 1988 season provided the most visible effort at worker placement, while the Eastern Airlines and Greyhound strikes provided other examples. By the 1990s, employers dealing with a labor strike showed less and less reluctance to hire replacement workers.

When workers appealed to the conscience of capital managers, pointing out that corporate-dictated economic changes meant irreparable harm to their communities, they met an indifference and cynicism far more sinister than Paxton's lyrics suggest. For example, managers of Massey Coal Group invoked competition from foreign, western, and nonunion producers to justify the need for company-by-company agreements in its dispute with the UMWA, which led to the strike of 1984–85. E. Morgan Massey, president of the coal group, explained that "multinational corporations do not have a great deal of national loyalty and even less loyalty to southern West Virginia" (quoted in Couto 1993: 180).

Yet, the corporate structure of Massey illustrated the confusion over "competition" in the industry. The Massey Coal Group was literally a subsidiary of a joint venture of joint ventures of subsidiaries of two parent corporations, Fluor and the Royal Dutch/Shell Group. The Royal Dutch/Shell Group owned mining interests in South Africa, and Fluor was developing coal mining in China with Massey's assistance. Some of Massey's subsidiaries in the Appalachian region provided the nonunion competition to its own union mines. In fact, Massey estimated that his company was the largest nonunion underground mining company in Appalachia, if not the country. In effect, Massey supplied some of its own competition within the Appalachian region, and its parent corporations supplied more competition in other countries.

Miners striking the Pittston Coal Company also confronted that company's conscience at a stockholders' meeting at corporate offices in Greenwich, Connecticut. One miner complained that the new contract required Sunday operations at the mine and that Sunday was the time he went to church. One Pittston officer responded that miners were using religion as a crutch. The miner agreed, "I use church to get through work during the week. That's my crutch in life, the whole meaning of it, because I hope to go to a better place when this is over." In a deeply cynical retort that no lyricist would dare phrase without risking charges of hyperbole, the company official suggested, "Come to Greenwich" (Couto 1993: 181). These labor conflicts in Appalachia expressed a dispute in American life over work and social capital for community. If portions of Appalachia resemble developing nations' conditions, it is because of American social policies. All Americans increasingly feel the consequences of these policies as social policy passed to the invisible hand the job of managing the social consequences of economic changes. Since 1972 the invisible hand has smothered social capital.

The corporate search for new and higher profits in a changed economy after 1972 meant new cost-cutting attitudes toward workers and their communities everywhere. For the first half of the twentieth century, private capital produced and reproduced a workforce for the industries it created through social capital investment (Gaventa 1980: 47–123; Hall 1984: Serrin 1992; Shifflett 1991). Coal towns, steel towns, and mill towns went up. When the need for this labor force diminished, social capital dried up, and coal towns began a decline that marks the region as a symbol of the problems of our postindustrial era. Steel towns (Serrin 1992; Town 1978) and some textile towns have followed that decline. Where the demand for a skilled labor force declines, so does incentive to invest in social capital.

The ups and downs of social capital in Appalachia suggest how the forms and amounts of social capital vary from place to place at the same time and from time to time in the same place (Uzawa 1988: 341). The changes in Appalachia suggest the manner in which American forms of social capital vary with the market's needs for workers. Our social capital invests public goods and moral resources primarily to produce and sustain people as laborers; it limits the community that it produces to the labor force. Since 1980, Americans have argued over whether the sources of the very few forms and limited amounts of social capital, such as job training or welfare and health care for children in poverty, should be public or private. Less often, we argue about the adequacy of the size and forms of social capital. We seem to agree that American workers and low-income family members need to face new and larger social and economic problems with fewer types of and lesser amounts of public social capital. In this context, community becomes an indirect consequence of policies to shape a workforce rather than a deliberate and intentional goal.

William Serrin, reflecting on Homestead, Pennsylvania, a declining steel town, lamented the ties of industry and social capital that diminish community. He contrasted the prosperity of Pittsburgh's white, upper-class, northern suburbs at the same time that "unattractive areas, be they old industrial areas, working class communities, or inner-city black and Hispanic areas were being written off. . . . Money was following money the American way. It was the mentality of the frontier: extract and leave. It was an unethical way for the country to live, but no one seemed to care"(Serrin 1992: 420).

Both liberals and conservatives fall short on supporting the broad goal of having social capital serve community needs, not just the needs of the labor force. Robert Reich, for example, hopes for an economy without community. Reich did not find tragedy in the passage of the steel mill and steel town of Homestead, Pennsylvania. "Why should we care about Homestead, or for that matter, about any town or city in decline? . . . Americans are always leaving some place behind; departures are in our ancestral genes . . . Homestead and its people . . . are separable" (Reich 1992: 16).

Reich's concern falls on the people as workers apart from their place. He finds the most important question to be: "How did the people of Homestead fare once they left? How did they make out in the transition from steel production to other work? The answer is, probably not very well. Most of them probably got jobs farther west or south in the service industry, making one-third to one-half the income they had in the steel mill." This Reich finds is "not so much the tragedy of an American steel town as it is the tragedy of modern America" (Reich 1992: 16). Reich is partially correct, the people of Homestead and the declining industrial areas of the United States are not better off economically. However, he misses the central point: people are people in community, and not just at work.

If we separate work from the place where people live, we invite further and worse tragedies for families and communities. If work is not tied to the maintenance and sustenance of community, then the types and amount of work may eventually and literally erode the ground, poison the air, disrupt families, and contaminate the water that supports community. This will not happen in all communities, however, only those where working people and poor people live, the people most vulnerable to unemployment as markets shift their demands for labor.

Indeed, economic capital, on its own, will invest social capital or ignore it for its own purpose of profit and not for public or social purposes. It will spend more on social capital goods and resources when the production of a labor force is profitable and less or nothing when it is not. The declining coal towns and steel towns of Appalachia suggest an economy of wealth that cannot sustain large numbers of people in the place they live and prefer to work. To achieve profits in bad economic times, the economy of wealth may require the literal destruction of communities and that many areas be simply "written off."

An unregulated market is likely to treat social capital goods and resources just like other commodities, according to Adam Smith. It will relate the cost of labor to its supply. When wages drop below the subsistence level, working-class people die. The supply of workers decline. The cost of labor increases. Wages increase to a level above subsistence. The numbers of workers increase. More workers, without a corresponding increase in demand for workers, depress the wages of workers. This drop in wages, naturally, sets off another effort of the market to adjust the supply and demand for people as workers by their wages. Smith concludes, in understated and morbid tones, "It is in this manner that the demand for men, like that of any other commodity, necessarily regulates the production of men; quicker when it goes on too slowly, and stops it when it advances too fast" (Smith, in Heilbroner 1986: 204). The housing crisis, the education crisis, and the health crisis in parts of Appalachia, and the inner city, are related. They are part of a deficit in the budget of social capital that has increased as public policy entrusted the distribution of economic benefits and costs to the "invisible hand."

Appalachia, Work, and Social Capital

Adam Smith's views would have us expect that the market would supply the amount of labor needed at different times and different places by regulating the number of people. We find evidence of this crude formula in Appalachia in the 1980s. The region's population grew by only 1.6 percent in the 1980s, compared to a national population growth of 9.8 percent. Each Appalachian subregion's different experience of economic change has meant differences in the number of people in the labor force and, consequently, different experiences with social capital (see Map 3). The Northern Appalachian subregion, with the decline of the coal and steel industries and changes in the manufacturing sector of its economy, lost population. The Southern Appalachian subregion, especially the metropolitan areas, which experienced increased economic activity and labor force participation, increased in population. Central Appalachia, the core of all definitions based on geography

Map 3. Labor Force Participation in Appalachia, 1990

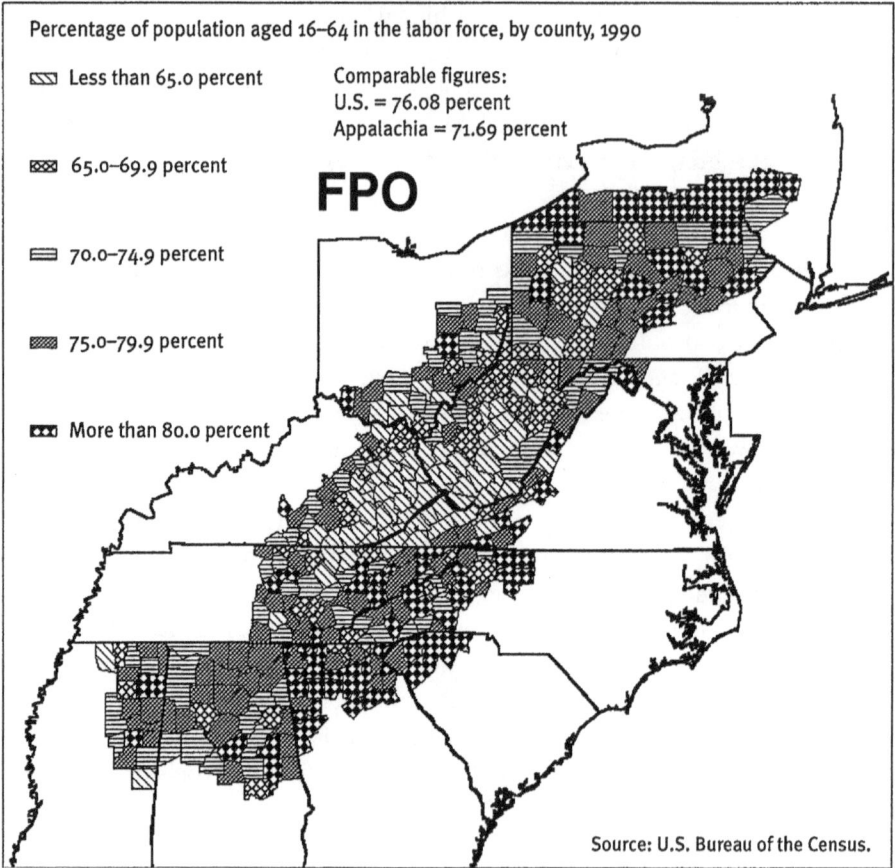

Percentage of population aged 16–64 in the labor force, by county, 1990

▨ Less than 65.0 percent

Comparable figures:
U.S. = 76.08 percent
Appalachia = 71.69 percent

FPO

▦ 65.0–69.9 percent

▤ 70.0–74.9 percent

▨ 75.0–79.9 percent

▥ More than 80.0 percent

Source: U.S. Bureau of the Census.

and economic need, had a severe decline in its coal industry employment. This meant a decade of outmigration during the 1980s that was reminiscent of the exodus of the 1950s.

Labor force participation correlates strongly with the change of population in Appalachia from 1980 to 1990. The higher the labor force participation, the greater the increase in the population of the county. In crude terms, people came to places of work and left places without work. That is only a portion of the portrait, however. In places of declining labor force participation, the number of children also declined, another means of decreasing the supply of labor. Correspondingly, the number of children grew in places of increased labor force participation. The increase in the population aged sixteen to sixty-four years explains a portion of this. That is, the working age population contains the childbearing age population and grows in the places of increased labor force participation.

Senior citizens seem to withstand the invisible hand's sweep of supply and demand. The size of the population over sixty-five years of age does not correlate strongly or significantly with labor force participation. This probably reflects the social capital we invested in those over sixty-five years of age through the 1960s' programs of Social Security, Medicare, and Medicaid. These three programs have increased the incomes of seniors, protected their income from medical bills, and greatly reduced the amount of poverty among them.

These programs are the dominant exception of the American proclivity to bind social capital to the market and to limit public sources of social capital. A comprehensive, comparative study of North American and European social welfare policies, the Luxembourg Income Study, found that American social programs target segments of the population rather than promoting social rights of all citizens or the working class (McFate, Lawson, and Wilson 1995: 705). These policies ordinarily produce levels of poverty that are higher than the levels in comparable nations, such as Canada, United Kingdom, West Germany, Netherlands, France, and Sweden (McFate, Smeeding, and Rainwater 1995: 31). This standard approach to social policy coupled with the economic transitions of the 1980s exacerbated the dismal record of the United States. By the late 1980s, the United States had higher rates of poverty among the nonelderly, more severe poverty than before, and sharply different patterns of poverty between racial minorities and whites (McFate, Lawson, and Wilson 1995: 700).

Social Security, Medicare, and Medicaid are exceptions that prove the rule that the limited public sources of American social capital are tied to work. Social programs for the elderly are social capital as a reward for labor force participation. The paucity of social capital for other age groups means these younger groups are more dependent on the nature and amount of work available. As Smith envisioned, the market increases and decreases the supply of workers apart from those who have left the labor force after serving in it. Table 2 provides the measures of correlation and significance for labor force participation and population.

Income plays a central role in increasing and decreasing the number of labor force participants. With inadequate forms of social capital, the working-age population depends heavily on the wages of work. This is not surprising. What is surprising, however, is how the relationship of income and labor force participation varies at different times. Thus, median family in-

Table 2. Social Capital Measures of Population

Population Measure	Percentage of Adults in Civilian Labor Force		
	1980	1990	Rate of Change, 1980–90
Rate of change in total population, 1980–90	R = .397 p < .0001	R = .585 p < .0001	R = .310 p < .0001
Percentage of population > 65 years of age			
1980	R = .122 p < .05	—	R = −.182 p < .01
1990	—	R = −.055 n.s.	R = −.192 p < .0001
Rate of change, 1980–90	R = −.045 n.s.	R = −.084 n.s.	R = −.084 n.s.

come, per capita income, and poverty all had strong and significant correlations with labor force participation that *increased* from 1980 to 1990. The social capital policies of the 1980s, whether by intention or not, provided less income for those who did not participate in the labor force. Poverty, in particular, correlates strongly and significantly with labor force participation. Ironically, however, labor force participation is higher in poor areas during times of more liberal social capital policies, like the 1970s, than at times of more rigid dependence on the market, like the 1980s. The measures of labor force participation and the correlations of labor force participation and poverty bear this out. The Jamestown dictum, "If you don't work, you don't eat," seems very applicable to American social capital at all times. Occasionally, at times of increased emphasis on market democracy, social capital policies modify that dictum to "If there is no work, you don't eat." The correlation and significance of the measures of labor force participation and income and poverty are given in Table 3.

By tying income to work and by providing low amounts of social capital, women in low-income, low-employment counties are pushed into work. That is, as labor force participation decreases significantly in low-income

Table 3. Social Capital Measures of Income

Income Measure	Percentage of Adults in Civilian Labor Force		
	1980	1990	Rate of Change, 1980–90
Median family income			
1980	R = .373	—	R = .130
	p < .0001		p < .01
1990	—	R = .696	R = .332
		p < .0001	p < .0001
Rate of change, 1980–90	R = .557	R = .627	R = .361
	p < .0001	p < .0001	p < .0001
Percentage of population in poverty			
1980	R = −.571	—	R = −.126
	p < .0001		p < .05
1990	—	R = −.719	R = −.261
		p < .0001	p < .0001
Rate of change, 1980–90	R = −.335	R = −.411	R = −.263
	p < .0001	p < .0001	p < .0001
Per capita income			
1980	R = .395	—	R = .045
	p < .0001		n.s.
1990	—	R = .567	R = .205
		p < .0001	p < .0001
Rate of change, 1980–90	R = .518	R = .517	R = .205
	p < .0001	p < .0001	p < .0001

counties, women remain in or enter into the labor force and thus become a larger proportion of a smaller labor force. Table 4 provides evidence of the correlation of increased numbers of women in small and declining labor forces and the factors that push women into a declining economy. The percentage of women in the labor force is higher in areas of high labor force participation. However, the percentage of women in the labor force increased significantly in those areas where overall labor force participation decreased in the 1980s. More women entered or stayed in declining workforces than expanding ones because they found themselves more frequently as the head of a household and/or with children in poverty to support.

Table 4. Social Capital Measures of Family

| Family | Percentage of Adults in Civilian Labor Force | | |
Measure	1980	1990	Rate of Change, 1980–90
Percentage of households with female head			
1980	R = −.055 n.s.	—	R = −.045 n.s.
1990	—	R = −.184 $p < .001$	R = −.109 $p < .05$
Rate of change, 1980–90	R = −.241 $p < .0001$	R = −.265 $p < .0001$	R = −.148 $p < .01$
Percentage of children in poverty			
1980	R = −.583 $p < .0001$	—	R = −.148 $p < .01$
1990	—	R = −.731 $p < .0001$	R = −.303 $p < .0001$
Rate of change, 1980–90	R = −.230 $p < .0001$	R = −.332 $p < .0001$	R = −.259 $p < .0001$
Women as percentage of labor force			
1980	R = .758 $p < .0001$	—	R = .257 $p < .0001$
1990	—	R = .645 $p < .0001$	R = .257 $p < .0001$
Rate of change, 1980–90	R = .632 $p < .0001$	R = −.579 $p < .0001$	R = −.189 $p < .0001$

Female-headed households have a stronger and more significant correlation with labor force participation in 1990 than they do in 1980. Again, inadequate social capital policies undermine families but produce new, female workers for declining labor markets. Female-headed households are more prevalent in places with lower labor force participation.

The poverty of children increases pressure on women to work in low-income, low-employment areas. Again, these measures correlate strongly, significantly, and inversely. The percentage of children living in poverty increases as labor force participation decreases. By 1990, the market mecha-

Table 5. Social Capital Measures of Education

Education Measure	Percentage of Adults in Civilian Labor Force		
	1980	1990	Rate of Change, 1980−90
Percentage of population > 25 years of age with high school education			
1980	R = .298 p < .0001	—	R = .255 p < .0001
1990	—	R = .447 p < .0001	R = .277 p < .0001
Rate of change, 1980−90	R = −.055 n.s.	R = −.105 p < .05	R = −.109 p < .05
Percentage of population >25 years of age with college education			
1980	R = .155 p < .0001	—	R = .450 p < .0001
1990	—	R = .416 p < .0001	R = .428 p < .0001
Rate of change, 1980−90	R = .251 p < .0001	R = .219 p < .0001	R = .045 n.s.

nisms of the 1980s had increased the correlation between labor force participation and the percentage of children in poverty. This suggests that although the market and surfeit of social capital may push more women into work in response to the threat to their children, the wages offered are far less effective in reducing the poverty of the new labor force participants. Women stay in disadvantageous labor forces. In areas with decreased labor force participation, the portion of women increased.

Just as market mechanisms reshape the family for labor force participation, they remake the labor force in terms of educational achievement. Table 5 shows that areas of high labor force participation have higher levels of education than do areas with low labor force participation. Once again, we find a much stronger correlation between labor force participation and education in 1990 than in 1980. Overall, increases in labor force participation have a modest but significant correlation with decreases in high school education. This may measure the expansion of low-wage, low-skill employ-

Table 6. Social Capital Measures of Housing

Housing Measure	Percentage of Adults in Civilian Labor Force		
	1980	1990	Rate of Change, 1980–90
Percentage of houses with > 1 person per room			
1980	$R = -.57$ $p < .0001$	—	$R = .234$ $p < .0001$
1990	—	$R = -.228$ $p < .0001$	$R = -.063$ $p < .0001$
Rate of change, 1980–90	$R = .291$ $p < .0001$	$R = .401$ $p < .0001$	$R = .302$ $p < .0001$
Percentage of houses with inadequate plumbing			
1980	$R = -.577$ $p < .0001$	—	$R = -.195$ $p < .0001$
1990	—	$R = -.542$ $p < .0001$	$R = -.182$ $p < .0001$
Rate of change, 1980–90	$R = .291$ $p < .0001$	$R = -.297$ $p < .0001$	$R = -.122$ $p < .05$

ment opportunities. The market found a way to increase participation in the workforce without increasing the social capital invested in the education of workers. At the same time, the market clearly built a labor force in the areas that had invested social capital in the high school and college education of its adult population.

Housing provides another measure of the public goods and moral resources that we invest in people as a workforce. Once again, we find strong and significant association of the quality of housing and labor force participation. Where labor force participation is highest, the amount of housing with overcrowding and inadequate plumbing is lowest. Surprisingly, however, increased labor force participation has far less impact on increasing social capital. Table 6, for example, indicates a modest but significant increase in overcrowded housing in areas with higher labor force participation. At the other end of the labor force spectrum, better housing becomes available at lower prices in places where labor force fortunes are declining. The

Table 7. Social Capital Measures of Health

Health Measure	Percentage of Adults in Civilian Labor Force		
	1980	1990	Rate of Change, 1980–90
Infant mortality rate, 1984–88	R = −.071 n.s.	—	R = −.084 n.s.
Age-adjusted cancer rate, 1983–87	R = −.261 $p < .0001$	R = −.205[a] $p < .0001$	R = −.032 n.s.
Percentage of population aged 16–64 with a work disability, 1990	R = −.707 $p < .0001$	R = −.773[a] $p < .0001$	R = −.355 $p < .0001$

[a] Dependent and independent variables are reversed.

change in housing with inadequate plumbing is in the direction we would expect: lower housing standards in lower labor markets.

In a strict market allocation of labor, supply and demand regulates the life and death of workers. At least Adam Smith thought so. A range of public policies has provided public forms of social capital that the market neglects, which somewhat mitigates this market mechanism of morbidity. Medicaid, for example, provides maternal and infant care for poor women in violation of strict market capitalism. As a consequence, perhaps, we find a low correlation between labor force participation and infant mortality, as Table 7 indicates. However, given the deficit in social capital, the market regulates the life and death of workers in other ways. Cancer rates correlate to labor force participation in small but statistically significant ways. Moreover, if a lack of social capital does not kill, it may certainly maim. Labor force participation correlates strongly, significantly, and inversely with disability. Where labor force participation is low, the rate of work disabilities is very high.

Market Democracy and Unadaptive Capitalism

The free market's halcyon days of the 1980s hid from view the new American challenges that were evident in Appalachia. Market democracy kept the invisible hand's secret: the efficiency of the market requires human sacrifice—sometimes temporary or enduring hardship, for example, unemployment, migration, or poverty; sometimes one's health; and sometimes even one's life. As the market received more praise, it demanded higher human costs, at least in Appalachia. Market democracy in the 1980s expressed the renewed faith of some Americans in limited government and individual self-interest as the final and best arbiters of public welfare and the public good, despite the higher human costs.

George Gilder expressed the unbounded confidence some had in the "high adventure and redemptive morality of capitalism" and the "altruistic creativity" at the foundation of capitalism. The task of reducing poverty, according to Gilder, entailed changing the poor, by extending values of family and faith as well as by freeing them from dependence on government programs (Gilder 1981: x). Charles Murray (1984) and other conservative social analysts of the 1980s not only advocated the market; they attacked public programs of social welfare. Murray attributed the economic stagnation of the late 1970s and early 1980s to the excesses of the social welfare programs of the 1960s and their consequence of removing incentives to work from low-income groups.

Such analyses lead inevitably to a solution of reduced social programs and to a toleration of hardship as an incentive for the poor and unemployed to improve their behavior. Murray combines a call for more limited government with the following assumptions: that individuals in poverty need more incentives to undertake their individual pursuit of self-interest; that a market economy offers prospects of success for anyone who undertakes that individual pursuit; that government has buffered the poor from the natural consequence of a lack of individual effort; and that families and churches provide the only morally justified social support of individuals. The aura of market democracy included the ethos of individual effort, a passion for reward, and approval for unlimited acquisition. Market democracy envisions the universal pursuit of individual self-interest as the organizing principle of civil society and as the surest avenue to achieve realistic approximations of the social good.

One critic of market democrats has portrayed them as political utopians (Kuttner 1991). In this utopia, mediating structures have the reactive role of charity, taking care of widows, orphans, and other "truly needy" persons. As an article of faith in the excellence of the market and the folly of government, these services are deemed "more generous, more humane, more wisely distributed, and more effective in [their] results than the services formerly subsidized by the federal government" (Murray 1984: 230). The clarity of this conclusion evidently comes from its premises, because no evidence is offered to support it.

Economist Robert Heilbroner refers to the forms of economic and social policies of market democracy as "unadaptive capitalism." In his 1993 attempt to discern likely paths for the American economy in the twenty-first century, Heilbroner incorporates much of Adam Smith's work and its social capital implications. He foresees a variety of capitalist economies, adaptive and unadaptive, rooted in national cultures and traditions, that will influence each nation's ability to adapt its form of capitalism to economic and social needs. He makes clear that the United States has all the characteristics of unadaptive capitalism, for which his prognosis is not bright. He argues that unadaptive capitalisms—those with restive and ideologically charged political traditions, weak structures of public administration, and unorganized union and corporate sectors—will "almost certainly not fare as well" as adaptive capitalisms will (Heilbroner 1993: 141). However, as he suggests, there is short-term, local benefit to unadaptive capitalism: unadaptive capitalism provides new jobs and higher wages to some workers, even if it ignores the long-term erosion of social capital, the distribution of benefits, and other costs of short-term prosperity.

Heilbroner explains that economics is a series of dynamic waves of social interventions that alter the productive capabilities of a society, its social composition, and even the relationship of the society to nature. Capital is wealth. Its value inheres in its use to create larger amounts of capital. The greatest accumulation of capital occurs when a new process or product displaces an existing one. To be among the few, early suppliers of a new market of high demand offers the avenue to greatest wealth. It also provides an incentive to look for existing products and processes to displace.

Appalachia's dominant industries declined because by substituting other goods for their products or introducing new processes to produce the same product, other producers could accumulate more capital. The dynamism of capitalism means that one set of production processes and products yields quickly to new products and producers. Deindustrialization and postindustrialization describe forms of capital accumulation that take place in new regions of the country and the world. Appalachia participated as one region in a global pattern of capital accumulation. At one time, one or more portions of the region attracted capital because of the profits to be made there; this is still occurring in parts of Southern Appalachia. At other times, one or more portions of the region lost capital because of the profits to be made elsewhere; this is occurring now in Central and Northern Appalachia. The divestment of capital must inevitably happen in the parts of Southern Appalachia that are enjoying good times now. According to Heilbroner (1993: 35–54), the dynamic nature of economics and the particular patterns of accumulation of capital generate "persistent and powerful tendencies to change."

Social Capital, Economic Roles, and Mediating Structures

In general, American public policy favors a market approach to social capital. Investments in social capital goods and services ordinarily come from private, not public, sources; they follow upon the needs of private capital and have as their central purpose the production, reproduction, and distribution of a labor force for private capital. When groups of people have subordinate roles in the economy, the social capital goods and resources invested in them are modest. When people have no role in the economy, even less social capital goods and resources are invested in them. Similarly, when a community's economic condition improves, so will the social capital invested in it.

The challenges of industrialization and postindustrial market economies are apparent in Appalachia (Couto 1991c, 1994), where declines in employment have triggered declines in social capital. Central to meeting this challenge is the role played by mediating structures: to supply social capital to people apart from their prospects of employment. Chapter 2 explains this role in terms of democratic theory.

Mediating Structures and the Democratic Prospect

In the 1830s, Alexis de Tocqueville commented about the unique American proclivity to form associations to deal with public problems. Given the problems of public drunkenness, Tocqueville mused, Americans are more likely to form an association to deal with the matter than are the French, who are more likely to approach public officials, or the English, who are likely to look to their nobles. Since Tocqueville's time, Americans have continued to assign a unique, primary role for voluntary associations in their democratic practice. The recent emphasis on mediating structures reaffirms the American proclivity that Tocqueville observed.

The democratic role of mediating structures is far more complicated than the continued recitation of Tocqueville's views permits us to understand. The recent scholarship on mediating structures and on social capital promotes a conservative political agenda, but this obviously reflects only one side of democratic possibilities. The social and political reforms of the 1960s expressed a preference for increased equality and communal bonds, and mediating structures and social capital played a role in that political agenda as well. This chapter relates mediating structures and social capital with two democratic theories: the *democratic promise* of limited government and market economics, and the *democratic prospect* of increased social and economic equality and communal bonds. It concludes that mediating structures promote the democratic prospect by advocating for or providing new amounts and improved forms of social capital.

Mediating Structures and Democratic Theory: The Social Perspective

The early scholarship on mediating structures presented their roles as a protest against the excesses of both market capitalism and government. Mediating structures defended liberty and community simultaneously against, respectively, the policies of government and the practices of capitalism. Robert Nisbet, for example, described intermediate associations as a countermeasure to the modern tendency toward centralization and organizational growth in government and the economy. Nisbet focused on the threat to intermediate associations from totalitarianism and authoritarianism, Hitler's Germany and Stalin's Soviet Union, and their efforts to increase and centralize state power. In these two contexts, associations that expressed particular loyalties or that nurtured individualism had to be either co-opted to the purposes of the state (in the case of totalitarianism) or eliminated (in the case of authoritarianism). Nisbet observed that the seeds of the success of totalitarian and authoritarian states grew where the "accustomed roots of membership and belief" in intermediate associations had been pulled (Nisbet 1962: 204).

Totalitarianism and authoritarianism conflict with democracy precisely on the role of intermediate associations, according to Nisbet. First, the monolithic cast of such states "arises from the sterilization or destruction of all groups and statuses that, in any way, rival or detract from the allegiance of the masses to the State" (Nisbet 1962: 205). Second, in totalitarian and authoritarian systems, the state serves as the absolute substitute for "all the diversified associations of which society is normally composed" (Nisbet 1962: 206). In military fashion, the nation mobilizes to eliminate not only independent or critical ideas and beliefs but the intermediate associations where such ideas and beliefs germinate and grow. Totalitarian and authoritarian states create a network of associations of their own to reach down "into the most intimate recesses of human life" and to create a new "network of functions and loyalties" (Nisbet 1962: 208). For Nisbet, the true horror of fascism and communism is the elimination of intermediate associations and the liberty that they nurture. "The absolute political community, centralized and omnicompetent, founded upon the atomized masses, must ceaselessly destroy all those autonomies and immunities that in normal society are the indispensable sources of the capacity for freedom and organization. Total political centralization can lead only to social and cultural death" (Nisbet 1962: 210–11). One can hardly imagine a firmer expression of the dread of state power.

Nisbet's work on intermediate associations articulates a yearning for community just as clearly as it does a dread of state power. "Historically," he writes, "our problem must be seen in terms of the decline in functional and psychological significance of such groups as the family, the small local community, and the various other traditional relationships that have immemorially mediated between the individual and his [sic] society" (Nisbet 1962: 50). Within these groups, individuals acquire primary human and communal bonds of friendship, affection, prestige, and recognition. When these groups decline, the bonds they produce may go with them. Nisbet explains the role of intermediate associations in terms of networks of support and trust: "At bottom, social organization is a pattern of institutional functions into which are woven numerous psychological threads of meaning, loyalty, and interdependence. The contemporary sense of alienation is . . . [partially] a problem in the institutional functions of the relationships that ordinarily communicate integration and purpose to individuals" (Nisbet 1962: 53).

Totalitarianism and authoritarianism are not the only offenders against intermediate associations. The enlarged and centralized economy also impacted intermediate associations adversely. Nisbet attributes the alienation he observed in the twentieth century to changes in *both* the economy and the state that began in the seventeenth century. These changes transformed traditional intermediate associations without providing new, alternative, and adequate associations that could play a central role in the moral and psychological life of individuals (Nisbet 1962: 52). Like Florence Reece and Adam Smith, Nisbet suspects that repressive action against intermediate associations by capital through the state explains the lack of new associations. Instead of pointing to J. H. Blair, like Reece, or to the strong arm of the magistrate, like Smith, Nisbet leaves his suspicion at a speculative level: "It is almost as if the forces that weakened the old have remained to obstruct the new channels of association" (Nisbet 1962: 73).

Nisbet far more clearly asserts that intermediate associations mitigated the alienation and excesses of market capitalism in the industrial era and made its success possible by preserving social order in a market economy. They continue the communal state that preceded and survived the modern age—the family, the geographic community of village, the guild, etc. The economic stability of nineteenth-century market capitalism came from these groups, which preceded it and which it adversely affected. "The natural economic order of the nineteenth century turns out to be, when carefully examined, a special set of political controls and immunities existing on the foundations of institutions, most notably the family and local community, which had nothing whatsoever to do with the essence of capitalism. Freedom of contract, the fluidity of capital, the mobility of labor, and the whole factory system were able to thrive and to give the appearance of internal stability only because of the continued existence of institutional and cultural allegiances which were, in every sense, precapitalist" (Nisbet 1962: 237).

Nisbet's advocacy of intermediate associations protested the excesses of industrial capitalism as well as totalitarian and authoritarian governments. He defended liberty from the state and community from industrial capitalism. However, Nisbet's twin concerns for liberty and community are less prominent in subsequent theories of mediating structures. These theories treat community, as Tocqueville did, as an outcome of liberty, and they criticize market capital far less than Nisbet did. For example, David Sills's early exposition of voluntary associations, which remains among the best (Sills 1967), excludes groups that deal directly with the economy, and emphasizes the community functions of intermediate associations in reinforcing the primary elements of personal identity that concerned Nisbet. Among the social benefits provided by spare-time, participatory, voluntary associations, Sills lists the integration of subgroups into the culture and institutions of the main group; the affirmation of values; decision making; provision of public services, such as health care and disaster prevention or relief; initiating social change; and distributing power.

Sills discusses the mediation role of voluntary associations in terms of the intervention of formal and organized groups and the state to promote an interest that preserves or strengthens the bonds of the individuals within the groups. This primary mediating role focuses on the state and the function of voluntary associations to distribute political power. Like Nisbet, Sills concludes that the power of dispersed associations balances and limits the power of the state, which is good politics.

Sills of course invokes Tocqueville and bestows on him the apparently high honor of being one of the first, truly modern social scientists. Tocqueville wins this honor because of his oft-cited observation that the need for liberty of association increases with public efforts to promote equality: "Among the laws that rule human societies there is one which seems to be more precise and clear than all others. If men are to remain civilized or to become so, the art of associating together must grow and improve in the same ratio in which the equality of conditions is increased" (Tocqueville in Sills 1967: 376).

The precise reason for this law of human society, and hence the increased need for the art of association, is the centralization of power in the state and its bureaucracy that comes with the extension of social and economic equality. Sills consequently ends up in the same camp with Nisbet. Both maintain the importance of mediating structures in dispersing power in society and in checking the modern tendency to concentrate power in the hands of the state and bureaucratic organization. Sills does not develop the importance of mediating structures in mitigating excesses of market capitalism, as Nisbet did. However, mass production certainly is one form of "equality of conditions" that Sills, following upon Tocqueville, cites as the reason for voluntary associations. Hence, we may infer support in Sills's work for Nisbet's twin concerns for liberty and community, the excess of the state and the market.

Sills's works as well as Nisbet's are untouched by the 1960s, an era that challenged the easy assumptions held about the contribution of mediating structures to democratic practice and the inherently democratic nature of American politics. The civil rights movement questioned race relations and broader issues of equality and their relation to American democratic practice. The women's movement asked similar questions regarding gender. The peace movement questioned representation and participation in decision making in liberal, democratic government. The student movement demanded increased representation and participation in processes that decided the nature and functions of the educational institutions of which students were a part.

These social movements created a concern with social and economic equality, rather than with the totalitarian or authoritarian state, in the scholarship on mediating structures. Some of this subsequent work reinforced the themes of Nisbet and Sills. It also introduced an emphasis on equality, rather than liberty, and criticized arrangements of social and institutional authority on the basis of their contribution to political and economic inequality. The Filer Commission, named after its chair John Filer, conducted a full-scale assessment of the relationship of the voluntary sector and democracy and dubbed nonprofit organizations "the third sector." Funded by John D. Rockefeller III in 1973, this group, formally titled the Commission on Private Philanthropy and Public Needs, spent four years and published seven volumes in its extensive study. The Filer Commission report promoted mediating structures to a place in the democratic trinity next to government and business. This Tocquevillean elevation extended to libraries, universities, and hospitals. The commission catalogued the underlying social functions of the third sector much as Nisbet and Sills had done before. Reflecting the influence of the 1960s, it also specified public policy or political roles in both government and the market, extrapolating from the general roles that Nisbet and Sills had discussed. Specifically, the commission suggested that the third sector initiates new ideas and processes, develops public policy, supports minority or local interests, provides services prohibited to government, oversees government, oversees the market place, brings the sectors together, gives aid abroad, and furthers active citizenship and altruism (Silverstein 1983).

Working largely on his own and at the same time, David Horton Smith portrayed the expanded political functions of voluntary associations in terms similar to those used by the Filer Commission. Smith surveyed the work of other scholars, including Nisbet, and included the social functions they attributed to voluntary associations in his own catalog of their functions. According to Smith, voluntary associations integrate individuals and groups into society in many ways, including countering social dislocations and fostering cooperation. Smith's work clearly bears marks of the 1960s in its concern for increased social and economic equality. According to Smith's survey, the voluntary sector serves two conflicting functions in society: both changing and defending the status quo. It preserves old and prevailing ideas and practices and embodies, represents, and supports the role of dominant government and business organizations and programs. In terms of social change, voluntary associations make up for the shortcomings of American politics, including those of other voluntary associations. They provide partially tested social innovations or social risk capital; definitions of reality and morality that counter prevailing definitions; a latent potential to mobilize social resources for the "right reason," such as disaster relief or social protest; the sense of mystery, wonder, and the sacred both in religious practice and exploration of human consciousness; and an element of play for society, including the search for novelty, beauty, recreation, and fun. The voluntary sector continues to liberate individuals and permits them to achieve a fuller measure of their potential, but the restraints against which they struggle include the social environment as well as government. Smith notes that the "'liberation' movement of women, blacks, the poor, the 'Third World' and other disadvantaged and disenfranchised groups" highlighted the "societal limits on people" imposed by economic systems, government laws and practices, and even portions of the voluntary sector—for example, schools, the family, and religion (Smith 1983: 337).

Nisbet and Sills portrayed voluntary associations as primary bulwarks of liberal democracy against the potential, intended and unintended consequences of abridgement of liberty by the efforts of government, such as

Hitler's Germany and the Stalin's Soviet Union. After the lessons about social change learned in the 1960s, other scholars incorporated mediating structures in their analyses of the limits of liberal democracy. Mediating structures became a modest part of social movements to promote increased forms of social and economic equality and to protest the abridgement of equality by political, social, and economic institutions.

The 1970s brought further scholarly reactions to the 1960s and new attention to mediating structures. The first explicit and lengthy study of mediating structures—the Mediating Structures Project, supported by the American Enterprise Institute, the business-initiated, Washington think tank—appeared in the late 1970s and emphasized, once again, a primary, if not exclusive, role of voluntary associations in helping to promote limited government. In the early stages of this project, Peter L. Berger and Richard J. Neuhaus outlined the public policy role of family, church, neighborhood groups, and voluntary associations—all mediating structures that "stand between the individual in his or her private life and the large institutions of modern society" (Kerrine 1980: 332). Although the focus of their forty-five-page essay was far narrower than Nisbet's, Berger and Neuhaus explained the stakes of mediating structures' involvement in public policy in terms remarkably similar to those of Nisbet and of the time preceding the social introspection of the 1960s. Berger and Neuhaus argued that their mediating structures could preserve limited government by substituting their efforts to establish community and equality for those of government: "America has a singular opportunity to contest the predictions of the inevitability of mass society with its anomic individuals, alienated and impotent, excluded from the ordering of a polity that is no longer theirs. And we are convinced that mediating structures might be the agencies for a new empowerment of people in America's renewed experiment in democratic pluralism" (Berger and Neuhaus 1977: 45).

Unlike Nisbet, who wrote in reaction to the rise of totalitarian and authoritarian governments of the 1930s, the Mediating Structures Project came in reaction to the American social programs of the 1960s. The project had the same concern as Nisbet, namely "to strengthen pluralism and voluntarism" and to reassert the self-limiting nature of state power in a pluralist democracy (Kerrine 1980: 331, 337). The context was postindustrial America and dramatic changes in the economic practices of corporations that had profound consequences for Americans. Unlike Nisbet, however, the project ignored the economic context of social problems and zeroed in on the remnant of the largest government initiative for social welfare since the New Deal: the Great Society.

The project lamented the costs exacted by government efforts since the New Deal to complete a vision of social justice. In a parallel to Nisbet's work, the project assumed that government programs displace the natural communities of kinship and fellowship within which people order their lives (Kerrine 1980: 334). The project protested government usurpation just as Nisbet had. It rejected government's using "the people" to legitimate public policy, arguing that the voice of "the people" as moral authority of the state lay in the multitude of communities that comprise society, not the pronouncements of a central authority (Kerrine 1980: 334). The target now was not Nazi Germany or Communist Russia but liberal America. The Great Society allegedly had supplanted communal networks with networks of its own. By so doing, critics alleged, the American government threatened the potential takeover of moral authority and produced ineffective programs that had little accountability to the people whom they were intended to serve. The goal of social justice, the project suggested, might be achieved better through mediating structures that were "'in touch' with the aspirations of most people" (Kerrine 1980: 334). This meant rethinking the proposition, rooted in the New Deal, that public responsibility to address human needs must be implemented by government (Kerrine 1980: 334). Completely missing from the project was any sense that the new forms and severity of human needs emerging in the 1970s might be related to new economic arrangements and practices rather than to government programs. Nisbet had emphasized that mediating structures mitigated the consequences of market capitalism. The new attention to mediating structures was absorbed with its efforts to exorcise the liberal government programs of the 1960s and to a lesser extent those of the 1930s.

In the meantime, some liberal social theorists continued to look to the social movements of the 1960s for examples of mediating structures' capacity to transform social policy (Bellah et al. 1985). Historical studies indicated that federal agencies within radical reform efforts of the Reconstruction, the New Deal, and the War on Poverty included the formation of mediating structures as a key component of their work (Couto 1991a).

Nationally, however, the Democratic Party moved to a conservative middle ground that ignored these politically transformative roles of mediating structures. Instead, it adopted some of the bias against government, including its own liberal past, in the new emphasis on mediating structures. By the 1990s, the Progressive Policy Institute, fittingly enough a radically centrist think tank for the moderate Democratic Leadership Council, had a credo of community, empowerment, and mediating structures. Like the policies of conservative Republicans, this credo asked more from mediating structures and less from government: "Unwilling to frame every public question in terms of a choice between government provision and market competition, progressives place new emphasis on the voluntary associations and institutions of community—America's 'third sector.' Government's role is to empower families, voluntary organizations, and institutions to solve their own problems, not to try to replace them with public programs or institutions. Community also means taking care of citizens in need and affirming the common civic values that unite us as Americans" (Marshall and Schram 1993: xvii).

This seeming agreement across the political spectrum ignores bothersome details about the relation of mediating structures and democracy. For example, proponents of mediating structures differ about their role. Some proponents suggest a minimalist role for mediating structures—that is, that public policy should protect and foster them and do them no harm. Other proponents suggest maximalist roles for mediating structures, ranging from participating in the design of public policy to conducting public policy as service deliverers. Among the maximalists are those who would provide mediating structures with public resources to underwrite their public policy role and those who are more inclined to leave the matter of fund-raising and resources to the mediating structures (Kerrine 1980: 333). Proponents also differ about what organizations are and are not mediating structures. At a minimum, community groups, voluntary associations, churches, and families make the most conservative list of mediating structures (Berger and Neuhaus 1977). Ethnic and racial groups and labor organizations expand the list of mediating structures for liberals and progressives (Kerrine 1980: 332).

There are other, more practical problems with the proposed policy roles for mediating structures in democracy. David Price, a political scientist, has extolled Berger and Neuhaus's suggestion that mediating structures offer a paradigm to empower poor people and "to do so where it matters, in people's control of their own lives" (Price 1980: 381) but cautions that trusting in mediating structures as social problem solvers ignores their short supply among the poor and powerless. Later studies of the problem-plagued inner city attributed its plight partially to the absence of mediating structures (W. J. Wilson 1987). According to Price, the efforts of Community Action Programs in the 1960s did not replace the mediating structures among the poor and powerless, they attempted to create some that were missing. Price chides conservative advocates for their naïveté in "'utilizing' mediating structures [without taking into account] the difficult process of facilitation and community-building that is required" (Price 1980: 382). Objections to public efforts to create and support mediating structures assume that they occur naturally. Price, like Nisbet, points out that mediating structures do not occur naturally. There may be genuine impediments to them. If we want them, we need to support their origins and continuation through public policy.

Price complicates the role of mediating structures in public policy and suggests specific criteria to determine their role. Not all mediating structures will have the same capacity for public tasks and building community. Even the same organization will vary over time and from place to place in its capacity. So, policy makers need to determine the capacities of a mediating structure to perform a specific task and to serve as a focal point of community interaction. Second, Price suggests that effective mediating structures must have characteristics beyond just local effectiveness. They must be inclusive, incorporating in their functions and membership some broader range of values that command allegiance from others outside the group.

In addition to these bothersome details about mediating structures and democracy, much of the consensus about them ignored fundamental differences about their political function. They are not merely bulwarks against totalitarian and authoritarian governments. They mitigate the social consequences of economics. They promote equality as well as liberty.

Mediating Structures and Democratic Theory: The Political Perspective

One might expect political theorists to address and to resolve some of the problems of the political nature and democratic role of mediating structures that social theorists assumed away. However, the immense literature of political science pays less attention to mediating structures than the comparatively scant literature on mediating structures pays to politics. By their absence, mediating structures appear irrelevant to political democratic theory. Political scientists ordinarily define politics as governing and government. Consequently, when nonprofit groups come under the lens of political science, they are viewed, like their for-profit counterparts, as interest groups focused on influencing the process and decision making of government. The American Association of Retired Persons, the National Rifle Association, and the Council of Philanthropy are examples of the type of voluntary associations likely to gain the attention of political scientists. They are mediating structures in the same sense as powerful lobbying groups for doctors and manufacturers are. As Sills described, they mediate between the interests of their constituents and public policy or the political process; they play roles within the game of politics as government and governing. For example, the work of Sidney Verba, Kay Lehman Schlozman, and Henry E. Brady (1995) assigns an essentially political role to the voluntary sector, which "in America shapes the allocation of economic, social, and cultural benefits and contributes to the achievement of collective purposes" (7). Only a portion of voluntary associations and activities are political, however, according to Verba and his colleagues. This political portion intends, or has the consequence of affecting, government action, either directly or indirectly (9). Nonpolitical volunteerism may have an indirect political content because it "can enrich the stockpile of resources relevant to political action" (8). Church work, for example, may provide opportunities to develop skills that are relevant for politics (17–18).

This study by three prominent political scientists goes no further than do the works of David Horton Smith and the Filer Commission in explaining mediating structures as a prerequisite for democracy. In fact, it does not go as far. Smith and the Filer Commission asserted the political nature of the social change efforts of mediating structures, however modest. Verba and his colleagues deal with political participation as "communicating information about citizen preferences and needs to policy makers and creating pressure on them to heed what they hear" (Verba, Schlozman, and Brady: 12). Three decades after social theorists incorporated the critiques of pluralism into their accounts of mediating structures, political scientists still explain the politics of mediating structures in terms of pluralism—competition among centers of power for influence.

More interesting than the general irrelevance of mediating structures in the work of political theorists is their apparent irrelevance even in the work of democratic theorists who are critical of pluralism! Although some social theories of mediating structures proposed after the 1960s incorporated social and political critiques in their discussion of the political roles of mediating structures, most political theorists writing after the 1960s either ignore mediating structures or warn of their antidemocratic role.

In their book *Poor People's Movements: Why They Succeed and How They Fail*, Frances Fox Piven and Richard A. Cloward (1979) did champion the liberation aspect of mediating structures. Their work, which situates mediating structures in social movements that protest and liberate groups from both economic and political forms of repression in American life, emphasizes informal organizations of mass mobilization and protest much more than formal organizations. Their work assumes the inability of democratic pluralism to redistribute social and economic resources meaningfully. It also assumes a fatal, antidemocratic flaw inherent in formal organizations, even mediating structures, which begin in social protest but then evolve to internal oligarchy and stasis (Piven and Cloward 1979: xv).

In his book *Strong Democracy: Participatory Politics for a New Age*, Benjamin Barber assembles a democratic theory with a heavy emphasis on community and suspicion about local organizations. His work is long on democratic renewal but short on an explicit role for mediating structures in the renewal process. Barber contrasts liberalism with the republican virtue of citizenship. Liberalism, he argues, promotes "thin democracy," while citizenship promotes "strong democracy." Levels of participation distinguish thin and strong democracy (Barber 1984: 132). Barber acknowledges that mediating structures may serve as schools for the civic education necessary for strong democracy. However, he warns about their serving in this role, pointing out that, to the extent they are parochial or particular to an issue or place, they may undermine democracy. Strong bonds among neighbors, Barber suggests, may separate them from others. In his view, communal bonds that divide subvert "the wider ties required by democracy— ties that can be nurtured only by an expanding imagination bound to no particular sect or fraternity. Strong democracy creates a continuum of activity that stretches from the neighborhood to the nation—from private to public—and along which the consciousness of participating citizens can expand" (235). Clearly, Barber is less than sanguine about the capacity of mediating structures to promote this broadened consciousness for the increased and improved participation of strong democracy. He suggests that only direct political participation, activity that is explicitly public, such as town meetings and neighborhood assemblies, succeeds completely as a form of civic education (235).

In *Discursive Democracy*, John Dryzek takes Barber's framework of criticism into further abstraction and away from practical considerations about mediating structures. Dryzek contrasts liberal and participatory democracies as two major democratic possibilities, not dichotomous but yet distinct. The pole of participatory democracy incorporates a sense of community. At that pole, according to Dryzek, "politics becomes increasingly discursive, educational, oriented to truly public interests, and needful of active citizenship" (Dryzek 1990: 119). At the liberal pole, "voting, strategy, private interests, bargaining, exchange, spectacle, and limited involvement" dominate politics (Dryzek 1990: 13). Dryzek compares these poles to the thin and strong democracy of Barber and contrasts them in terms similar to Barber's. However, the set of political institutions at Dryzek's participatory democratic pole is empty! We find instead a hypothesis that participatory democracy and community require discursive democratic institutions (Dry-zek 1990: 40).

In a somewhat similar vein, Joshua Cohen and Joel Rogers (1995a,b) deal explicitly with the political theory of associations and democracy, but, except in the case of labor organizations, they pay little attention to the ordinary mediating structures that social theorists pin their democratic hopes on. Ironically, the explicit consideration of the politics of associations goes no further than David Horton Smith's in explaining the political functions of mediating structures and implies an empty set (Young 1995), just as Dryzek did.

Jeffrey M. Berry and his colleagues undertook another explicitly political examination of mediating structures in *The Rebirth of Urban Democracy*, their study of neighborhood associations in five large cities. Their examination of the literature on democratic participation led them to conclude that "social scientists have largely given up on participatory democracy" and those who had not given up did not offer a coherent set of guidelines for reforms of current, inadequately democratic practice (Berry, Portney, and Thomson 1993: 213). In contrast to the work they reviewed, and in keeping with the thrust of this argument, Berry and his colleagues found that neighborhood associations increased their members' bonds with others and increased political equality. They did so when they provided their members with opportunities for representation and participation in social and political processes. Thus, Berry and his colleagues support the contentions of Barber about "strong democracy" but offer optimism about the place of mediating structures in achieving it and empirical evidence to support their optimism.

Likewise, when Sara Evans and Harry Boyte looked at movements to increase social and economic equality, they found mediating structures. Their book, *Free Spaces*, offers historical evidence about the capacity of mediating structures to contribute to participatory, democratic, reform politics in their role as "public places in the community . . . the environments in which people are able to learn a new self-respect, a deeper and more assertive group identity, public skills, and values of cooperation and civic virtue . . . settings between private lives and large-scale institutions where ordinary citizens can act with dignity, independence, and vision" (Evans and Boyte 1986: 17). These efforts at broad political, social, and economic change and especially the free spaces they create offer the glimmer of solidarity and discursive democracy. Tracing several social movements over the past century, Evans and Boyte find that local groups resisted race, gender, and class discrimination overtly and covertly in free spaces.

In *Fighting Back in Appalachia,* Stephen L. Fisher deals explicitly with community organizations in Appalachia and their real and potential political role for democratic political reform and renewal. Like Barber and Dryzek, Fisher concerns himself with community in participatory forms of democracy. He recognizes that some elements of the analysis of free spaces, community, and democracy are ideals that are insufficiently grounded in experience to determine what specific forms of them are transformative. Indeed, although an advocate of community and community organizing, Fisher, like Barber, understands that some local organizing efforts may be parochial and reinforce racial, gender, and other antidemocratic biases. Consequently, free spaces, for Fisher, are transformative and democratic when they provide a place "where 'people's history' can be connected to a systemic critique of the political economy; where participants can begin to see the connection between their concerns and those of other exploited people; where members can come to confront issues of racism and sexism; and where people can start to envision new alternatives to the world in which they live" (Fisher 1993: 329).

Fisher is primarily concerned with community organizations in Appalachia that conduct forms of resistance to preserve or achieve some public service or quality essential to the continuation of their communities. His analysis suggests how we might study the democratic, transformative nature of mediating structures. Understandably, he offers no easy answers. Instead, he suggests that relating the democratic process to mediating structures requires an analysis of how local histories fit into the contours of the political economy of capitalism, including its international nature. This large task breaks down into several smaller but still challenging and complex questions. How can local efforts successfully challenge dominant centers of power? How do we promote the values of mediating structures, such as churches and community organizations, that support resistance to centralization and to unjust forms and expressions of power and challenge those values of the same groups that reinforce racial, gender, and other antidemocratic biases? What are the political forms and class dimensions of cultural transformation involved in the changes brought or sought by mediating structures? Fisher challenges analysts to explain culture and community as spaces of political action, locally and globally; to explain how the needs and grievances that inspire local political action are rooted in ubiquitous structural processes occurring at a political, economic, and cultural level far distant from the local grievance (Fisher 1993: 327).

Fisher's work exemplifies a rare instance of the explicit, careful consideration of mediating structures and democratic political theory. His work may also explain why so few political scientists emulate his efforts. He requires that the political nature of culture, social class divisions, and the economy be included in an analysis of mediating structures and democracy. Fisher adds economics as well as differences of class, race, gender, and culture to the list of elements necessary to examine the relationship of mediating structure and democratic politics. Covering so much analytical literature and then requiring that analysis be grounded in local histories of small, out-of-view communities and of organized efforts to defend or enhance them requires a depth and breadth in areas far beyond the normal matters of political science—governing and government. In his study *Power and Powerlessness: Quiescence and Rebellion in an Appalachian Valley*, John Gaventa (1980) showed how this broader scholarship could be done. He grounded new and rich political theoretical considerations and a conceptual framework on power and powerlessness in the history and experience of popular rebellion in one Central Appalachia area. Fisher does comparable work with the theoretical considerations and conceptual framework of community organizing. Both works suggest the possibilities of finding within Appalachia concrete examples of political scholarship that illuminate democratic possibilities and roles of mediating structures.

With Fisher we also reach the limits of political theorists' considerations of mediating structures and democratic practice. He also brings us to a realization of the complexity of their relationship and to its empirical examination.

Mediating Structures and Social Capital

Robert Putnam's work synthesized the social and political theorists' scholarship of mediating structures, social capital, and democratic theory. It gave mediating structures uncommon attention from a political theorist and supported the conservative social theorists' views on nongovernmental approaches to the economic and political changes of the 1970s and 1980s. Putnam's study addressed questions about democracy, economic development, and civic life (Putnam 1993: xiv). He found that groups such as sports clubs, cooperatives, mutual aid societies, cultural associations, labor unions, and other voluntary unions, a rich array of mediating structures, affect the efficacy of political institutions. Interactions among people in these groups and organizations create horizontal networks of civic engagement that help participants solve dilemmas of collective action. These same networks bolster the performance of the polity and the economy (Putnam 1993: 115, 175–76). Mediating structures provide building blocks of horizontal and vertical networks that social capital binds together into a foundation for democratic practice.

Borrowing from the work of others, Putnam describes social capital as the "features of social organization, such as trust, norms, and networks, that can improve the efficiency of society by facilitating coordinated actions" (Putnam 1993: 167). Social capital underwrites all transactions, private and social, economic and political. Social capital, unlike private capital, is the by-product of social activities and the social side of commercial transactions. In daily interactions, structured by mediating structures, people learn trust, social norms, and effective networks for public action. A plethora of mediating structures creates a dense horizontal network and many opportunities to acquire the social capital of trust. A dearth of mediating structures creates a thin horizontal network and fewer opportunities to acquire trust or other forms of social capital. Putnam is prescriptive: "Those concerned with democracy and development . . . should be building a more civic community. . . . [and aiming for] local transformation of local structures rather than reliance upon national initiatives" (Putnam 1993: 185).

Putnam's work reinforced the easy assumptions Americans make about the relationship of voluntary associations and democracy, first noted by Tocqueville. It offered renewed hope of finding solutions to public problems that did not require government intervention and, perhaps, support. Putnam concludes by invoking the patron saint of American voluntary associations. "Tocqueville was right: Democratic government is strengthened, not weakened, when it faces a vigorous civil society" (Putnam 1993: 182).

Putnam tied social capital explicitly to mediating structures, seeing their role as social capital entrepreneurs. However, Nisbet, writing three decades before Putnam, goes further than Putnam does in conceptualizing mediating structures as social capital entrepreneurs. Putnam relates social capital to the virtues of social interaction, trust, loyalty, and cooperation—moral resources (Putnam 1993: 169)—but Nisbet identifies a material base as well as a moral base to social capital. He explains that intermediate associations—family, church, and local community—drew and held peoples' allegiances because "these groups possessed a virtually indispensable relation to the economic and political order. The social problems of birth and death, courtship and marriage, employment and unemployment, infirmity and old age were met, however inadequately at times, through the associative means of these social groups" (Nisbet 1962: 54).

Nisbet sees a crisis in the dearth and decline of intermediate associations because they no longer provided the material base of social capital by which people produced and reproduced themselves in community: "Family, local community, church, and the whole network of informal interpersonal relationships have ceased to play a determining role in our institutional systems of mutual aid, welfare, education, recreation, and economic production and distribution" (Nisbet 1962: 54). Nisbet relates the failure of intermediate associations to provide the psychological and symbolic functions of social capital—that is, its moral element—directly to their diminished capacity to perform the material and economic functions of social capital.

The renewed emphasis on mediating structures in the 1980s came with and from the ideological stature of market democracy. Declining commitments to government regulation and social policies and programs to promote equality stimulated a search for new sources and stocks of social capital. Berger and Neuhaus found them in mediating structures. Mediating structures could supplement or replace public programs to address social problems. Robert Putnam's work supported the conservative revision of the political role of mediating structures. It ignored and diminished the economic function of mediating structures and the material side of social capital. Social capital, in Putnam's work, consists almost exclusively of moral resources.

Social Capital as Moral Resources for the Community

Defining social capital as moral resources expresses a limited criticism of market economics. The economists' expression of the human community falls far short of the community envisioned by the political and social theorists of mediating structures and social capital. The moral virtues of mediating structures counteract the social alienation implicit in the individualism that is embedded in market relations. Individualism—or, more precisely, individual interests—formed the first moral basis for the politics of capitalism. But individualism limits human relations to the advice, let the buyer beware. Robert Nisbet deals directly with the communal failings of market economics from the inception of capitalism. Specifically, the alienation implicit in human relationships that are guided only by market concerns for instrumental, individual self-interest and reward marks the moral failure of the political economy of capitalism. Nisbet debunked the false promise of totalitarian politics to "rescue" masses of atomized individuals from their intolerable individualism (Nisbet 1962: 245). However, he did not thereby advocate market democracy. Intolerable individualism grows in the soil of the alienation endemic to capitalism and its overbearing emphasis on self-interest. Totalitarian government did not invent intolerable individualism, and market democracy cannot remedy it.

Counteracting the individuating alienation of market relations requires moral resources, as Albert O. Hirschman (1984) explains well in his essay "Against Parsimony." Hirschman laments the narrow focus of economic inquiry on the market of buying and selling, a focus that transforms human beings into human calculators of the monetary costs and benefits of a limited range of possible actions or decisions. This narrow focus often misses changes in values. People may develop preferences for public goods (cleaner environments, for example) and begin to consume different products (biodegradable products, for example). A change in behavior stemming from changed values eludes economic inquiry that explains behavior strictly by price differences. Health concerns, for example, may curb the smoking behavior of an individual even if cigarettes are cheap. Hirschman also laments the primary concern of the field of economics with the production of private goods. The narrow focus on the pursuit of profit misses noninstrumental or selfless activities by which people strive to produce truth, beauty, justice, liberty, community, friendship, love, or salvation. These selfless activities have uncertain and nonmonetary outcomes. Efforts to produce them may exceed their value, which violates the concept of instrumental action for profit. An individual may try to produce a work of beauty, such as a painting, yet fail to produce anything of economic worth. In the narrow focus of economic, instrumental activity, this effort amounts to unproductive time. Even successful efforts to produce a nonmonetary outcome (increased racial justice, for example) violate the instrumental logic of calculated, rational actions of consumption and production, which are the predominant assumptions of market economics.

Hirschman advises expanding the domain of economics to include noninstrumental action, because the production and consumption of valuable noninstrumental outcomes differ from the consumption and production of monetary goods. Noninstrumental action combines striving for an uncertain outcome with attainment, to some degree, of that outcome. Striving and attaining replace production and consumption and mark the difference between noninstrumental and instrumental action. Noninstrumental action is rational because an individual makes gains, although they do not take the form of personal, material wealth. People attain nonmonetary values like justice, community, and friendship to some degree by the *process* of striving and not merely by the produced *outcome* of their efforts.

> He who strives after truth (or beauty) frequently experiences the conviction, fleeting though it may be, that he has found (or achieved) it. He who participates in a movement for liberty or justice frequently has the expe-

rience of already bringing these ideals within reach . . . This fusion of striving and attaining is a fact of experience that goes far in accounting for the existence and importance of non-instrumental activities. As though in compensation for the uncertainty about the outcome, the striving effort is colored by the goal and, in this fashion, makes for an experience that is very different from merely agreeable, pleasurable, or even "stimulating"; in spite of its frequently painful character it has a well-known "intoxicating" quality (Hirschman 1984: 92).

Part of the intoxicating quality of noninstrumental action, striving on behalf of values, comes in the feeling of being a "real person" and of belonging to a group. In economic terms, noninstrumental action represents an investment in individual and group identity (Hirschman 1984: 92). In political and social terms, noninstrumental action may provide a glimmer of solidarity and community, the thick horizontal network of Putnam's social capital.

Hirschman describes noninstrumental action on behalf of values as a moral resource with unique properties. Unlike the resources of instrumental action and private capital, moral resources increase through use, rather than decrease, and diminish if not used (Hirschman 1984: 93). In simple terms, permitting another driver to merge into my lane while driving does not exhaust my capacity for courtesy for the day. The function of moral resources extends further than the individual acts of courteous and discourteous drivers. The system of traffic depends upon individual acts of courtesy, a minimum supply of moral resources, to keep several lanes of traffic flowing. Although permitting a driver or drivers to merge before me into my lane may modestly delay my travel, it assists everyone to move at a slower but reasonable rate. My courtesy to another driver, if extended by other drivers, benefits the whole flow of traffic (Hirschman 1984: 94). Excessive courtesy has its individual and systemic limits, however. Permitting every car to merge into my lane may halt the traffic in my lane, delay my arrival at work, cause late arrivals at work for the drivers in the lane behind me, and encourage drivers in the stalled lane of traffic to change lanes hastily, putting others at risk for an accident. The middle ground of alternating merge combines courtesy with efficiency and requires modest sacrifice of individual well-being.

Moral resources have a floor as well as a ceiling to benefits. Centrally planned economies demand too much of moral resources, according to Hirschman. Market economics, with its assumption that the social order is more secure when it is built on self-interest rather than love or benevo-

lence, expects too little of moral resources (Hirschman 1984: 93). Once a social system, such as a market democracy, becomes convinced that benev-
olence is unnecessary if "interests" are given full scope, "the system will
undermine its own viability which is, in fact, premised on civic behavior and
on the respect of certain moral norms to a far greater extent than capitalism's official ideology avows" (Hirschman 1984: 94). Returning to our driving example, once a traffic system instills considerations of individual benefit above courtesy for social benefit, there are no grounds to honor an
alternating merge system. Merging becomes a contest of individual wills,
with dented fenders and human injury as its outcomes.

Social Capital as Market Mitigations and Public Goods

Ironically, just as Nisbet explained, it is moral resources that make markets
work. Moral resources mitigate the destructive alienation embedded in market relations and support the noninstrumental efforts of those who counter
market forces.

The advocates of market democracy have paid little attention to the dark
side of markets, such as negative externalities and inadequate public goods.
Even Putnam's work does not include mitigating market failures among
the social capital roles of mediating structures. If left alone, the market
would ignore negative externalities and its other shortcomings. Transactions about the production and consumption of private goods and services
may have effects on people other than those directly involved in buying and
selling (Heilbroner and Thurow 1994: 189). Smoke from industrial smoke-
stacks darkens houses in the area and places contaminants in the air that can
cause pulmonary disorders. The costs of these effects are negative externalities to the people who have to clean their houses extra hard or pay medical
bills without receiving any direct or individual compensation from the profitable output of the factory. Negative externalities are rooted in the rational, instrumental logic of the marketplace. If I do not have a problem, I have
no incentive to take on the costs to solve it. Positive externalities are rooted
in their similarity to public goods. If an office complex landscapes a portion
of their property and places a fountain in a grassy knoll, the owners of that
complex cannot prevent people who walk by from enjoying the respite of
grass and flowing water in an urban environment.

Adam Smith envisioned an appropriate role for the state in the case of
negative externalities. The state, he wrote, has "the duty of protecting, as far
as possible, every member of the society from the injustice or oppression of
every other member of it" (quoted in Heilbroner 1993: 71). The state may

protect some members of society from the consequences that the actions of others have upon them. Public regulations provide the ordinary means to curb the consequences of negative externalities. Regulations may result in making costs that had been passed on to the public, like smoke leaving a chimney, the responsibility of the person passing them along. Regulation may mean holding someone liable for damages resulting from their actions or making them responsible for instituting new practices that reduce the source of the adverse consequence of past practices.

Left to their own devices, the natural laws of the market would also provide a dearth of public goods. Public goods, such as a lighthouse or the weather service, have unique properties that inhibit incentives to provide them through the market. First of all, the consumption of a public good by one person does not interfere with its consumption by another person. Thus, unlike with the consumption of food, clothing, or health services, the benefit that a lighthouse provides to one boat owner does not diminish its supply for another boat owner (Heilbroner and Thurow 1994: 186–89). The consumption of a public good by one consumer does not change the quality or quantity of it that is available for use by other consumers. Public goods are not exclusive. One person cannot deny another person the use of a weather forecast. Finally, public goods are provided by public decisions about what public goods to purchase and how much of them to buy.

People who do not own boats have little incentive to contribute to the construction of lighthouses. But if only boat owners of a particular locality paid for a lighthouse, the costs to them would soar beyond its reasonable worth. Boat owners have even less incentive to provide for a lighthouse from their own pockets because they cannot limit the benefits of the lighthouses exclusively to those who support its construction. Occasional boaters in the area and landlubbing tourists could use the lighthouse at no cost to them.

Market rationality leads one to attempt to enjoy as much benefit of public goods that are supplied by others without contributing oneself to their provision. It leads others to cease supplying them once their costs exceed their benefits to the contributing individuals. Because of these characteristics, public goods are not left solely to the rational, instrumental calculations of the market to supply. The adequate supply of public goods requires that government take revenue from everyone to pay for them. Even Adam Smith, no advocate of government intervention, relegated to the state "the duty of erecting and maintaining certain public works and certain public institutions, which it can never be to the interest of any individual, or group of individuals, to erect and maintain because the profit would never repay the expense . . . though it may frequently do much more than repay it to a great society" (Smith 1937 [1776]: 651).

It falls to the public realm to decide what public goods are, which ones to purchase, and how many of them are enough. When guided by market democracy, government produces little public support for public goods. Conservative economists have a magic like Merlin's apprentice to transform what are thought to be public goods, including lighthouses and the weather service, into the realm of private production and profit. Only national defense seems beyond the ken of conservative economists' capacity to privatize. Even in this area the 1980s showed how some political conservatives, if given the chance, attempt privatization in the realm of foreign affairs, where even economic conservatives fall short. The Reagan administration's arrangement to sell missiles to Iran and to use the cash to supply arms to the contra rebels in Nicaragua represented an effort to conduct national defense policy separately from the political decision-making framework for public goods. Oliver North took the further step of soliciting contributions from wealthy individuals, thus privatizing this alternative national defense policy, which had been disapproved by Congress.

There are few pure public goods such as lighthouses. The distinction between what is and what is not a public good is a political issue rather than a simple economic decision. For example, education and sanitation are not pure public goods, although they are often provided by the government. Jurisdictional boundaries may exclude some people from the use of schools or sanitation services precisely because unlimited access is neither possible nor wise because the support for them is provided by a limited public within some boundaries. Government officials most often decide who pays and who uses public goods. Other factors may exclude people from the use of a public good as well. School segregation excluded African American students from one set of public schools and required them to attend another set of schools supported by the public but at a much reduced level. The Supreme Court decision in 1954 to ban school segregation came on constitutional grounds. In political terms, however, *Brown v. Board of Education* suggested that "separate but equal" public goods represents a *political* decision to construct and maintain *economic* differences that support social divisions of superior and inferior individuals, such as white supremacy.

The wake of conservative administrations in both the United States and Britain in the 1980s halted any momentum to extend public goods. They asserted a market democracy that preferred the market to government and that turned political issues into economic decisions. The impact on public goods of market democracy appeared more dramatically in Great Britain, where the net of public goods had been cast more widely than in post–World War II America. British national industries were privatized. In the United States, the remnant of the Reagan recall of government included the "reinvention of government," which substituted the market for the government in the provision of public goods and services. Private capital entrepreneurs gained more public trust with the provision and management of what had been public goods, such as schools, health care, and prisons. The redistribution of wealth that went to the already rich was balanced with a new emphasis on moral resources and mediating structures for those who had less wealth and economic prospects than before. Part of this conservative makeover included a limited scope for mediating structures that accentuated moral resources more than the economic base of social capital.

The full range of roles for mediating structures includes providing social capital by mitigating the market failures of negative externalities and inadequate public goods. Ironically, this explicitly political and economic role has a great deal to do with moral resources. How can a community's members trust and cooperate with each other when some of them support political decisions to construct and maintain economic differences that support social divisions of severe needs and excess privileges amongst them? When market democrats construct new, disparaging economic and political myths about social and economic inequality, they erode the moral resources of trust and cooperation that they advocate.

Dealing with market failures, whether those manifested by inadequate public goods or negative externalities, involves considering the proper fit of politics and economics or the discursive democracy that John Dryzek described. What are the range and nature of public goods? Who should have access to public goods? What public goods are impaired because of negative externalities? Who should bear the costs of removing negative externalities? The resolution of these questions entails a political decision about the adequacy of the market to remedy the social problems it creates and about the very nature of social problems. Mediating structures have a role in these political decisions that Putnam and the advocates of market democracy ignore.

Social Capital and Social Class

The economic role of mediating structures to mitigate market failures involves the democratic problem of equality. Julian Wolpert's analysis of generosity in America indicates a problem of distribution among philanthropies: "them that has, gets." Wolpert studied contributions to nonprofit organizations in eighty-five metropolitan statistical areas. He found that support for amenity services, programs intended to enhance the variety and quality of life, exceeded support for social services, programs intended to reduce inequality. He found that amenity support increases as people contribute more to nonprofit organizations in general. Support for amenity services is also greater in places where per capita income is increasing and where the political and cultural ideology is liberal (Wolpert 1993: 6–7). Wolpert found that nonprofit organizations were tied to their source of contributions by geographic area as well as by the nature of their services: "Nonprofits have become locked into a process of largely providing services and amenities to their own local donors and are not organized to provide more generous support for redistributive services." They have not overcome "the impediments to retargeting support between service sectors and from places of affluence to places of long-term distress" (Wolpert 1993: 37). The charitable pattern of nonprofits does little to bridge differences between pockets of affluence and pockets of poverty. Nonprofits do not make up for deficits in social capital, nor do they redistribute resources sufficiently. The uneven support for nonprofit organizations from area to area and the predominance of support for the provision of amenities in all areas has an adverse impact on the places with a concentration of low-income residents and higher amounts of social need (Wolpert 1993: 7). Indeed, in areas with concentrations of the neediest people—such as the country's inner cities, central Appalachia, the rural South, and parts of the Southwest—nonprofits are overwhelmed by the needs they face (Wolpert 1993: 31; 1994).

Others have expressed a similar concern about the adequacy of mediating structures as social capital entrepreneurs to redress social and economic inequality. Glenn Loury (1987) stressed that mediating structures may produce and reproduce the socioeconomic class structure. Pierre Bourdieu (1986: 241–50) develops this in substantial detail, explaining that the various forms of capital have the capacity to produce and reproduce themselves.

Bourdieu explains, for example, the social construction of labor—human capital—in terms of the history and recurrent need of financial capital for social stability: "Capital is accumulated by labor (in its materialized form or its 'incorporated,' embodied form) which, when appropriated on a private, that is, exclusive basis by agents or groups, enables them to appropriate social energy in the form of reified or living labor" (Bourdieu 1986: 241). Bourdieu explains social and cultural capital not as resources that may lend themselves to financial capital, as Nisbet viewed them, but as another form of exchange that financial capital initiates. He faults economic theory, as Hirschman did, for ignoring the economic nature of social and cultural capital, especially their class structure. Bourdieu defines social capital in terms of class or networks of relationships, calling it "the aggregate of the actual or potential resources which are linked to possession of a durable network of more or less institutionalized relationships of mutual acquaintance and recognition—or, in other words, to membership in a group—which provides each of its members with the backing of the collectivity-owned capital, a 'credential' which entitles them to credit, in the various senses of the word" (Bourdieu 1986: 249). People have different amounts of social capital depending on the actual or potential resources, the size of the network to which they are linked, and the amount of economic and cultural capital the members of that network have. Social capital is never independent of the other forms of capital, according to Bourdieu.

The network of social capital requires regular institutional maintenance to produce and reproduce "lasting, useful relationships that can secure material or symbolic profits" (Bourdieu 1986: 249). These networks are the products of investment strategies "individual and collective, consciously or unconsciously aimed at establishing or reproducing social relationships that are directly useable in the short or long term, that is, at transforming contingent relations, such as those of neighborhood, the workplace, or even kinship, into relationships that are at once necessary and elective, implying durable obligations subjectively felt (feelings of gratitude, respect, friendship, etc.) or institutionally guaranteed rights" (Bourdieu 1986: 249–50). Socioeconomic standing, or class, obviously influences the makeup of these networks, but so do family, neighborhood, church, and other mediating structures. Here again, we find moral resources precisely as described by Hirschman as investments in individual and group identity. In Bourdieu's work, however, these moral resources are invested to maintain class differences rather than reduce them, precisely as Wolpert described amenity services.

Cultural and social capital are social forms of economics, according to Bourdieu. Inequalities of economic capital and its social correlates persist by their capacity to reproduce themselves in identical or expanded forms (Bourdieu 1986: 241). Economic capital, as a rational, instrumental actor, institutes social games to make sure that wealth and poverty are not determined by chance. It is of course possible to beat the odds; to pass from poverty to wealth. This is part of the social game invented to prevent significant redistribution of wealth. If it were not possible to beat the odds, the many people who are not wealthy would not keep coming to the table despite a frequent lack of success. Players may beat the odds but not change them. Bourdieu's radical criticism of market capitalism has a great deal in common with the economic part of Nisbet's conservative advocacy of mediating structures. Likewise, the far more conservative Glen Loury suggests, as Bourdieu does, that economic capital may transform even mediating structures, such as the family, and their communal bonds. Financial capital influences the forms and amounts of social capital in order to preserve the social norms of the acquisition and value of financial capital. Wolpert's study (1993) of differences in the amounts of charitable contributions and in the nature of charity (amenity or redistributive services) provides empirical support for Bourdieu's theoretical assumptions about capital and reproduction and evidence for Loury's concern for too little social capital in places of need.

The works of Wolpert, Nisbet, Bourdieu, and Loury suggest the necessary but not sufficient role of mediating structures in redistributing social capital across class boundaries. Social capital is a moral resource if it provides directly or advocates for the social or political provision of health care, education, environmental quality, housing, safety, and the other "factors of production" of community for those who are in need of them and have far less of them than others. When these factors are provided according to the market, they reproduce class distinctions or the forms of financial capital, including market failures.

Adam Smith anticipated this development of inequality of social capital and its relationship to market capitalism. Two hundred years before Wolpert and Bourdieu, Smith made room for the strong arm of the law as well as the more frequently mentioned invisible hand of social benefit. The strong arm of the law preserves economic inequality in society. Smith also explained that the market established who were inferior and superior. The division of labor, the first market innovation that increased productivity, also divided members of society. Socioeconomic differences, according to Smith, are "not upon many occasions so much the cause, as the effect of the division of labour" (Smith 1937 [1776]: 15). Differences in wealth and property helped to finance and establish the division of labor and other early market mechanisms of mass production. Those market relations then fixed and exaggerated social differences.

Just to be clear about the relation of great wealth and poverty, Smith links them. "Wherever there is great property, there is great inequality. For one very rich man, there must be at least five hundred poor, and the affluence of the few supposes the indigence of many" (Smith 1937 [1776]: 670). In the euphoria of the mythical magic of market democracy, it is easy to overlook that Adam Smith himself would have understood that the poverty and human needs of Appalachia, and other parts of America, exemplify deficits and inequality in American public policies of social capital that are part of market capitalism.

The emphasis on limited government since 1980 has meant an increased reliance on mediating structures for the production of social capital's material goods. Government increasingly contracts with mediating structures for the provision of mental health services, day care, homeless shelters, child protection, home health care, legal aid, family planning, respite care, and preschool programs. In some cases, such as mental health and literacy, government provided incentives for the initiation of mediating structures in order to create a set of providers with which to contract (Smith and Lipsky 1993: 3–11; Douglas 1987; Hansmann 1987; Ware 1989). According to some, this support has had negative consequences on the contracting mediating structures. Democracy demands accountability for public funds. Consequently, government support of mediating structures has required increased professionalization of nonprofit services. This development implies a shift of norms from those of the local community to those of the government agency providing funds (Smith and Lipsky 1993: 79–81). It is precisely this change that conservative advocates of mediating structures lament. Both Nisbet and Berger and Neuhaus, for example, prefer mediating structures to remain under local control operating by local norms. This is accomplished more easily by forgoing forms of government support and contracts.

Without the resources of government, however, mediating structures may be inadequate to the task of providing even a minimal supply of needed goods and services. While it may be correct that local churches and civic organizations can run food banks and soup kitchens effectively and efficiently, it does not follow that churches and civic organizations have the resources to alleviate the problem of hunger (Smith and Lipsky 1993: 27). It is this gap between the resources of mediating structures and the needs that they address that invites government participation with additional resources (Salamon 1987: 100) and risks renewed concern with centralization and government intrusion.

The partnership of mediating structures and the public sector may entail different forms of welfare systems tailored to fit the curious contours of limited government *and* public forms of social capital. Liberals find contracting attractive because it extends the boundaries of the welfare state and supplements the resources of families and organizations affected by problems (Smith and Lipsky 1993: 18). Mediating structures substitute for government action at times of reveling in the promise of limited government and provide the wax and wicks for a thousand points of light. Conservatives like contracting with nonprofit organizations because they prefer private, not public, initiative and enterprise.

The celebration of the free market in the 1980s went hand in hand with an effort to return to views of social responsibility that allegedly preceded the 1960s and the social movements and public policies identified with that decade. In the 1980s, public policy narrowed community to fit the contours of local situations and resources rather than expanded it to provide bonds among people separated by geographic and socioeconomic distances. Mediating structures, like community, became "a vehicle for devolving social services to nongovernmental providers to enhance individual responsibility and reduce claims for public spending" (Smith and Lipsky 1993: 208).

Mediating Structures and Democratic Theory

The complex relationship of mediating structures and democracy remains behind a veil of more than a century of veneration for Tocqueville. Social capital, the provision of goods and services to meet human needs, expresses the moral resources of trust and cooperation. A paucity of these goods and services expresses market virtues of individualism and self-reliance. Unadaptive capitalism wants it both ways: few publicly provided goods and services for human needs but lots of social capital, moral resources, for social problems. It doesn't work that way, and no amount of praise for mediating structures can change that.

Lester Salamon senses a complicated relationship and offers three very different and contradictory propositions about the relationship of mediating structures to democracy, which our examination bears out. Salamon conjectures that mediating structures may be a *prerequisite* to democracy; an *impediment* to democracy; or *largely irrelevant* to democracy. In the first view, mediating structures are prerequisite to democracy as part of the Anglo-American conception of civil society, a separate sphere of social activity that exists between the family and the state. This sphere preserves social values and counteracts the excesses of the state and of individuals. A rich network of autonomous groups protects isolated individuals from the overweening power of the state and creates social bonds that constrain individualism and make cooperation possible (Salamon 1993: 7). This theme is present in Nisbet, Sills, and the conservative social theory that followed the 1970s and championed community without attention to its economic foundation.

In defense of the second proposition, that mediating structures impede democracy, Salamon offers the criticisms from nineteenth-century France and Germany. Political and social theorists, including Hegel, found voluntary associations to be instruments of privilege and wealth that mediated between individuals and institutions in order to prevent change and to defend the status quo. This theme is present in the social criticism of the 1960s that championed new forms of social, political, and economic equality and in the critical assessments of social capital by Bourdieu and Loury.

Salamon approaches the third proposition, that the nonprofit sector is largely irrelevant to democracy, with his own empirical evidence. Focusing only on public-benefit service organizations, Salamon finds "a set of organizations that, while potentially important to the promotion of democracy, is, for the most part, *disengaged* from politics" (Salamon 1993: 19). Only 3 percent of the 3,000 agencies he surveyed devoted half or more of their expenditures to advocacy on behalf of the people they served. Only 18 percent reported having *some* involvement in advocacy activity. This latter portion did not vary very much with the age, size, or field of service of the agencies, although larger, multiservice, and community development agencies reported slightly higher rates of political involvement than others did. Wolpert offers further evidence for Salamon's third assertion.

A theory of democracy, mediating structures and social capital lies implicit in Salamon's propositions. First, democracy provides for liberty. Much of the social theory on mediating structures (Nisbet; Berger and Neuhaus) emphasizes liberty. Second, democracy works to reduce class distinctions. This is explicit in some treatments of mediating structures (Sills) and implicit in the research on mediating structures in social movements (Evans and Boyte; Fisher). Finally, democracy requires direct advocacy of those in need or indirect advocacy by others for them. This advocacy extends to affecting public policy.

James Morone explains that, historically, American democracy combines fragments of this triad of liberty, equality, and political action in fragile, kaleidoscopic arrangements that change frequently. Morone is concerned with explaining how Americans overcome their prejudice against government and support increased government action to achieve their goal of community. Deep-seated individualism, the bedrock of liberalism, promotes a fear of public power. Deep-seated communitarianism, the bedrock of the republican tradition, promotes a desire for direct, communal democracy (Morone 1990: 1).

A sidelight of his study suggests that if mediating structures express the democratic wish of American political life, they also express some of the dread and distrust of government action on public problems. Community institutions, voluntary organizations and mediating structures harbor the hopes of some Americans that somehow people can put their government aside and rule themselves directly. Putnam found that community organizations promote effective public institutions. Morone suggests that in another context and historical setting community organizations may provide ineffective and irrelevant surrogates for effective public institutions (Morone 1990: 29). The impulse for voluntary associations, which Tocqueville chronicled, harbors the fear of public power. James MacGregor Burns traced this fear to a uniquely American "negative liberty" that defends personal interests *against* government rather than "the capacity to expand their liberties *through the use of government power*" (Burns 1978: 157). The Founding Fathers' fear of the despotism of the past centuries and fear of an unknown future under majority rule combined to create checks and balances for minorities and majorities that prevent them from seizing the apparatus of the state in American government.

American liberty expressed freedom *from* government rather than freedom *for* some common purpose *through* government. Even presidents who expanded government to pursue increased social and economic equality did so primarily by attacking some government institutions, such as the national bank or the courts, as the legacy of their opponents who championed the interests of the privileged few at the cost of the needful many (Burns 1978: 163–64). American government has as a central task to circumscribe the public realm in as little area as possible and to conduct surveillance of government to prevent it from straying from its publicly imposed limits. The American Revolution gave birth to a political tradition with more concern for limits on government than for its public purpose (Morone 1990: 30). As much as possible, Americans were to pursue life, liberty, and happiness *without* government, rather than through its actions. Mediating structures, in part, provide the means for public, but not government, action— a surrogate for government action.

Morone's work provides a useful analytical framework within which to examine the relationship of mediating structures with democratic practice. The democratic wish is suspended between the democratic promise of limited government for individual liberty, which has roots in the dread of government and trust in economic markets, and the democratic prospect of social and economic equality, which is rooted in a yearning for community. The democratic wish moves toward one pole or the other and shifts its elements, including mediating structures, with each shift. Much of the literature on mediating structures, especially social theorists such as Nisbet and Sills, places them in the democratic promise of limited government.

Morone implies a broader democratic role for mediating structures. He delegates to them the task of creating "a communal imagination that is part of the government" (Morone 1990: 30) within the American political tradition. In Morone's assessment, mediating structures bring communal imagination to government by working out the vague possibilities for increased democratic practice in the law. John L. Lewis and the United Mine Workers of America (UMWA), for example, brought working people more prominently into American democratic life by promoting union organizing through Section 7(a) of the National Industrial Recovery Act. That section asserted that employees "shall have the right to organize and bargain collectively through representatives of their own choosing, and shall be free from the interference, restraint or coercion of employers of labor." Lewis took this as the Emancipation Proclamation for labor. The UMWA began extensive organizing of the coalfields and increased its strength and that of other unions as well (Morone 1990: 162–67). It was during one organizing drive of this time that Florence Reece penned her line, "Which side are you on?" Later, in a manner similar to organized labor, civil rights groups and organized groups of the poor took the vague provisions for "maximum feasible participation" in programs of the Office of Economic Opportunity and established new norms for citizen representation and participation in a broad range of government programs, agencies, and processes—such as public hearings (Morone 1990: 227–33).

Salamon's three propositions about mediating structures and democracy—impetus, impediment, or irrelevance—hold the key to the democratic role of mediating structures. They do so not as one or the other but in combination. Mediating structures are a prerequisite to democracy. They preserve the liberty of citizens to act on public matters apart from government. They permit their members representation and participation in the sociopolitical arrangements of the neighborhood, community, nation, or state. They are instruments of rather than impediments to democracy when they forge bonds of trust and cooperation beyond the boundaries of their own group to persons and groups outside of it. They are relevant to democracy when they provide directly or advocate for the social or political provision of goods and services to meet human needs and reduce socioeconomic inequalities. The test for the democratic nature of mediating structures involves the stringent test of all three elements—liberty, equality, and political action—not only one of the three.

Democracy requires mediating structures because they embody explicit or implicit protests against reducing community to the narrow economic base of market capitalism. Mediating structures provide the moral resources for community that make market capitalism possible. Their moral resources mitigate the flaws and failings of the market's negative externalities and inadequate public goods. They prevent the narrow political economy of the least adaptive and more savage forms of capitalism, those premised exclusively on market relationships, from imploding into a black hole that emits neither the light nor the warmth of community. Mediating structures reach their democratic potential when they expand social capital from a narrow economic base of market capitalism and advocate for new forms and increased amounts of public and socially provided goods and services to reduce human need. This expansion entails organizing at the local level, as Putnam pointed out. A more civil society does require local participation and transformation. Social capital is not merely a local matter, however. The forms and amounts of social capital come also from the national institutions of politics and the economy. Putnam limits social capital to the realm of local moral resources. This serious limitation ignores the role of mediating structures in the social and political provision of material goods and services such as health care, education, housing, employment, environmental quality, and the other factors that literally produce and sustain people in community. Mediating structures reach their democratic potential when they produce, directly or through advocacy of social and political provision, new forms and larger amounts of social capital, including the economic base of human community; when they provide their members representation and participation in the sociopolitical organizations of neighborhood, community, state, and nation; and when they expand their members' sense of common bonds with others and thus increase trust, cooperation, and collaboration.

Fully Democratic Mediating Structures

The relationship of mediating structures and social capital varies with different formulations of the democratic wish. An emphasis on the democratic promise of limited government suggests that mediating structures are a prerequisite to democracy and that social capital should have private sources closely tied to the market. An emphasis on the democratic prospect suggests that mediating structures pursue the democratic prospect through organized action and advocacy for increased social, economic, and political equality and that social capital should have public forms separate from the market.

The aversion to government that is present in market democracy may undermine the democratic nature of mediating structures. It may express a preference for the market to replace government and for economics to replace politics to mediate the social relationship of groups and individuals.

The preference for government action that is present in some forms of the democratic prospect undermines the democratic nature of mediating structures when it accepts government action as a surrogate for participatory democracy. In the reasonable middle ground between the democratic promise and the democratic prospect, mediating structures exercise their democratic potential by extending trust, cooperation, and other moral resources from local organizations and institutions into broader, horizontal and vertical, organizational and institutional networks. This trust and moral resource may be measured by advocacy for the provision of new forms and larger amounts of public goods to reduce social, economic, and political inequalities. This is not an empty set in American politics nor is it an empty gesture in American life, as the next section makes clear.

PART II

The Democratic Prospect
of Mediating Structures

Part I explained Appalachian poverty as one example of the neglect of social capital in market economics. It also explained the complex relationships between mediating structures and democratic theory. However complex, the relationships are clearer when we see them in action. Mediating structures provide or advocate for more and improved social capital. This part of the book provides stories of community-based mediating structures doing that and thus makes clearer the relationship between mediating structures and social capital. Individually, these stories portray our Tocquevillean faith in community-based action and the reasons we extol mediating structures as the stage upon which the best elements of the American character play their roles. Together, the stories show how some mediating structures, those based in communities, work to promote the democratic prospect.

Community-based mediating structures mitigate the consequences of severe deficits of social capital, which are the failures of market capitalism. The human needs, poverty, unemployment, and depleted social capital of Appalachia manifest what Pierre Bourdieu called *savage capitalism* and what Robert Heilbroner termed, less stridently for American ears, *unadaptive capitalism*. Whatever the term, the Appalachian conditions and American practices of Part I provide the context of the work of community-based mediating structures described in this part. In keeping with Part I, this part details what more than a score of community-based mediating structures have done in attempts to remedy inadequate forms and amounts of social capital in American life.

The roles of community-based mediating structures extend beyond nursing the wounds that market capitalism inflicts. They include efforts to revive and sustain the democratic prospect of increased amounts and improved forms of social capital. These efforts express the value and worth of groups and individuals that are redundant or marginal to the labor needs of the market. Community-based mediating structures, such as those described here, sustain the hope and vision of human worth that exceeds market or labor value and the bonds of community that exceed market relations of exchange. Community-based mediating structures produce a longer list of public goods than do the advocates of limited government and market democracy. The long list of public goods discussed in this part of the book expresses the different forms and amounts of moral resources as well as the material base of social capital, such as housing, health, cultural expression, education, family support, and child development. It asserts the role of community-based mediating structures in Appalachia and elsewhere as social capital entrepreneurs, a role made necessary by market and related political shortcomings. Appendix A lists the organizations that have been included in this work and a brief synopsis of their role in social capital.

This part provides grounding for the democratic theory of mediating structures and applications of the generalizations presented in Part I. One of the generalizations we shall draw from the lessons of mediating structures is that good ideas have to travel. This part brings good ideas and good practices to print. The stories portray both the potential and the problems of mediating structures as vehicles of the democratic prospect of improved forms and increased amounts of social capital.

Each chapter in this part of the book tells stories of the different dimensions of mediating structures and democratic theory. Chapter 3 examines the social theorists' dimensions of the pluralist politics of mediating structures. The members of the Dungannon (Virginia) Development Corporation, for example, created dense horizontal networks in their efforts to bring new forms of health services, educational programs, housing, and cooperative and profit-making enterprises to their community. The Brumley Gap (Virginia) Concerned Citizens group developed new forms of support and trust during its five-year-long, successful effort to block a hydroelectrical project that would have flooded its community. The Appalachian Independence Center provides for the liberation and self-actualization of people with disabilities who live in and around Abingdon, Virginia. The Southern Empowerment Project trained opposition leaders. The Appalachian Center for Economic Networks acquired risk capital for new, small enterprises. The Council of Senior West Virginians pursued changes in public policy.

Chapter 4 deals with the political theorists' dimensions of the transformative and participatory politics of mediating structures. The experience of the Bumpass Cove (Tennessee) Concerned Citizens group illustrates the role of mediating structures in expanding the imagination of people. Its efforts to stop toxic waste dumping in their area and to clean up that which had been dumped in the past imparted new skills of political participation, higher estimations of self-worth and community worth, and more stringent standards for the accountability of public officials. In a similar manner, the experiences of the Western North Carolina Alliance, the Appalachian Ohio Public Interest Center, the Appalachian Peoples Action Coalition, the Appalachian Alliance, and Roadside Theater illustrate, respectively, discursive democracy, dialogical community, free spaces, transformative change, and cultural transcendence, which are the means and the ends of the democratic prospect.

Chapters 5 and 6 describe the economic efforts of several mediating structures. These efforts entail the most difficult and important but least successful tasks of community-based mediating structures in promoting the democratic prospect. Chapter 5 examines efforts to mitigate market failures, including the work of the West Virginia Primary Care Association to support health care for people for whom market forces did not provide; the efforts of the Ohio Valley Environmental Coalition to deal with the negative externality of environmental degradation; the Virginia Black Lung Association's protection of victims of that occupational disease; the support of the Federation of Appalachian Housing Enterprises for the work of fifteen housing groups that run against the tide of depleted housing conditions; and the West Virginia Education Association's conduct of a statewide strike in 1990 to increase funding for public education.

The accounts of Chapter 6 explain the efforts of mediating structures to provide improved and increased forms of social capital. For example, Clay Mountain Housing provides a limited supply of affordable housing at the local level. The Appalachian Communities for Children provides new and higher standards of human services for children and families in Jackson and Clay Counties in Eastern Kentucky. The Kentucky Small Farm Project devolved responsibility for resources to the very local level. SafeSpace invested in the worth of the women and children who endured physical abuse and worked to prevent the abuse of others. Marketing Appalachian Traditional Crafts attempted, with some success, to bring new and higher values to the market relations of producers and consumers. The Southeast Women's Employment Coalition had only limited success in improving employment opportunities for women but contributed much more successfully to the development of the skills and organizational capacity of its member groups.

As Part I explained, the Appalachian region has a serious shortage of social capital. This part explains that it also has an abundance of exemplary mediating structures. These organizations change. The descriptions offered here provide a picture of their work at one time, about 1990. Appendix B provides background on how and why these groups were selected.

Efforts of community-based mediating structures to redress the severe and all-too-common problems of workers' health, environmental degradation, poor housing and sanitation, and related problems renew the glimmer of the democratic prospect. The specific steps needed to make that glimmer into a shining image of our democratic prospects become clearer in the successes and limitations of the community-based mediating structures that we discuss in this part.

Catherine Guthrie conducted almost all of the interviews for this section and wrote the initial drafts of the synopses of each group upon which the narratives are based. She is coauthor of this section.

CHAPTER 3

Social Dimensions

Mediating structures have a more prominent place in the social theories of democracy than in the political theories of democracy. The early social theorists of mediating structures and the neoconservatives who followed them attributed to mediating structures many essential democratic roles, especially those related to forming dense, horizontal networks of civic engagement; expressing support and trust among people; training opposition leaders; liberating individuals for self-actualization; promoting ideals and values; and increasing citizens' participation in public policy formation.

For the social theorists of democracy, the primary role of mediating structures is to protect community from government and, secondarily, to protect it from disruptive economic forces. Robert Nisbet and early proponents of mediating structures extolled them as bulwarks against authoritarian and totalitarian states. Neoconservatives extended their dread of government to liberal American policies of the 1960s and renewed a call for mediating structures to implement public policy. Later, at least among some conservatives, that call implied that mediating structures should replace government policy. Despite this last development, the social dimensions of community-based mediating structures provide a solid foundation for improved policies of social capital and the democratic prospect. This chapter offers the social dimensions of mediating structures in that light rather than as an alternative to politics or as an agent of market democracy.

Dense Horizontal Networks

Robert Putnam gave the social dimension of community-based mediating structures an explicitly political consequence. In his work, civic associations create horizontal networks of civic engagement that increase the efficacy of political institutions. Social capital binds these networks together with trust and other moral resources. The more developed the civic associations, the denser their horizontal networks and the stronger the bonds of social capital among them. Few community groups illustrate the dense horizontal networks that arise with community development efforts better than the Dungannon Development Corporation (DDC) does. The DDC also illustrates Putnam's caution, "Building social capital will not be easy, but it is the key to making democracy work" (Putnam 1993: 184).

Dungannon, population 360, is in Scott County, one of the poorest counties in southwest Virginia. Located between the rugged coalfield region to the north and the more prosperous farming country to the south and east, Scott County lost about 8 percent of the population in the 1980s, and its population is "graying"; one in six of its residents is over sixty-five years of age. In 1990, more than 20 percent of the county's population fell below the poverty level, and per capita income was about two-thirds of the national level. The economy in Dungannon included a few local businesses. Attracted by the area's second-growth timber resources, Louisiana Pacific opened a waferwood construction board plant outside of the town in 1986, which employed 80 people initially and 110 people after ten years of operation. When it closed, the plant was the largest private employer in Dungannon's history.

At first glance, the town appears to be one of thousands of withering rural communities with declining infrastructure, employment, and services. However, Dungannon differed from the stereotype. In fifteen years, largely through the efforts of the DDC, Dungannon gained a town center, a sewer system, several education programs, a bank, a new post office, a library, a health clinic, a maternal and infant program, a volunteer fire department, and even a laundromat. These are services that many Americans can take for granted, but getting them to Dungannon meant running against the tide of decreasing population and increasing poverty that erodes social capital. DDC's achievements provided a record that any political incumbent would be happy to run on. The DDC brought new and more social capital. These programs extended far beyond the town of Dungannon and served 7,000 people in the surrounding area of Scott County.

Other local development efforts preceded DDC and shaped what would become its approach and determination in community development. Many of the initial board members of the DDC, for example, participated in development efforts to establish a community health center in the mid-1970s (Couto 1982). Contamination of Dungannon's water supply, a well, presented a community health problem that Anne Leibig, the community health center administrator, addressed after medical services started. She found funds for an improved water system available through community development block grants. In order to apply for those funds, Dungannon needed a town manager. Leibig assumed that role. After two attempts, Dungannon got the funds for the water system.

One development effort literally followed another. A volunteer fire department followed the establishment of the community health center. Then, Leibig responded to local requests to begin a women's club, which took as its first project the acquisition, relocation, and renovation of the town's railroad station. The Clinchfield Railroad planned to raze the structure, which had long ago stopped serving as a depot for rail passenger service. The club's success in this effort meant the preservation of an historic town building and the provision of a new resource, The Depot, which provided space for additional community programs and activities. Each new project seemed to require some new group, and each new group made the horizontal network of development efforts grow wider and denser.

Eventually, a group turned to economic development. A group of women wanted to improve insurance benefits and sanitation at the sewing factory in Dungannon. The Liberty Shirt and Blouse sewing factory, which was the economic base of Dungannon in 1979, employed about 100 women. Working conditions at the factory were bad. "It was your typical sweatshop scenario," recalled Nancy Robinson, who later became head of the DDC. Leibig helped the women organize. They painted the building and made renovations that improved the appearance of the interior of the factory. They accomplished a portion of what they set out to do. Their success contributed to their decision to continue in such efforts by organizing the DDC.

This modest beginning put DDC within the networks of development that had emerged around Leibig's efforts. Soon DDC became the center of the network. DDC related particular objectives to a broader goal of "total community development." As Nancy Robinson explained in a boilerplate paragraph used in funding proposals, "We are interested in economic development as a part of total community development. We cannot count on economic development from the outside to come in and provide us with jobs. Outside developers are interested in the nearby coal deposits, timber in the National Forest, and the water resources of the Clinch River, but they do not look to the development of our *total* community. We feel that we must look to our own resources to build a stable economic base."

This approach brought attention to education and housing needs. The DDC managed The Depot for the Women's Club and began education programs there. Within five years, DDC had established a range of programs from literacy to community college degrees. DDC worked out arrangements with Mountain Empire Community College in Big Stone Gap, about fifty miles from Dungannon. Some three hundred students had taken classes by 1985. Thirty students had completed certificates as nursing assistants, three in business management, and six had earned associate degrees in education or business. Seventeen other students had completed their high school graduate equivalency diploma (GED). A community library began in 1986 through the efforts of volunteers and residents.

In addition to these individual achievements, the education program spawned new community efforts. A history class developed into the Dungannon Historical Society, which gained grants from the Virginia Foundation for the Humanities for a slide-and-tape presentation on the history of Dungannon. The nursing assistants provided a new supply of health care providers, whose labor was partially absorbed by a Maternal and Infant Health Outreach Worker (MIHOW) program that DDC sponsored. This program provided prenatal care for women at risk for problem pregnancies that might result in low birth weights or birth defects. The program monitored and provided child development until the age of three. By 1992, MIHOW enrolled and served about fifty women annually. When its first set of toddlers reached three years of age, they "graduated" to the local Head Start program.

The education program developed a vertical network with other education programs as well as a horizontal network with community development efforts. Project READ provided adults basic education programs to establish or improve basic literacy skills. This program fed into the GED program, which in turn provided new students for the community college courses. In addition, the project provided tutoring for school children and support and training for parents to assist their children in achieving success in school. Project READ established offices and hours in two surrounding and larger communities. In a short span of time, the Education Committee of DDC established a series of concentric and overlapping learning circles. DDC not only succeeded in attracting new resources to Dungannon, it also sent services to adjoining areas.

The networks that supported these programs were as amazing as the programs themselves. The VISTA program provided Project READ its two staff members. Other funds for the program came from the Virginia Literacy Foundation, the Appalachian Community Fund, the Appalachian Regional Commission, and the Association for Community Based Education. The committee's success gained the attention of the PBS and ABC television networks, which included Dungannon in their cooperatively produced and nationally televised, prime-time special, *A Chance to Learn*, broadcast in September 1986.

The housing efforts of DDC did not proceed as quickly or as successfully as its education programs. DDC originally intended to build an apartment complex. After repeated failures in trying to work with the Farmers Home Administration (FmHA) to secure funding of the complex, the DDC pursued other avenues to develop affordable rental property in the area. The delays caused by the lack of success with FmHA actually benefited the DDC, which discovered that community residents preferred single-unit homes over an apartment complex. By the mid-1990s, DDC had constructed the first of twenty planned low- to moderate-income houses on ten acres of land that it purchased.

The central goal of economic development, increased employment opportunities, proved to be an elusive and disappointing target for DDC. In an effort to increase jobs in Dungannon, DDC helped start a second sewing factory in 1983 that would operate as a worker-owned cooperative. The thirty-eight employees bought shares and attended classes at The Depot that led to an education certificate in clothing manufacturing, management, and marketing. The following year, the other larger, privately owned factory burned down, and the absentee owners decided to relocate rather than rebuild. The co-op factory declined to expand and incorporate the ninety workers left out of work by the closing. So the DDC began work to establish yet another sewing factory, named Phoenix Industries for the mythical bird that rises from the ashes of destruction.

To give Phoenix its wings, DDC invoked the networks of assistance it had established in prior efforts at development. The Tennessee Valley Authority (TVA) offered to move a surplus building to Dungannon from a site of its scaled-back nuclear construction program. TVA also provided surveying and engineering assistance, and its retirees association provided volunteers and contributions to support DDC's efforts. In addition to relocating the TVA's building, DDC borrowed $50,000 to build a cinder-block building that it would lease to Phoenix Industries. The National Guard and Paramount Coal Company prepared the site, Flatwoods Job Corps did the electrical wiring, Rural Area Development Association did the necessary construction, and Louisiana Pacific provided some seed money and the waferboard for the roof.

The committee overseeing Phoenix Industries established employee-friendly policies. Forty-three women who attended the certificate program in clothing manufacturing, management, and marketing wrote the personnel policies for the factory, which called for profit sharing with employees and with the community to stimulate other locally owned and managed businesses. While policies emerged, delays pushed the opening of the new factory back to 1988. Overcoming these delays tested the continued determination of DDC, the Phoenix committee, and their capacity to hold their networks together.

The biggest delay in the construction and opening of the factory was caused by the lack of an adequate sewer system in the town that would allow the building to operate "up to code." A representative from the planning district submitted a Community Development Block Grant (CDBG) for a sewer system for the town of Dungannon, however the grant did not score high enough for funding. According to Nancy Robinson, there were several reasons the grant was not awarded. First, Dungannon faced competition for grants from larger cities such as Norton and Big Stone Gap, which are within the same planning district, called "Lenowisco" for Lee, Norton, Wise, and Scott counties. The grant submitted for Dungannon did not mention any matching funds, which were required for the project, and part of the grant was poorly written. Robinson and an intern met with a representative from the planning district, who agreed to let them rewrite sections of the grant. They rewrote it and also found some matching grant money through the Virginia Water Project. In the next funding cycle, the town of Dungannon was awarded $500,000 to begin building a sewer system. Working with the planning district in this fashion showed the dividends of the pattern of partnerships that the DDC had developed through the years with state and federal agencies.

This period of time marked the height of DDC's economic development efforts. The activity around the development of the sewing factory encouraged a bank to move into the town. DDC touted the community-owned factory as an alternative solution to small rural communities' economic problems. The amount of assistance DDC received enhanced its reputation as one of the most successful community development organizations in the region. DDC's history seemed to support the contentions of social theorists about how effective mediating structures could be in accomplishing local development efforts without intrusive government involvement. More precisely, however, DDC seemed to suggest how mediating structures could leverage and multiply public resources from public sources.

The failure of the sewing factory within a year came as a severe disappointment. Clearly, the apparel industry is intensely competitive. Robinson, however, looked internally for the primary reasons for failure. Despite all the training and advice, Robinson felt the women of the factory simply made a poor decision in selecting a manager. The choice for manager was between a man whom all the women liked and a woman whom, Robinson estimated, the community saw as "stern and difficult at times." Robinson believed that the woman was the better candidate for manager, and she expressed her opinion in favor of the woman. "People like myself were saying, 'Forget the personalities, go with what you know to be true about what will happen.'" Robinson brought her concerns to the board but, in her words, "got labeled a trouble maker." DDC began to unravel at the moment of its largest and most successful venture. Robinson resigned as the director of DDC one month before Phoenix opened because of intense frustration with the management situation and personal conflicts between members of the DDC and Phoenix boards of directors.

Phoenix Industry's failure was particularly and personally devastating for Robinson. She had worked for four years to build a successful industry for the women in the community. Her work with local government agencies had been difficult, and the failure of Phoenix bolstered the smug skepticism of DDC's critics. She recalls: "Our government agencies wanted to see us fail. They did not want us to be successful. In fact, when we tried to get some private capital, they wrote us a letter saying, 'We don't think you can do what you say you are going to do.' We had everybody watching us. All the government agencies were watching us. That's why I'm so bitter, because it never should have failed."

The Phoenix factory failure was even more devastating because the other cooperative sewing factory had failed shortly before. Again, Robinson looked to the working relations of members of the cooperative, rather than to market or other extraneous forces, to explain the failure: "It's amazing how, when you empower people, how complicated things become. They didn't understand that you needed managers just like in other businesses. So when a manager would try to say something, someone else would say, 'You can't tell me that, I own just as much of this business as you do.' That was our biggest problem. There was a lot of dissension. They forgot that it still had to be managed like a business, no matter what kind of business it is.

That was the downfall of the cooperative." Shortfalls of the moral resources of social capital contributed to DDC's two greatest failures, the closing of both garment factories.

However, the supply of social capital that DDC had built up enabled the group to continue after these failures. DDC's dense horizontal networks continued to support programs of recreation, education, and community services. Each program had a committee and developed other programs, such as the library, maternal and infant health services, and summer youth programs, that involved more people on more committees. These programs put residents in face-to-face relations of assistance and help. The Crisis Fund, for example, helped up to 250 people a year with short-term general assistance, such as food vouchers, medication, and furniture and clothing after fires. The Crisis Fund also provided seeds and plants for summer gardens. Another program, Self Help and Resource Exchange (SHARE), also expressed the willingness of residents to assist one another.

These dense networks sustained Nancy Robinson personally, in spite of her many troubles. As she dealt with the frustrating delays in the opening of the Phoenix Industries, her house burned and all her possessions were destroyed. Teri Vautrin, DDC staff member, graduate of The Depot's education programs and a friend of Robinson, wrote the following poem, which was published in the *Dungannon Times*, a quarterly newspaper of the DDC, in 1987:

About Friends (For Nancy)

Friends call you in the middle of the night crying
and in the middle of the afternoon laughing.

Friends tell you how great you look when you've had no sleep
and no make-up on
but you need to hear it anyway.

Friends say the right things at the right times
and sometimes the wrong things at the wrong times
but it doesn't matter.

Friends hold on
hold out
hold vigils when there is illness or troubles
but mostly
friends hold tight.

Friends laugh at you
with you
in spite of you
and for you
when there is no laughter left in your heart.

Friends have
ears to listen to your sad tunes
lips to smile with you at good times
arms to hold you and hug you
and hearts to love and love and love you.

I love you.
You're my friends.

DDC made deliberate efforts to restore and improve the horizontal networks and their stock of social capital, including friendships. DDC staff and board members participated in a workshop on conflict resolution. The group also received some assistance in redesigning their organizational structure. The group moved from a hierarchical model to a circle model. They eliminated the position of executive director and added those of "project coordinators" for specific DDC efforts. They also designed a new system of accountability between staff and board members.

DDC took on new initiatives as they began to work on environmental issues in the 1990s. The natural environment had always played some role in DDC's development strategy. Indeed, DDC was one of the few organizations in Scott County that raised issues of timber use and industrial emissions related to plans to open the Louisiana Pacific plant. The Nature Conservancy identified the Clinch River in southwest Virginia as one of the twenty "Last Great Places" because of the incredible diversity of plant species and shrinking habitat in the area. The increasing attention on the ecology and beauty of the area prompted DDC to explore ecotourism as economic development. DDC hoped that the Nature Conservancy would buy the 400-acre Rikemo Lodge property on the Clinch River and allow DDC to manage it for ecotourism. The DDC wanted to renovate the lodge for overnight guests, create a campground, hiking trails, and possibly a canoe rental business. They hoped also to establish an information center for tourists who came through the area. The Nature Conservancy did purchase the property from the CSX Railroad Company and leased the operation of the lodge to DDC. Initial experience with the lodge was successful, with heavy bookings by visiting members of the extended families of the area.

In the midst of continuing and new activity, the Phoenix building served a new effort in social capital. Although there were no sewing machines in the Phoenix building, it provided dormitory space and a meeting hall for groups of college students and other youth who come to Dungannon to discover and invest in community. Through a new volunteer program, DDC brought hundreds of students in small groups for short periods of time to help rehabilitate houses in the area. These student volunteers provided resources to the housing program of DDC. In 1992, for example, DDC completed twenty minor and two major housing rehabilitations, as well as constructing one new house. During their five-day stay, the students learned and utilized basic construction skills. They also met with DDC leaders to discuss the reasons for and consequences of poverty in the area. On "Appalachian Issues" night, volunteers confronted stereotypes of poverty and "hillbillies." The session was one of the highlights of the volunteer program. Subtly, the example of dense horizontal networks that support community development and rejuvenation provided students a model for community, networks, and social capital in their own lives. Their time in Dungannon instructed them in the adage that DDC had taken as its motto: "When we join caring hands, we give birth to community." Their time in Dungannon also made them part of the DDC's broad horizontal networks.

Support and Trust

Robert Nisbet preceded Putnam with work on "intermediate associations" by three decades. Nisbet compared the function of intermediate associations to primary institutions that sustain and promote friendship, affection, prestige, and personal recognition. Like Putnam, Nisbet portrayed intermediate associations as dense horizontal networks of support and trust. Putnam extends this discussion to the impact of support and trust on civic culture and political efficacy. Nisbet emphasized the role of support and trust for personal freedom to balance government's tendency toward, at best, impersonal organization and, at worst, political repression. Nisbet also anticipated a role for mediating structures to mitigate the social consequences of industrial capitalism.

The Brumley Gap Concerned Citizens (BGCC) group in Washington County, Virginia, exemplifies Nisbet's ideas of an intermediate association dealing with capital development. Brumley Gap's remote location, small and stable population, and its residents' attachment to a particular place mixed land, families, and friends into a commitment to a way of life and "a belief in the harmony of God's creation" (Blanton 1979: 100). BGCC functioned to defend local values and personal freedom from the intrusion of private capital rather than from the state. In the annals of recent community organizing in Appalachia, BGCC retells a dramatic version of the David and Goliath confrontation (Alexander 1993). Once again, David, the ordinary "little" people of Brumley Gap, prevailed. They did so because of the ability of local leaders to mobilize mutual support and trust to express a sense of community and a determination to defend that sense and the place that supported it.

In 1977, Appalachian Power Company (APCO)—subsidiary of the largest investor-owned electric utility in the United States, American Electric Power (AEP)—announced its plans to build the world's largest pumped-storage, hydroelectric facility in one of the nation's smallest, most tight-knit communities, Brumley Gap in southwest Virginia. A pumped-storage facility combines a high and low reservoir of water and exchanges the supply between them just like pouring water from a pitcher to a glass and then back into the pitcher. During winter mornings and summer afternoons, times of peak demand for electricity, the water is released to generate electricity. It then remains in a basin at the base of the mountain until the evening, a time of low demand, when it is pumped back up to the reservoir with electrical power from underutilized plants, often, though not in AEP's case, nuclear plants. The water is made ready to begin the process again the next day. Although this arrangement uses more energy than it produces, it is profitable because pumped-storage facilities add to the rate base upon which regulated industries earn profits and reduce unutilized generating capacity. In the case of Brumley Gap, the pumped-storage facility would have added $2 billion to AEP's rate base.

The proposed facility required flooding the valley and displacing 139 families, several churches, and a few small businesses. The Brumley Gap Concerned Citizens fought adamantly for five years to save their homes and farms. They celebrated their victory on October 30, 1982, when APCO announced its withdrawal from the proposed project.

Richard Cartwright Austin, a United Presbyterian minister and "environmental theologian" from neighboring Scott County, Virginia, came to Brumley Gap in May of 1978 to talk to citizens about the proposed pumped-storage facility of the Appalachian Power Company. Austin lived near Powell Mountain and opposed a second pumped-storage project proposed for that site. He was in the process of organizing a coalition of AEP customers to oppose both projects and wanted to include people at Brumley Gap. Prior to Austin's visit to Brumley Gap, several families there had hired their own lawyers to oppose AEP's plans, but no one had made an effort to organize local residents. Mike Wise, owner of the general store in the valley, supported Austin's efforts and agreed to spread the word about them. That was on Thursday. On Monday, May 10, 1978, more than 100 residents gathered at the Davy Crockett Coon Hunters Club to listen to Austin describe the project and make suggestions on how to challenge it. Austin recalled, "I've never had a clearer experience of working as a catalyst. Everybody was ready to do something, but no one knew where to start" (Blanton 1979: 101).

Describing that first meeting, Lee McDaniel, who became prominent in the organized defense of Brumley Gap, remembered:

> People are speaking, but there's not a lot of chattering, not a lot of laughter, and the kids are even quiet. There's about 150 people there and everything is quiet just like there's a hurricane coming. It was just like [we realized], "We have been had."
>
> Dr. Austin got up there and told us about the proposal. He knew what was goin' on and he explained it to us. He said that we live in the United States and this is a democracy and people have rights and "You all have certain property rights. People cannot come and take your land without eminent domain and without proving a need for it."
>
> Well, after he said his little speech, it was as if the cloud had been lifted and the bright lights were turned on and the dancers had begun. That place got to hummin' and heads started laughin' and everybody in there was just as happy as they could be. It wasn't ten minutes until we had a president, Samuel Dickenson, a schoolteacher in our valley, a vice-president, Gale Webb, who's a big old politician in our valley, and we had Levonda McDaniel, the first secretary. We named ourselves [the Brumley Gap Concerned Citizens] and we pledged [money] that night; each family that could afford it would give $100.00. (Alexander 1993: 5–6)

To save their valley, the BGCC had to challenge the American Electric Power Company; the Appalachian Power Company, which had thousands of dollars to spend on public relations and environmental studies; their local government, the Washington County Board of Supervisors, who were convinced by AEP/APCO that the project would bring in millions of dollars of tax revenues to the county; and even a center of the state's land grant university, Virginia Polytechnic Institute and State University, which had agreed to conduct an environmental study for APCO (Blanton 1979: 101).

The eventual success of BGCC stemmed from six strategies adopted that very first night of the BGCC. Four of the strategies dealt with the economics and politics of protest:

- resistance should begin at the preliminary permit stage;
- resistance to pumped-storage must focus upon economic and energy alternatives, not simply upon environmental protection;
- resistance would require legal expertise; and
- resistance would need to reach out to embrace the entire seven-state American Electric Power service area.

The other two strategies took cognizance of the specific communities involved. First, those at the meeting agreed on united opposition against both the Powell Mountain and the Brumley Gap proposals. Finally, and in Austin's opinion the most important of the six strategic decisions, those at the meeting agreed that the people with the greatest stake in the outcome, most particularly the people who would be pushed from their homes and farms at Brumley Gap or Powell Mountain, would lead the resistance.

The members of BGCC had a fierce loyalty to their homes that rooted the trust they had in one another. They proceeded with less hope in their ability to prevail and more a sense of duty to try to preserve the land, their land. Lee McDaniel suggests, "It's hard to explain what's precious about life here" and then explains it precisely: "I think it's something about the earth. A sort of communion with the Lord when you can go out there and plow your fields and produce half of what you eat. Most people here realize they're not really college-educated types, yet within themselves they are secure" (Alexander 1993: 5). Gale Webb, who was to become vice president of BGCC, added, "Our roots are here in this valley, and no other place would ever seem like home to most people here. My wife and I, along with our children, have worked hard, sometimes day and night, to have a little place we would call our own here in the valley" (Alexander 1993: 3).

Studying BGCC ten years after events there, Dawn Alexander described BGCC in terms that suggest Nisbet's primary institution: "A reverence for tradition, culture, family, heritage, and religion spurred on those involved in the Brumley Gap struggle. People did not want to give up land that had been in their families for centuries. They refused to walk quietly away from the close-knit community which they had built up over the years. Many of the younger people fought more to protect the community's elderly from heartbreak than they did for themselves. Others wanted to be able to pass on their land—and their values—to their children" (Alexander 1993: 23).

Some residents combined anger with their reverence of tradition. One resident lamented, "There isn't much of this heritage left in America. The way the ground almost talks to you when you turn it. A place with birds and deer and other things looking at you, shy, from the cover of the trees. And now them wanting to come in here like a little bit of Hitler, a little bit of Napoleon, to make it all end" (Alexander 1993: 7).

Local organizing in Brumley Gap began with a campaign to raise money. One of the decisions made at the first meeting was that every family should try to give $100 to get the group started and to begin the bank account for the inevitable legal fees that the BGCC would incur in its fight. Bake sales, raffles, and other fundraising events became common in Brumley Gap. These events helped raise money, but they also pulled the community together. BGCC also set up a citizen-band patrol system to spread the word from house to house if anyone sighted utility trucks on any of the roads in the valley.

Community organizing assumed new forms in reaction to the steps that APCO took. In June of 1978, residents of Brumley Gap received registered letters from APCO requesting formal permission to come on their land to begin elaborate geological examinations and surveys. The letter reminded them that Virginia law permitted them to enter the land without permission. A few people thought the resistance was over. A few vowed to use force against any company workers on their land. In between these responses, Austin sought to support people in some organized show of peaceful resistance. BGCC agreed to participate in workshops on nonviolent resistance. When APCO's second round of registered letters came, BGCC called the media and burned the letters in a bonfire of resistance. Lee McDaniel expressed the new confidence and tactics of BGCC: "We're going to be nice and peaceful about the whole thing. When they come in with their earth moving equipment, they're going to have to run over us!" (Austin 1984: 121).

Shortly after the fiery response to the second round of letters, BGCC conducted a "Save Brumley Gap Festival." On the first day of the festival, however, deputy sheriffs traveled throughout the valley delivering more bad news to all those who had received APCO's letters. The sheriff's summons requested residents to appear in court to show cause why they should not be enjoined from impeding the company's work to proceed. It took a few days for the shock of the summons to wear off and to recognize that the group had actually won its first skirmish with the company. As Austin interpreted it, "The people had successfully called AEP's bluff. AEP had not attempted to force its way onto anyone's land. AEP had not even attempted to deal with any valley resident individually. The valley organizing and peaceful resistance training had been effective enough to convince the utility it must deal with the people as a group" (Austin 1984: 122).

Whatever bonds the residents of Brumley Gap had before, APCO's action now brought them together as defendants in a legal injunction lawsuit. Residents articulated a new appreciation for what they had. Mike Wise, a crossroads of information at his store, put his attachment in terms of mutual support. "If I need a piece of equipment, I know I can get it from a neighbor. If I need a helping hand to move something, here I know I can get it. If we had to move into a city, I'm afraid we'll lose those things." They also articulated a deeper appreciation for their home. For example, as Cricket Woods explained, "You get up each morning and look at the valley. It's always seemed pretty, but now you take it in more, appreciate it more. I always look up in the hills at Pinnacle Rock when I'm working outside, and I thank God for my life here. If I have to leave, then I'll just thank him for letting me live in the valley all these years" (Blanton 1979: 100).

The citizen's group next approached local and federal policy makers to stall the project. The Washington County Board of Supervisors had already endorsed APCO's project. BGCC members attended board meetings pressuring them to set up a citizen's advisory committee to study the issue. These local organizing efforts did not make much impact on the direction of the project, but they were useful for BGCC to practice their leadership and participation skills and to bolster local support. Ultimately, they needed to convince the Federal Energy Regulatory Commission (FERC) to deny AEP/APCO preliminary permits for the pumped-storage project.

Forty residents of Brumley Gap and five allies from West Virginia traveled to Washington, D.C., to attend the FERC permit hearings on June 25, 1980. Early in the morning, they stood outside the FERC building and prayed. Later, all forty-five of them piled into the conference room to listen as FERC commissioners addressed the Brumley Gap case. What was expected to be a fifteen-minute approval of preliminary permits turned into a ninety-minute argument. One FERC commissioner, Matthew Holden, favored delaying the decision on the preliminary permit until the results of a study commissioned by the Brumley Gap Concerned Citizens regarding the feasibility of the project were available. The chairman decided to allow Brumley Gap to submit their study, but he also let them know that unless the study contained a "strong showing of conceptual wastefulness of the Brumley Gap project" that the permits would be granted.

This was an unexpected decision and a clear victory for the BGCC. It prevented investment in the project and postponed any damage to the valley. FERC had denied only one preliminary permit previously. A routine matter of government extending to energy companies the benefit of the doubt regarding new capacity turned into the largest protest the federal government had ever experienced at such an early stage of planning (Austin 1984: 123). By the time the AEP did receive its preliminary permit from FERC in August 1982, more than two years later, the county board had withdrawn support for the Brumley Gap project, and the Powell Mountain site was not accessible because of opposition from local officials there. On October 30, 1982, the utility announced that it was abandoning its plans to pursue the pumped-storage facility "as part of a deep, cost-cutting program" (Austin 1984: 123).

Residents understood that several factors, in addition to their own opposition, contributed to AEP's decision. Catherine Dickenson, for example, had three additional explanations. "First, you have to give God the credit. I think the Lord was on our side number one. And number two, the news media that covered the story that was great for us. And number three, the economy at that time was on the down-slide." Rising interest rates made borrowing huge amounts for the pumped-storage facility far less attractive to AEP. Without a doubt, however, the opposition of BGCC stopped preliminary and damaging work in the valley that would have started a momentum of expenditures and justified more work later.

As with other matters of the five-year struggle, the celebration showed signs of family trust and support. Madge Lilly, a resident of Brumley Gap for eighty-four years, described her reaction to the news with explicit reference to family and neighbors. "Somebody called me and told me they [APCO] had pulled out. And, well, I just went out, the children was over at the barn and workin', and I went out to the yard a screamin' and a cryin' and clappin' my hands. And they said, 'Momma, what's the matter?' I said, 'Oh, they've pulled out.' And here they come. We got in the car and we put some old red ribbons on the car and we come plum down here [Abingdon] a blowin' our horn." (Alexander 1993: 21–22).

Other residents joined in the celebratory motorcade. Austin's truck bore a sign that read, "We won because we were right." Another vehicle's sign said, "Nothing is impossible with God." Lee McDaniel recalled that "In the valley that night, everybody was huggin', and kissin', and cryin', and runnin' up and down tootin' car horns" (Alexander 1993: 22). Later, citizens participated in a service of thanksgiving at a local church. After the service, a feast was held to celebrate (Austin 1984: 123–24). Following the feast, residents sang "The Ballad of Brumley Gap," which Doris Beach had written during the first summer of the crisis. Five years after their efforts began, the concluding verses expressed satisfaction with those efforts.

The mountain folks all figgered two can play the game.
They prayed together and read the laws and said, "Now that's a shame.
But you boys should know better. You ain't playin' by the rules.
Just keep your machines off our property. You ain't takin' us for fools."
Them mountaineers will put a stop to a high-handed corporation.
They're showin' people everywhere just who controls this nation.
Of the people, by the people, for the people just like us.
Two hundred years and going strong, and still, "In God We Trust!"
So-o-o! Everybody Clap! For Brumley Gap! (Alexander 1993: 21)

After their victory celebrations, the Concerned Citizens still had some business to attend to. They had some money left over, which they voted to put toward their new firehouse and to create a community center. These buildings joined Mike Wise's general store as the center of community life in Brumley Gap. Most residents in the valley are satisfied with the firehouse and the community center. A few, however, were disappointed that the left-over money was not given to the Coalition of American Electric Consumers, which had supported BGCC and now had financial problems of its own. Other residents also recalled that some members wished that the money could have been spent on a project other than the firehouse. Ideas included a seniors center, a youth center, and a gardening co-op.

These other options had insufficient support because after five years of defending their community, local residents were tired. They wanted, most of all, to return to and enjoy the quiet life they had fought to preserve. Rees Shearer explained, "A community goes through a long struggle and they're tired. They're proud of what they do, but they're tired. They've done their debt, and when that struggle or a like struggle moves to another community, there may be some people who are willing to make a little bit of a tie-in, but few, unfortunately." Lee McDaniel put her retreat to quiet times in more personal terms. "I had corns on my ears (from listening to so many people). It was constantly something. [I had] no personal time. That's when I forgot about having a boyfriend and I haven't had one since" (Alexander 1993: 35).

Residents of Brumley Gap continued to educate their children about what happened so that they would be prepared if they ever faced such a crisis. At a ten-year celebration of their victory, Rees Shearer entertained the children with a poem:

Come gather round children throughout the land,
And learn how your parents for Brumley Gap did stand . . .

Without their resistance to the company's plan,
God's creation would now be diminished by man. (Alexander 1993: 30)

Without support and trust among neighbors, there would have been no resistance.

Training Opposition Leaders

For David Sills, mediating structures intervene between group members and the state to promote, preserve, or strengthen the interests and bonds of the group. This function distributes and disperses power. Ironically, this dispersion of power requires consensus and conflict. "By disseminating ideas and creating consensus among their members, they [voluntary associations] create the basis for conflict between one organization and another. And, in the process of doing so, they also fulfill certain new and autonomous centers of power to compete with it" (Sills 1967: 376). This process also helps to "train potential opposition leaders in politically relevant skills" (Sills 1967: 376). This was certainly true in Brumley Gap. It applies as well to the Southern Empowerment Project (SEP), which dealt directly with power, opposition, and related political skills as its primary and intended outcomes.

In 1986, five community organizations in Appalachia and the upper South acted upon a common problem: they were all having difficulty finding qualified community organizers as staff. They decided to train organizers through a new organization that they would start, the Southern Empowerment Project (SEP). Carol Ford, past president of Save Our Cumberland Mountains (SOCM), one of SEP's founding groups, recalled, "We just didn't have the where-with-all to educate these people [new staff] to bring them up to speed or the time to give to them. We needed people who could just come on board and be walking and running as they go in." Until SEP, there was no training program for rural, southern community organizers. Each SEP member group often had a handful of applicants for staff positions who had some training or experience, but they often came from outside the region. The training these prospective staff members needed included developing sensitivity to the racial, historical, and cultural characteristics of the Appalachian and Southern region. Ford recalled, "the resumes [were] coming through from New York, Chicago, and Missouri. . . . They didn't understand us, our ways, our language, the different idioms, and we didn't really understand them."

SEP established a six-week summer program to train twelve to fifteen participants in community organizing. Graduates of SEP's program increased the pool from which grassroots groups could hire staff. SEP also provided leadership skills training for the board and staff members of its groups and exchanges among its groups. The four board meetings each year plus the numerous training sessions that SEP sponsored helped groups confront problems and address tough issues, such as racism.

Finding qualified and experienced community organizers provided the impetus for SEP's formation, but it was neither a uniquely Southern nor Appalachian problem. The Center for Community Change (CCC) in Washington, D.C., examined the scarcity of organizers nationally (CCC 1992: 3–6) and found a decline of young people among community organizers. Some were not interested in personal and social fulfillment at the workplace at the cost of low pay and professional and economic insecurity. It was also difficult for young people interested in organizing to find out about social change jobs. And nonprofit groups were less willing to hire them than before, finding it too time consuming to take on young, inexperienced organizers. SEP, of course, dealt only with the last factor.

Ford was inclined to blame schools and education for the lack of committed community organizers among young people, pointing out, "They [young people] are not even aware there is something to be interested in or that there is anything to challenge their minds or challenge their way of doing things. It's just like everybody being programmed into these little boxes. . . . They [schools] suppress self-expression. There is nothing for an organizer, you know, that spurs people to ask questions or to look at themselves or situations around them."

SEP attracted both recent college graduates, many from outside the region, and individuals from within SEP member groups that were moving from a member-leadership role to a staff-organizer role. Ford recalled that the original vision of SEP included finding a way "for leaders coming up through organizations to be able to come through this and be able to organize. . . . to develop our own resources. . . . to develop our own people here."

The six-week summer training program included both classroom instruction and field placements with SEP member groups. Interns participated in the full six weeks or in just part of the program. Full-time interns traveled to four different training sites in three different states—Kentucky, Tennessee, and North Carolina—and spent two weeks in field placements with two SEP member groups. Many of the participants in the training had already been hired by a SEP member group; however, a small number of applicants came through independent of any SEP organization with the hope that the training would help them find a job. SEP helped the interns who were not currently employed write a resume and find a job as an organizer.

The tuition charge of the SEP training covered all expenses except travel to the different training sites. SEP member groups were charged half of the total fee for their staff members whom they sent through the training. Participants not hired by a SEP member group paid full tuition for the six-week training. If a member group hired a SEP graduate after the training, the member group paid any remaining tuition expenses. The internal revenues, including summer training fees, covered approximately 25 percent of SEP's budget. Foundations and local and national church agencies were the largest donors to SEP. SEP member groups paid dues of $150.

SEP trained leaders within its member groups by encouraging them to conduct workshops in conjunction with the six-week summer training. These experiences for members were challenging but not threatening. Most of the workshops, such as "Holding a Public Official Accountable," involved either a simulation or an activity that combined the theory and practice of advocacy in a real-life situation that permitted leaders to reflect on their experience. Both the organizer trainee and the workshop leader, who was a member of one of the groups, benefited from the activities.

SEP emphasized direct-action organizing as the primary avenue to social change. Direct-action organizing involves people directly in challenging the system of distribution of goods and values, including social capital. SEP contrasted its emphasis with five other approaches to social change: service, advocacy, litigation, education, and mobilization. SEP's distinct emphasis came from its member groups, which extolled six goals for SEP:

- fostering democratic values;
- changing unjust institutions;
- empowering individuals;
- winning issues;
- building strong organizations; and
- overcoming racism, classism, and sexism.

The curriculum for the organizer training was grounded in these six goals of direct-action organizing. The curriculum also stressed the distinct roles of organizers, leaders, and members in community-based, member-run organizations. Advocacy and direct service also got some attention during the first week of the training.

While SEP developed and trained qualified staff members, it also modeled internal, organizational democratic processes. SEP's structure resembled a member-run and member-controlled organization, and members, board members, and staff had clearly defined roles. Staff members did not vote or attempt to influence the direction of the board, but they did facilitate the work of the board. They pointed out the tasks to accomplish, made sure they got done, and saw to it that everyone had the information they needed. They even made suggestions. The control of the group, however, remained with the members. Representatives of SEP's group members wrote the by-laws of SEP and made the hiring decisions for SEP staff. Ford recalled, "We wanted someone who would listen to us and was answerable to us and would not put themselves into directing us. We were advanced leaders and we were not going to let anybody there, or in the future, be directed. We were going to direct the flow of SEP and how it would go, and that was really pertinent, and part of the deciding factor in who was hired."

Initially, the SEP board hired June Rostan as SEP director. Rostan came with extensive experience for her work. She had served successfully on the staff of the Highlander Research and Education Center, working with labor unions in the region. After that, she served on the staff of the Coal Employment Project, which advocated for employment opportunities for women in the coal industry. Rostan had also received a three-year Kellogg National Fellowship in 1985, which provided a new opportunity to learn about social problems and social problem solving.

The board and staff have faced some challenges as they have grown. SEP has expanded from the original five groups to ten groups. Adding new groups has helped strengthen SEP but it also highlighted the importance of maintaining some continuity on the board while its new members were coming in. SEP has lost one founding member group, the Tennessee Valley Energy Coalition (T-VEC). The irony of the inability of a support and resource group such as SEP to help sustain the existence of one of its own members disappointed SEP staff, and gave them a sense of their limits.

Similarly, while direct-action organizing bound SEP members together, it excluded Native American groups that SEP would have liked to have as members. SEP informally approached leaders of several different Native American groups in the area about becoming SEP member groups, but with no success. Ford concluded, "They have a different way of doing things than we do. So, there may be barriers there. We have to really look at that. How can we meet their needs instead of just expecting them to be a part of what we are, as we are? That's a growth experience."

After six years of its work, SEP carried out a long-range planning process that articulated its mission. Ford explained. "Until we did our long range planning this past year, we never had a mission statement. We just understood that this was what we wanted to do, but we had never put it down as a mission statement." Just as David Sills suggested such group's missions might be, SEP's mission statement reads as a declaration of opposition and a search for new centers of power: "The Southern Empowerment Project is a multi-racial association of member-run, member-based organizations. The mission of SEP is to recruit and train a pool of community leaders to become organizers to help citizens organizations in the South solve community problems by challenging racism and social injustice and standing with the oppressed."

Through training, workshops, and board meetings, SEP has taken on a unique role in Central Appalachia and adjoining areas of the South to train leaders to oppose the current distribution of political and economic power. SEP strengthened the individuals and groups that passed through the program. It also strengthened a regional movement for social justice. Through its multiracial board and workshops on racism, SEP broke down some racial barriers between its predominantly white member groups in the Central Appalachian region and its predominantly black member groups in North Carolina and Tennessee. These connections helped SEP groups' members to recognize common threads of social and economic inequality and to promote action for the democratic prospect.

Liberation and Self-Actualization

David Horton Smith's work integrated previous work on mediating structures with the personal, political, and societal changes of the 1960s. According to Smith, mediating structures could liberate members of disadvantaged and relatively powerless groups from the societal limits imposed by deficits of social capital. Equally important, they could liberate the members of these groups from the pejorative stereotypes of others that they might have internalized to one degree or another. The process of liberation within mediating structures contains elements of free spaces. As Evans and Boyte point out, "For some this [self-actualization] means intellectual development, the process of becoming increasingly analytical, informed, and self-conscious about the nature of one's life situation and problems. When this occurs for a whole category or group of people, the process is often referred to as 'group conscientization' or 'consciousness-raising' (for example, among blacks, women, the poor). Seldom does such special personal growth occur on a broad scale outside voluntary groups and movements" (Evans and Boyte 1986: 337).

According to Smith, participation in voluntary associations for the liberation of members of restricted groups has other benefits. It provides members of those groups training in leadership that would not be possible otherwise. Skills such as running meetings, public speaking, or administering a budget come with leadership roles in voluntary associations (Smith 1983).

Smith did not mention the physically disabled, but the movements of liberation and self-actualization of the 1960s spilled over from the civil rights and women's movement and touched the lives of many other groups and individuals. The Appalachian Independence Center expresses that spillover and the power of mediating structures in liberation and self-actualization for the physically disabled. Work disabilities are only one form of physical disabilities, but their prevalence in Appalachia illustrates the place of social capital in poverty. The counties with the highest rates of work disability are clustered in the poorest area of the region, that with a declining demand for a labor force, Central Appalachia. The proportion of disabilities in a population reflects the investment of social capital in the production of healthy people; specifically, investments in illness prevention and prenatal care. Services for the disabled reflect another form of social capital investment. Over the past two decades, groups of the disabled have organized to acquire new and improved services. The Appalachian Independence Center is one illustration of these efforts to expand social capital to prevent disabilities and to invest in disabled people as members of a broader community.

The Appalachian Independence Center (AIC) in Abingdon, Virginia, began in 1988 when a group of physically disabled residents expressed concern that persons with disabilities were not receiving the services they needed. They acted upon that concern and established a center that offers a diversity of services: technical assistance, training in independent living skills, community education, peer counseling, information and referral, support groups, and advocacy. Through these services, AIC works to eliminate architectural and attitudinal barriers and to help disabled persons achieve independent lifestyles.

Handicapped Unlimited, a volunteer group of disabled persons, preceded the Appalachian Independence Center organizationally by twelve years. Members of Handicapped Unlimited met once a month at an Abingdon restaurant to discuss issues facing people with disabilities. These monthly meetings also served as a support group and an important social event for many people. However, accessibility problems and the personal problems of its members eventually exhausted the efforts of the all-volunteer group. By the time Jeannette Seitz joined Handicapped Unlimited in 1985, the group had tried several times, without success, to get a grant to start an independent living center. Seitz, who later became a board member for AIC, recalled,

"One of the reasons we needed a center was that there was so much to do with a handful of volunteers people couldn't handle it all." She and others reasoned that they could accomplish more on behalf of the disabled community if they could start a center and pay some staff people. Federal funds made state grants available to begin and operate centers for independent living. Seitz and a few other leaders arranged to meet with representatives from the Virginia Department of Rehabilitative Services about submitting a grant. They eventually did so, and in 1988 they received funds to open the AIC and hire several staff members.

AIC did not start with one specific issue, as had the Brumley Gap Concerned Citizens. Its organizers started with a broad mission, more akin to that of the Dungannon Development Commission, "to foster an improved community environment." Similarly, AIC, unlike BGCC, did not want to restore a disturbed environment but intended to disturb and change their environment so that persons with disabilities "could better achieve their maximum level of independence." This mission encompassed activities ranging from legislative advocacy to peer counseling. The founders of AIC were also deliberate in whom they chose for their first board of directors, making sure they had an attorney and an accountant as well as many other skilled and enthusiastic members. Additionally, at least 51 percent of the board's members had to be disabled. Multiple issues and a skilled board provided keys in the stability and success of the center.

AIC had many successes during its first five years, due directly to the Americans with Disabilities Act (ADA). This federal program provided states with funds to support groups that proposed programs of independent living for people with disabilities. Seitz noted that due directly and indirectly to the work of AIC on the provisions of ADA the public buildings in Southwest Virginia grew more accessible. Yet, according to Seitz, the biggest successes were the achievements of the individuals whose lives have been directly improved by the personal attention they have received through the Center. "Knowing that all those people have been served," she said, "that their lives have been improved because of us, to me, that is the greatest thing."

Greg Morrell, AIC's executive director, concurred that the major accomplishment of the center's work is

> seeing our participants take more control of their lives; becoming more integrated into the community; their self-esteem growing; being more independent. When I say independent I mean not that they are doing

more things for themselves but that they are taking charge, advocating for change in the way that people view people with disabilities; breaking down those myths and misconceptions, the attitudes, through community education. We are role models trying to project a positive model through community education; advocacy with businesses, community leaders, [and] governmental officials about the need of having buildings accessible and integrating people with disabilities in community settings.

The AIC program ACTION (Advocates Committed To Independence and Opportunities Now) shows how AIC pursued its goals. The AIC board began ACTION because its previous work to develop assertive and effective leaders had not succeeded. The Center only had a handful of people willing to speak up in front of groups, at town or county councils, or in front of the media. Seitz explained that the group "was starting to look like a small group of disgruntled people." She felt that they needed "to show that it was more people, that it was a bigger group." ACTION intended to train disabled persons to become leaders who could advocate effectively for themselves and other disabled persons.

However, Morrell and Seitz found that the group of people they selected had other needs that had to be met before they could jump into advocacy or even advocacy training. "When we pulled [the group] together," Morrell recalled, "they had been isolated for such a long time that their intercommunication skills weren't very good." Seitz remembered the New Year's Eve party she helped organize at the Center for the ACTION group. "They really were sitting around the room staring at each other. They didn't know what to do. They didn't know how to initiate conversation. We had to beg them to take refreshments. And they just felt like they were being bothered. It was almost sort of comical. You would think it was a sitcom."

Morrell and Seitz had not anticipated these problems and backed up to look at them and for a new starting point. They found it when they realized central differences among people with disabilities. Although both Morrell and Seitz are wheelchair-bound, they had received their injuries in high school, after they had had opportunities to participate in social settings and "life without disabilities." Many of the participants in ACTION, however, had been disabled from birth or early childhood and had lived most of their lives in relative isolation. Morrell understood the difference between his perspective on life and that of many of the other participants. "What they consider a privilege, like going to a restaurant, Jeannette or I see as a right." The goals of ACTION were adjusted. Work on social skills would precede advocacy training. AIC helped individuals gain self-esteem through counseling and support groups. Staff developed support groups for people with multiple sclerosis, cerebral palsy, and visual impairment.

AIC also conducted community education to break attitudinal barriers. Much of AIC's work on shaping attitudes about people with disabilities was done with children without disabilities. The ACTION group began to meet with children in schools and church groups to introduce them to people in wheelchairs and to educate them about what it was like to roll rather than walk through life. Morrell explained this work in terms of asserting and sharing the self-esteem of the disabled—pride not pity.

> It's kind of like with people who are black. If you have never been around a person who is black and your parents or other people have given you a stereotype of that person, or through TV or whatever, you've got this image and you may be afraid of that person. And with people with disabilities the same thing happens to us. But the more you are around people with disabilities, as the more you are around people of color, you learn each has their own different personality. And then there are people out there that are really nice people who have disabilities and there are people out there who are jerks. That's the way life is. But you have to see them as human beings first.

Morrell used this comparison to show the importance of personal contact between people with and without disabilities to break down attitudinal barriers and to raise the civil rights issues of the disabled. This required covering the basics. In educational presentations, for example, he asked his audiences whether voting and making a phone call from a public phone were rights or privileges. After receiving assurances about their nature as rights, he pointed out that if you were in a wheelchair you might not be able to exercise either one of these "rights" because of access problems.

AIC has had some difficulties in their history, most notably, they have high staff turnover. Morrell lamented that it was difficult to attract knowledgeable people who had skills because AIC did not have the resources to offer sufficient medical benefits for their employees. "We have some people out there that would be good employees but they get more money to stay at home than if they were to come here and work. They want to do it and their self-esteem would improve, but they have medical conditions, and if you lose medical benefits and you are a person with a disability, you have lost quite a bit because you never know what will happen."

Other organizational problems involved AIC members. Some of its members used the Appalachian Independence Center only for the limited purpose of acquiring funding for a single accessory. They did not become involved further, and this frustrated Morrell. "We may get people referred to us as a funding source, which is a good and bad thing. We may hook them in because of this funding source. People can have a ramp put into their home or their bathroom modified. That may be their first opportunity to get into our system. . . . The bad thing is that all they want to do is get that piece of equipment or home modification and leave. . . . They don't understand this whole concept of independent living and trying to gain some control over your life."

As much as Morrell and Seitz wanted more disabled people to participate, they also anticipated that participants would move on to independence from them. They were not concerned with building their membership. Seitz explained, "We want them [AIC participants] to go off on their own. That is our mission. We don't want them to need us anymore. So we actually get more excited when that happens and they are going off and doing their own thing and they don't have anything to do with us anymore." Morrell added, "That person may be no longer with us because they are active in the community, which is better."

The Appalachian Independence Center's unique location, the Appalachian region of Virginia, created problems of fitting in with other centers like it. Several times a year the directors of the ten independent living centers of Virginia came together for a directors' council and strategized on how they could work together on statewide and national issues. Morrell attends the directors' council meetings but saw them as time consuming and without relevance to the needs of the people in the rural areas of Southwest Virginia. "What happens a lot is that we come together in Richmond and they are talking about crazy things like mass transit, subways, and things like that. We'd like to have a road paved down here." Morrell saw a large rural/urban gap between the needs and problems in Northern Virginia—the Greater Washington, D.C., area—and those in sparsely populated southwestern Virginia. On the other hand, he also faced a gap between his own resources and local needs. The inability of the AIC staff to help people outside their own area troubled staff members. They frequently got phone calls from people in an adjoining area, which was in the coalfield region and did not have an independent living center, but AIC could not serve them. Nor could AIC refer these callers to adequate nearby services, because there were none.

Morrell and Seitz reflected the liberation process and self-actualization that they promote. They expressed confidence in their ability to find opportunities and resources to help individuals take advantage of the new laws and incentives for creating independent lifestyles for themselves. A primary path to these new opportunities and resources followed the implementation of federal and state laws locally. However, Seitz also foresaw an enduring need for the Appalachian Independence Center's one-on-one work, work that the federal and state levels could not replicate directly but only indirectly through contracted services with the AIC.

Promotion of Ideals and Values

David Horton Smith described the voluntary sector also in terms of "commitment to some value, ideal, or common interest" (Smith 1983: 331). By their commitments, community-based mediating structures provide society with a large variety of partially tested social innovations or, in Smith's terms, social risk capital. The Appalachian Center for Economic Networks (ACEnet) expresses the commitment of mediating structures to reduce poverty in its efforts to develop new forms and amounts of economic enterprise in Appalachian Ohio.

The resurgence of the market economy after 1980 dealt Appalachian Ohio, the southeast portion of the state, a severe blow. Per capita income declined relative to the national figure. In 1990, Appalachian Ohio stood at 72 percent of the nation's per capita income, down from 78 percent in 1970 and 81 percent in 1980. Workers in the manufacturing sector lost work. Their percentage of the workforce declined from 34 percent in 1970 to 22 percent in 1980 to 16 percent in 1990. This change in the labor force meant less income and increased poverty, especially among children. In 1990, 25 percent of the children in Appalachian Ohio were in poverty, compared to 16 percent in 1980.

ACEnet experimented with new ideas for economic development within eight counties of Appalachian Ohio. It began in 1985 as the Worker Owned Network (WON), an organization intent on developing worker-owned cooperatives and replicating the successful cooperatives of the Mondragon area of Northern Spain. Ten worker-owned cooperatives and many small businesses in the Athens, Ohio, area arose from this initial effort. One of them, Casa Nueva, a worker-owned Mexican American restaurant in Athens, started with twelve displaced workers and grew to employ thirty-nine worker-owners, each of whom earned between $7 and $9 an hour.

After this initial success, the WON staff began exploring other models of economic development. They established an innovative small business incubator, the Cooperative Business Center, which provided space for up to twelve small businesses in its start-up stage. The facility provided each tenant reduced rates on fax, computer, copier, and laser printing services. This business incubator opened in October 1991 with nine tenants and thirty-nine jobs among them. It soon reached full occupancy.

The Cooperative Business Center marked the end of WON's strategy to develop businesses through worker cooperatives. WON's experience revealed that success was limited in a firm-by-firm strategy. The systemic nature of rural poverty required a regional approach to change relationships between firms and markets, among firms, and between firms and support organizations in a region. In 1991, WON changed its name to ACEnet to reflect the expanding scope of its economic development work, which had grown to include training programs for low-income individuals, networking with manufacturing firms, and accessing capital for small business start-ups.

ACEnet established the following goals for itself:

- design and implement innovative models for economic development;
- enable organizations and individuals to develop strategies, based on continual learning, which empower people and their communities;
- encourage more cooperative, collaborative, and inclusive relationships in and among the public and private sectors; and
- initiate networks of businesses, policy makers, economic development groups, and others committed to similar goals.

ACEnet took lessons from regions in Denmark and Northern Italy, where small firms with less than twenty employees cooperate to meet niche market demands with the support of local banks and schools. Over a relatively short span of time, these areas had experienced dramatic increases in the number of firms, employment, and per capita income. For example, from 1970 to 1985 the Emilia-Romagna region of Italy, according to proposals submitted by ACEnet, moved from seventeenth to second place in regional per capita income. ACEnet's new approach maintained WON's emphasis on democratic processes in the workplace, such as those used in the Mondragon projects, but shifted the emphasis from individual business enterprises to the economic network of a region. WON's disappointments taught ACEnet the importance of finding lucrative niche markets. ACEnet's new strategy of developing flexible manufacturing networks (FMNs) attempts to meet niche markets with goods produced by a combination of small firms contributing to a single product rather than a single firm taking on complete responsibility for the product. In a well-developed example of a flexible manufacturing system, each firm is likely to belong to a dozen or more of these FMNs and is continually forming new networks that produce custom or short-run items in response to changing markets. As firms expand, new firms join existing networks, and new networks form to fill new market niches; new workers are drawn into the firms, dramatically increasing the employment opportunities in the region.

ACEnet's only unsuccessful initiative was a crafts cooperative that shut down after eighteen months of operation. The organizers could not find a market that would provide the crafts makers a reasonable wage. ACEnet works with micro enterprises or with firms that are sole proprietorships, partnerships, or family businesses with less than ten employees. Generally, these enterprises do not have regular access to loans from commercial banks and have needs that can be met with loans under $15,000. ACEnet established an initial network of forty local manufacturing firms around the emerging niche market of accessibility products for the disabled. With their cooperating firms, ACEnet has designed the following products:

- an accessible kitchen unit, which includes adjustable cabinets and counter tops;
- a wall-mounted, adjustable desk;
- a free-standing, Shaker-style, adjustable desk; and
- a gardening tool (the Appalachian Easy Weeder) with a handle designed for ease of use by people with limited grip or hand strength.

ACEnet created a for-profit subsidiary, Accessible Designs/Adjustable Systems Inc. (AD-AS), to manage and market the products developed by this network. ACEnet sees the market for products for the disabled as growing due to the passage of the Fair Housing Amendments and the Americans with Disabilities Act, the growth of the over-65 age group, and the related, rapidly increasing demand for accessibility. Some of the manufacturing firms involved in AD-AS grew and began a worker-training program. This growth and training for new jobs lie at the heart of the network concept that ACEnet facilitates and promotes. ACEnet collaborated with manufacturing firms, the Athens County Job Opportunity Basic Skill Training Program (JOBS), the local Job Training Partnership Agency (JTPA), the local vocational school and technical college, and low-income groups to establish a job training program to place low-income people who needed permanent jobs into the network's manufacturing firms.

ACEnet also entered the specialty food market. Its "Specialty Food Initiative" informed and trained local farmers and individuals in product development for emerging markets. Its training component included an introduction to entrepreneurship for trainees to determine if they were interested in starting their own business. The program also included a Kitchen Incubator, a fully equipped kitchen that met all health codes, which was available for rent to people interested in testing or producing their food products.

One of the biggest challenges in creating a supportive community for small business and manufacturing firms is gaining access to capital. ACEnet staff members identified the following major capital gaps for microenterprise development:

- start-up funds are very difficult to obtain, especially if the potential entrepreneur has no personal collateral;
- banks and loan funds do not know how to package loans for joint projects;
- funds for the research and development of new products or lines of products are perceived as being quite risky;
- microentrepreneurs without a credit history or with a poor credit history (who will make up a large portion of the individuals served through the proposed project) have a difficult time beginning a banking relationship.

To address these challenges, ACEnet had a four-part strategy for helping meet the capital needs of small firms and businesses. Included in the strategy was the creation of an ACEnet loan fund; closer work with existing loan funds; coordination with banks in the development of a loan guarantee program to enable microentrepreneurs to get loans sooner; and creation of a pathway of training to support low-income entrepreneurs and lower their risk as they become business owners. June Holley, ACEnet director, looked forward to the day when ACEnet's track record of success would enable her to say to the banks in the Athens area, "Hey listen, these folks are part of this network and we know them. We have been working with them. This person is a 'small shot,' they are not going to have that kind of collateral and yet we want you to do this on character."

Holley understood that financial capital was part of a process. "It is lots of steps and pieces. It's building a relationship." WON began with a budget of $15,000. After six years, some ten business start-ups, and one hundred new jobs, ACEnet's track record meant an infusion of capital and an annual budget of $300,000. Finding capital resources and innovative ideas, then putting them to work to create work and income epitomized ACEnet's social risk capital efforts and one bridge to an ideal of a political economy that sustains and values community.

Public Policy Participation

David Horton Smith emphasized that voluntary associations also test social innovations that challenge dominant government and business institutions and practices and the assumptions upon which they rest. ACEnet does that. So does the Council of Senior West Virginians (CSWV), which evolved from a creature of government programs to their monitor and critic. During that change, the central purpose of CSWV remained the same, "to gather direct evidence on the needs of seniors and provide public education on means of meeting them." CSWV illustrates the complex relationship of mediating structures and public policy.

CSWV began just six years after the passage of the 1965 Older Americans Act, which President Lyndon B. Johnson initiated as part of the Great Society programs. The act provided federal resources to address the needs of older Americans. It established programs for seniors, such as Meals on Wheels, as well as senior centers, commissions on aging, and area agencies on aging. According to Mike Harmon, CSWV's first executive director, CSWV grew from the desire of some of these agencies' leaders to have "an independent group of seniors to help advocate some of the things that weren't getting addressed by anybody." State program officials called an organizational meeting of agencies' staffs at which CSWV began in 1971. Later, programs for disabled people would replicate this effort to organize constituents. The organizational structure of the regional and county senior groups established by federal legislation provided CSWV its framework to organize. The countywide senior centers provided excellent places to find, meet, organize, and recruit seniors for CSWV.

Many of the original board members of CSWV came from the senior centers' leadership. Harmon recalled scheduling meetings at the senior centers on the nights when they had potluck dinners. "These meetings would bring in 25 to 100 people." The directors of seniors' programs supported these organizing efforts. Harmon also recalled receiving support from the staff of the West Virginia Commission on Aging. He would use their phone. Often the Commission would reimburse his transportation costs to the regional CSWV meetings. With firm footing within programs for seniors, CSWV membership grew quickly to 3,000. Modest membership dues of $1, later $2, removed financial barriers to membership, but provided only a portion of CSWV's initial budget of $15,000.

Tim Dent, CSWV's director for most of the 1980s, understood that his board's informal long-range goal of the CSWV was "to change the rules of the game in West Virginia." As he put it, "The creation . . . of a strong, grassroots based senior citizens' organization, which can affect not only state legislation but is a key to winning a major new piece of social legislation, will bring an element of participatory democracy to our state. Now, people are expected to only cast votes for politicians and do nothing until the next election. This must change. Public figures must be held directly accountable to the citizens."

Initially, CSWV had no staff. This left a great gap between the limited letter-writing campaigns and Dent's long-range goal. Harmon had helped close that gap after he became CSWV's first executive director in 1974. Harmon, in his mid-20s at the time, had worked in a regional program for seniors as his civilian service alternative to the draft and military service in Vietnam. When he finished his work there, CSWV had just received a small grant from the West Virginia Commission on Aging that permitted it to hire Harmon as its full-time director.

Harmon found an able and willing group of people with whom to work. In particular, he found an abundance of leadership skills. "These people had been doing this stuff all their lives. It was just a matter of finding them and getting them, and recruiting them into the group. Especially with the elderly, there is a tremendous amount of knowledge there. People have spent most of their lives working with the union or some other organization and they know a lot of this stuff. It's a lot easier for them to come into the group and do the teaching than it is for you to recruit people that don't know anything about this stuff and try to teach people how to be leaders or whatever."

In some instances, Harmon found that CSWV provided seniors a new vehicle to continue rather than start their advocacy of ideals and values. "We had a really good active delegation from McDowell County . . . because the seniors down there had this history of involvement with the UMW [United Mine Workers]. Like the only thing going on in McDowell is coal mining. . . . Those seniors would get to our meetings no matter what. I think that they traveled in the Commission on Aging vans but they would have got to the meetings one way or the other because they were very tuned into the importance of organizing and working on this legislation. They had been through all that with the UMW."

Working among capable people with leadership experience in organized settings saved Harmon a great deal of effort. He found he could call people through the senior center network, tell them what he needed, and arrange a date for getting it done. His contacts took care of the local arrangements and publicity. "I would just drive in there and there would be 75 to 100 seniors all chomping at the bit."

Over twenty years, CSWV members chomped on several bits, including health care reform, rural transportation, accessibility and in-home services for the elderly and disabled, utility rates, and government accountability. These issues have brought them into several coalitions with other groups. For example, CSWV's efforts to hold down costs of electricity eventually led to support for the Brumley Gap Concerned Citizens, through the staff time CSWV gave to the Coalition of American Electric Consumers.

CSWV formed a 501(c)(4) sister organization, the Coalition on Legislation for the Elderly (COLE), in order to focus more time and resources on direct lobbying efforts in Charleston. Through COLE, CSWV was able to team up with other grassroots groups, such as the Citizen Action Group, and sign on groups to help pass legislation on behalf of the elderly. In addition, CSWV worked in coalition with the National Council of Senior Citizens, the National Health Care Campaign, the West Virginia AFL-CIO retiree locals, Mountain State Health Care Campaign, and the National Long Term Care Campaign. Eventually, CSWV and COLE divided over how to deal with the new Republican administration's changes in public policy. Personality differences exacerbated the program divisions and created long-lasting hard feelings.

In carrying out its work, CSWV consistently targeted the state and federal legislation and agencies responsible for administrating programs for seniors. In the beginning, seniors were not always well received at the capitol. Harmon recalled, "Back when we first got started, legislators were down right hostile. They were sarcastic. You would talk about a bunch of old people wanting to get this bill passed and they would be telling jokes about old people." Harmon gauged the success of CSWV both by the reception accorded seniors by their legislators and by seniors' own enthusiasm for influencing legislation. "I think back in the old days when it [lobbying] used to be almost a dirty word to some people, lobbying was not necessarily a positive thing, and people sort of timidly approached it. . . . One of the things that we tried to do in our meetings was to try to impart that this is our government. It belongs to us. And the only way that we are going to make it work is to get directly involved and express our opinion and try to influence that."

CSWV identified the needs and priorities of seniors through an annual survey. Each member could vote on priorities for CSWV. The 1993 survey identified the following as the top priorities: (1) universal access to health care with in-home long-term care, (2) prescription drug cost control, (3) monitoring aging programs, (4) implementation of the public transit bill, and (5) several other issues related to taxes and utility rates. The small staff of CSWV and board members worked together through monthly board meetings to strategize and pursue the goals identified by the membership.

By 1990, CSWV, through its coalition work, gained information, disseminated it, and educated others about health care reform issues centered on the elderly. The centerpiece of its effort, the Continuum of Care Project, anticipated the need to reform health care. As Dent explained in a 1991 report to CORA,

> For the past ten years the survey of senior needs has shown that the current health care system which forces seniors into expensive nursing institutions or leaves them isolated and unable to meet basic daily needs is unacceptable. Our chaotic service delivery "system," the cost of health care, and West Virginia's rising elderly population make an organizing campaign to achieve a fully funded, comprehensive long term care program essential. The health care needs of all Americans, and the necessity to establish basic health care needs as a right for all, should also be a growing concern to seniors. Not only are there major gaps in health care services for the elderly, but a coordinated health care system cannot be created without taking into account how the cost of health care for seniors will impact on a national health care system. We cannot reform health care only for non-seniors; nor do the majority of seniors want increased health benefits for themselves alone. ("CSWV Proposal to CORA: Continuum of Care Project," CORA, Knoxville, Tenn., January 31, 1991, p. 4)

A later coordinator of CSWV, Maggie Meehan, characterized much of the CSWV membership as "good government watchers." Many of the current members were retired teachers, union leaders, or have some other experience in community leadership. Meehan observed that because CSWV members "have been active [in their past careers], they see that it is easy to become advocates on behalf of the frail." Other members were what Meehan called the "old, old." They were people whose eyesight and hearing had failed and were too tired to be involved in political activism any longer. These members understood the importance of monitoring government procedures and policies, but "they don't get upset about it. For many of these members as long as services are delivered they don't care whether . . . there is conflict of interest, whether budgets are cut, or whether there is too much money being spent on administration."

After twenty years, CSWV faced its own problems of longevity. In the early 1990s, staff turnover, missed funding deadlines, and other factors placed internal stress on the organization. Externally, organizations in its environment had changed. Harmon recalled using the phones at the Commission on Aging to save costs and using the vans of the local and regional service agencies for members' transportation. However, after twenty years the Commission had its own legislative and administrative battles to fight. The presence of an independent, organized set of seniors could sometimes mean criticism and opposition. For instance, CSWV participated in a lawsuit to protest the closed-door meetings held by the Commission on Aging, the Area Agencies on Aging, and several key legislators who considered and approved reducing the number of Area Agencies on Aging from nine to four. A notation in the budget digest was decided by the budget conference committee cochairs rather than in "full and open conference." CSWV opposed the decision process because closed-door meetings are unconstitutional. It also protested the decision because it meant fewer agencies were responsible for supervising more local senior programs under the Older Americans Act with no increase in resources to do the job. CSWV, along with Common Cause, the League of Women Voters, and Citizen Action Group won their case concerning the closed-door meeting. Thenceforth, the budget digest had to be prepared in full and open conference. However, winning the right to open conferences did not change the decision on the reduction of the number of area agencies. Nor did the conflict win friends for CSWV among the agencies that held the closed-door sessions.

Harmon pointed to a political process of representation and participation as the major achievement of the CSWV, rather than a single issue. "That was one of the things that I felt that I did a good job at . . . getting people convinced that this government was their tool and if they left it alone it could screw up." In the course of twenty years, as CSWV evolved from an instrument of federal policies to an independent organization that monitored them, CSWV never attempted to substitute for government, nor did it displace its function as a mediating structure. CSWV proceeded with two beliefs: only government can meet the great needs of seniors, and only organized groups of seniors can "cause our government to meet its responsibilities."

We Are Here to Complement Them

The social dimensions of mediating structures have more political functions than social theorists suggest. These theorists are concerned that mediating structures protect individuals and groups from incursions of authoritarian and totalitarian governments or even from overbearing government programs. Leaders of community-based mediating structures do oppose government intrusion. Just as often, however, they welcome government resources. Their relationship with government programs varies over time, from place to place, and depends on the people involved. Leaders, such as Nancy Robinson, director of the Dungannon Development Corporation, expect more assistance from local public officials to acquire public funds for their programs. They expect government to support local initiatives.

Indeed, government often has. Community-based mediating structures have built sets of networks among its members that include government programs. In addition, the entrepreneurial skills of community-based mediating structures leveraged large amounts of federal, state, and local funds. Leaders within these mediating structures find ways to meet the eligibility requirements for programs and to do what is necessary to compete for government and private capital funds. Looking back on fourteen years of organizing in the community, Nancy Robinson found that the Dungannon Development Corporation's biggest success was "surviving as long as we have as a community group. We are still here despite people not wanting us to be here, despite the agencies not wanting us to be here, but we have also shown them that we are not here to hurt them, we are here to complement them. It took a while to gain their trust."

CHAPTER 4

Political Dimensions

The social dimensions of the democratic prospect of community-based mediating structures provide a starting point for portraying their political dimensions. Mediating structures can transform and improve a set of political, economic, and social arrangements. Most theorists of the democratic prospect, however, give them little attention. This inattention is all the more remarkable because these theorists extol political transformation through expanded imagination, discursive and dialogical communities, free spaces, transformative changes, and transcendent communal bonds—all of which may be found in community-based mediating structures. Just as no one political theorist includes all these elements in a single theory of the democratic prospect, so too no one community-based mediating structure illustrates equally all of these political dimensions in its work. Each contains elements of all of them, however.

The political dimensions of community-based mediating structures encompass a space in which people have the time to develop their common bonds and discuss alternative economic, political, and social arrangements to transform the status quo. These political dimensions have more to do with imagination than voting. They measure the worth of individual human beings rather than the value of their incomes or economic roles. Community-based mediating structures create moral resources for their members in the process of expanding social capital for others. These moral resources transcend time and space. They put local people in touch with efforts of social change in different places at the same time and in times past. The intended benefits of their change efforts link local people with the generations that will follow them.

Expanded Imagination

According to Benjamin Barber (1984) "strong democracy" differs from "thin democracy" by degrees and forms of participation. He defines strong democracy as "politics in the participatory mode where conflict is resolved . . . through a participatory process of ongoing, proximate self-legislation and the creation of a political community capable of transforming dependent, private individuals into free citizens and partial and private interests into public goods" (Barber 1984: 132). Barber is skeptical and cautious about community-based mediating structures in strong democracy. He advocates a dense horizontal network of social capital and democratic practice without a direct role for mediating structures in that network.

Barber concedes that mediating structures may serve as schools for the civic education necessary for strong democracy if these structures expand the imagination of their participants by offering their members the opportunity for direct political participation (Barber 1984: 235). This opportunity transforms local residents from private individuals into collaborative citizens who work to transform partial and private interests into public goods. Expanded political imagination and personal and communal transformation are hallmarks of the Bumpass Cove Citizens Group.

Bumpass Cove is located in eastern Tennessee in rugged, mountainous country along the Nolichuckey River, not far from Johnson City. The mountains above Bumpass Cove had been mined for lead, manganese, and other minerals for almost 200 years. In June 1972, the Bumpass Cove Environmental Controls and Minerals Corporation obtained a permit from the state to operate a sanitary landfill for household garbage in one of the old mining sites at the head of Bumpass Cove. Hazardous waste could be deposited there but only with the permission of the state Division of Solid Waste Management. In an adjacent mining site, the "old Fowler site," the state issued a tentative approval for a liquid waste incinerator.

Between 1972 and 1979, residents of Bumpass Cove complained about the truck traffic going to the landfill. Prior to 1972, eighteen-wheel tractor-trailer trucks rarely traveled the quiet, narrow road up Bumpass Creek. Less than one year after the landfill was opened, however, large trucks became a regular occurrence. The trucks obeyed neither speed limits nor weight limits. They often splattered mud from the road on the children waiting at school bus stops. Hobert J. Story, whose small house sat a few feet off the road, initiated and presented a petition to the Washington County court with more than 100 signatures requesting that weight and speed limits on the Bumpass Cove road be reduced, posted, and enforced.

Story was a native of Bumpass Cove, but he had lived most of his working-age years away from the area. He returned home with a work disability that kept him housebound and in a place to watch the trucks all day long. Initially, Story fought against the speeding trucks on his own. When he observed trucks that seemed to be carrying chemicals, which the state permit did not allow, he began a record of trucks and dates. Many of these trucks entered the landfill late at night and on the weekends, sometimes leaking liquids with strong odors. Story regularly asked state officials to investigate the operation of the landfill. In a 1975 letter to the governor, he wrote, "When the wind is blowing southernly [*sic*] a distinct smell of these chemicals can be detected for three miles." In another letter, Story asked the governor and the state commissioner of public health to conduct tests at the landfill. He was willing to bet the "farm," literally, that hazards to people's health existed. "If these tests reveal no source of contamination or health hazard, no source of possible water or air pollution or contamination, I will at the conclusion of these tests assign to the State of Tennessee the equity in my home and the source of my income for a period of one year to help defray the cost of the investigation, provided the State of Tennessee will, in case of finding the tests positive and there is definite proof of contamination, order the closing of the Bumpass Cove Landfill" (H. Story to Ray Blanton, May 31, 1975, Archives of Appalachia, East Tennessee State University).

Story tried unsuccessfully to get others in Bumpass Cove to join his efforts to pressure the health department to investigate the landfill. Many community residents considered Story unreliable and his complaints unfounded exaggerations of a nuisance. Linda Walls, Story's niece, remembered, "Hobert Story had singlehandedly tried to stop them. See, he would talk to people, but no one would listen. He was a drunk. . . . He couldn't get nobody to listen to him. My daddy was his brother, and sometimes my daddy would listen to him. They drank, you know. People just thought Hobert was a drunk."

People began to listen in July of 1979, when flooding due to heavy rain washed barrels of toxic chemicals from the landfill into Bumpass Creek. With the environmental threat within sight and smell of everyone along the swollen Bumpass Creek, people took notice. The barrels appeared on Saturday, and over the weekend people met and decided to stop the trucks from bringing in any more waste and chemicals. On Monday morning, at

7 o'clock, more than 200 people gathered and formed a human road block-ade that halted the trucks. Some of the idle trucks leaked some of their contents right in front of the protesters. Residents called the fire department to come out and wash the road.

The dramatic standoff at the roadblock encouraged some of the residents of Bumpass Cove to imagine what else was possible. They set out to stop the trucks permanently and formed the Bumpass Cove Citizens Group (BCCG). BCCG asked the county to close the road to the landfill because the bridge on the road had a three-ton limit that the trucks hauling the waste exceeded. The school bus's use of the same bridge strained the nerves of the parents of the bus's passengers. The county commissioners agreed about the risk and closed the bridge to the trucks. The road closure did not stop the trucks for long. They found an alternative route to the landfill. Finally, the state health department ordered a halt to dumping in the landfill regardless of the route taken to get there. BCCG had stopped the trucks!

With outside assistance, some of the leaders of BCCG undertook new goals for the group and the community. The first of these goals dealt with health. In early October, some members of the BCCG went to a workshop on hazardous waste problems at the Highlander Research and Education Center in New Market, Tennessee. Highlander had supported citizen efforts in labor organizing and civil rights in the South since the 1930s (Glen 1988; Horton and Freire 1990; Horton 1991). BCCG leaders learned ways to track who did the dumping, what they dumped, and the health risks associated with chemicals.

Following the workshop, Mary Lee Rogers and her husband went to the state offices of public health in Nashville to research what had been dumped. Rogers recounted this visit: "They took us in a big room. . . . They put us in a conference room, big long table, and they carried in pile after pile after pile of papers in there. They was not in any order, they hadn't never been. We put it together. All of this information we put together and made a little booklet of what went in, how much went in at a time, what the health effects [could be]."

After completing the booklet, Rogers and some other BCCG members had a meeting with a local health department official. They found, for the first time, that they had information that enabled them to be effective and, to their surprise, threatening. As Rogers recalled,

> We were at this meeting and the big man at the health department was saying this [chemical] was not in there [the landfill] and that [chemical] was not in there and at last he said, "How in the world would *you* know

what was in there?" The health department had made it so confusing. We could go down there, and any file we asked for they could hand to us, it could be in Greek and we wouldn't have known a thing about it. Now we spent all that time and effort at the Highlander Center and made that little booklet up. And we handed him the little booklet we made. It showed all of the chemicals and the risks. And he said, "Where did you get that?" If it hadn't been for the people at the Highlander Center teaching us how to go about finding this information, we wouldn't have known what to go down there and look for.

BCCG became involved in a network of support from July of 1979, when it incorporated as a formal organization, to the following summer, when they succeeded in closing the landfill. BCCG received grants from the Youth Project to involve the young people of Bumpass Cove in the organization. Several leaders were awarded SALT (Southern Appalachian Leadership Training) fellowships through Highlander. BCCG also received help from the Center for Heath Services at Vanderbilt University. The Community Health Effort Support System of the Center provided a small grant of $2,500 to assist the BCCG in their organizing efforts. In the summer of 1980, the Appalachian Student Health Coalition, another program of the Center for Health Services, conducted a health fair, which provided free physical examinations for Bumpass Cove residents. The examinations suggested that residents had higher than expected rates of respiratory problems. In addition to monitoring what came into their area, BCCG members became involved in matters beyond their community. They helped form a statewide citizens coalition to deal with hazardous waste, TEACH (Tennesseans Against Chemical Hazards).

The outside assistance, publicity, and momentum of their group gave Bumpass Cove residents far more attention than they were accustomed to, and encouraged some of them, especially the women of BCCG, to imagine a changed Bumpass Cove. Linda Walls, a BCCG leader, had modest but dramatically changed hopes for increased recreation, health care, cultural activities, and community bonds: "Our hopes were to better this community, to have a community center where everybody could get weekly or monthly meals and have our children a place to go, have parties, and let them have like a community center like they have in other areas in the cities and all that. That was our plan: continuing to monitor the landfill and keeping people healthy."

Their expanded imaginations were a mixed blessing. They had a vision of a new and better community. They also had new insight into the politics of their problem and the limits of their power. Gail Story's expanded political imagination brought sadness: "We wised up. In some ways that was really good and some ways that was really sad. . . . We lost the innocence that we had of just living here and feeling like the government was protecting us. . . . We learned not to trust, and that's a shame—not to trust the health department, not to trust the government, to learn to trust yourself and check things out. . . . To question, that's what we've learned."

The citizens of Bumpass Cove expected more from their state and local health department officials, and when they did not find it, they began to demand more of them. Gail Story believes that "Before us [BCCG], I don't think any group actually had questioned the health department or made them to be accountable to anything. . . . They sure as hell was not trying to protect any group or regulate anything." Rogers qualified that lesson: "The health department has regulations but they don't allow anybody to enforce them." Her biggest lesson was, unfortunately, the same as Gail Story's and not a positive one: "Do not trust your health department!"

This new attitude of questioning and independent information gathering changed some women by degrees. Others it changed rapidly and completely. Story, in particular, changed her views about women because of her work on the landfill. "When we started . . . we stayed at home. We raised kids. We raised gardens. I don't think I even drove at the time. I mean it was like 'a woman's place was in the home,' and that's the way it had always been." Linda Walls noticed the change in Story and a lesser change in herself (and other women leaders of BCCG). As she explains: "[Gail] is outspoken now, and that's good because she won't let anyone run over her anymore. . . . She's learned a lot from this, and I have too, but I wasn't naive to the same extent."

The women also learned new appreciation for Hobert Story, despite his alcoholism. Gail Story remembers him as a kind man who did not intimidate women as other men did. She found qualities of leadership in him. "Hobert had a way of making you feel like you'd done something good, and it made you want to do something else. Hobert had a pretty yard; he would work in it all the time. But the time when the trucks were stopped in the road, his house was right beside the road, and we near wore his yard out. There were men sitting on stumps and whittling and chewing tobacco, spitting. I said, 'Hobert, we wore your yard out.' And he said, 'I can always grow more grass, but I can't grow friends.' I'll never forget that. He loved having those people there."

Despite their new appreciation for one another, for their newly developed skills of research and collective action, and for their work in questioning the actions of officials, the women found it difficult to keep people active after their initial success in stopping the trucks. Some members of the group were content with stopping the trucks from dumping and were put off by the complications of more action for change.

Some change was simply not feasible. Environmental degradation had gone too far to allow Bumpass Cove to be restored to its condition before the dumping began. Efforts to remove the toxic materials from the landfill made a bad situation worse. A backhoe ruptured several barrels during a removal effort. People who lived nearby were asked to evacuate their homes while the chemicals either evaporated or were covered with topsoil. Officials judged that further removal efforts would only make the toxic materials airborne and risk additional exposure to the people of Bumpass Cove, to those living along the route of removal, and to the next environment where the rotting and leaking barrels would be stored. The problem was no longer local. People in other places were involved. Story recounted that BCCG "had two choices, and they had to pick the lesser of the dangers: either take it out or leave it in. To leave it in was the safest. It wasn't the safest for us, it was the safest for the rest of the world." Deciding to leave the chemicals in the landfill, according to Linda Walls sapped the group of its vitality and mission. "There was nothing to meet and talk about, because there was nothing else we could do."

Pursuing compensation for damages through court action also deterred the group's imagination for broad community change. More than eighty residents entered a long, drawn-out lawsuit that dissipated the BCCG. Story recalled "that lawsuit that helped bust the group up," this way: "People were starting to want to settle. They were wanting the money. They started seeing the dollar signs and forgetting what we was really fighting."

Soon it was no longer clear what BCCG was fighting, because it seemed to be fighting everyone, including its own members and leaders. Internal disagreements, mistrust, and accusations developed within a year of the roadblock. At a BCCG meeting in June 1980, the president of the group presented newspaper clippings that reported the 1960s redbaiting of the Highlander Center. His actions began a "red scare" that divided the group. Gail Story, Linda Walls, and other officers of the BCCG countered these attacks. They deposed the president and took him to court after he attempted to dissolve the charter of the BCCG. Story answered the former president's attorney's questions about her travel to Highlander. She admitted she went and explained why she went. "I just got a fifth-grade education. [I] got married when I was fourteen years old. . . . These people come and they offered me an opportunity to learn." The court found for Story and the other plaintiffs, clarified the legitimacy of the new officers of BCCG, and placed a restraining order on the former president.

These conflicts within BCCG gave Story confidence and reason to reinterpret her actions. Like Florence Reece almost a half century before her, Story explained, in a letter to the local newspaper, "What we was doing was what we had a right to do as citizens of the United States."

> To Whom It May Concern:
> I am Gail Story and I would like to reply to my neighbor. First of all, I am not communist and I have never been approached by anyone that claimed to be communist. Highlander is just the name of a place that has a library and people like me who can go there and learn things, that we should already know, about the rules and the laws of our country. Things that we as people of the United States have a right to get such as information that is of public record. As for me, I am proud to be American and I love God and the United States and I am proud to be American and I would never do anything to slander anyone.

The combination of false accusations and the compromise of BCCG's original goals began a process of decline as rapid as the group's initial growth. In part, the attention that the BCCG received helped to undo the group.

Even after the days of organized protest and collective action for change ended, however, an increased imagination of the democratic prospect remained. The children of Bumpass Cove changed as a result of their participation in the struggle. One of the children, now grown, attained a degree in environmental studies. Former leaders pointed to the change in individual women and their new attitudes. They also took some credit for helping to bring the issue of hazardous waste to national attention and for inspiring others to take action. As Walls concluded, "The problem is national now. A lot of problems have been solved simply because people got together. I think they have used our example. . . . They said, 'Look what happened in Bumpass Cove. . . . This is what happened to these people. It's not going to happen to us.'"

Ironically, the expanded political imagination of the citizens of Bumpass Cove led to less trust in public officials as well as more trust in themselves. Internal divisions tore at the group, but communal bonds developed as well. The strong democracy of Bumpass Cove led to conflict and collaboration, discovery of a greater sense of how politics operate, empathy for others, and inspiration for people far distant from Bumpass Cove as well.

Discursive Democracy and Dialogical Communities

The political participation of strong democracy involves people in political discourse about common values. Amazingly, political theorists find few instances in American politics of community-based mediating structures that promote genuine discourse and dialogue. They are crowded out by private interests that express themselves in the limited politics of voting and exchanges of influence.

The Appalachian Ohio Public Interest Center (AOPIC) and the Western North Carolina Alliance (WNCA) provide glimmers of the discursive democracy that sustains and grounds hope in the expanded politics of the democratic prospect. AOPIC did this by stimulating public discourse about severe poverty and ruinous environmental conditions. WNCA organized hundreds of North Carolina citizen-members and conducted workshops for many more local residents to oppose a nuclear waste facility, challenge clearcutting in the national forest, and protest the construction of superhighways into the mountains. Their efforts promoted dialogue about community values and a common future.

Appalachian Ohio Public Interest Center (AOPIC)

AOPIC began in the early 1980s in direct response to budget cuts implemented by the Reagan administration. The university and small businesses of its home base of Athens, Ohio, provide some refuge from the economic hardships of southeastern Appalachian Ohio. They also provide a supportive location for community-based mediating structures. Two other groups in this study, the Appalachian Center for Economic Networks (ACEnet) and the Appalachian Peoples Action Coalition (APAC) were located in the Athens area too, and all three groups shared information and staff talent. Faculty and staff of Ohio University, located in Athens, also supported some aspects of the work of these nonprofit organizations. Bob Garbo, one of the founders of AOPIC, recalled its discursive beginnings: "The end of the world came in 1980 when we all realized that the end was here for all the social services and community organizations. We saw the community organizations as not popular, not funded, and certainly being squashed. We began talking about pulling together a coalition to raise funds to keep the concept of a people-owned organization going."

Garbo, along with local professionals—university and even some public agency staff members—staged a rally for the continued public support of human service programs. The rally drew more than 1,000 people from Athens and surrounding counties to participate in a march and to listen to the event's featured speaker, U.S. Senator Howard Metzenbaum. AOPIC grew in the early 1980s, and began to take on issues in this poor rural area that other groups, particularly government agencies, could not or would not address. Carol Kuhre, a founding member who later became AOPIC's director, recalled, "All of us who founded the organization were friends and we communicated with each other about what we perceived the needs of the region to be. . . . We all had done social change work together and were communicating with each other on a regular basis about our struggles. I think that some of those people who were with government agencies felt strapped as to what they could do with their agencies. So, the need was to form another organization that could do some of the more up-front, political work that would probably be real controversial. . . . We could use [it] as a bridge organization to larger issues."

Within eighteen months of its beginning, AOPIC joined the statewide Ohio Public Interest Campaign (OPIC) as its first rural branch. The initial issues the group worked on included a toxic dump in Hocking County, north of Athens; subsidence and water supply, a problem related to longwall mining in counties to the west of Athens; and a battle over the cost to consumers for the extension of utilities to rural areas, where new electrical lines often cost exorbitant amounts, telephone services of lower quality than those in urban areas cost more, and water utilities also carried higher fees. The last issue resulted in some clear victories of improved services and lower rates.

AOPIC helped form Citizens Organized Against Longwalling (COAL). Longwall mining in the area left deep cavities underground that changed the course of aquifers and caused subsidence or cave-ins of the surface. AOPIC and COAL documented a seven-foot drop in the water table; springs and wells that went dry; and roads, houses, and barns that were damaged by subsidence. AOPIC addressed its protest to federal and state regulatory agencies with responsibility for supervising the mining activities of the Southern Ohio Coal Company, a subsidiary of the American Electric Power Company. This experience prepared AOPIC to provide research and organizing assistance to local residents who addressed varied threats to water, soil, and air from eighty known industrial hazardous waste sites and seven superfund sites in the area.

Becoming part of the OPIC/Citizen Action coalition was an exciting move for the young group. They now had a statewide agenda. They could use the OPIC/Citizen Action reputation when appealing to funding sources. Occasionally, they could ask the OPIC staff to assist them with certain tasks.

There were costs for this affiliation as well. AOPIC's efforts could get lost within the larger organization, and the statewide publicity for OPIC diluted recognition for AOPIC's local effort. The group considered the difficulties of remaining part of a statewide coalition and determined that the benefits of participating in OPIC/Citizen Action outweighed the costs.

With time, however, AOPIC's top priority became fund-raising. It struggled to address OPIC's statewide agenda and to meet its own budget. Growth and management problems led to funding problems and organizational crisis. Eventually the staff dwindled to one person, and AOPIC almost folded in the mid-1980s. Remarkably, AOPIC overcame these problems and created a new vision for the 1990s. Kuhre organized and facilitated intensive workshops on the future of the organization, which involved fifty-six people during four daylong sessions. "We gave the organization a new mandate and direction," she recalls. Kuhre became the director and was determined "to take the organization back to where we were as original founders, to the basic grassroots organizing around both environment and poverty. And by God, return to that because that's what we can do that they [government organizations] can't do because of their constraints. . . . Every community needs a group that is a little bit weird. Don't you think?"

AOPIC set out to further discursive democracy and the dialogic community. It did so by "building the organization, providing training to other groups in the area, and thinking creatively and boldly about the possible ways to solve southeastern (Appalachian) Ohio's economic and environmental problems." Kuhre felt that AOPIC had "moved from a reactive position to an active, visionary role."

> We have been responding to the cries of this dump going in here or that dump going in. We have been organizing like field workers. But it comes time to say, "If we don't want southern Ohio to become the world's dumping ground, we have to create a vision of what we want here instead." So we try to take those same people who got riled up and say, "Just because your problem was solved, don't drop out. Stay with us as we move toward a vision of the development we want." What we have done is figure out a strategy for doing economic development out of the waste stream.

By 1993, AOPIC had 350 members in twenty-nine Appalachian Ohio counties and undertook a program of rural regeneration with explicit social capital dimensions. Kuhre remembered, "We started out with the citizens complaining about the dump going in next to them and the groundwater contamination, and we are saying to the same people, 'Let's also talk about creating something new.'" Rural Regeneration emerged as a collaborative venture of education, government, labor, nonprofit, and religious groups and the private sector. The AOPIC Rural Action Center proposed to coordinate the efforts of these groups to "create jobs and work on job-retention and expansion, improve the infrastructure of the region, and improve the quality of life in the region through citizen mobilization."

The process of rural regeneration called for:

- Inventories of natural, human, and market resources;
- Inclusive community-based assessment and planning processes;
- Identification and training of community leaders;
- Identification, training, and coordination of community volunteers;
- Integrated "economic literacy and on-the-job training" for the employed and those on public assistance; and
- Sustainable economic development projects based largely on the needs and resources of the bioregion.

Rural Regeneration fulfilled part of the role that AOPIC saw for itself in the community. It facilitated discussions among traditionally adversarial groups and the search for compatible solutions to local and regional problems. For example, AOPIC helped health advocates in the community and the university cooperate to provide health care to low-income families. Previously, advocates and the university community had not seen each other as accessible, yet the university, with its resources and information, had the potential to make a substantial and positive impact in the surrounding communities. Kuhre exclaimed, "Look at this resource! I mean we have 850 specialized faculty, and we are sitting in one of the poorest counties in the state. What the hell is going on around here?"

As an example of AOPIC's effective yet low-profile work and success in creating common ground, they helped initiate a program for medical students at the university to make home visits to low-income households. This project cooperated with the local Head Start program as well. AOPIC also wrote a proposal, at the request of the medical school, for a free clinic and free dispensary for drugs. The success in working with the university involved a combination of strategic planning, diplomacy, and pressure. Kuhre commented that AOPIC's cooperation with the university "is another form of organizing."

It's not just organizing low-income people. It's organizing also among those who have the power, and people who want to do something but just don't know how, or won't dare, or won't do it alone. We are intentionally mining the university for its skills and resources and the ability they have to assist small groups. And some of us are learning that not everyone over there is going to charge them $250 an hour to consult. That, in fact, they can call here and I can find a chemist or a physicist or somebody to assist these groups and nobody ever charges anything. So we are like a brokering institution. A common denominator is being built and I see no end to that.

Kuhre looked for common ground in other places as well, such as between miners and environmentalists. "Reconciling conflicting interests begins with listening and learning the integrity in their argument and saying, 'Listen to them. Don't dismiss them. Listen to each other!'" Kuhre calls this "working in the little way" and found hope in its difficult but measurable progress.

Another founding member of AOPIC who worked with a local poverty agency saw value in AOPIC's advocacy work, which other agencies were not able to do. Many antipoverty agencies sought the cheap way to solve poverty, in contrast with AOPIC's program of rural regeneration and institutional reform. "It's much less expensive to hire a bunch of us and have us think we are doing something than it is to really deal with the issue of poverty."

The new direction built on past success, and especially the hope of change and improvement through political action. Kuhre summarizes:

Maybe the most valuable thing is that [AOPIC] demonstrates that citizens—given even a little bit of encouragement—can act on their own issues and are willing to do it. . . . An awful lot of [college students] run through this place as interns or somehow come in touch with us. I never dismiss the fact that they somehow get a sense that not everyone operates according to corporate America, that there are people out there who live by a different story—and they live it all their life. They live a different story. . . .

There is so much hopelessness in this society, not just for young people. One of our founding attorneys . . . said, "We have to give people hope even if we have to lie." Now, I wouldn't carry it that far, but there is a need, a desperate need, for people to see that some things work and [that] people care. They are not just out to fleece their own pockets or get bigger titles or something. Some people have to demonstrate that. We don't do that perfectly, but we are trying.

The Western North Carolina Alliance also illustrates discursive democracy and dialogical community on environmental issues. WNCA had several common features with the Bumpass Cove Citizens Group. Both groups were in geographic areas where poverty rates were higher than the national average and per capita incomes were lower. In both areas, people worked hard just to get by. These conditions encouraged the desperate search for new jobs and for economic activity even at cost to the environment. In Bumpass Cove, these environmental subsidies meant toxic materials. In Western North Carolina, subsidies meant that plus the demand that the environment go an extra mile to support an extractive economy that took more from the community than it gave.

WNCA began when a local woman, Esther Cunningham, read about the Appalachian Alliance's land study in *Mountain Life and Work,* a publication of the now defunct Council of Southern Mountains. That study examined landownership and land use in Appalachia (Appalachian Land Ownership Task Force 1983). The study provoked concern among some Western North Carolina residents, such as Cunningham, about oil and gas development in the Nantahala and Pisgah National Forests, which make about 30 percent of the land in the western counties of the state. In this region of the state, one's backyard, or what once was once a family's home place, is likely to be national forest. With the help of the Appalachian Alliance, an emerging group of citizens concerned about the hazards of oil and gas drilling received a grant from the Needmor Foundation to hire staff and begin the Western North Carolina Alliance.

The threat of oil and gas exploration and drilling proved minimal and soon faded. However, other environmental issues and threats emerged, including extensive clearcutting within the Pisgah and Nantahala National Forests, discharges of the carcinogen dioxin and other toxic materials into the Pigeon River in Canton by plants of the Champion International Paper Company, and the threat of a proposed nuclear waste dump in the area. Although WNCA members struggled with all of these problems, they focused most of their attention on stopping extensive and accelerated clearcutting in the national forests. Elmer Hall, a member of the WNCA Forest Task Force, explained that WNCA has always addressed other issues, but challenging U.S. Forest Service clearcutting has been the mountain that has overshadowed all of the others: "It was how we raised the most money and got the most press, and it is an ongoing issue. So it is easy to become familiar with and know how to deal with it. But it is just one small segment of what the organization's purpose is."

WNCA's successful campaign "Cut the Clearcutting" aimed to reform Forest Service management. Through organizing local chapters and developing leadership, WNCA got more than 20,000 signatures on a petition that its members presented to the Forest Service supervisor in North Carolina. The petition asked that the forest plan be changed to eliminate clearcutting. WNCA participated in discussions on the forest plan and conducted a protest called "The Plan is a Sham!" which disputed the Forest Service's 1992 plan. Clearcutting declined as a result of many factors, among them the WNCA's discursive democracy, which countered pressure on the National Forest Service to raise its own income with revenue from the timber clearcutting industry.

The flurry of activity and victories around the "Cut the Clearcutting" campaign helped WNCA's membership grow to 800 members in 1993. Another dialogue about community ensued. The majority of residents in Western North Carolina considered WNCA members "outsiders." "Our basic division," Hall explained, "is between people who moved here, transplants, those [of us] who are not native, and locals who make up well over the majority, maybe 70 percent, of the population. Almost everyone in the WNCA (90 percent) are people who weren't born in this area . . . a middle-class, retiree, hippie, intellectual, academic, university constituency." A sense of community clashed with class and environmental concerns, as Hall explained: "To be concerned about the environment, you have to be free to think beyond your own immediate concerns. If you are having trouble paying the bills and getting food, it's really hard for the larger concerns about the larger community to be part of your consciousness."

The character of WNCA's membership provided both strengths and weaknesses. It attracted environmental activists, as both staff and leaders who shared commitments to protect the natural environment of Western North Carolina. A more diverse membership would have included the direct, active participation of "local" people and more concern for their economic well-being. WNCA made an effort to diversify and expand its membership. Its efforts to combine advocacy on environmental issues with a concern for local economics required discussion within WNCA as well as discussion between WNCA and other groups. But discursive democracy and dialogical communities do not come easily. The WNCA conflicted with other organizations in a fight to clean up the Pigeon River, polluted by Champion Paper. The WNCA found few allies in their position. The local union, for example, was "the strongest, most vocal opponent of cleaning up the river." Other social justice groups were not interested in supporting a cause that would threaten workers. Hall suggested that the lack of a middle ground between jobs and the environment had set groups fighting each other: "There is a problem and even a distrust between people who just see themselves as working for social justice and people who just see themselves as working for environmental protection."

Members of the WNCA gained support and credibility in Western North Carolina for the results they achieved and how they achieved them, but this did not come without difficulties and disappointments. As Hall put it, "Changing a federal bureaucracy (the way it works) that is also aided and abetted by a voracious timber industry is no easy task. . . . But it is a back-yard issue for everybody, one way or another here, because the national forests are so much a part of Western North Carolina and also the tourist industry and everything, people's quality of life. Part of the disappointment is working on a campaign that never seems to end. You get tired sometimes of the same issues."

WNCA built its strength and credibility on the forest issues and main-tained it at some internal costs. Individuals associated with Earth First! be-gan a civil disobedience campaign in the area that surpassed the tactics of WNCA and the tolerance of residents, including some WNCA members. Earth First! members chained themselves to the doors of some of the For-est Service buildings in North Carolina. At the time, the WNCA was the only group known for opposing the Forest Service, so some people believed that the WNCA had a hand in this activity. Hall recalls, "We were accused by the timber industry of spiking trees and being irrational . . . being gra-nola eaters, and all sorts of things like that. . . . We had several members write in angry letters and resign because of the confusion."

Local negative response came from action on other issues as well. In the late 1980s, the WNCA developed a Transportation Task Force, which fo-cused on stopping a new highway from being built between Erwin, Ten-nessee, and Asheville, North Carolina. This position tarnished the WNCA's image again. Media reports suggested that the WNCA opposed any new road building, a position WNCA had never adopted. Hall explained how that image created new opposition and problems in conducting discursive democracy:

> WNCA got the public picture of being against roads, against jobs, against development; a "no growth" kind of thought. So much so that our local chapter had been meeting for years here at the Presbyterian church and

some of the elders of the church got a resolution passed saying that the WNCA could not use their church anymore. So we had to move to the volunteer fire department. The reason being that there were real estate agents working in Mars Hill and other parts of the county, and Chamber of Commerce types that didn't want their church being used by a group against development."

The WNCA dealt with the classic dilemma of jobs versus the environment. AOPIC dealt with the environmental damage that comes from an insufficiently regulated industry. The experiences of both WNCA and AOPIC show that the development and perseverance of discursive democracy and dialogical communities are not easy. Their recurrent efforts may even make it seem to some as though no work is being done. They are there, however, at the pole of participatory, strong democracy. The discourse and dialogue they spark light the way to adapting market capitalism in ways that prevent or mitigate its excesses.

Free Spaces

The Appalachian Peoples Action Coalition (APAC) worked on issues that affected low-income people in the area surrounding Athens, Ohio. Low-income residents, with assistance from leaders of other nonprofit groups in the area, began this group in 1987. APAC held monthly meetings that featured a potluck supper and often a guest speaker. Its programs helped low-income citizens address health, housing, social service, and job training issues. APAC also operated a used furniture store. The APAC programs mitigated the poverty in the area very modestly. The meetings and the bargain furniture store, however, provided free spaces, which are an important political dimension of community-based mediating structures and their provision of social capital.

Free spaces offer a tangible form to efforts that promote the democratic prospect. Tracing several social movements over the past century, Sara Evans and Harry Boyte found that groups restricted by race, gender, and class discrimination regularly develop free spaces, where people discover new democratic potential within themselves and new political facts about the world. They construct networks and contacts with other groups, expand identities beyond themselves, and take more control of public matters (Evans and Boyte 1986: 188). Free spaces offer the glimmer of strong democracy, dialogical community, and, of course, the possibility of democratic institutions.

Top: Dancers at the opening celebration of the This and That Laundromat in Dungannon, Virginia. (Photo courtesy of the Dungannon Development Corporation)

Above: Nancy Robinson (left) and Barbara Green (right) present Kitty Cole, a training supervisor, with an "Appalachian Sister" award for her work on housing needs in the Dungannon, Virginia, area. (Photo by Cathy Guthrie)

Virginia Madge Lilly feeding native trout in a stream in Brumley Gap, Virginia. (Photo by Cathy Guthrie)

View of Brumley Gap from the firehouse. Water from the proposed dam at the gap would have submerged this area where new numbers for the fire trucks are being made. (Photo by Cathy Guthrie)

Executive Director Greg Morrell and board member Jeannette Seitz of the Appalachian Independence Center.

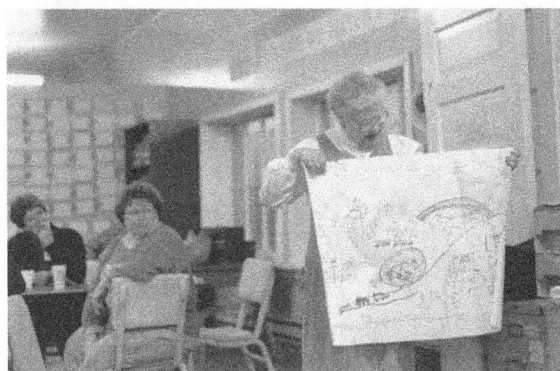

Above: Left to right: organizers Linda Walls, Gail Story Sams, and Roxy Wilson in Wilson's yard, which overlooks the road leading to the landfill in Bumpass Cove, Tennessee. (Photo by Cathy Guthrie)

Left, top: Bob's Appalachian Back Scratchin' Band tunes up as another member of the Appalachian Peoples Action Coalition (APAC) works on GED homework before the start of the monthly membership meeting.

Left, bottom: APAC member explains a community analysis drawn at a Highlander workshop to other members at a monthly meeting. (Photo by Cathy Guthrie)

Top: APAC members include a potluck supper in every monthly meeting. (Photo by Cathy Guthrie)

Bottom: Roadside Theater improvises at the Appalachian Identity Center in Cincinnati, Ohio. (Photo by Cathy Guthrie)

In its work for and with low-income citizens of the greater Athens area, APAC developed several different free spaces where people could receive support and help. It influenced the policies of the county welfare department, children's services agency, and the local court through direct action and education. The free spaces it developed come about in different ways. Some spaces became freer by becoming less public. Dean Ferrell, the president of APAC in 1993, recalled that the receptionist's desk at the Welfare Department used to be "out in the open. Everybody sitting in the room could hear the conversation of people who spoke to her." Ferrell and other APAC members pointed out the need for privacy and made a recommendation to the department that the receptionist be accessible but removed from the rest of the waiting room. This simple change made a big difference. It recognized the right of low-income families to privacy and self-respect.

APAC began a "court watch" program to make public space more accountable to the public. Many of the people with whom APAC worked felt they were being treated unfairly in court. APAC members sat in on hearings and maintained a silent presence to witness the treatment the judge gave to low-income people, especially juveniles. It seemed to Ferrell that "if your dad didn't play golf with the judge, it made a difference in how you were treated in the courtroom." Kathryn Lad, an APAC staff member, explained, "Part of the issue of respect involved how people are treated in the courtroom when no one is watching. Just the presence of court watchers tends to change the atmosphere and respect of the courtroom." Reflecting on its first five years of operation, Dean Ferrell explained APAC's reputation for making what is public more accessible to more people. "APAC is best known for helping people cut bureaucratic red tape involved with so many government assistance programs. Since many social workers are familiar with APAC, problems often get solved before they reach the courts. Intervention achieves results. The main purpose of APAC is to gain a better way of living for low-income people through unity. When we have helped one of us, we have helped us all."

APAC helped its members become more informed about available services in the area by inviting guest speakers to come to meetings and talk on topics of general interest. For example, APAC invited the director of Children's Service to one of their monthly meetings. Peg Winkler, treasurer for APAC, explained the benefit she got from the meeting. She shared with the director "the image of Children's Services . . . that they take away children," and learned in turn of services the agency offered to children in their homes.

Just outside of Athens, APAC operated the Bargain Furniture Store. All of the furniture was donated, fixed up by APAC volunteers, and then sold at very low prices. Paul Rutter, who worked as the assistant store manager, explained that by fixing up used furniture, APAC also recycled and helped the community: "This throwaway society is ridiculous . . . We can reclaim it and resell it to somebody at a low price. It helps us to maintain our advocacy work and also our organization; helping one another to help ourselves. And if we help ourselves, we help other people. It's a round-robin." Initially the Bargain Furniture Store was open only on the weekends, but it expanded its hours and its space.

APAC members decided to start the store because they wanted a project that would reach more people. Although the majority of the store's customers were there to find furniture, they found other things as well. The store became a social center. Lad, whose office was in a small room at the end of the Bargain Furniture Store, observed, "Some of the people come in here to shop *and* to talk to Paul. They feel very connected with APAC. They may not be a card-carrying member, but they feel connected. . . . [It is important] for people to be able to come down here and to have a place where it is comfortable . . . to come in a shop where they have friends, where they can talk about things." Lad also pointed out that the store was "a place for young men to come and hang around. And there aren't very many organizations that attract men that age. It's a place they can work, and it's a place for them to do the kind of things that men like to do." She added, "Working and volunteering gave them a sense that they had a job. They would come and do what you would normally be paid for doing, but as members of APAC [they] were volunteering to keep the place going."

APAC was not in its work alone. Federal programs helped APAC provide some community residents work and skills. For example, Paul Rutter, the assistant manager of the store, was employed through Green Thumb, the Senior Community Service Employment Program. A grant from the Department of Labor, under the Older Americans Act, paid seniors minimum wage for working up to 20 hours a week in a nonprofit agency. The Green Thumb program began in 1965 through the efforts of the National Farmers Union and its concern with increases in rural poverty. By 1990, the program had grown from a pilot with 280 participants to one with 18,500 participants working in more than 10,000 nonprofit and government organizations (Salsbury 1990). APAC's Bargain Furniture Store also became a site for the Community Work Experience Program (CWEP). Many of APAC members received some form of public assistance and could now work their required hours through volunteering at APAC through the CWEP program.

By 1993, APAC had a dues-paying membership of about 250. Membership dues for 1994 increased to $2 per year and entitled members to a

10 percent discount on anything bought at the Bargain Furniture store. APAC also had an emergency loan fund and emergency transportation service for members. Membership was important to the group, but APAC aimed to benefit people other than its members. Kathryn Lad explained, "People who feel that they are connected with APAC . . . [are] like circles that go around."

The path to the democratic prospect, like the path of social movements, will have free spaces such as those created by APAC, spaces that provide settings between private lives and the large-scale institutions. Community-based organizations need physical spaces where its members can act "with dignity, independence, and vision," as Evans and Boyte pointed out, and as the following hymn, sung at a APAC membership potluck meeting, expressed:

> Give me oil in my lamp.
> Keep me burning, burning, burning.
> Give me oil in my lamp, I pray.
>
> Give me oil in my lamp.
> Keep me burning, burning, burning.
> Keep me burning to the break of day.
>
> Give me love in my life.
> Keep me sharing, sharing, sharing.
> Sing Hosanna, sing until the break of day. (Sevison 1952)

Transformative Politics

Free spaces, according to Stephen L. Fisher, are transformative and democratic when they provide a place where people connect local events to a systematic critique of a broader political economy. The Appalachian Alliance attempted this complex and extensive transformative task explicitly. In 1977, the Alliance coalesced grassroots groups in response to massive flooding throughout the central Appalachian coalfield region, which left an estimated 20,000 people homeless in the region. Eastern Kentucky and West Virginia were hit hardest. Although the initial issues of the Appalachian Alliance were the floods and related damages, the Alliance quickly moved on to other issues, including needs for human services, environmental problems, unfair taxation, and government accountability. The stated purposes of the Alliance were "to support individuals and communities working to gain democratic control over their lives, work places, and natural resources;

to help build a unified voice in Appalachia; and to change public policy through direct action." The Alliance's booklet, *Report From the Colony*, offered an overview of the region, its problems, and the political-economic origins that guided its actions. After ten successful years of coalition work, the Appalachian Alliance closed in 1987, when its steering committee voted to put the organization "into a period of resting." The ten-year history of this organization provides insight into the problems and prospects of transformative politics.

In 1977, staff members and leaders from several grassroots groups and organizations from the region gathered at the Highlander Center in New Market, Tennessee, and formed the Appalachian Alliance. The first meetings of the Alliance drew about 100 people. A strong coalition emerged with an agenda common to people throughout the Appalachian region, from Pennsylvania to Georgia. June Rostan, Southern Empowerment Project director and a former steering committee member, who lived in Tennessee at the time of the floods, recalled that the founders of the Alliance "looked at things from a regional perspective because . . . they knew that it wouldn't suffice just to do things on a state by state basis . . . they wanted to put pressure across the state lines and say, 'This [flood] has hit several states of the Appalachian area. Let's use this as an opportunity to get organized around some things and not just respond to the flood.' " The steering committee agreed to meet four times a year, planned an annual membership meeting, and set membership dues. Finally, it established different task forces to work on specific issues. The Alliance focused initially on immediate housing needs and then related issues. Rostan recalled "a real drastic need . . . for housing. In fact I can remember during that time, you could see all of these house trailers when you traveled to eastern Kentucky from here. People needed land, too. . . . land became a critical issue." Accordingly, the Alliance took up issues related to land. It set up a group to monitor the implementation of the 1977 Surface Mining Control Act.

Although the Alliance was involved in many projects in its ten-year history, the Appalachian Land Ownership Study stands out among its notable achievements. Grants from the Ford Foundation and the Appalachian Regional Commission made it possible for the Appalachian Alliance to conduct this landmark study of land ownership patterns in Appalachia. The Alliance's member groups sent representatives to the Highlander Center to participate in training for research. The newly trained participants took this knowledge back to their groups and begin to research land owning in their state and counties. The Land Ownership Study researched more than 19 million acres of mineral and surface acreage in six Appalachian states.

The study found that people who lived outside of the counties owned 72 percent of the property surveyed. Eventually the University Press of Kentucky published the completed study, an irony that Rostan and others noted: "[The Alliance] had a hard time trying to find someone to publish it. . . . Finally the University (Press) of Kentucky published it. . . . Of any University that has ties to the coal companies, that's it, that's the one . . . UK." The size and success of this study set a benchmark and precedent for participatory action research in America (Park, Brydon-Miller, Hall, and Jackson 1993).

Once the study was completed and published, organizing work began. A letter of invitation to the annual meeting of the Appalachian Alliance asked for help to determine ways to use the study in communities across the region. One year later, the announcements of the 1981 annual meeting reported on the publicity the Land Ownership Study had created throughout the region:

> In Kentucky . . . the study has brought statewide attention to the problem of lack of taxation on unmined coal . . .
> In Alabama . . . the findings of the study prompted an all-night filibuster against [a] bill (that would have lowered taxes) . . .
> In Tennessee . . . the study prompted a resolution in the state legislature to call for an investigation . . .
> In Madison County, North Carolina . . . the study's findings have led the county to begin to investigate the impact of leasing for new minerals . . .
> In West Virginia . . . the regional papers have all picked up the story.

Not every group involved in the Alliance followed the study with a plan of action, but there were some outstanding successes. A number of organizations gained strength and direction from participating in the study and used the study to form new organizations that brought about long-term change. The founders of the Kentucky Fair Tax Coalition (KFTC) gained knowledge on issues and organizing through their involvement with the Land Ownership Study and the Appalachian Alliance. Eventually, KFTC led a successful campaign to reverse the broad form deed law, which had severely limited landowners' control over the surface of their land if a third party owned the coal beneath it. KFTC's successful campaign relied on the cumulative information concerning land ownership and taxes and the skills this research provided to the future organizers on this issue. The Western North Carolina Alliance also got its start through the Land Ownership Study. David Liden, a former staff member of the Alliance, became the first coordinator for WNCA. The study helped explain the tax inequities and poor tax base of West Virginia. The new specifics of these problems helped renew strong dissatisfaction with the poor quality of public services, including education. The West Virginia teacher strike of 1990 began in a coal mining county severely impacted by absentee landownership and the tax advantages of the coal companies, which the land study had revealed.

As one Alliance task force worked on the Land Ownership Study, other task forces worked on health care, housing, the status of women, energy, education, nuclear waste, and cooperative economic development. The Alliance was especially interested in monitoring the response of the U.S. Department of Housing and Urban Development to the 1977 flood and the responses of other regional agencies, such as the Appalachian Regional Commission (ARC) and the Tennessee Valley Authority (TVA). Rostan recalled that many grassroots organizations criticized ARC for taking a bricks-and-mortar approach to development and making too small an investment in human and social capital. During the 1980s, the Reagan administration decreased funding for the ARC and for the community development work of the TVA. TVA's modest community development remained crucial to efforts such as those in Dungannon, Virginia. The Alliance monitored and criticized the nuclear construction program of the TVA, which remained the nation's largest until the economics of nuclear power undermined TVA's determined efforts to ignore them.

In the years following completion of the land ownership study, the Alliance had more energy than focus. The advent of the Reagan administration offered a new focus for the Alliance, just as it had offered the impetus to the organization of the Appalachian Ohio Public Interest Center. Rostan recalled:

> There was a flurry . . . as soon as Reagan got elected. People were saying, "Maybe in a way this is good. We can organize better because there is a real clear opposition here." . . . But then people kind of settled in. I guess to a certain extent the Alliance had a tougher time deciding what to do after the Land Study was finished.
>
> There was some frustration toward the end about how to move an agenda and how to find the areas where people could agree to move stuff forward. There were philosophical differences about the most effective way to get things done. There were people within the Alliance that thought organizing and building membership organizations was one of the best ways to get things done, and others who didn't.

In the early 1980s, the Alliance published two more booklets, *National Sacrifice Area* (1980) and *Appalachia in the Eighties: A Time for Action* (1982).

Although the Alliance's goals were not as clear as they had been in the aftermath of the flood and in the years of the land ownership study, the coalition continued to grow through the 1980s. It attracted more than thirty member groups and addressed almost as many issues. An Alliance pamphlet exemplified its openness to many groups and the spectrum of issues they were willing to tackle. It asked, "Which Are the Issues of the Appalachian Region?" The answers were: unemployment, oil and gas, taxation, water pollution, toxic waste, health care, energy, strip mining, land, labor, coal, environment, housing, occupational health and safety, women, education, and nuclear power. If those were not enough, the pamphlet asked readers for more: "What Are *Your* Issues?"!

The openness of the Appalachian Alliance to issues and groups suggested flexibility but also an inability to agree on priorities. The health problems of the new director stymied priority setting further. Frustration followed delay. The Alliance had raised money and put a lot of energy into hiring its new director. When his illness forced him to resign, the steering committee lacked the energy and other resources to go through the process again. It made more sense to the board members, Rostan remembers, to close the Alliance at a positive moment rather than let it fizzle out. She recalled, "There was a sense that a lot of things had been accomplished as a result of the Alliance and that maybe it was just time to put it to rest. . . . We said we can go on with the organization, but there are times when you need to call it quits and do it on a high note, do it not when you are falling apart but have accomplished some things."

Despite the well-organized structure of the coalition and the need for a regional group, the Appalachian Alliance never applied for recognition as a tax-exempt 501(c)(3) organization. Rostan speculated that "maybe people figured it might not last forever, that because it was a coalition it was the sum of its parts, [and that] the money could be channeled through other organizations in the region." Throughout its ten years of operation, the Alliance relied on the Highlander Center and the Commission on Religion in Appalachia (CORA) to broker and administer foundation funds for it. These arrangements usually worked fairly well. However, since Highlander controlled the flow of the Alliance's money, and perhaps because many of the early meetings and training were held at Highlander, the Highlander Center received credit for the Appalachian Land Ownership Study, one of the Alliance's most successful projects.

Despite the frustrations and staff problems, the steering committee meetings and the annual meetings of the Alliance continued to be valuable for staff members of many groups. They provided the only political regional meetings of grassroots groups in the region at the time. Until it reached a "dormant" period, the Alliance exemplified many of the transformative efforts that Fisher looks for in free spaces.

Political Transcendence: Singing Across Dark Spaces

In addition to transforming the current political conditions of their members, the political dimensions of community-based mediating structures put their members in touch with other people like themselves, who, in previous times and places, had tried to transform the conditions they faced. Fran Ansley and Jim Sessions (1992) suggest this transcendence in their account of the takeover of the coal preparation plant of the Pittston Coal Company during the long and eventful strike of 1980 (Couto 1992). Strike organizers conceived the takeover tactic to invoke the memory of the sit-down strikes of the 1930s and to tie their strike to the traditions of the American labor movement. In addition, the striking miners, their families, and their supporters converted a modest local swim and tennis club into Camp Solidarity and hosted tens of thousands of supporters who visited them from around the nation and the world. Eventually, the solidarity of the strike incorporated the traditions of the American labor movement, the strength and energy of union members in other parts of the country, and the Solidarity movement of Poland.

The cultural expression of current events and conditions and their ties to the past and the future of a community provide groups with social capital to create and recreate communities that transcend time and space. Songs written about the Bumpass Cove effort and other songs used at the Appalachian Peoples Action Coalition indicate the role and power of cultural expression in change efforts. Florence Reece's words, from a song written in the middle of a 1930s coal strike, have entered the lexicon of American expression, and its sentiment transcends the time and place of their origin.

Roadside Theater, an ensemble drama company, dealt specifically with culture as social capital. Roadside Theater was one part of Appalshop, a nonprofit arts and educational organization located in Whitesburg, Kentucky. Appalshop began in 1969 as the Appalachian Film Workshop with funds from the now defunct federal Office of Economic Opportunity, the command center of the War on Poverty. Roadside Theater began at Appalshop in 1975 with its specific challenge being "to find a theatrical form and dramatic content that made sense to the rural people who live in the Appalachian mountains of east Kentucky and southwest Virginia, a people for whom there was no written body of dramatic literature or tradition of attending the theater." Roadside Theater shared the challenge of preservation, perpetuation, and celebration of Appalachian culture with Appalshop's eight other projects: Appalshop Films, Headwaters Television, Appalachian Media Institute, Educational Services, June Appal Recordings, WMMT-FM Radio, Appalshop Center Programs, and the American Festival Project. Roadside met its original challenge of finding a theatrical form and content that was relevant to the Appalachian region by developing plays, educational initiatives with local schools and school districts, tours, community residential theatre, and cross-cultural exchanges, including artistic collaborations. Through the work of its ensemble of performers, writers, and administrators, Roadside helped to achieve Appalshop's overall mission as well as helped to introduce and strengthen "grassroots theater" in communities across the country.

Roadside's first play, *Mountain Tales and Music*, combined traditional tales that ensemble members and other members of Appalshop remembered being passed down in their families. For its dramatic impact, it relied on the language and narrative of traditional stories of the region, not on stylized costumes or sets. The simplicity of the play permitted Roadside to perform without a formal stage and thus almost anywhere—classroom, libraries, church basements, halls of community centers, etc. The company followed its first success with a series of productions with the same formula. Roadside's dramatizations of Appalachian history and culture dispelled the hillbilly stereotype and brought its audiences back through time and space to celebrate the strengths and to ponder the struggles of people and groups in the Appalachian region.

From its inception, Roadside toured locally, nationally, and internationally. In 1984, the National Endowment for the Arts recognized Roadside's work with a five-year award that allowed the ensemble to expand its touring program. It also challenged the group to relate regional material to audiences around the country. Ensemble members realized that for their work to have a lasting impact in the communities they visited outside the region, the company needed to help those communities discover, express, and validate their own culture. They developed one- to two-week community residencies, which took the place of their practice of one- to two-day engagements. The longer residencies permitted the ensemble to work with people in the communities it visited and to help them discover their own cultural resources. In doing so, Roadside turned the model of national touring on its head. Rather than importing a temporary dramatic expression like a museum exhibit, it developed each community's dramatic expression from within (Salmons-Rue 1994).

Typical of Roadside Theater's residencies was a one-week residency in Cincinnati, Ohio, hosted by the Urban Appalachian Council (UAC) and the Appalachian Community Development Association in 1992. Roadside combined presentations of traditional Appalachian culture with workshops designed to build pride in the local urban culture of the UAC members. The UAC served neighborhoods in Cincinnati that were heavily populated with people who had migrated from the mountains to the city. It provided migrants from the mountains a horizontal network of support, social capital, while the recent arrivals adjusted to city life and battled pejorative, hillbilly stereotypes. Roadside's work in Cincinnati included workshops for a women's group at the Appalachian Identity Center, staff and adult education tutors of the Urban Appalachian Council, public school teachers in Cincinnati, and the Covington (Kentucky) Youth Group. At the end of the week, the Roadside ensemble presented the play, *From Dublin to Dayton*, which recounted migrations from Ireland to Appalachia and from Appalachia to industrial centers of the Midwest. Roadside's residency in Cincinnati emphasized traditional Appalachian culture but troupe members also spent time telling and listening to stories from UAC members about their own experiences in the city. The troupe members posed five questions and a request to the people with whom they worked:

> Who is the oldest member of your family living now?
> Who is the oldest member of your family they remember?
> Can they remember one story about this oldest family member?
> Do they remember any giant, ghost, or fairy tales from their childhood?
> Do you?
> Tell them!

In trying to explain how Roadside's residency would help strengthen the urban Appalachian communities in Cincinnati, Pauletta Hansel, program and advocacy service director for UAC asked, "Why should you be proud of being from Price Hill or North Side or the East End if that has never been presented as a thing that had any worth?" Hansel interpreted Roadside's residency as helping people find their common experiences and their worth.

The outcome of the residencies varied from place to place, but Roadside intended to have a lasting impact wherever they carried out a residency. Donna Porterfield, the managing director of Roadside, underscored that mission: "Our question is always, what happens to the work after we leave? It can be many things. It can be that the arts presenter has some new people on the board that are more representative of the community. It can be a teacher that teaches in a different way. It can be a community trying to write a play." During a year-long residency in Haysi (Dickenson County), Virginia, Roadside pulled together the Appalachian Agency for Senior Citizens, the Haysi High School drama class, a community history club called Mountain People and Places, and the local Baptist church. The groups produced a play, written by the high school drama students, and conducted four community festivals celebrating local history and life. When Roadside summarized its work in Haysi, it emphasized the personal aspects of the political transformation to which they contributed: "[The residency] did not eliminate the economic problems in Dickenson County, but it did help change individuals' lives and the way the county regards itself. The residency has made visible the indigenous resources for further community cultural and economic development."

Other programs of Roadside Theater included cultural exchanges with Chicano artists in San Antonio, Texas, through the Guadalupe Cultural Arts Center; another exchange with Zuni singers, musicians, and storytellers in New Mexico; and an ongoing relationship and exchange with Junebug Productions, an African American company in New Orleans with ties to Freedom Summer of Mississippi in 1964. Roadside also explored the responsibility of higher education institutions to their communities and worked for three years on a Community Based Arts Project with Cornell University's Center for Theater Arts. Through their work in communities in Appalachia and throughout the United States, Roadside Theater contributed to the movement for social change by celebrating the stories, art, creativity, and experience of everyday life. The ensemble added social capital where it traveled through its leadership development. It encouraged students, teachers, senior citizens, and others to tell their stories and create a lasting appreciation for their own culture and who they are.

The development of appreciation for one's culture combined local, particular events and universal, transcendent experiences in a curious mix. Dudley Cocke, who directed Roadside, expressed this mix in describing the company and its work: "The soul of the work is Appalachia but our works are not solely Appalachian. That is why the plays are appealing to those who aren't Appalachian. This is intentional. By intensifying our particular experience we find commonalities shared by all people" (Bienko 1992: 8). Pauletta Hansel, who sponsored the week-long Cincinnati workshop, understood the universal element of a particular, intense cultural expression as the process of naming oneself and claiming one's past: "There's a way in which 'Appalachian' might be irrelevant. But in one way people's knowledge and pride in their own culture and heritage can be what helps to sustain and empower them. So it's not necessarily particular things out of the mountain history or particular Appalachian cultural traits that might necessarily provide that sustenance but more the act of naming them and claiming them."

Progress in Process

Community-based mediating structures can promote the democratic prospect in distinct but related ways. People may be transformed by their efforts to transform their situations and by the dialogue and discourse *among* and *within* community-based mediating structures that happens as part of those efforts. Free spaces expand people's political imaginations about community and enable some people to transcend their own local, transformative efforts by establishing communal bonds with other people who made efforts like their own in other free spaces of other times and places. This link to other democratic efforts makes clear to them that the democratic prospect is work in progress. This insight sustains them even when they fail or do not model perfectly discursive, dialogical communities. Community-based mediating structures stir our imaginations about the possibilities of such communities and consequently our own transformed possibilities within them.

CHAPTER 5

Economic Dimensions I:
Mitigating the Market

The political dimensions of the democratic prospect measure a transformed and improved set of political, economic, and social arrangements. In practice, community-based mediating structures express economic transformations by mitigating market failures, which this chapter deals with, and by providing more social capital and improved forms of it, the topic of the next chapter. The political and social dimensions of mediating structures are far more familiar to us than their economic dimensions are. Conservative advocates of mediating structures assume the soundness of market economies and even use the market as an analog for democracy. Thus, some advocates assume away the basis of the economic dimension of community-based mediating structures. Nevertheless, markets do fail, and when they do, mediating structures may stem the depletion of social capital, deal with externalities, protect the vulnerable, run against the economic tide, and increase the supply of public goods.

Confidence that the market will provide for the common good supports the democratic promise of limited government and pervades American public policy. Policy analysts generally assert that only market failures justify public policy interventions (Weimer and Vining 1989: 29–93; Stokey and Zeckhauser 1978: 291–319). At times other than market failures, according to the common view of policy analysts, government's primary and appropriate hands-off role assures the unimpeded functions of the efficient natural laws of the market. American public policy and social values ordinarily seek to promote financial capital. Market democracy does this with more than ordinary enthusiasm and with little heed to adverse social costs and consequences, such as unemployment and poverty. However, the market does have two central and often ignored shortcomings: it does not supply public goods adequately, and it ignores the negative consequences of profit seeking. These failures undermine and may even literally destroy communal bonds and social responsibility. When mediating structures act to preserve community, they concomitantly mitigate the consequences of too few public goods and too many negative externalities of profit seeking. In this manner, the familiar social and political roles of mediating structures implicitly convey their less familiar economic roles.

Countering Market Forces

The tie between social capital and the workforce means that social capital is depleted when work declines and disappears. When coal miners lost work to new production methods—as they did following World War II, in the 1960s, and in the 1980s—the social capital of coal mining communities declined. Each period of change in the coal industry resulted in outmigration, as workers and their families sought economic opportunities elsewhere, first in the urban areas of the Midwest and later in the urban areas of the South.

Health care was a casualty of this industrial decline and subsequent depletion of social capital. Health care has a special relationship with coal mining. John L. Lewis, the legendary leader of the United Mine Workers of America (UMWA), intended to provide fewer but much better paying jobs through the mechanization of coal mining that followed World War II. He also intended to finance new forms of social capital through a stable, prosperous coal industry. Labor contracts that permitted capital-intensive mining mechanisms displaced one-third of the workforce but also established industry-supported, social capital funds for hospitals, clinics, rehabilitation, retirement, and survivors' benefits (Krajcinovic 1997). Later, in the 1970s, efforts to compensate for and prevent black lung disease provided some of the initial impetus for reform of the UMWA (B. E. Smith 1987). The reform administration of the UMWA reinstituted the emphasis on health care, especially primary care clinics in West Virginia. The West Virginia Primary

Care Association (WVPCA) continued the legacy of the social capital policies of the UMWA and other labor unions and took up a critical role in health care in West Virginia after 1980.

By the early 1990s, West Virginia depended on community health centers for the provision of health care more than any other state. In 1992, seventy primary care centers located throughout West Virginia served almost 300,000 registered patients, who made almost 1 million visits in the forty-seven medically underserved counties in the state, which constituted 85 percent of West Virginia's fifty-five counties. The patient base of the clinics equaled about one-sixth of the state's population of 1.8 million people. Seventy percent of the health centers' patient visits involved Medicaid or Medicare patients or patients without health insurance. The centers of the WVPCA provided in excess of $14 million of uncompensated care in 1992. The centers represented an investment in health care that the market did not provide. In simplest terms, the services of the WVPCA and its member health centers mitigated a market failure in the provision of health care to poor, elderly, unemployed, and underemployed residents of West Virginia.

The development of the current extensive network of West Virginia health centers resulted in part from the work of the United Mine Workers, who established innovative health centers in the 1950s (Krajcinovic 1997). The UMWA revived that work in the 1970s during the early administration of its reform president, Arnold Miller. Since then, many of the UMWA centers have become community owned and operated. The large number of centers resulted from the health care needs of communities in very rural and mountainous areas of the state where transportation was difficult.

Though the centers were run by different organizations and served different communities, they all shared a number of characteristics. They were nonprofit and community owned. The majority of them were in rural areas. They all treated patients regardless of their ability to pay. They included and sometimes emphasized preventive health care and health education in their services. The West Virginia Primary Care Association provided an umbrella, support, and unified voice for the centers, its mission being "to protect the interests of primary care, to ensure that there is access to the underserved, and to be an advocate for primary care."

Jill Hutchinson, executive director of the WVPCA, explained the central importance of the community health centers in the provision of health care.

You wouldn't have any health delivery system to speak of [without the seventy health centers]. We have centers in areas where there's no other place to go. For example, in the northern part of Greenbrier County, you go to the community health center there, or I don't know where you go. The problem is this, you may be thirty miles away from a hospital, but thirty miles in West Virginia could be an hour's drive. Mileage is nothing. It's driving time. Also, you may have a private doctor ten minutes down the road, but that private doctor might not see you. He may see Medicaid patients, but he probably won't see you if you don't have insurance.

So where's that person going to go? If it's Northern Greenbrier Medical Center—I'll use that as an example because they are isolated and very small—and they close, those people are in trouble. . . . The Tug River Center down in Gary, in the southern coal fields, has expanded over into another part of McDowell County, and they see more people than they can handle. If they close their doors, I have no idea what will happen to those people. I really don't. And many of them don't have transportation, which is one of the biggest issues we face. I can't even be scientific about it. I'm saying if they close, those people have no place to go.

The WVPCA supported these local efforts to provide health care by meeting some of the centers' fundamental needs. Local health centers needed resources—personnel and reimbursements for uncompensated care—to be able to provide their services. A host of constantly changing state and federal regulations affected those resources for better and for worse, and staff members needed help to keep up with them. The WVPCA provided training for administrators, staff, and board members to acquire and maintain skills to attract and maintain the resources they needed.

The crucial role of resources affected WVPCA's own development. The 1980s brought federal changes in funding for health services. The federal government combined funding for different human service programs into block grants to the states, which could decide how to allocate those funds. States had the option to include funds that previously had gone to primary care clinics into the block grant or to maintain a separate funding stream directly to the health centers. West Virginia was one of a handful of states to select the block grant option.

The West Virginia Primary Care Study Group, which looked after the interests of primary care providers at the time, split into two parts over the decision on federal funding. Federally funded health centers within the study group calculated that block grants would mean less federal funds for primary care and opposed them. In response, they established a new group, the West Virginia Association of Community Health Centers, and parted company with the other health centers within the study group that had supported the block grant.

The state rescinded its choice of block-grant funding shortly after making it, but the two groups of health centers remained divided. For the next decade, the West Virginia Primary Care Study Group represented the interests of the nonfederally funded health centers, while the West Virginia Association of Community Health Centers represented the federally funded centers. The Association gained momentum and strong associate members, such as the UMWA and the Bureau of Public Health. Eventually, by the early 1990s, the two groups reunited into the West Virginia Primary Care Association (WVPCA), which represented all community health centers regardless of their major funding source. This organizational history underscores the function of state associations in monitoring and protecting the supply of resources to their members and illustrates how programs of social capital resources easily become wedge issues.

The reconstituted WVPCA provided services such as continuing education, training, and workshops for the health care administrators and clinicians of its members. Workshop topics included medical record keeping, confidentiality, and malpractice. Board members and staff of the various health centers provided much of the training and technical assistance for the association. Jill Hutchinson, executive director in 1992, explained: "We have great expertise in some of these folks that have been around for eighteen years. We have one health center that does wonderful board training. We utilize them to do trainings at other health centers." WVPCA's five-member board, consisting of health center executive directors, oversaw a budget derived from federal grants, membership dues, and income from workshops and conferences.

The community health centers that were members of WVPCA operated in low-income areas, among migrant workers, and among the homeless. Some of the centers were large operations with satellite clinics in nearby areas; others were small, storefront clinics that provided free services in urban areas through voluntary health care providers. Despite this array of providers, the association provided a unified voice in the West Virginia legislature. In 1992, WVPCA's legislative work won an increase in the uncompensated care funds to a level of $3.2 million. This fund reimbursed primary care centers when the patients did not have the resources to pay for services. In addition, the association won approval of Medicaid reimbursement of physician assistants, who provided many services in the clinics. The association's vigilance in the legislature protected the interests of primary care centers in the face of health care reform provisions and the increasing competition of hospitals and changes proposed by insurers.

Hutchinson described the WVPCA in terms of supporting a network of social capital entrepreneurs:

> If [WVPCA] didn't exist, what you would have is an all-volunteer organization of health center administrators trying to pull together things that they don't have time to do; things like education. . . . How would they bring the training that was necessary? We brought in a national speaker to talk about how to fill out cost reports. You would have a bunch of volunteers trying to scamper around to do this and try to take care of their health center. . . . Where would they get their technical assistance? The health department certainly doesn't have that charge necessarily, nor do they have the time to do it. We've always had an organization in West Virginia of some kind. It's hard to think of not having one.

In addition to brokering among resources and needs of its members, the WVPCA brokered between federal and state resources and the needs of health care providers. This role was especially important for the uninsured and for recipients of Medicaid and Medicare, who made up 70 percent of WVPCA members' patients. As Hutchinson explained,

> We stand on the front lines of trying to get the state Medicaid agency to move on things. . . . We provide continuing medical education for clinicians. We serve on every committee known to man. . . . We narrowly focus down sometimes on our state issues and hopefully try not to forget the federal issues, which are to insure that the community health center dollars are there and are increased, that the migrants, the homeless, . . . and all those other hundreds of people that pour into community health centers are protected and . . . programs for them increased, where appropriate.

Hutchinson ascribed the success of primary care in West Virginia to a three-way agreement among the state department of health, federal agencies, and the WVPCA. As in any cooperative arrangement, every partner brought something to the table. WVPCA brought the ability to broker resources from federal, state, and foundation sources, along with the ability to deliver its own technical assistance and that of other agencies effectively. WVPCA played an active and reactive role in its partnership. It brought to the attention of state and federal officials the needs of primary care providers in the state and also monitored the funding and regulatory environment in which the providers worked. This work took specific forms, such as efforts to station eligibility workers in the clinics to assure that patients who were eligible for state and federal programs were enrolled. Of course, reimbursement for enrolled patients reduced the amount of uncompensated care the clinics had to provide for patients who were eligible but not enrolled. Monitoring federal and state legislation and regulations and surveying member clinics to get their reactions enabled the WVPCA to "nudge and cajole" effectively. Without Medicaid and Medicare, the market would underproduce health care in rural, low-income areas. Without community-based mediating structures, public programs to mitigate such market failures would not be as effective as they are.

Dealing with Externalities

Environmental degradation provides a classic, textbook example of the market failure of negative externality. Emissions from a smokestack pollute the air and deposit ash and chemicals in areas surrounding it. Emissions that travel to higher elevations return to earth in distant places. Adam Smith and others understood that government would have to intervene to curb negative externalities such as these. In practice, legislation and regulations have addressed and improved environmental quality. However, the state often has to be prompted to act, and often it is mediating structures that do the prompting.

In 1989, the Ohio Valley Environmental Coalition (OVEC) began to address environmental problems in the tri-state area of Kentucky, West Virginia, and southern Ohio with a very specific nudge. BASF, a German-owned chemical company, proposed constructing and operating a hazardous waste incinerator near Ironton, Ohio. Dianne Bady, director of OVEC, helped start the group. Bady had moved to southern Ohio from northern Wisconsin, where she had gained experience working on environmental issues. She recalled that OVEC grew slowly from an initial meeting of a handful of people who "got together and decided we didn't like the idea . . . of a toxic waste incinerator to bring waste in from all over the country." After an eight-month fight, BASF withdrew its plans.

Once OVEC claimed victory over the proposed Ironton incinerator, it did not have to look very far for other issues to work on. Aristech Chemical of Haverville, Ohio, utilized a deep-injection well to dispose of hazardous waste. The well leaked. A BASF plant in Huntington, West Virginia, burned chemical wastes. OVEC found abandoned chemical waste dumps along the Guyandotte River near Huntington. Ashland Oil's petrochemical refinery in Catlettsburg, Kentucky, spurred citizen outrage about the general environmental degradation of the area.

OVEC members successfully uncovered and publicized evidence about these conditions and pressured state and federal agencies to take appropriate actions. Aristech agreed to close its well. BASF's burning practices were reported in *Chemical Week,* leading to additional state inspections. Eventually, the federal government promulgated new regulations on boiler waste burning. West Virginia officials agreed to cover the surface of the chemical waste dumps to reduce exposure from contaminated dust. State and federal inspections at Ashland Oil's refinery increased, and the environmental quality in the area improved.

Accurate documentation and analysis of the various problems by active OVEC members helped the group gain credibility among the media and with the agencies in charge of enforcing environmental regulations. The members had the technical skills to prepare expert opinions and testimonies for public hearings on a variety of environmental concerns. For example, OVEC worked with the Affiliated Trades Construction Union to successfully challenge the state of West Virginia's attempt to lower the dioxin emission standards in a move to accommodate the operators of a proposed giant paper pulp mill.Through their expertise, a small handful of people effectively advocated for increased and improved environmental quality on behalf of the larger membership. State and federal agencies recognized and sometimes even welcomed the knowledge and careful research of OVEC. For example, in the case of the leaking injection well utilized by Aristech Chemical, according to Dianne Bady, "It was a situation when the environmental agency in the state of Ohio seemed to want to do the right thing, but the company was putting up such a big fight that the state regulators seemed to welcome us getting involved. So they were getting pressure from the other side too. And then eventually the U.S. EPA [Environmental Protection Agency] fined the company, Aristech, and the company has agreed to close the offending well, or rather, to stop dumping in it."

OVEC's expertise on issues spread across three states and three different EPA districts. Kentucky, Ohio, and West Virginia were each in a separate EPA district. The divisions of these political jurisdictions required OVEC to spend vast amounts of energy dealing with the fragmented administrative structure of an integrated ecological system.

OVEC's reputation did not go unchallenged as it pressured local industries to comply with state and federal environmental regulations. As they began to address Ashland Oil's violations of pollution regulations, "there was a real intense effort to discredit us," Bady recalls. "The white-collar workers at Ashland's corporate headquarters—ten miles upwind of the refinery—had an Ashland Oil employee action group newsletter which regularly told blatant lies about [us]. Some Ashland Oil employees tried to claim that OVEC was 'anti-jobs,' that 'we were trying to destroy the tri-state economy,' and that OVEC's actions against them were 'self-serving.'" The charges circulated, but they did not change public perceptions of Ashland management among the residents who lived downwind from the refinery. Downwind residents had health problems, such as skin burns and breathing difficulties, as well as property damage, such as pitted glass and blistered paint on houses and cars.

Many of the affected residents sued the refinery for personal and property damage. Although this drew attention to the problem, the lawsuit frustrated some of OVEC's organizing work. Kim Baker, a former OVEC organizer, recalled that "a whole lot of our potential membership became wrapped up in a great big litigation [that] turned all of their voice over to their attorneys" and, to make matters worse, "settled for a paltry sum."

OVEC members used video documentation of illegal emissions to pressure Ashland Oil to reduce them. OVEC's videos documented violations of clean air regulations by picturing the "opacity" of the emissions. OVEC members shared their videotapes with the Kentucky Division of Air and asked for stronger enforcement of existing regulations. Ultimately, Ashland Oil signed an agreement with the state of Kentucky to pay $7.7 million to clean up and monitor its operations ("Ashland Oil Forced to Pay" 1993). Ashland financed the implementation of a 24-hour-per-day video surveillance system that transmitted images to the Kentucky Division of Air Quality office in Ashland. If residents suspected that Ashland had exceeded its emissions limits, they could view the videotapes. The company also agreed to implement safety measures and to increase monitoring at their hydrogen fluoride alkylation unit, another direct result of OVEC's suggestions and pressure.

As OVEC monitored and exposed violations of industrial polluters, it underwent a transition. For its first three years, OVEC had operated on a purely volunteer basis. Only in August of 1992 did the group receive its first foundation support, from the W. Alton Jones Foundation, which OVEC used to hire a small staff. OVEC then received grant money from the Town Creek Foundation, the Florence and John Schumann Foundation, the Public Welfare Foundation, the Appalachian Community Fund, the Commission on Religion in Appalachia, and other foundations.

In the process of looking for and receiving the funding, OVEC evaluated its work. It decided to move from an advocacy to an organizing model, that is, from the focused actions of a few, active, protesting "experts" to the mobilization of local residents adversely affected by environmental degradation. Dianne Bady worked closely with Pete McDowell from the Partnership for Democracy, who helped her develop a plan and a strategy for this move. She recalled, "It was in that process of deciding where we wanted to go and how we were going to get there that we realized the distinction between advocacy and organizing and realized that we needed to focus more on organizing." McDowell helped her to understand, she said, "that the only way the group was going to be able to be long term and sustainable was to focus more on organizing, to get more people involved rather than maintaining its status as an advocacy group where it's really just a few people who are doing everything."

The group moved toward an organizing model by hiring Kim Baker, who had experience as an organizer with the Council of Senior West Virginians and who also had had training with the Southern Empowerment Project, two groups we have already met. OVEC's staff also contracted with Joe Szakos from Kentuckians for the Commonwealth (KFTC) to be their "organizing mentor." He worked with OVEC's three new staff members on ways they could begin to involve more people in the activities of the group. Subsequently, OVEC began one-on-one contacts with people, holding small house meetings, building leadership among members, and developing spokespersons for the group.

Transforming the board of directors into a board that better represented the membership proved to be a slow and difficult process. The original board was top-heavy with professionals who had contributed to the credibility of OVEC. Bady felt that OVEC "needed to get more people on the board that didn't have any technical training but that were involved in fights in their own communities." Ironically, some of OVEC's success actually impeded the recruitment of new members. Baker, the newly hired organizer, recalled, "The people in the community said, 'Well, I'm sure glad that you all are taking care of this stuff. . . . I don't see that it takes a whole lot of people to do it, and I'm glad that you all are fixing it.' Organizing's more difficult when people have that perception."

Although OVEC drew heavily on the successful organizing model of Kentuckians for the Commonwealth, the group realized it could not possibly duplicate KFTC's successful legislative efforts. OVEC needed to influence the policies of three states and the administration of three federal districts. An intense legislative or organizing strategy in all of them would spread the staff far too thin. Because of this and other differences, OVEC worked to build strong relationships with statewide groups such as the Ohio Environmental Council, the West Virginia Environmental Council, and the West Virginia Citizens Action Group to make legislative efforts in their respective states.

The first Clinton administration brought in some hope for the environmental movement, but OVEC recognized that immense challenges remained. Bady observed, "We now have a new federal administration, which has pledged to be environmentally responsible. Can we step back and assume that new agency officials will solve the problems with no help from us? No way! . . . At the state level, things in West Virginia and Ohio show few signs of positive change. These state agencies are underfunded and understaffed and often seem to lack the ability or desire to deal with the tough issues now being faced, unless they are forced to by massive citizen pressure." That pressure demands that the state require industries to take note of externalities and to address them.

Protecting Some from Others

Negative externalities may adversely affect the health and well-being of specific individuals and groups—risks for injury and illness that occur at work, for example. Some risks are inevitable, while others are preventable. For example, proper ventilation and other dust control methods may reduce the risk of black lung for coal miners. Adam Smith understood that the state might intervene in cases of injustice or oppression (Heilbroner 1993: 71). It is uncertain whether he would have understood black lung as injustice or oppression. Certainly, many economists, legislators, and coal operators today do not see it that way. Some mediating structures, on the other hand, play a role in expanding public awareness of the human costs of market failures and in making sure the risks of labor, such as occupational illness, are factored into the cost of doing business (Judkins 1993).

No single problem signifies the failure of the market more clearly than factors that imperil life and health yet still remain conditions of employment. No single problem of Appalachia stands out as clearly as worker disability (see Map 4). In a startling analysis, Gary L. Burkett, a medical sociologist, found that the vast majority of counties with the highest rates of work disability cluster in the Central Appalachian area of Eastern Kentucky, southern West Virginia, Southwest Virginia, Southeast Ohio, and a northern tier of East Tennessee counties. They are all coalfield counties or contiguous to them (Burkett 1994).

The Virginia Black Lung Association (VBLA) organized and served dis-

Percentage of population aged 16–64 with a work disability, by county, 1990

▨ Less than 7.0 percent

Comparable figures:
U.S. = 8.90 percent
Appalachia = 11.98 percent

▨ 7.0–9.0 percent

FPO

▤ 9.1– 12.0 percent

▨ 12.1–15.0 percent

▨ More than 15.0 percent

Source: U.S. Bureau of the Census.

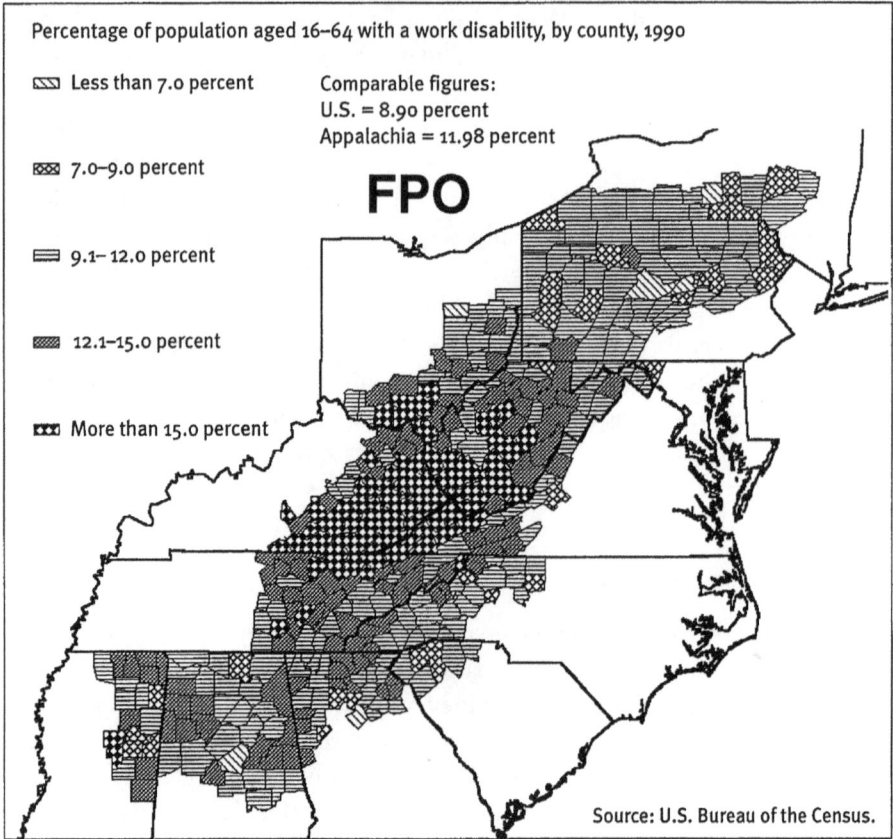

abled miners and their families who were trying to change black lung regulations. The VBLA began in the 1970s as part of the regionwide movement to gain recognition of, compensation for, and prevention of black lung disease. VBLA declined in the early 1980s as the leadership dwindled and economic conditions worsened in the Appalachian region. The group renewed activity in January 1988 with new leadership, energy, and members—men and women, union and nonunion, old and young. In its recent history, the VBLA has provided an example of how a grassroots group can grow from a support group with a few dozen members into an important political force of more than 1,700 members that protected current workers and compensated former workers for the market failure of occupational illness and disease.

VBLA's renewed activity in 1988 redressed the consequences of changes in black lung regulations. Since their inception in 1970, black lung regulations have varied, making it easier or more difficult for miners to gain recognition of and compensation for their claims of black lung. Initially, approval rates for claims were as high as 75 percent, according to Marilyn Carroll, director of the VBLA. In 1976, new regulations cut approval rates in half, down to 37 percent. In 1981, with the onset of the Reagan administration, changes in the Social Security Administration's regulations restricted eligibility by stricter medical standards. The new standards led to a 4 percent approval rate of new claims for black lung benefits. The standards grew so tough that many disabled miners lost the black lung benefits they had won earlier! The Reagan Department of Labor reviewed past cases, appealed some, and in some cases even demanded that miners return benefit payments they had received over the years. The VBLA called this collection of so-called "overpayments" "the most intolerable of procedures adopted by the Department of Labor." In one instance, a miner shot himself when he received notice that he owed the government $32,000. For Carroll, these changes illustrated that "This is not about health care. This is about money."

Despite these changes, seven years intervened between the new regulations and the revitalization of VBLA. According to Carroll, the devastating economic conditions in the coalfield regions during the early 1980s deterred organizing. In addition, many of the leaders from the original movement in the 1970s had died, and the movement lacked leaders. Carroll was instrumental in reactivating the VBLA. She had gained organizing experience through the Council of Southern Mountains and Highlanders' Southern Appalachian Leadership Training (SALT). She had also worked in the area with a local association of retarded citizens. Her work to establish legal services in the Southwest Virginia coalfield area provided her first involvement in legal issues associated with black lung cases.

Once underway again, VBLA addressed the impact of the 1981 regulation changes on overpayments, the medical standards used for determining eligibility, the needs of widows, the solvency of the Black Lung Benefit Trust Fund, and the presence of coal dust in the workplace. VBLA revived the National Black Lung Association (NBLA) and started working on drafting new legislation with NBLA groups as far away as Chicago and Indiana.

In the beginning, it was not evident that VBLA would be able to exert so much influence. Carroll described the gradual process of reviving the association. "We had our first meeting in 1988, but it really starts before then. . . . We talked with individuals for four months before we even called a meeting, and that preparatory time was really critical to finding out what the needs were. . . . We worked, from August until January . . . on an individual, one-to-one basis." Carroll recalled that in the beginning the people were more interested in what had happened to them individually than in working on legislation.

> Our beginning came out of the law office where we were housed. You had really hard-working people, taxpaying individuals, who came in and felt like they were being shafted after working for the coal companies a lifetime. And they would come in and they would say, "I was good to them. Why are they doing this to me? What have I done?" And when they started realizing they hadn't done anything wrong, they started realizing that there was a need . . . that it wasn't just an individual breakdown in communication between one man and the company, that it was a practice of their policy. . . . It became a whole education, self-education. That's what we did for the first six months or so. . . .
>
> In the beginning, we looked like a self-help therapy group. There was a lot of screaming and carrying on. There was a lot of blaming doctors. I do hold the doctors responsible for some of the things they do, but in the beginning it was more of people talking about what had happened to them individually. And then, they saw a pattern, and it became focused on trying to find a solution, and we moved more toward dealing with the legislation. We all realized quickly that the doctors we felt were selling out to the companies would sell out to anybody if the price was right, and it was the format, the system, that needed to change. So that's what we started doing.

The next step in revitalizing VBLA was getting people together throughout the six coal mining counties of Virginia to share stories and realize common problems. When the group began meeting, its members found common ground. The miners and their families recognized that their most common problem was the federal government's demand for payback of benefits in appealed cases.

Many of the members of the VBLA were union members who had experience with group process, which helped make the organization strong. Immediately, the group decided to charge membership fees, print up membership cards, begin fund raising, take accurate meeting minutes, and appoint officers. VBLA looked inward for leadership.

> We began with the notion that everybody had a place and a talent, and it would be our responsibility to find a place for them. Some of the things we faced in the beginning are not issues now. But in the beginning the lack of formal education was a problem for a lot of our members because they felt intimidated by it. They felt like they didn't have some of the skills that

were needed to do some of the jobs, and they felt badly about themselves. You see, there was an esteem problem. . . . What we did in the beginning was we worked where we had talent. Herbert Endicott has a real ability to sell caps, T-shirts and so on, so we just turned him loose. And membership also. Leonard Justius lives in an isolated community in Hurley, but he knew everybody there, and we would have meetings of fifty to ninety-five people. He worked on membership in his particular locality. It just depended on their local area and what they felt was necessary.

Carroll looked back on the first year of the VBLA as one that helped individuals build confidence and a foundation of group strength and leadership. "One phrase we kept hearing all the time in those meetings that first year or two was 'I'm just a dumb coal miner.'" Carroll recounted how the group fought the self-perception of "dumb coal miners." It took its meetings seriously. The members read the minutes out loud and made sure the acoustics in the room were such that the members who couldn't read or were hearing impaired could also hear and participate in the meetings. Instead of focusing on illiteracy and lack of education as a weakness, the group focused on the strength of experience, good memories, and speaking skills. Carroll recalled, "At one point, one of the wives said, 'I make a motion that we have no dumb coal miners in this organization.' And the motion carried. So we took care of our 'dumb' problem. The last time the 'dumb coal miner' thing came up, I said, 'You aren't too good at reading and writing are you?' And they said, 'No, we're not.' I said, 'Have you seen a coal miner who was very poor at talking?' They said, 'No.' And I believe that was the end of the discussion."

Within two years, the VBLA began to make contact with congressional representatives from the area. VBLA staff collected the stories of their members and shared many of them during a 1990 testimony before the U.S. House of Representatives Subcommittee on Labor Standards. The testimony included the story of Homer Anderson:

A typical case is that of Homer Anderson, who came home from World War II a hero to work in the mines. After working 22 years in the mines, with hours upon hours of overtime, he was diagnosed June 27, 1973, as having second stage Black Lung. Several physicians, highly qualified "B" readers examined him and confirmed disabling black lung. The Labor Department physicians found him disabled with black lung. After drawing black lung benefits for 8 years, he was notified by mail one day to pay back the total amount, $63,000 in 30 days. He was denied benefits in federal court, stating the coal company outweighed him in evidence with

33 to 7 x-rays. His case is now on appeal. Twelve years after his initial application, he is still trying to earn his black lung benefits.

In coordination with the National Black Lung Association, which had elected a VBLA member as its president and a VBLA staff member as its secretary, VBLA drafted a black lung reform bill addressing issues of benefit repayment, survivor benefits, attorney fees, and medical evidence. VBLA's bill was introduced to the House in May of 1993 and passed. A Senate bill, introduced in November, failed.

Although VBLA has put less emphasis on prevention, it has monitored and supported the prevention efforts of others. Calvin Dunford, chairman of the VBLA, recalled going to Washington to lobby and meet with an undersecretary of the Department of Labor. "He told me the mines was clean enough that you could eat off of the floor. And I told him that he was mistaken. That I had run those tractors . . . where the dust would run from under the wheels just like you was running through water. And I asked him was the company taking care of their own dust samples. He said absolutely. So two weeks after we came back is when they caught this bunch down here at Grundy with fraud of those dust samples."

Even if they could get good legislation passed, leaders of the organization realized that continued vigilance would be necessary to keep benefits. Vince Carroll, general counsel for the VBLA, warned, "While the number of people employed in coal mining over the coming decades may well be less, the increasing dependence on coal for energy, the installation of new technology, such as longwall mining, and the increasing number of extremely dirty truck mines will maintain and expand the existence of this disease."

Translating human need into public policy follows a twisting and torturous path. Carroll worried about morale, keeping the effort going, and, most of all, maintaining faith in people.

> The faith is not in the government or in the big industry but the faith is in people. . . . Jim Sessions from CORA [Commission on Religion in Appalachia] said something . . . that I can't get out of my brain for the last couple of years: "One thing we need to recognize in Appalachia is the strength that is there because we have the community networking and the support groups. The hope is not from the outside but from what *we can give* to the rest of the world." That's true because of the immense amount of strength that is here. And any organization that is successful has to work from this strength rather than denigrating its weakness. That's what we attempted to do. From the family strength and from the union background and from the fact that everybody deserves the world's

respect, these are the things that we're really about. We are not really about changing the law.

Carroll felt that the membership was dedicated to winning despite the setbacks, compromises, and disappointments associated with trying to pass legislation to protect the vulnerable. "That's one of the interesting things to me—that they can think long term, they know how hard the fight is, and they are focused on a long, hard haul. And I wonder, does the rough job of coal mining prepare those families for that, because you know you are not going to have an easy day when you go to those mines."

Running against the Tide

As Julian Wolpert's study of American charitable giving shows, the tide of social capital runs in the direction of donors' benefits rather than recipients' needs and toward areas of affluence rather than areas of poverty (Wolpert 1993). Mediating structures buck this tide to attract social capital to areas of need. The Federation of Appalachian Housing Enterprises (FAHE), for example, brings social capital to areas of Central Appalachia.

The Federation of Appalachian Housing Enterprises began in Berea, Kentucky, as the housing program for the Human/Economic Appalachian Development (HEAD) Corporation (Poage 1996). FAHE developed because low-income housing providers in the Appalachian region had common needs, including a mechanism for obtaining capital for low-cost housing. In 1980, after three years of operation, HEAD's housing program incorporated separately as FAHE. By the early 1990s, FAHE served fifteen housing groups in the Central Appalachian region in a federation of mutual assistance and support to make home ownership possible for low and very low-income families in Central Appalachia. The board of directors had an executive director and one representative from each member group.

In the 1980s, the members of FAHE constructed 623 new homes, rehabilitated 1,393 homes, repaired 4,031 homes, and weatherized 7,880 homes and other structures. FAHE members served 13,127 families during this time. By the early 1990s, FAHE members were constructing 100 new homes and rehabilitating 150 houses annually. FAHE helped its member groups achieve their mission to improve the housing conditions of low-income families by holding their network together, sharing talent, presenting a strong voice in Washington, D.C., and their state capitals, and devising new ways to secure capital for low-cost housing.

FAHE deliberately invested new forms and amounts of social capital in low-income areas because of the worth of the people there and because it viewed such housing itself as part of a sustainable community. David Lollis, FAHE's executive director since 1980, explained:

> Home ownership is just as much a dream for low-income families and individuals as it is for the more affluent. Home ownership encourages the same desirable results for low-income families as for others—pride and self-esteem, a sense of belonging in the community, family stability, and a healthy environment for children. But in today's world we have closed off this opportunity to nearly half of our rural families and individuals.
>
> The need is for modest, well-built, energy-efficient houses, that are warm and dry, that have clean running water, and indoor bath and toilet facilities. The need is for building community, so that folks have a reason to live there and to work together to solve their problems. The need is for resources for local groups who have joined together to support and help each other through the development process.

FAHE created economies of scale for its member groups to deal with the tasks of writing proposals for large grants and administering them. For example, FAHE secured and administered a Comprehensive Employment Training Act (CETA) grant from the U.S. Department of Labor. Through the CETA program, FAHE member groups enrolled unemployed people in their areas and trained them on the job in work crews. Since its successful beginning, FAHE has developed many programs designed in response to the resource and technical needs of its member groups. These programs include a home loan fund, which lends money at interest rates of 1 to 3 percent; home ownership and maintenance counseling to ensure success in home ownership for first-time homeowners; technical assistance to member groups to ensure quality construction; a construction loan fund, which makes short-term, low-interest loans to member groups that have secured permanent financing; technical assistance to member groups in housing program design and business and financial management; resource development, fund-raising, and capacity-building for member groups; and advocacy for members and for rural low-income housing on the local, regional, state and national levels.

These programs required that FAHE acquire and manage capital for low-income families. For many families, acquiring capital through government programs or banks to build a new house or improve a rundown house was often impossible without FAHE's assistance. Lollis explained FAHE's leveraging role: "We are trying to figure out what's the problem, what's the bank telling us is the reason they won't do it, [and] what's the government saying. . . . Then [I] go to a foundation to see if we can create something that solves that problem and opens that door. That's what we are here to do."

For example, Lollis successfully negotiated funds from the James C. Penney Foundation to provide small loans in case a new homeowner is faced with replacing a major appliance, such as a refrigerator or water heater. If in Lollis's estimation the homeowner does not have sufficient funds to pay for the replacement, the fund covers the cost, then FAHE sets up a process for repayment. Getting the payment reserve fund to cushion such cash flow problems, he explained, "gave the banks the security they felt they needed" to lend money to FAHE's participants.

Lollis explained that the Federation was motivated first of all by the demands that the member groups put on them; secondly by the dramatic need for housing in the region (see Map 5); and third by its own reputation for good work. Lollis believed that "once you've done some things well, it really does feed on itself as long as you stay on top of your game."

> Being part of the Federation is like a "Good Housekeeping Seal." We have a good reputation. Our builders meet a certain standard. So if it's a FAHE house, it is going to be a house that's well built. So we just can't let any group in with full membership without their going through an apprenticeship period where they really can demonstrate they can build a quality house, they can relate to the communities in positive ways, they can counsel people on home ownership, and they can run their financial affairs and produce a financial statement.

In addition to its screening process, FAHE underwent a peer review process for its lending programs. Lollis explained that FAHE is "in many ways a mortgage banker, but we're not subject to the same regulations [as banks]. . . . We realized we needed to set standards and do peer reviews so that we would be able to say that we're very conscious of our need to regulate ourselves."

Much of FAHE's strength and innovation came from the challenges it overcame, such as raising money for overhead costs. As a "second-level organization," a term Lollis used to describe FAHE's regional scope and coalition-like nature, FAHE had a difficult time raising money for the backup and indirect services it provides. To make matters worse, FAHE absorbed much of the overhead of its member groups. Funding sources, especially foundations, preferred to fund programs of direct benefit rather than the indirect support services that made programs possible. Thus, FAHE found fund-raising increasingly difficult, despite its proven success.

The Federation addressed this funding problem by charging members for

Map 5. Substandard Housing in Appalachia, 1990

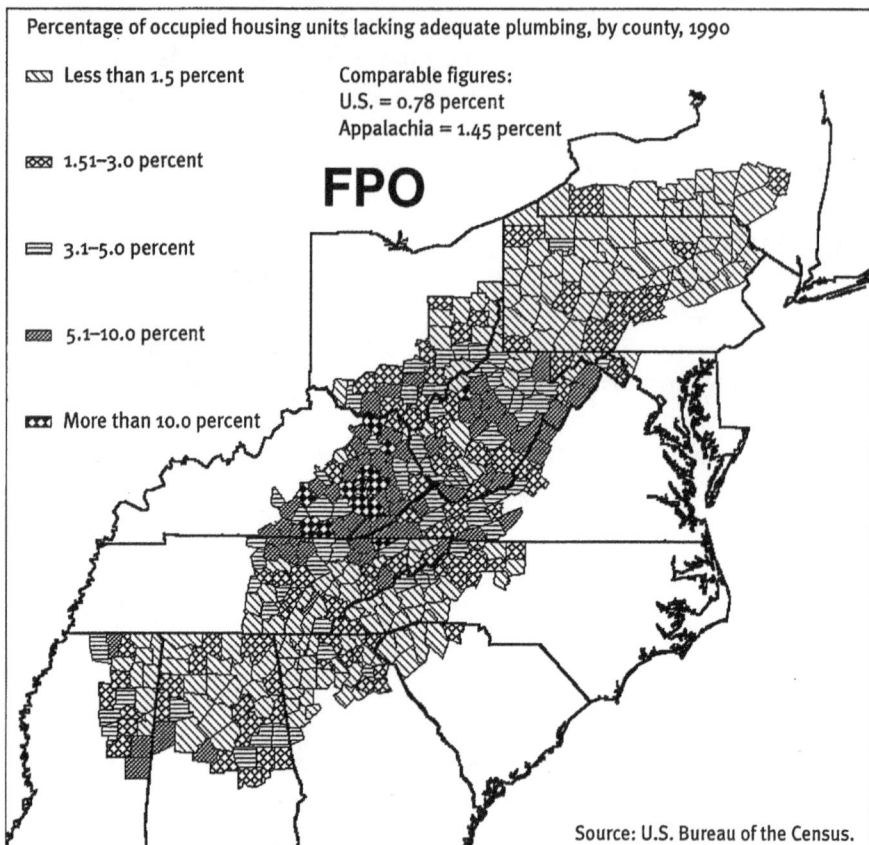

Percentage of occupied housing units lacking adequate plumbing, by county, 1990

Less than 1.5 percent

1.51–3.0 percent

3.1–5.0 percent

5.1–10.0 percent

More than 10.0 percent

Comparable figures:
U.S. = 0.78 percent
Appalachia = 1.45 percent

FPO

Source: U.S. Bureau of the Census.

some of the services it offered them. FAHE encouraged its member groups to seek funding for services that FAHE rendered, such as inspections, and to pay for them. The Federation also hoped to generate some income through the rehabilitation of an historic city block in Mt. Sterling, Kentucky. The Mt. Sterling Housing Corporation, organized by the FAHE staff and board of directors, obtained several million dollars in Community Development Block Grants and Home Loans to renovate several old buildings in Mt. Sterling for rental units for the low-income elderly. This rehabilitation represented a new venture for FAHE into construction and rehabilitation, rather than supporting another group to do that work.

The lack of adequate housing resulted from much greater economic and political problems of social capital, and Lollis understood FAHE's limitations in providing a service rather than organizing for policy changes. But Lollis also understood decent housing as more that just a service. He observed,

"You can't do everything. You have to really decide what you're going to do and try to do that well. So we produce houses. We try to work with families in such a way that we really empower them as individuals and help them take care of their own lives. . . . Housing can be a thing in the community that can be used to build some pride, and then people can begin to take an interest in their communities."

As Lollis considered the difficult tasks of the group as it moved into its second decade of work, he commented, "If I were going to arrange the world, I would arrange it a different way, but I can't do that. But I can figure out how to make the system work. . . . How to get a person from where they've been abused by the system to where they can begin to understand the system well enough to make it work for them." FAHE hasn't rearranged the world, but it has made social capital flow uphill.

Increasing the Supply of Public Goods

Part of the tension between the democratic promise and the democratic prospect entails the range of public goods and the amount of public resources that the public should provide. Mediating structures play an economic role in advocating for broader definitions of public goods and new and larger amounts of public investment in them. Formulas for supporting public schools reflect the market's proclivity to provide according to resources rather than need. Affluent suburbs have better schools and lower taxes than rural or inner-city school systems. Education provides a good illustration of the relation between social capital and market failure in the provision of public goods.

The West Virginia Education Association (WVEA) addressed the disparity in funding public education. Its work illustrates the role of community-based mediating structures in the political determination of the nature of public goods and the amount of social capital to invest in them. The WVEA's power to advocate for education reform came from its membership of more than 17,000 teachers, about three-fourths of the state's total 22,000 teachers, and from its affiliation with the National Education Association (NEA). Although it has been involved in many important issues in its long history, WVEA gained national notoriety in the spring of 1990 when it organized and initiated a statewide teacher's strike. At the time of the strike, WVEA was more than 125 years old and had its headquarters in Charleston; it had thirty full-time employees, some stationed at its headquarters and others in field offices. WVEA worked in all of West Virginia's fifty-five counties.

The strike followed a decade of attempts to reform the West Virginia school system. These efforts began with a court case in 1980, *Pauley v. Bailey*. Parents of a school child in Lincoln County, a low-income county in this low-income state, felt that their child deserved as good an education as children in the wealthier counties in the state. The state supreme court agreed somewhat but decided that it needed a definition of the state constitution's provision for "a thorough and efficient system of free schools." It gave Judge Arthur Recht the job of defining that provision and determining whether the state's funding provisions for public schools met the Constitution's provision for "equal protection." Recht undertook the task for the supreme court in a forty-day, nonjury trial. Recht found that West Virginia schools lagged the nation and that the Lincoln County schools were inadequate by West Virginia standards in areas that conveyed a thorough and efficient education—curriculum, personnel, facilities, materials, and equipment. The "Recht decision" prescribed subjects to be taught, number of minutes of instruction, curriculum goals, and even, in some cases, classroom methods. It also found that the state's system of public school financing was unconstitutional, due to the glaring disparities in educational opportunity and quality of school facilities that it produced. Among other measures, reforms such as a statewide property reappraisal and a Uniform School Funding Amendment were recommended.

The legislature acted upon a few of these measures, but by 1987 many leaders within the WVEA were ready to strike to elicit the enactment of more reforms. The executive committee of the WVEA failed to get the 65 percent approval they needed from their delegate assembly to authorize a strike that year. Jackie Goodwin, director of communications for WVEA, recalled, "At the eleventh hour in the legislature, the key legislative leaders came in and talked to our county presidents and wooed them into holding off this strike. . . . The legislative leaders said, 'Oh, don't strike!' And they promised them the sun, moon, and stars, and that just didn't materialize." The unfulfilled promises and agreements made by the legislators in 1987 created more support for the strike in 1990.

In between those times, in 1988, the Appalachian Education Laboratory (AEL) surveyed conditions of rural education in West Virginia and outlined some of the reasons for the unequal distribution of revenue and resources to the different counties in West Virginia. Of the total funds spent on public education in 1988, 27 percent came from the local county, 65 percent from the state, and 8 percent from the federal government. All of the counties had regular levies, and some counties had additional levies to increase the funds for education. Voters in very rural counties often did not approve additional levies. The AEL study pointed out that these small, low-income counties had very high property tax rates in order to generate revenue for general public expenses. In rural areas, the school districts also had to shoulder the costs of maintaining roads for bus transportation and for footbridges over streams for students who lived far off the main road. The high property assessments plus the added transportation costs created a heavy tax burden on rural West Virginia residents and provided strong disincentives for them to take on additional levies (Coe and Howley 1989: 5). More populated and affluent counties did not have similarly high levies, because they gained needed revenue through levies on commercial property. There were also big inequalities between West Virginia and the rest of the nation. In 1990, West Virginia's average teacher salary of $21,904 was the forty-ninth lowest in the U.S. The major goal of the impending strike was to create a salary increase for West Virginia teachers from the state, *not* from local sources.

Matters came to a head in 1990. Days after emergency meetings of the presidents of the county education associations and the executive committee of the WVEA, teachers in ten counties went on strike on Wednesday, March 7. By March 15, teachers in forty-seven counties were out on the picket lines.

As thousands of teachers demanded a pay increase, the governor and legislators explained that resources for funding education were not available. However, WVEA responded with four solutions for generating needed capital. The WVEA called first for the repeal of the "super tax credit." This credit, first adopted in 1985, was part of the unsuccessful effort to attract the Saturn Motor plant to West Virginia, which General Motors ultimately located in Tennessee. West Virginia was left with a new "corporate tax structure that benefited a small number of the state's largest companies," 90 percent of which were coal companies, according to a revenue fact sheet that the WVEA prepared for the 1990 legislative session. It stated, "Clearly, a state which has no money for teacher and school employee salary increases can't afford to subsidize a handful of coal companies in order for them to reduce coal mining jobs. We must repeal the super tax credit." WVEA also proposed increasing the taxes of landowners who owned more than 1,000 acres. This proposal targeted absentee landowners, particularly coal companies. The Appalachian Land Study estimated that two-thirds of the private land of West Virginia belonged to such absentee landowners, who paid little tax. The third proposal was to increase the personal income tax on individual incomes of more than $60,000 per year. The WVEA pointed out that in 1987 the legislature had closed some loopholes in the tax code and reduced the upper-bracket income tax rate by half, from 13 percent to 6.5 percent. WVEA suggested an increase to 9.5 percent. The final proposal suggested changes in property tax appraisal, including a general increase in property taxes and the appraisal of commercial and natural resource property by state rather than county offices, in order to create more uniform and equitable appraisals.

After a week and a half, striking teachers and students returned to school on Monday, March 19, after the executive committee of the WVEA came to an agreement with legislative leaders over reforms in the educational system. The first reform action involved a series of town meetings in order for teachers and community members to air frustrations, discuss problems, and search for solutions. Eventually, the WVEA took information from these meetings and other sources and negotiated an education reform package during a special session of the state legislature. The reform package included a $5,000 pay raise for teachers over a three-year period, the institution of a faculty senate in each school to give teachers more say in school policy, a mentor teaching program that transferred the skills and experience from some selected veteran teachers to new teachers, reforms in the teachers retirement system, and a mandatory teacher evaluation process.

Clearly, the reform package negotiated by the WVEA was a victory for West Virginia teachers. Jackie Goodwin, director of communications at WVEA, explained how the salary increase translates into better education. "If teachers are concerned about making a decent wage and not being able to pay their bills and not having their retirement secure, and not having insurance, and having a sick child . . . how can they go into the classroom day after day and do a good job teaching? They have a load of things on their mind. Their problems outweigh the problems they see in the classroom. . . . [When] you have happy teachers, good working conditions, good benefits, that transfers into the program." The WVEA also believed that higher salaries would help attract and retain teachers in West Virginia. Many teachers living on West Virginia's boarders with Ohio, Kentucky, and Maryland were crossing the state border for salaries that were sometimes $5,000 to $7,000 higher than those offered in their home state.

Although the strike resulted in positive change for teachers and schools, it did not achieve the broad, increased-revenue goals that WVEA had proposed. By 1993, WVEA concluded that "the bright prospects of the strike settlement had little chance to continue because of a lack of financial support." New regulations and additional batteries of tests could not make up for a lack of financial support for improved instruction (Meadows 1992: 2). WVEA continues to advocate for an excess acreage tax, repeal of the super tax credit, and higher severance tax on coal companies. It has also turned to other matters of social capital, including integrating students with special needs, keeping the school building authority financially sound, and securing a teachers' retirement system.

The positive outcome of WVEA's actions appeared a few years later. A 1998 national survey of public schools gave West Virginia a grade of "C" for allocation of resources; only seven states scored better. West Virginia was also given an "A" for adequacy of resources and an "A" for equity, the highest grade of any state (*Education Week* 1998).

Fewest Resources, Greatest Needs

Holding housing, health care, and other forms of social capital to its money belt by its invisible hand, market economics distributes social capital inadequately, dispensing the fewest resources to those in greatest need. Even when a good is regarded as public, such as education and some forms of health care, the market will err unfailingly on the side of too few resources to support them. In all these instances, the democratic prospect's only hope is the mitigation of market failures. Mediating structures embody and express that hope.

CHAPTER 6

Economic Dimensions II: Providing Social Capital

In addition to their efforts to mitigate market failures, community-based mediating structures transform political, economic, and social arrangements by providing improved forms and increased amounts of social capital. They bring public and private resources to areas and groups of people that would not otherwise have them. Community-based mediating structures invest these resources in people whom the market has disinvested or neglected. This chapter tells stories of community-based mediating structures providing social capital locally, establishing higher stages of welfare development, devolving responsibility, investing in individual and group identity, transforming market values, and improving the supply of social capital.

Once again, these economic roles make community-based mediating structures purveyors of the democratic prospect. Social and political theorists, such as Nisbet, who advocate mediating structures as the expression, defense, and preservation of communal bonds among people, imply an economic role for them. The advocacy of mediating structures implies the hope of preserving some form of communal bonds in the face of the radically individual and alienating nature of human relations mediated solely by the economic considerations of the market. Robert Bellah and his colleagues also premise their prescriptions for a "good society" on new institutions that reject the paradigm of Lockean individualism that we can create a good life simply by striving for individual comfort and security (Bellah et al. 1992:

86). They fault the political economy of the free market explicitly for its moral failure to distribute work and income more equitably (Bellah et al: 1992: 82–110). This advocacy replaces a limited concept of community, based on mutual self-interest in accumulation, with a broader concept with less pecuniary values. Thus, some advocacy for mediating structures, even when it supports limited government, rejects the narrow political economic foundation of market democracy that substitutes economics for politics.

Providing Public Goods Locally

Glenn Loury links social capital to inequality. He asserts that "some communities have too little of it" and that socioeconomic differences may flow from different forms and amounts of social capital. Consequently, the production of local public goods remedies market-generated, socioeconomic inequality. Community-based mediating structures, such as Clay Mountain Housing, provide housing as "local public goods" in a redistribution of social capital.

Clay Mountain Housing, Inc. (CMH) in Clay, West Virginia, began in 1988 to help local low-income residents acquire decent housing through partnerships with other nonprofit organizations, banks, and government programs. In its first five years of operation, CMH assisted more than 100 families to either purchase a home or rehabilitate an existing home. CMH was a member of the Federation of Appalachian Housing Enterprises.

Kathy Britt and Clara Deyton founded CMH in 1987. Britt, a Catholic nun, found initial inspiration for CMH's efforts in a study undertaken by the Rural Homelessness Project, a joint undertaking of the Covenant House, a day shelter for the homeless in Charleston, West Virginia, and the Charleston Coalition for the Homeless. The study, *It Ain't Much But It's All I Got*, found that large numbers of people in three rural West Virginia counties were living in "unsafe, unsanitary, and unhealthful structures" (23). The study also found that public agencies, such as the U.S. Department of Housing and Urban Development (HUD) and the West Virginia Department of Human Services, were actually contributing to the problem, by ignoring substandard housing and allowing landlords to continue to rent substandard units. After the report was completed, Kathy Britt focused on the housing problems in Clay County, one of the three counties studied.

Britt asked Clara Deyton, a Clay County native, to join her in an effort to begin CMH. Through her connections with church funding sources and foundations, Britt began to look for funding. Deyton, with her connections to the community, began to generate local support for their work. CMH pursued its goal "to make home ownership and safe, decent, affordable housing a reality for low-income families in the county" by helping low-income people acquire grants and loans for housing, constructing new homes, rehabilitating old ones, and advocating for renters through HUD and Legal Services. Britt and Deyton also assisted families on loan payment options and housing maintenance.

Britt and Deyton targeted the Farmers Home Administration (FmHA) as a good candidate for their first source of loans. "They had been in housing for eons, but . . . they had only made seven loans in nine years" in Clay County, Britt explained. For the first year and a half, Britt and Deyton worked out of the back of their cars. They traveled throughout the county, talking to people about their housing needs while helping them fill out FmHA applications. Periodically, they held membership meetings in the public library. Their initial work with FmHA began a challenging but rewarding relationship with the agency. "We made friends with the Farmer's Home. Well, we had two reps. The first one was not really cooperative. The people did not want to go back because of the way they were treated. But he didn't stay very long with us. . . . Then he was replaced with a person we didn't know and we made friends with him right away. Clara is really good at this. . . . She gets along very well with Dave. She can handle him and he takes things from her. . . . He has the money, we have the families."

Clara explained the supportive role that CMH plays for families as they go through the loan application process. "We keep in close contact with the families, or we try to. Also, if there is anything that falls down in the communication, like if they don't hear from Farmer's Home, or we don't hear from the family, we either contact the family or the family will contact us and say, 'You know, I put that application in three months ago and I haven't heard anything.' So, if that happens, I will call Dave and say, 'What happened to this application?' So then he tries to find it, because he knows if he doesn't then I am going to get on his back."

Clay Mountain Housing increased its programs with time, setting up their own revolving loan fund and beginning to work with other agencies and housing coalitions. CMH gained support from the West Virginia Housing Development Fund for three different loan programs: HOME repair, the Home Improvement Loan Program (HILP), and the Low-Income Assisted Mortgage Program (LAMP). These programs channeled federal housing program funds to Clay County. Each had different requirements and application procedures. With the knowledge they had acquired, CMH staff could assess a family's housing needs and help them choose the best program to apply for.

The staff's success in helping those with low incomes obtain loans resulted from their work at forming positive relationships and building partnerships. Britt explained, "I think if you can form some kind of working relationship with groups such as Farmer's Home or the bank or other agencies in the county, I think that helps build up your credibility. . . . You are connecting to what is already in place. I think that is favorable." These relationships created opportunities for innovation, or what Deyton called "creative lending." CMH also indirectly influenced national and state housing policy through their affiliation with larger housing coalitions such as the Federation of Appalachian Housing Enterprises (FAHE) and West Virginia Community Works.

As CMH grew, Britt and Deyton had to make some organizational transitions. Their own homeless condition improved. After working from their cars initially, they moved from one borrowed office space into another, then finally into the old post office on Main Street in Clay. They now had an office in Clay in which to do the administrative work, which had increased with their success. Attendance at membership meetings declined, however, as a result of their having an office and a permanent phone number that people could use to ask questions and get assistance on loan procedures. CMH added a VISTA worker to its staff to help the group continue reaching out to people in the field as administrative duties kept Britt and Deyton office-bound and attendance at meetings dropped. CMH also hired a full-time construction supervisor, who worked with job trainees. Britt and Deyton hoped to eventually develop CMH's own construction crew.

Although CMH focused solely on obtaining loans and grants for housing rehabilitation and construction, the impact of their work went beyond building homes. Deyton had many before-and-after pictures of the dozens of houses that CMH had helped rehabilitate, but in her view what was less visible was more important. She maintained, "When you change people's housing situation, you change their whole life, because you build their self-esteem." Pictures of rehabilitated houses preceded stories of women who went back to school and of children who were no longer ashamed to invite friends home to play.

CMH's work was only one part of the changes that Britt saw in Clay County. Looking back on more than two decades of work in the county, in 1997 Britt thought people had no more money than before but more awareness of possibilities. She attributed this to television, the necessity of looking for opportunities because of cutbacks in welfare programs, and the proximity of Charleston. She pointed with special emphasis to education, reporting that education and the military had reversed their place in the opportunity ladder of local youth. Not only do more kids finish high school, she estimated, but twenty go on to some form of college for every one student who did so twenty years ago. In this mix of change, CMH promoted housing as a public good and produced housing locally in new and improved forms.

Higher Stages of Welfare Development

Community-based organizations, such as Clay Mountain Housing, may provide new and better services and thus develop improved stages of welfare. Observing social welfare provision worldwide, Alva Myrdal suggested three stages in the development of social welfare programs. The first, a paternalistic conservative stage, aims to cure the worst of social problems and depends on private charity and public relief. The second stage, a liberal era, attempts to pool risks to prevent some social problems and reduce inequalities through limited forms of social insurance. The third, a social democratic stage, attempts to prevent social ills through protective and cooperative social policies (Smith and Lipsky 1993: 15–16). The first stage of social welfare provision coincides with the democratic promise of limited government. It mitigates the worst failures of the market without conceding the inadequacy of the nonprofit and voluntary sector to redress the worst social problems. Social policy is left largely to the healing touch of the invisible hand. Within this first stage, market democracy individualizes social problems as well as social remedies to them. The second and third stages of social welfare provision match, in varying degrees, the democratic prospect of greater social and economic equality.

Community-based mediating structures play a role in the swings between the first and the higher stages of social welfare policies. They are surrogates for government action when public policy revels in market democracy, as it did in the 1980s. They provided the wax and wicks for a thousand points of light in the 1990s. At other times, during the 1930s and 1960s, when the democratic prospect of increased social and economic equality and extended communal bonds tugged at the democratic wish, mediating structures witnessed for the need and efficacy of public action to address and redress human needs. At any time, mediating structures may provide a level of service that improves on the current standard of social welfare available.

Appalachian Communities for Children (ACC) works to improve the quality of education and community life of children in Jackson and Clay Counties in Kentucky. The organization began in the mid-1970s as an advisory board working to staff, sustain, and improve three preschool programs

Table 8. Percentage of Children in Poverty in Appalachia, 1970–1990

Region	1970	1980	1990	Rate of Change 1980–90	Rate of Change 1970–90
United States	14.86	16.00	17.55	9.68	18.07
Appalachia	18.91	17.02	20.33	19.44	7.52
Northern	13.31	14.20	19.65	38.35	47.62
Central	34.98	25.68	30.10	17.20	−13.95
Southern	22.60	18.00	18.63	3.51	−17.58
Metropolitan counties	14.41	14.36	17.53	22.13	21.64
Northern	10.65	12.38	17.69	42.90	66.08
Central	20.63	17.67	22.87	29.47	10.85
Southern	19.71	16.61	17.18	3.42	−12.82
Rural counties	23.19	19.29	22.80	18.21	−1.69
Northern	16.42	16.06	21.60	34.46	31.53
Central	36.25	26.33	30.67	16.48	−15.38
Southern	25.77	19.46	20.29	4.27	−21.29

Source: U.S. Bureau of the Census, *Current Population Survey* and *Poverty in the United States*, 1991; and *County and City Data Book*, 1975 and 1985.

in Jackson County. ACC's program grew to include adult education, health and family life, in-school tutoring, and long-term community development. The work of the Appalachian Communities for Children dramatically illustrates new and higher standards of programs and services for children in areas of chronic and severe poverty.

As ACC began its work, Central Appalachia was in the midst of improved fortunes, due largely to a boom in coal. Family poverty decreased between 1970 and 1980, from 30 to 19 percent of all families. Child poverty decreased from 35 to 26 percent during the same time. Family income as a proportion of median family income nationally also increased from 1970 to 1980, from 58 to 71 percent. The coal boom inevitably busted, and the economic decline brought on hard times. By 1990, family incomes had dropped to 61 percent of the national median income, almost back to the 1970 figure, and 22 percent of the families and 30 percent of the children were living in poverty (see Table 8 and Map 6). Jackson and Clay Counties were even deeper pockets of poverty than Central Appalachia as a whole. In 1990, almost one-half of the children of the two counties were in poverty, about one-third of families were in poverty, and family income had declined to 42 percent of the national median family income level.

Map 6. Children in Poverty in Appalachia, 1990

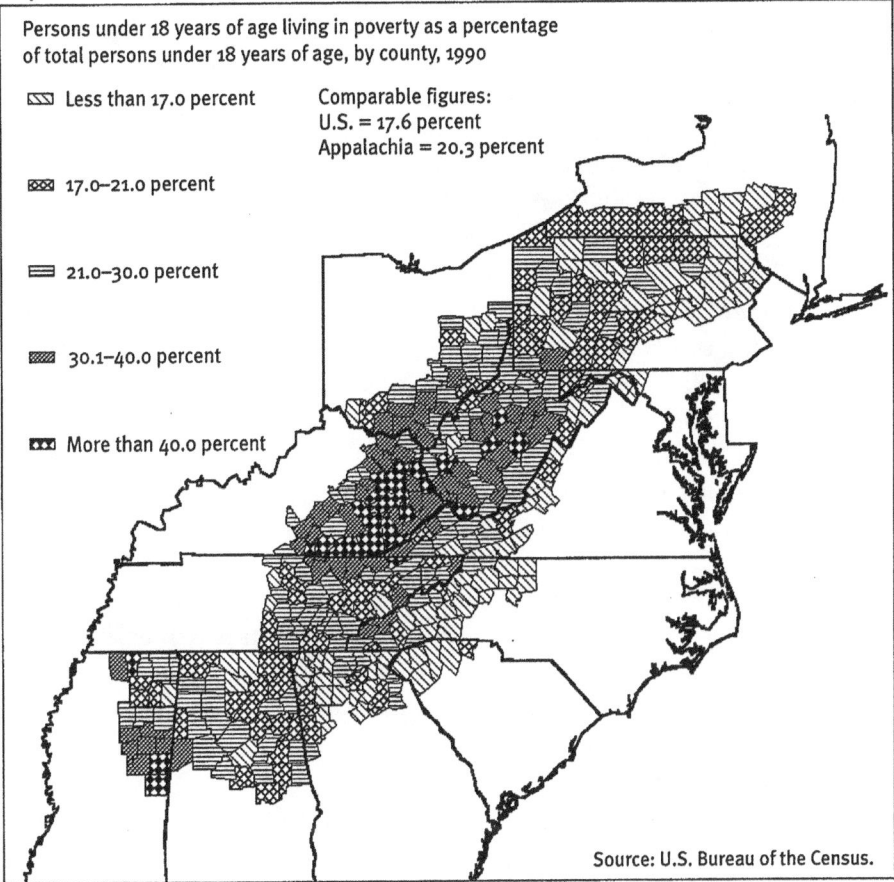

Persons under 18 years of age living in poverty as a percentage
of total persons under 18 years of age, by county, 1990

Less than 17.0 percent

Comparable figures:
U.S. = 17.6 percent
Appalachia = 20.3 percent

17.0–21.0 percent

21.0–30.0 percent

30.1–40.0 percent

More than 40.0 percent

Source: U.S. Bureau of the Census.

In 1973, during better economic times for the area, a group of parents in
Jackson County, Kentucky, had come together over their concern that three
preschool programs in remote areas of the county were going to close due
to lack of funding. The parents took their concern to the Save the Children
Federation (SCF). SCF gave financial support that—combined with continued albeit reduced funding from the programs' primary sponsor, the Kentucky Youth Resource Center (KYRC)—kept the programs alive. This effort began a relationship between local leaders and Save the Children. SCF
urged the parent group to incorporate as a nonprofit organization, which it
did. In 1975, the parents group started the Appalachian Communities for
Children.

Over the next decade, ACC acquired three buildings in Jackson County to house their preschool programs and to begin community programs. ACC started informal General Equivalency Diploma (GED) classes for parents of preschoolers who had not completed high school. SCF staff served as advisers and resource people to the new programs, but ACC members ran the organization. In the process, they kept records and developed organizational skills, which in turn developed strong membership control and leadership within ACC. In 1985, the initial preschool programs were terminated due to lack of funds from KYRC. ACC, however, continued to organize in other aspects of community education at the three centers and began to develop tutoring programs in the Jackson County schools.

All of the school and community programs that ACC offered relied on community people teaching community people. ACC recruited and trained local residents as "paraprofessionals," the same term ACC staff used to describe their teachers and tutors. This training helped parents become more involved in their children's education and has also helped adults feel comfortable in educational programs. Training local people to be tutors bridged what Judy Sizemore, artist in residence at ACC, described as a "cultural gap" in Jackson County between educators and low-income parents. She explained, "The [class] rift between educators and parents was intensified by a very real cultural gap. Parents who had not completed high school, or in many cases eighth grade, often felt intimidated by educators, and some educators looked down on undereducated parents, feeling that they had nothing of value to contribute to their children's education."

ACC helped close the cultural gap in other ways. Its GED program gave parents the opportunity to complete their high school degree. ACC created an in-school tutoring program in the Jackson County schools, with parents trained as tutors. They also brought parents into the schools to lead art classes. The parents' tutoring skills and the enthusiasm of students for the new programs impressed school administrators and teachers. Many low-income mothers, once considered a problem by some school officials, became a "valuable community resource." ACC received state and national recognition for the cooperative relationships it has built with the Jackson County schools.

The supportive network that ACC created among parents and Jackson County schools preceded the 1990 Kentucky Education Reform Act (KERA), which required such networks. Schools with a high percentage of students on the free or reduced-fee lunch program had to implement family resource centers to link schools, parents, and social services. The schools could apply for funding to staff the resource centers. Through the skill of ACC staff, the

Sand Gap and Tyner schools in Jackson County received top ratings in the grant selection process in the first two years of KERA. The Tyner School subcontracted with ACC to staff the parent involvement and literacy programs at the family resource center.

ACC's work gave the Jackson County schools a head start on KERA's changes. Sizemore commented that before KERA there was a sense that some of the hands-on activities in ACC's innovative math program were "fluff." In her view, the schools "weren't really picking up on the concept that this is real, this isn't something extra, this *is* the curriculum." In some ways KERA legitimized the work that ACC was doing. Sizemore explained, "All of a sudden, they say, 'Well, those people were right.'" "What makes us different," suggested Judy Martin, director of ACC, "is that we didn't just tack parents on the resource centers." At schools where the relationships between parents, teachers, and administrators had not been nurtured, and where resource centers had just "popped up," the new KERA programs and their higher standards faced the task of building such relations and integrating them into school programs.

After a few years, ACC expanded its original work into neighboring Clay County. It acquired a building in downtown Manchester for its Clay County Learning Center. During the day, the center housed adult literacy classes, GED tutoring, and classes for pregnant teenagers and new mothers. Carolene Turner, an ACC staff member, noted that before ACC started working with pregnant teenagers, the health department in the area had more young mothers requesting assistance with pre- and postnatal care and counseling than it could handle. The health department had 100 young women on their waiting list for assistance when ACC obtained a grant to start the Resource Mothers program to assist young mothers needing support, services, and counseling. ACC's efforts have helped relieve the health department's overload. Because community people, not agency employees, staff the Resource Mothers program, Carolene believes young mothers are more willing to seek counseling. "If you are from a health department and you go to make a home visit, they [the mothers] are all tense because they think 'Okay, she's sure to look down to see what I am doing, and they are going to report back.' If they don't like what they are seeing, . . . they are going to come and take my child away. . . . [The young mothers] feel more comfortable with us." ACC, with support and assistance from the University of Kentucky, also began the Mountain Scouts Cancer Screening program in Clay County to supplement services to test for cervical and breast cancer and provide referrals for treatment.

Left to right: Executive Director Marilyn Carroll, President Calvin Dunford, and staff member Sister Carolyn Brink of the Virginia Black Lung Association in Richlands, Virginia. (Photo by Cathy Guthrie)

The long-term financial support from the Save the Children Federation's Appalachian Sponsorship Program made ACC's longevity possible. ACC had more than 1,000 children who received assistance through SCF. The sponsorship covered administrative costs and salary for ACC staff to oversee the programs. The administrative support that SCF provided allowed ACC staff to develop and to take on more projects, such as the Jobs Training Program Act (JTPA) program. With stable support, ACC staff members were better able to follow the development of new federal and state programs and to bring their services home.

The close ties with SCF have meant scrutiny, reflection, and analysis for ACC, which advanced ACC's case that they were a strong and accountable organization. Clearly, SCF regarded ACC as a model program. The Bush administration did as well, apparently. The Points of Light Foundation selected ACC as one of only seven programs in the country to participate in

House built by a member group of the Federation of Appalachian Housing Enterprises and new homeowner Vicella Adams, Letcher County, Kentucky. (Photo courtesy of David Lollis, FAHE)

Directors of the member groups of the Federation of Appalachian Housing Enterprises (FAHE) in a group portrait they entitled "Windswept." David Lollis, executive director of FAHE, is in the center of the first row, wearing sunglasses; Nancy Robinson of Dungannon Development Commission is fifth from the left in the first row; Kathy Britt of Clay Mountain Housing is in the second row, second from the right. (Photo courtesy of David Lollis, FAHE)

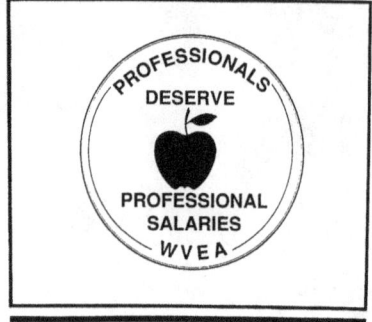

The West Virginia Education Association made a graphic case about the salary needs of teachers by showing bites from the apples of the national rankings of West Virginia in terms of the estimated average salary ranking of its public school teachers. (Courtesy of West Virginia Education Association)

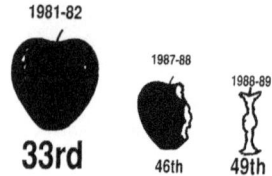

The West Virginia Education Association celebrated achieving the pay increase that it sought. (Courtesy of West Virginia Education Association)

The adrinka cloth produced by participants in the Community in the Classroom workshop hosted by the Appalachian Communities for Children (ACC). Taken from African and African American culture, the adrinka cloth depicts symbols chosen to tell the story of a group. (Photo by Cathy Guthrie)

its "Family Matters" project. SCF laid out the lessons learned from ACC's experience:

- A long-term programmatic and financial commitment to a community-based organization provides a stable base for growth and leverage to attract other funds;
- The development of strong local leadership contributes to the impact and sustainability of a community-based organization;
- Volunteer hours, required of participants, create a sense of equality and greater self-development;
- A successful program requires continuing training in technical skills and self-development;
- ACC's success follows from attention to the special needs and concerns of the women it serves and from support for their own course of development; and
- ACC supplements local institutions, rather than competing with them. (Sizemore 1990: 27–36)

This last element of success contributed to higher stages of welfare development and some frustrations. In contrast to the feeling of family within

Participants in the ACC's Community in the Classroom workshop. The poem being read and the symbols shown were inspired by the adrinka cloth project. (Photo by Cathy Guthrie)

ACC, the dealings of ACC staff with local professional people were marked by "underdog" status. Martin expressed frustration because many local professionals discount ACC's work instead of giving ACC staff credit for putting the local counties in a position to compete for and attract new funds for education and human services: "We do things. We stretch ourselves. We work our buns off. We put all kinds of effort, real investment into it. And we get it to a certain point to where it's attractive to other people and then they take it away from us. . . . They say, 'Really, professional people should be doing these things.'" Finally, there was the frustration of fighting for continued community control in the present as a means to assure the future of the programs. When the revenue streams stop, other agencies and professionals have less interest in the programs. For the sake of the future of the programs, ACC worked to keep them independent enough to develop community stakeholders and to preserve the opportunity for community people to continue them.

Devolving Responsibility to the Local Level

Both conservative and progressive social policy theory call for mediating structures to take an expanded role in shifting responsibility for social welfare to the local level and to nongovernment providers (Smith and Lipsky 1993: 208, 213–15). The Kentucky Small Farm Project (KSFP) exemplifies the devolved and local role of community-based mediating structures in providing new forms of social capital. Both the conservative and liberal ends of the mediating structure spectrum—Berger and Neuhaus (Berger and Neuhaus 1977; Neuhaus 1980) and Bellah and his colleagues (1992), respectively—speak of this practice as the principle of *subsidiarity*: nothing should be centralized at a higher level that can be decentralized and conducted locally. Unfortunately, the history of the Kentucky Small Farms Project also suggests that devolution is not enough. When routine enters into small-scale, local programs, the sense of ownership and the participation of members may dwindle, just as it does in large-scale, centralized programs.

The Kentucky Small Farm Project began in 1981 as the Grass Roots Farm Project. Ervan Hontz, a former VISTA worker, directed the project for its first ten years and then retired in 1992. Hontz envisioned KSFP organizing clusters of poor families in the Eastern Kentucky counties of Wolfe, Lee, and Breathitt to help them increase their incomes and improve their nutrition through assistance with farm and garden management. Its goals were to help poor families save money by producing their own food and to gain extra income through sales of produce. Since its beginning, the major projects of the Kentucky Small Farm Project have been livestock and garden seed supply for co-op families in these three counties.

During its first decade of operation, the KSFP served more than 300 families in twenty communities. Co-op membership cost $5 per year per family, which covered some of the cost of the seed and fertilizer each member received. Members were organized into cooperatives, which included at least five families in the same community. The president of each co-op represented their communities on the board of directors, which met quarterly.

The Heifer Project International supplied KSFP families with beef cows, milk cows, milk goats, pigs, sheep, chickens, rabbits, and bees. The Heifer Project emphasized animal "pass-ons," in which the first female offspring was passed on to a neighbor. If the pass-on program succeeded, then over a period of time the community became self-sufficient in the maintenance and supply of the animals. The Heifer Project and the Christian Appalachian Project also helped KSFP obtain garden seed.

KSFP also depended on outside resources to rehabilitate members' houses. The Heifer Project International connected the KSFP with church groups through its affiliation with the Church of the Brethren. Beginning in 1983, five to six church groups willing to donate time, skill, and money came down each summer to repair the floors, ceilings, and roofs of co-op members' houses. Two members of one such church work crew, Pat and Bill Stoughton, succeeded Hontz as director in 1992. They had come to Eastern Kentucky with work crews from their church in New Jersey before moving down to take over the directorship.

Over the years, members received the vital services of donated animals, seed, fertilizer, and housing repairs, but, in the opinion of their new directors, they had too little sense of ownership of their organization. Pat Stoughton expressed frustration that her new emphasis on member control and leadership brought conflict. "When we started putting the new stuff in, fund-raising activities, putting in new ideas on empowerment, one group up and quit . . . because they did not want to make their own decisions. They told us, that is what they hire directors for, to make decisions." There was success in leadership development with the animal management committee, which had representatives from all three counties. The committee members formed their own set of rules and regulations, evaluations, and training sessions for recipients of Heifer Project livestock. The animal management committee members also helped the co-ops communicate with each other about animal pass-ons when they were ready. Coordinating pass-ons, formerly solely the responsibility of the directors, was a task that members now managed.

The Stoughtons worked to develop outside resources as well as member development. They designed a newsletter specifically for churches to keep them informed of KSFP activities and to ask for help on specific projects, such as clothing distribution, furniture and appliance distribution, an emergency fund, a "Christmas train," and an education fund. The education fund gave six college students from co-op families $100 each to buy books and supplies.

KSFP's subsidiarity had limits as well as benefits. The emphasis on service from groups outside the area and on self-help of co-op members kept KSFP from becoming a force for broader change efforts in the communities. The high level of poverty and the incredible energy that the families had to put into just getting by also took away from organized efforts at change. KSFP acknowledged its limited role. An appeal for funding explained, "While we realize that the end result of these efforts will not change all 325 families, we hope to make their lives a little more tolerable as they continue to live in poverty."

Investments in Individuals and Group Identity

Social capital violates the first premise of market economics by investing in groups because of common bonds of identity rather than for tangible prospects of profit (Hirschman 1984: 92). SafeSpace began in the mid-1970s as an informal network of safe homes in rural east Tennessee to shelter battered women and their children. Ultimately, it developed into a model state and regional organization, which provided emergency services for battered women and advocacy on and education about domestic violence. SafeSpace provided social capital to victims of domestic violence directly. Indirectly, it also served them by creating public awareness, empathy, and better services.

After moving to rural Cocke County, Tennessee, Dianne Levy, the founder and director of SafeSpace, became aware that some of her women neighbors were being beaten.

> I had a friend locally who ran the community grocery store, which was a cement block building, 16 by 10 feet, a very small grocery [in a] very remote mountainous area. I was concerned about this woman because I thought she had a skin disease. Most every time I saw her she was covered in strange kinds of things on her skin, which I couldn't identify.
>
> I was interested in herbs and healing in those days. So one day I finally said (because you don't talk about those sorts of things right off hand), I said, "Gee, what is this on your hand? Maybe we could use some comfrey or goldenseal on this thing to make it better." She looked at me like I was from another planet and said to me, "These are bruises." And she proceeded to tell me things that I should have known and should have seen, but I had no idea what I was looking for. She was beaten regularly by her husband who was an alcoholic—who was a brutal, violent man, who assaulted her and the children. She kept piles of quilts in her car because at any moment during the day or night she knew that she might have to leave the house with her children and likely have to spend the night in the woods. She would take the quilts out of the car, throw them down in the ditch and cover the kids up with the quilts.
>
> This store that she called a store had a dozen onions. It had three cans of beanie weenies and a couple packs of cigarettes. . . . She had maybe $50 worth of groceries in the store. On another occasion, I said "Gosh, is this really worth your time? To sit here all day? How much business are you actually doing?" She said, "Ah, I'm not here to make money. See this

building?" (It was a block building, very small, and it had two front windows and a door, no back door, had a wood stove in there and bare floor.) "Do you see this building? See that door? See that steel door? See, the windows have bars in them. This is made so he can't burn this place down. He can't get to me in here. I can lock ourselves in here."

Eventually, one Christmas Day, Levy's friend mortally wounded her husband while defending herself during another of his drunken assaults. She was convicted of second-degree murder. In light of her husband's widely known violent abuse, she received a sentence of lengthy probation without any time in prison.

Through conversation with her women friends in the community who also had stories of violent abuse, Levy realized that there was a need for shelter and other services. She sheltered a few women in her home and began informal counseling. She had moved to Cocke County deliberately to leave a stint of political activism behind and, she said, "was not looking to get involved." Nevertheless, she became involved. She explains, "After about a year, I called many of these people who had been calling me asking me to help. I said to them, 'We need to have a meeting.' We formed a task force, that was in about '79. There was a group of about ten people that came together. That was the core." Levy and three other women from the area formed a loose network of safe houses and a hotline. They worked for several years on a volunteer basis.

From the beginning, Levy knew that the groups would have to move beyond providing services. As she states, "We were not going to be a social services organization. . . . We were looking into social change, and we were clear that providing temporary shelter to families was necessary and important, but we had to impact the entire community and the state to see change." The real change that SafeSpace leaders envisioned was better protection of battered women and their children through the law and criminal justice system. Levy had noticed that neither law enforcement officers nor the courts adequately protected women and their children. "The cops couldn't arrest anybody unless they saw the beating happen. Women couldn't possibly prosecute because while they were waiting for a case to come up in court, they would be reassaulted. The state could only intervene if the children were at risk, and then its action would be to remove the children from the mother and leave the mother in the violent situation, totally destroying the family."

The fight to change the system began in the early 1980s, when Levy and other leaders created a statewide coalition, the Tennessee Task Force Against Domestic Violence. Levy and the task force drafted and lobbied for several important legislative remedies, including a bill to strengthen the order of protection. This order enabled women to remain in their homes with legal support for the restraint of the perpetrator. Another example was Safe-Space's championing of the probable cause arrest bill, which allowed law enforcement officers to assess the situation in the home and make an arrest if there was probable cause to believe that a crime had been committed. Before this bill was passed, law enforcement officers were required to see the actual assault before they were able to make an arrest. SafeSpace leaders also lobbied successfully to secure a tax on marriage licenses to provide funding for battered women's shelters in the state. SafeSpace leaders explained to CORA, in its 1992 funding request, "We encourage the system to provide the assistance due these families. Where necessary, we work to change those systems that will not respond. We are an activist organization struggling for social change." Although Levy did a lot of advocacy work herself, the passage of the bills would not have been possible without the support of volunteers, many of them formerly battered women. Each year, SafeSpace took many battered women to Nashville for the Grassroots Lobby Day.

Levy credited SafeSpace's success to its ability to collaborate with others. "We have very high credibility. Our work is good. We have helped a great many people in this community. We helped the district attorney. We helped the judges. We help the law. We're helpful. We actually make their work easier." Success also required conflict—fighting for SafeSpace as well as battered women. Levy explained,

We have battled our battles. I mean our battles as far as being pariahs and worrying about being stoned in the community and being called witches and love hens and all the red, pinko-lesbo kind of thing. That stuff is pretty much over. We have very high credibility in the community. We know how best to impact this change or that change. We know what directions we need to go in. Our problem is simply the battle to keep the cash coming on. It takes an enormous amount of my energy, which remains a reason I'm very resentful. I still have to struggle. So much of my time is taken up for the fund-raising. There are lots of other things that I need to be doing.

SafeSpace improved police work by training law enforcement officers to recognize domestic violence. Levy herself conducted law enforcement training at Walters State Community College. SafeSpace staff also trained sheriffs' departments in six rural counties as well as Tennessee state troopers and police from ten local municipalities. In a summary of their work, Levy commented, "We have noticed the improvement in arrest rates and attitudes toward battered women since this training began. I feel very lucky because there's not too many people that actually get to see the results of their work. . . . I've actually seen change happen in the communities and that's a nice thing."

While Levy and other leaders continued working on change at the institutional level, some of the most important change was happening on a personal level at the shelter SafeSpace operated. The women who came to the shelter usually stayed for about one month. As Levy recounts,

> Many women come to us thinking the beating they have received is very much their own fault, a personal problem, a family problem. When the realization hits them that this is a problem that many families suffer, that it is not just happening in their homes and that it is not their fault, the relief and the hope that surface is a wonderful thing to see. In the shelter, they come to realize that they are not helpless. They are not hopeless. They have worth, they have skill, they have the ability and power to change their lives.

Many of the women who worked in the shelter were themselves formerly battered women. The contact that these volunteers had with women in shelter was an essential aspect of SafeSpace's work. Sheltered women invested moral worth and dignity in each other. Levy emphasized the importance of this aspect of the work:

> We really encourage women to come back as volunteers because some of the most powerful stuff that goes on in this work is what goes on around the kitchen table and how women help one another and share their stories and politicize themselves. . . . It's just being in tears, then they become angry, from anger comes rage, and from rage comes change. So that's the way they bring each other along. I always like to think that they do feel ownership.
>
> I think that some women actually do feel that this is their shelter. There are women who leave the shelter after they are out of a crisis and then they continue to come back to visit. We have to ask people sometimes not to return. To that degree, there is a great deal of ownership. You know, this is my home, and I want to come in here and see my family. Women

build support networks that they keep on an official basis; our policies mandate that half our board has got to be formerly battered women.

SafeSpace successfully created better laws and empowered women to achieve a higher degree of physical safety. Despite these accomplishments, however, there was a large cultural problem that required work, according to Levy. "Our society is violent. Everywhere we look we see women and children victimized. We watch it for entertainment. . . . In front of the TV every night you watch a drama you're watching women being stalked, you're watching women being terrorized, you're watching them being raped, murdered. . . . We entertain ourselves with watching women, children being threatened and assaulted. We are desensitized by this violence. It surrounds us."

As part of SafeSpace's work to change the culture of violence, Levy created a curriculum for sixth graders that taught nonviolence. Many schools, Levy noted, were teaching family life curricula, but very few of them addressed sex roles or nonviolence. SafeSpace staff taught about family violence, dating violence, and rape prevention, hoping that they could help give children the skills to "make the kinds of decisions which will lead them on a nonviolent path toward conflict resolution in their homes and in their lives." Dianne Levy commented, "If next year we had enough people so that we could teach this curriculum to each grade level, before I was dead we might be able to close the shelter." Whether SafeSpace closes or not, its work invested new and better resources in a previously ignored group, battered women. Its investment, along with those of thousands of other women's groups, produced a portion of the less violent society it sought.

Transforming Market Values

MATCH, Marketing Appalachian Traditional Community Handcrafts, worked with a network of craft makers and, initially, a set of churches to create alternatives to the market's supply-and-demand arrangements. Ben and Nina Poage worked for more than ten years to establish a regional marketing cooperative for more than thirty craft groups in nine states. In addition to the horizontal networks that MATCH established, the Poages attempted to bring moral resources into the market for crafts. MATCH marketed crafts for its predominantly low-income members; filled the role of a support group for the craft makers, 85 percent of whom were women; and initiated the revitalization of historic Olde Towne Berea, Kentucky. Its work suggests how moral resources hold together the thick, horizontal network of Robert Putnam's social capital. MATCH had many successes but eventually ceased operations in 1986 as a result of increased competition for handcrafts, loss of leadership, and difficulty in maintaining funding.

MATCH began as an expression of the church social ministry. Nina and Ben Poage wanted to replicate the practice of churches buying crafts from third world nations and selling them to their congregations. The Poages thought that the church could do the same thing for Appalachia, an American third world region. They began with a federation of craft groups eager to participate in marketing projects. Marketing through the church involved the publication of a catalog with each MATCH group and its products featured on a separate page. MATCH sold the catalog to churches, which were then supposed to sell the catalog to their congregations. The approximately 30,000 catalogs sold better than the crafts. When orders did come, new problems developed. MATCH did not have a warehouse or an inventory. It relied on the individual crafters to keep up the supply of the items MATCH had advertised. The crafters often did not have inventory, and consequently some orders went unfilled.

Ben Poage recalled one lesson in trying to market a phantom inventory. "One group . . . made one item and they took a picture of it and put it in the catalog. It was the only copy of the item they ever made. It was cheap and it was cute. It was some carving. . . . We got orders hand over fist for that. [It was] probably the most ordered thing in the whole catalog. And we had to write them back and say, 'I'm sorry, but they don't make that anymore.'" Until MATCH started accumulating and storing crafts in their warehouse, they did not have much control over the quality or size of the available inventory.

MATCH changed its name, Marketing Appalachia Through the Church, to Marketing Appalachia's Traditional Community Handcrafts, when it moved beyond the church in its marketing scope. Ben Poage looks at this transition as the secularization of MATCH. Part of the transition to diverse markets included MATCH's establishment of its headquarters in an old train depot in historic Olde Towne Berea, where the Poages set up a warehouse to store the crafts and where they also eventually opened a retail store. As part of its branching out into new markets, MATCH also began working with member groups on color schemes for quilts and pillows and developed its own line of products.

Although business management became a priority for MATCH as it moved into secular markets, Nina Poage, the executive director, did not lose touch with the grassroots base and cooperative spirit that were the foundations of the group. The odd combination of grassroots organizing and serious business challenges was part of what Poage considered "rehumanizing the market place." Rehumanizing took place on three levels: production, consumption, and community development. On the production end, MATCH worked closely with the low-income membership of the MATCH member groups, especially women, to help them find alternative and satisfying work in the home. On the consumption end, MATCH believed it was sensitizing consumers to both the struggle in Appalachia and the rich traditions in the region. The craft groups became important community social settings for low-income women to share their concerns about the community and about their work. In working with the women, Nina Poage was amazed that "the same need that was in Pennsylvania was in Georgia or North Carolina or West Virginia and Virginia—the needs were the same for the women particularly in all these areas." MATCH staff realized that many of the women did not have high school diplomas or driver's licenses. The lack of education and mobility contributed to low self-esteem for many of the women. Through MATCH, both GED classes and driver education classes were organized for a number of member groups. The classes were held at craft group meeting places. MATCH staff helped train craft groups in grant writing and accounting.

Nina Poage explained the importance of the craft groups as support networks and safe places for educational training for women. "The women that we were working with would not go down to the courthouse and say that they didn't know how to read. Their men wouldn't let them go down to the courthouse . . . [because that was] a real reflection on them; it was a reflection on the family. But when she went to the craft group, that was her world, and she could do whatever she wanted to in that world. . . . She didn't have to go down to the courthouse and embarrass him. It was a safety net. The craft groups were safety nets."

Producing crafts through a cooperative cottage industry model such as MATCH is not generally considered controversial. Quilting bees, whittling, and crafting shuck corn-dolls suggest a homey, peaceful, and quaint lifestyle. However, women who became income earners threatened the patriarchal structure of some households. Nina Poage recalled, "We had a lot of stories about the men. When the women began to sell to the cooperatives, the men were extremely jealous because the women were making more money than the men in the household were. We had a lot of men, on several occasions, who just took the quilts out and burned them because it was a real threat to their lifestyle. We had to deal with that constantly."

MATCH's approach to "rehumanizing the market place" on the consumer end involved several different tactics. The original tactic MATCH emphasized was connecting the consumer with the producer by providing brief biographies of them. This was easily done through the MATCH catalog, in which the advertisement for a particular product provided a biography of the producer. Rehumanizing the market through their retail stores was more difficult. "It's hard to sensitize people to the Appalachian culture when they are buying crafts in a retail outlet," Nina recalled. Ben Poage pointed out MATCH's effort to portray a positive image of Appalachia to consumers: "I think we were culturally sensitive. . . . The members did not want any dirty-face kids showing [in the catalog], even though they existed and there's a political reason why they exist."

A tactic Nina used to sensitize people to the needs as well as the talent of the Appalachian crafters was by writing "fictional" stories based on real situations she had witnessed among MATCH member groups. In two of the stories, one about "Sadie" and one about "Mary Jane," the young women saved their families from total despair by bringing in some extra income through the quilts and dolls they marketed through MATCH. The Poages hoped that these stories added extra value to the products sold through MATCH.

Although MATCH had moved beyond the church, the church continued to be involved in helping MATCH market their products. Clergy attempted to sensitize their congregations to problems in Appalachia and to the worth of the traditional culture through articles in their church bulletins. The United Methodists wrote a piece on MATCH that explained, "Appalachia's people have much to share with us. Their beautiful crafts, handmade with personal care and love of giving, are only one physical manifestation of their deep spirituality and human expression. . . . The working crafts persons in MATCH are seeking to enter your lives through their products, to share a bond of friendship through their handmade craft. They seek not a handout, but a hand up. If we fail to work for love, liberation, and justice with and for our neighbors, we are crusted by the poverty of ourselves." Women in Appalachia who were working through MATCH took a place among women of the Christian tradition.

We remember the faith of Mary, an unwed mother, who said, "Yes," to the unknown. We remember the faith of Anna, woman of God, prophetess, who recognized the long-awaited Messiah of her people. We remember the faith of Lydia, seller of purple goods, who heard the Word of God and became the first Christian convert in Philippi. We remember the faith of Junia, apostle of the Church, coworker and prisoner with Paul, and likewise we should remember the faith of women crafters in Appalachia who are working against tremendous odds to change their lives and build their community.

Underlying the work to rehumanize the market at the level of both producer and the consumer were the idealistic, cooperative principles in which Ben and Nina Poage deeply believed. During the fast-growing and successful years of MATCH in the mid- to late 1970s, the Poages believed that MATCH was on the cutting edge of what they explained as a "third wave" of economics in the postindustrial era the nation was entering. They incorporated the ideas of E. F. Schumacher (1973) and Alvin Toffler (1970) to express their own beliefs in cooperative principles and the revitalization of cottage industries as a viable alternative to traditional labor: "In the 1980s, (the beginning of the post-industrial era?), people producing their items at home, saving fuel, time and the effort necessary in factory commuting plus saving the added cost of hiring some one to sit with the kids, not to mention minimizing the potential of family disruption (the wife working outside the home is a frequent cause of spouse abuse and divorce in Appalachian families) may well forecast a new style of production in the nation."

The hope and enthusiasm that the Poages felt about MATCH's potential was supported by the trend in the 1970s of young people who were making simple lifestyle choices. The Poages believed that individual expression and self-sufficiency had become important elements of a lifestyle for many young people. Sharing the tasks and profits of a communal system went along with those goals. They expressed great hopes that they associated with the millennium:

By the year 2000, the handcraft industry will be on the cutting edge of the "new third wave" by returning to old historic values, the cooperative concept of working together and sharing profits from that work.

In the year 2000, MATCH will be producing at its maximum because of the training that will take place during the late 1970's and 80's. Our 8,000 crafters will have tripled to almost 25,000 and no crafts person will be forced into the Northern "big city" migration stream which uproots and separates families. Cooperative ownership of the producers' own marketing facility will be a reality in every Appalachian crafts community and the preservation of our region's rich heritage which make a positive statement about Appalachia and its people will have been achieved.

MATCH stopped operations in 1986, far short of the millennium and the goals the Poages had enumerated in the mid-1970s. The early 1980s were not kind to MATCH. The Appalachian Regional Commission (ARC), which had provided MATCH with funds, was cut back by the budgets of the Reagan administration. Some of MATCH's member groups reached self-sufficiency and began to compete with MATCH for foundation funds. Without federal funds, the market imposed a stricter and more exacting test on MATCH. Two of the three retail stores MATCH managed were not breaking even. There were staff problems. Nina Poage left MATCH as the executive director in 1983 to return to school, taking her dynamic leadership and talent with her. She succinctly pointed to one lesson she had acquired: a group needs "somebody who is really experienced and who is really willing to work full-time, night and day, and has enough vision to keep things rolling along. They just didn't find that person. They tried several managers."

When the Appalachian Regional Commission cut MATCH out of their funding, MATCH lost $35,000 of its annual budget. MATCH's leaders also began to realize that foundations preferred to give money to local groups rather than umbrella groups such as MATCH. It was at this point, about 1984, that Ben Poage got a grant to conduct long-range plans for a number of MATCH member groups. Through the process of long-range planning, he began to see the benefits in strengthening the member groups and eventually phasing out MATCH's role as the umbrella group.

Despite the disappointment of not seeing MATCH survive until the millennium, the Poages identify a number of accomplishments of the group, including the standardization of quilt size and labeling and the revitalization of Olde Towne Berea. "When we started, we were the only [ones] down at the train station. Now I think there is something like fifteen stores." Nina sees that her contact with the women in MATCH groups helped their children see more opportunities for themselves. "I think what we did was we opened up some of the ideas that they could go to school, they could leave home and become something of an active, productive person in the community in addition to staying at home and being a family production center."

Ironically, MATCH's accomplishments improved the market for Appalachian crafts, a market that others filled. Mass production, including machine-made quilts, addressed the market when the country look became fashionable. In astonishment and dismay, Nina Poage points out that beautiful Appalachian quilts—many of them made in third world nations—are now available in Sears, J. C. Penney's, and other department stores.

Increasing the Supply of Social Capital

Pierre Bourdieu emphasized the deliberate social role and class functions that social capital may have. Social capital varies with the economic and cultural capital that members of a network have. Networks of groups with low-income members have less cultural and economic capital than networks with high-income members. Social capital thus reproduces social roles and class differences, especially in a market economy and a market democracy. It becomes a resource to prevent the accumulation of financial capital by those who do not have it and the loss of financial capital by those who do have it (Bourdieu 1986: 241). Social capital is never independent of the other forms of capital in terms of its origins and its contribution to the potential resources of a network and its parts. Bourdieu's insights into social capital imply that mediating structures not only have to establish a network but, if they are to serve the democratic prospect, must work to increase and change the social capital of existing networks. The Southeast Women's Employment Coalition (SWEC) suggests how this may be done and, once again, the difficulty of increasing social capital to promote the democratic prospect.

SWEC was one of many groups that sprang up in the late 1970s to focus on "nontraditional occupations" for women. The United States Department of Labor defines a nontraditional occupation as any occupation in which men or women represent fewer than 25 percent of those employed in it. Groups such as the Coal Employment Project targeted coal mining as one such occupation. Women and Employment took on the building trades in West Virginia. SWEC initially focused on highway construction jobs for women. President Jimmy Carter's Executive Order 1126 required federal contractors to have affirmative action goals and guidelines. The Comprehensive Employment Training Act (CETA) encouraged programs to train people in nontraditional occupations. The changed political climate encouraged leadership to combat what SWEC came to call occupational segregation. Eventually, SWEC served an equally important role as a support group for executive directors of more than a dozen nonprofit organizations in the Appalachian region, which had been started by and for women in the late 1970s and early 1980s.

In the spring of 1979, Leslie Lilly, director of the Southern Appalachian Leadership Training program (SALT) in Kentucky, pulled together a group of women leaders in the Appalachian region for a meeting at the Highlander Center. About sixty women attended the meeting to discuss stories about government programs, sexual harassment in the home, and the struggle "to find and create answers for the economic desperation" of women in economically depressed areas and communities in Appalachia. The women recognized the need for an organization and met again in the spring to begin the Southeast Women's Employment Coalition. Lilly became its first executive director.

Betty Jean Hall was at that time a SWEC board member and director of the Coal Employment Project. She recalled that Lilly saw three things that needed to be addressed concerning all of the women's groups that were springing up: "[The women], one, didn't know each other; two, didn't have any experience for the most part in leading anything, because they were women and hadn't been given that opportunity; and, three, we were sort of being set up to compete against each other [for funding]." Hall found the quarterly board meetings invaluable as a "free space." She remembers them as "a forum, an outlet, a growth opportunity, and an education opportunity for all these women that were running these organizations that did not have any experience." The executive directors of twelve groups in six different Appalachian states made up the members of the SWEC board of directors.

SWEC board meetings developed into important places for women to find support and to learn new organizing skills. They often featured workshops on various topics that would be useful to directors in their local organizing efforts. SWEC "invested" in its member groups. It brought a staff member from the Center for Community Change in Washington, D.C., to lead a workshop on the development of organizations; it had a workshop on Executive Order 1126; and it held grant-writing workshops. Later, when SWEC recruited representatives from groups of African American women, the board began to address racism as well.

SWEC helped its members with fundraising and broke some of the "rules" in doing so. Hall recalled that in the beginning many of the groups felt like "the people that were funding them were trying to pull them apart." Specifically, Hall recalled that women's groups competed among themselves over the same few funding sources. SWEC helped ease the tension among groups and gave women with no experience in fundraising a chance to see how things were done. Hall recalled SWEC's two joint fund-raising trips to New York:

> It drove the foundations crazy. They couldn't understand how five groups were coming at the same time to potentially compete against each other. . . . It was beautiful to watch in action. . . . We may have nine meetings scheduled in two or three days with nine different funders. . . . We got really good at figuring out who they were picking up on. . . . And we

would all quit talking about ourselves, and all of us would focus on [the group they were interested in]. . . . We could do it without talking to each other. . . . Everybody would sort of look at each other and it worked. It was really nice.

Eventually, SWEC developed its own issues, but choosing an issue campaign for the coalition to work on was not as easy as providing its members with support. The leadership in SWEC was divided over whether the group should focus on organizing the "80 percent"—that is, the women in traditional jobs such as waitresses and clerical workers who did not receive fair pay or benefits—or whether the group should focus on advocacy for nontraditional jobs. Hall said the issue was never totally resolved among the SWEC board members. Eventually the latter view prevailed, because more external support and opportunities came with the procurement of highway jobs for women.

SWEC launched its campaign for highway jobs just as the political climate for the equal employment goals of SWEC changed. Beginning in 1981, the Reagan administration cut travel budgets at the Office of Federal Contract Compliance and laid off its investigators. A limit was also placed on the number of cases that could be litigated through the Equal Employment Opportunity Commission, which enforced Title VII of the Civil Rights Act. Knowing it was going to be an uphill battle, SWEC filed a complaint in Washington against all fifty states and their departments of transportation for not enforcing equal employment hiring guidelines for women.

The highway campaign was not as successful as SWEC had hoped. The group had some impact on state policies in Ohio and generated interest in the campaign in Kentucky, but its efforts never grew into the national and regional movement that it had envisioned. On the other hand, some of SWEC's efforts were too successful for them to handle. An ad SWEC ran in the *Louisville Courier-Journal* asked women interested in well paying jobs in occupations in which few women were employed to call or write SWEC. The ad tapped a reservoir that flooded and submerged the capacity of SWEC to respond.

Other difficulties SWEC faced included problems created within the SWEC member organizations. The executive directors of these organizations would leave for three or four days at a time, three or four times a year, to attend SWEC meetings, which took their attention away from their work with their own groups. SWEC never included the membership of its member organizations in its meetings and workshops. In addition, SWEC had a hard time finding "new blood." Its board was composed of executive directors who were interested in keeping their positions, and not many new groups were forming, so few new executive directors joined SWEC.

SWEC also had other challenges in the 1980s involving funding and leadership. The Ford Foundation had launched a new program for domestic rural poverty and women's economic issues. Ford had said it would fund SWEC for five years as part of this initiative but then decided to reduce the funding to three years. In 1986, Lilly left the group as the executive director. She took with her the adrenaline and energy that ran SWEC. After Lilly left, SWEC's focus shifted to research projects. It produced the notable study *Women of the Rural South: Economic Status and Prospects* (B. E. Smith 1986), which used participatory research to document women's experience in finding jobs, supporting their families, and fighting poverty. Although this and other studies published later by SWEC influenced discussions on women and poverty in the region, the group never regained its original energy. The group went through two more executive directors before closing its doors in the summer of 1991 as a result of more funding problems.

Hall will always remember that the SWEC board "was the one place for people to go and let off steam and help each other solve their own problems." From time to time, Hall mentions her SWEC days to her male colleagues at work, but she says they can't grasp the importance of those days. "These men just can't understand what this could have been that you are still talking about. It's been dead for five years, so what does it matter? But it does matter." Hall carries with her the memories of how SWEC disrupted some networks and created others. Either way, SWEC increased the amount and improved the forms of social capital for the women whom it served.

"Down Payments" on New Communities

Mediating structures may improve the forms and increase the amounts of social capital. However, the amount of social capital, such as housing and physical security, that they can produce depends heavily on their willingness and ability to advocate for changes in public policy, such as the resourceful efforts of Clay Mountain Housing and SafeSpace. In addition to some form of broad advocacy, mediating structures need leadership to present new challenges to members in order to maintain the dense network of social capital and to keep it in good repair, as the experience of the Kentucky Small Farms Project shows. The contexts of the work of mediating structures include the strong links of existing social capital with class distinctions and inequality, as Pierre Bourdieu has pointed out. Not surprisingly, the efforts of some mediating structures, such as MATCH and SWEC, fall short in their efforts to transform and increase social capital. Within this large picture are cameos of success in increasing the moral resources of social capital, such as increased confidence and mutual support among members of community-based mediating structures. These forms of improved and increased social capital endure as investments in improved forms of community yet to be completely realized.

PART III

Mediating Structures
and Social Capital

The local nature of many community-based mediating structures limits the attention they receive. At the same time, their ubiquity gives them a taken-for-granted quality. For these and other reasons there is too little systematic analysis of community-based mediating structures. Part II outlined the work of twenty-three local, little known, community-based mediating structures and described their roles in confronting poverty and community decline and in promoting the democratic prospect. This part analyses the broader, common issues that underlie the experiences of these mediating structures and others like them in promoting the democratic prospect.

This part takes its direction from the work of the Center for Community Change (CCC). On its twenty-fifth anniversary, CCC issued a report on the lessons it had acquired in promoting community change in low-income areas in all parts of the country (CCC 1992). These lessons became the basis of the protocol we used in interviewing members of the community-based mediating structures we studied. The lessons of the CCC and the questions we subsequently developed are listed in Appendix B. They reveal that an elaborate set of leadership, organizational, and historical factors lie beneath the sometimes superficial and almost always unexamined assumptions that we make about mediating structures and democracy. Mediating structures do not occur naturally, nor can their democratic nature be taken for granted.

The chapters in Part III report on the lessons to be drawn from the work of community-based organizations and change. Chapter 7, for example, examines the means used to create and maintain community. This involves practical questions with which every community-based mediating structure must deal. What is community and who belongs to it? How do differences of race, class, gender, and age impact on different, and sometimes conflicting, perceptions of community? What are the various forms of representation and participation of community members in community-based mediating structures? How do community-based mediating structures keep their members involved? How do they create and share new visions of possibility for their community? How do community-based mediating structures deal with the challenges of change and continuity within their own life cycles?

However great their goals, mediating structures have mundane matters of management to which they have to attend. Chapter 8 does not provide a "how-to" manual, but it does explain how our group of community-based mediating structures managed to run efficiently and accountably. Not surprisingly, we found that their success depended on learning from the experiences of others, forming coalitions around issues and needs, and gaining stable financial support.

Chapter 9 examines the quintessence of leadership—change. For mediating structures, three lessons seem to stand out in their efforts to change: that the development of services and organizing for advocacy are compatible; that social and economic changes are long and difficult processes with no cookie-cutter shortcuts; and that successful change depends on adequate financial and human resources, including leadership, from both within and outside of the local community of effort.

The syntax in these chapters signals two different levels of discourse: the present tense is used to present generalizations about community-based mediating structures; the past tense signals evidence taken from the cases described in Part II. This device intends to make clear that the evidence taken from the mediating structures we studied comes from a particular time and is reported in Part II. Everything changes. The groups in our study have moved on to new issues, faced new challenges, and changed because of them. Sadly, several of the leaders we interviewed have passed away. The past tense does not indicate that a group has ceased to exist. It simply means that the evidence used for the generalizations of this chapter comes from a particular time and place. The present tense describes generalizations that we believe extend beyond any particular time and place.

Catherine Guthrie did the preliminary analysis of the interviews used in this section.

CHAPTER 7

Creating and Maintaining Community

The Center for Community Change's twenty-five years of work taught it that "the most successful [community-based organizations] . . . are those that find ways to keep the community intimately involved" (CCC 1992: 67). Continued involvement is an essential element of mediating structures' provision for the democratic prospect. They provide new forms and larger amounts of social capital when they offer their formal and informal members new forms and larger amounts of democratic representation and participation in the sociopolitical organizations of neighborhood, community, state, and nation. This representation and participation increase members' sense of common bonds with each other and with others beyond their community and thus increase their capacity for trust, cooperation, and collaboration. Community-based mediating structures have three formidable tasks related to creating and maintaining a sense of community: to impart to their members a renewed and expanded sense of community that embraces new and unfamiliar people; to embody in their operations the moral resources of trust, caring, and other expressions of community; and to assert a sense of solidarity to friends and foes with whom they deal.

Several factors assist them in their formidable task. Despite all the nostrums of market democracy on self-interest, people do act on behalf of common purpose and thereby increase social capital. As Albert O. Hirschman argues (see Chapter 2) and as Chapter 6 illustrates, social capital invests in the identity and higher human values of community. Like other moral resources, action on behalf of community may increase community even if it falls short of achieving some idealized version of it. As people discover the efficacy and value of their efforts on behalf of some common purpose, they may discover a community—perhaps one too full to maintain, but exhilarating in its expression nonetheless. This chapter examines the challenges that face mediating structures in creating and maintaining community.

The Community Must Feel It Owns the Organization

Community involvement comes with some sense of ownership, and that requires deciding who is a member of the community and who is not. These questions appear to have obvious answers until they are asked, and then easy answers sometimes cause organizational difficulty and conflict. What is the community that this organization serves, and who belongs to it? What do they need? What changes are required to meet their needs? Who should provide that change? How much change is enough? These large questions require answers that become basic decisions about the purpose and functions of organizations. Having asked these related questions, the organization must then involve its members in answering them.

What or Who Is Community?

Most concepts of community invoke a particular place and people in geographic proximity—a common culture in a close-knit neighborhood, small town, or holler. Many groups have this form of community. For example, the Appalachian Peoples Action Coalition had members living in the area in and around Athens, Ohio. The Dungannon Development Corporation brought people together around a host of development efforts in one small town in southwest Virginia. Similarly, Appalachian Communities for Children and SafeSpace provided services to people with similar needs in a specific geographic area.

Community-based mediating structures sometimes bring people together around a general need of many people living in the same place. The Brumley Gap Concerned Citizens group, for example, was concerned with plans to flood its community for a hydroelectric storage lake. A common threat such as this, or the pollution that Bumpass Cove experienced, affects a very large number of people, and it can bring almost everyone in a community together. In such cases, mediating structures give local residents the capacity to address a common threat to the social capital that sustains their community.

In other cases, community-based mediating structures bring together a distinct and limited set of residents within an area. The Appalachian Independence Center, for example, brought together people with physical disabilities who were living in and around Abingdon, Virginia.

In some cases, the community of mediating structures clearly has far less to do with local residence and much more to do with the common characteristics or bonds of people spread over a wide area. The Appalachian Ohio Public Interest Center brought people together around policy problems and preferences. Their residence determined whether they fell under the jurisdiction of the policies they addressed, but this was secondary to their policy interests. The Council of Senior West Virginians and the West Virginia Education Association are both examples of groups with members who remain part of the group's community even if they move to another part of the state. The Virginia Black Lung Association had a community that continued even when a victim of black lung moved from Virginia. The criteria for membership in VBLA related to one's legal standing, a health condition, and place of residence. Indeed, even death may not sever membership in a black lung association. The surviving dependents of a black lung victim may maintain their claim to benefits and consequently to the services of VBLA. Policy preferences and other bonds may unite members of a mediating structure from more than one place. Similarly, some mediating structures have a community of members who are clients for their services apart from considerations of where they live or their common culture. The Appalachian Center for Economic Networks in Appalachian Ohio, for example, worked with people who owned and ran small businesses or who would have liked to do so. Thus, it served a community of small entrepreneurs primarily and local residents secondarily.

Mediating structures may provide a communal bond among their members that is or can be stronger than local residence and/or common culture. Members of community-based mediating structures share a community greater than the accident of time and space. The nature of this bond may be more than some local residents want and explains why not everyone in place-based mediating structures, such as the Bumpass Cove Citizens Group, are group members.

The community members of mediating structures are not always individuals. For example, the Federation of Appalachian Housing Enterprises and the West Virginia Primary Care Association assembled groups, not individuals, into a community that addressed similar issues and problems, such as housing, or that provided similar services, such as primary care. These communities are organizations of similar service providers. In other cases, such as the Southern Empowerment Project, the community of a mediating structure may be groups that are clients with a need for common services, such as staff and leadership development. These groups can be loosely combined, as in the case of the Appalachian Alliance, MATCH, and SWEC.

Common cultural characteristics cast the broadest bonds of community with the loosest ties. For example, Roadside Theater created a temporary community with every one of its performances. This community was an audience for a dramatic performance. Its common bond was short-lived. The audience members came and went with only the slightest knowledge of one another, and they may never have assembled or expressed the same interest again once the performance was over. Precisely because of its lack of other bonds, the audience of a cultural performance may temporarily portray a profound, unique, bond dramatically, as in the case of the singing across dark spaces in the Pittston strike, discussed as transformative and transcendent politics in Chapter 4.

The depth and richness of common human bonds may be most poignant when people who may otherwise be strangers discover them together. Even the very simple, ephemeral action of joining in the chorus of a song or standing to applaud a dramatic performance offer those glimmering moments of solidarity, the "free space," and the promise of a meaningful community that we discussed in Chapter 2 and described in Chapter 4. The power of that cultural expression keeps mediating structures such as Roadside Theater going, but the ephemeral nature of its audience-communities also requires that the group develop more stable and enduring community ties. For this stable, ongoing communal tie, Roadside looked to its parent organization, Appalshop, as its anchor community and sponsor. Obviously, Roadside could not continue long without an audience that comes together as a temporary community.

An ongoing community of people in need does not increase social capital or improve the democratic prospect until its members act to express their common human bonds through the social, political, and economic roles of mediating structures. The very wide range of community, from an audience brought together for the brief time of a performance to a set of residents with lifelong roots in the same place, suggests three elements of the community of the democratic prospect: the wide variety of "dialogical communities," the time over which that dialogue takes place, and the intensity of that dialogue. A community of groups centered on administrative tasks, such as the West Virginia Primary Care Association, plays to its members as an enduring audience of a specific community just as Roadside Theater plays to its temporary audiences as members of a broad community. All community-based mediating structures, it would seem, have to convey to their members some sense that they are part of a community taking part in an important dramatic narrative, however varied, that transcends their own time and place.

All community-based mediating structures have more than one community. Roadside Theater participated in several communities simultaneously, including its audience, its sponsoring group, and its parent organization. Similarly, many different communities may participate in a community-based mediating structure simultaneously. For example, within the Appalachian Independence Center, the community of people with disabilities included communities of both the mentally and physically disabled. Among the latter, there were communities of those born disabled and those who had become disabled later in life. These communities may be broken down further by type of disability (cerebral palsy, paralysis, or blindness) or by cause of disability (auto accident, birth defect), and these communities within communities may take on different tasks and goals. For example, paralysis brought on by an auto accident involving a drunk driver may foster a small community to work on policies to prevent drunk driving.

This plethora of communities can fragment the members of a community-based mediating structure and divide their allegiances. To avoid fragmentation and division, skilled leaders hold communities together through representation and participation, involvement, and renewed vision of the common bonds that they all share. In some cases, leaders may fail to hold a broad community together. Issues may divide members of a group and foster breakaway groups with stronger, narrower bonds. The Bumpass Cove Citizens Group, for example, had an intense internal struggle over the sources of assistance they received from organizations outside of the community. Charges of communist influence flew through the air and divided the group. The Western North Carolina Alliance encountered opposition from local residents who treated as "outsiders" those group members who valued recreational and environmental issues more than economic development of local natural resources. Both the WNCA members and their opponents lived in the area, but length of residence and cultural values divided one community from another. As the remarks of Benjamin Barber suggested in Chapter 4, community obviously comes in many forms and may unite people as well as divide them.

The sense of community ownership of a community-based mediating structure involves, at the very least, clarity on membership in the community. Residence in a location and participation in a common culture do less to establish communal bonds than do ties engendered by common problems, needs, willingness to deal with issues, or involvement with programs. In addition to geographical place, mediating structures may bring people together around common interests, needs, or threats and provide them the space from which to do something with or about them. Community expresses assets and efficacy as much as it expresses needs.

Race, Class, Gender, and Community

The decision about who is or is not a member of a community eventually involves issues of race, gender, and class. Here, the democratic prospect and social capital require increased and improved forms of inclusion. Some community-based mediating structures, such as the Appalachian Independence Center and the Southeast Women's Employment Coalition, work specifically to address matters of inclusion and participation for groups in public programs and the job market. Other groups, such as the Appalachian Communities for Children, with its adult education programs, may deal indirectly with the question of broad social and economic inclusion by improving the education, health, or housing of all the people they serve.

All groups, however, have to deal with the questions of increased and improved inclusion internally as well. The West Virginia Education Association had a minority affairs committee and minority representation, even though the state's African American population was only 3 percent. In general, the mediating structures discussed here have low rates of African American membership and participation. In some cases, no attention was given to racial minorities because they were not present in specific, limited locations such as Brumley Gap. In other instances, the small population of racial minorities explains their absence from organizations. In most counties of Central Appalachia and its adjoining counties, the African American population is about 2.2 percent. Most counties in rural Appalachia have African American populations of less than 1 percent. This may explain the low number of members, but race plays other roles even in these organizations.

Even predominantly or exclusively white community-based mediating structures may work with members of other races in the course of their organizing. This may produce conflict that requires members to express values of inclusion. For example, in Bumpass Cove, an African American male from the federal government visited leaders of the all-white Bumpass Cove Citizens Group. His presence prompted four phone calls and one visit to the home of his hosts with warnings to "get that nigger out of here." Not everyone joined in the racism, but it was trying and divisive. One of his hosts recalled, "They was calling us 'nigger lovers' . . . They [the visitors] were high officials from the United States government. We were privileged that they would come up here. And I still back [their visit] up, if it's mentioned. I had to fight for a long time and I had to defend myself a long time for what I did. I still tell them, when it's mentioned, 'Yes, I did and I'll do it again. And if you don't care enough to fight for your children, *I'll* fight for your children.'"

If the group adopts inclusive policies, its staff may also expect external challenges to them. The Appalachian Communities for Children served no black families in Jackson County and few in adjoining Clay County. The staff structured their teen program with visits to and from black teens in the nearby city of Richmond, Kentucky. ACC also had an African American resident join its staff in a VISTA position, which required her to have a driver's license. Her efforts to acquire her license were reminiscent of previous efforts of other African Americans to register to vote in the rural South. The examiner would not let her take the test at first because the car, which she had borrowed, had a brake light that did not work. The next time she attempted to take her driving test, members of her church brought three cars for her to use, confident that one would meet the examiner's demanding standards. That time, he refused her the test because none of the church members' insurance policies covered her. He was challenged when he permitted a white woman, connected with ACC, to take the test in a car loaned by a friend whose insurance policy did not include her. A staff member recalled how this became a test of bonds among the staff: "We said, 'All twenty of us in the JOBS class will come down and support you.' Just to let her know, we're friends and we're going to be her fan club. But if it takes it, we will file a discrimination suit or whatever. But it is her call."

Other groups took similar deliberate action to include African Americans. The Virginia Black Lung Association, for example, worked for racial parity among its volunteers. In addition, it included the Black Lung Association of McDowell County, which has a relatively large concentration of African Americans. McDowell County's black lung association was 90 percent African American.

Organizations that are statewide and have many members, such as the West Virginia Primary Care Association and the West Virginia Education Association, have the best base for developing a broad, inclusive membership of rich and poor, urban and rural, black and white people. The Council of Senior West Virginians worked with the Charleston Black Ministerial Alliance and the West Virginia Black Baptist Convention. Other regional efforts may make deliberate efforts to be inclusive. The Appalachian Alliance included community-based mediating structures in black communities hit by the floods that sparked its initial organizing. Typically, coalitions of groups are dependent upon their member groups for initiatives to be racially inclusive. The Federation of Appalachian Housing Enterprises broke with this dependence to initiate a program of its own in an African American community outside of the Appalachian region. The Southern Empowerment Project, very conscious about the racial composition of its board and members of training sessions, made a point of including areas outside of Central Appalachia that had large African American populations.

The Southeast Women's Employment Coalition made more efforts than most other organizations to integrate and break down racial barriers. Although SWEC did not achieve what it had hoped in its advocacy work in the 1980s, it had some success in its work on racism at its board meetings. SWEC was criticized by a Ford Foundation program director for spending too much time on process, at the expense of practice, but the process of integrating the SWEC board and carrying out painful and enlightening discussions on the topic of racism had lasting effects. Betty Jean Hall recalled that "in the beginning it [SWEC] was very, very white." By 1982, SWEC had recruited some African American members who had been instrumental in starting organizations, including Sophia Bracy-Harris, Sara Davis, and Gardenia White. Betty Jean Hall recalled that including the African American women on the board was awkward at first. "You know, they came into this room full of lily-white women and obviously were on parade, sort of like being asked to join a sorority. It was just that kind of feeling. . . . I guess two of them were just absolutely adamant on walking out, and the third one talked them into staying." The workshops that SWEC pioneered on racism made deep impressions on the women who attended them, and inspired them to address racism, homophobia, and issues of disabilities within their own groups (Weiss 1993: 160).

The inclusion of women in the membership and leadership of community-based mediating structures presents far less of a problem than the inclusion of racial minorities. Many times the nature of services, such as domestic violence, or the makeup of the membership allows for a prominent place for women in an organization. The WVEA had more female members than male, almost the same ratio as that of all teachers in the state: 60 to 40 percent. In some cases, a gender division of roles still survives despite the increased participation of women. The Appalachian Peoples Action Coalition had more men involved in the management and daily operations of the furniture store and more women in charge of the conduct and participation of member meetings. In other cases, such as with the Dungannon Development Commission, women are clearly in charge of all aspects of the organization.

The community-based mediating structures of this study not only include women; more often than not women lead them. In many cases the gender emphasis has been intentional. Southeast Women's Employment Coalition provides an obvious example of the effort to supplement the skills of women who directed agencies. Appalachian Center for Economic Networks had a specific training program for women in manufacturing. SafeSpace was also deliberate on its emphasis on women in its services and administration, although it included men on its staff and in its education and law enforcement programs, and the administrative assistant was male.

The one area of inclusion that provided our community-based mediating structures the fewest problems was class. Most of our community-based mediating structures operated in low-income areas of Appalachia and made clear that participation and membership was for people with low incomes, that is, members of the working class. The Council of Senior West Virginians expressed itself as working class because of the strength of labor unions in its state and the experience of its members in them. Clay Mountain Housing worked exclusively with low-income individuals and families.

The inclusion of people from lower income groups presented a problem for a few of our groups, however. Roadside Theater has been deliberate in including working-class people and low-income communities among the audiences for its traveling show in addition to its usual patrons in universities and theaters. Perhaps the Western North Carolina Alliance had the largest problem of class-related inclusion. Most of the group's members were "newcomers," people who had moved to the area for its environment and lifestyle. In general, the members were better educated and better off financially than the longtime residents of the region. WNCA had some characteristics of a club, as well as a community-based mediating structure, and socioeconomic class divided its members from local residents. One staff member explained:

It's a cultural thing. Newcomers tend to join things and relate to organizations that way. The people born and raised here don't do that. They just call up their neighbors. They don't see the need of an organization because they are kind of organized in their own way. What's been important to us is that we need both. A lot of newcomers have new ideas and energy and know what some of the problems are in the region, and they will be related in a certain way. We also need the people who were born and raised here to have that grounding in what's real. And they are the most effective.

Of course, local people can and will organize to deal with clear threats to them, as they did in Bumpass Cove and Brumley Gap.

In addition to reflecting the communities of which they are a part in varying degrees, community-based mediating structures may also provide a glimmer of a community in the making, a community marked by less exclusion. Participation in these communities requires new democratic practices, to which we now turn.

Keeping Community Members Involved

Once established, communities need to be maintained. Mediating structures that make continued constituency building and organizing a part of their ongoing programs have a much higher chance of success and longevity. As the Center for Community Change observes: "We have learned that organizations must push themselves constantly to organize and involve their members. We have also learned that we err if we relate only to a staff person and neglect board members, who may give us a much better picture of how connected and accountable the group is to its community" (CCC 1992: 67).

Community-based mediating structures may focus on involving members of a primary community at times and a secondary community at other times, depending on the issue at hand. The Virginia Black Lung Association, for example, focused on its primary community of disabled miners and their dependents; its members worked with other groups, agencies, and legislators in order to achieve their goals and objectives. They depended on the media to establish and maintain their relationship with informal and secondary members of the VBLA, people who supported their cause. The West Virginia Primary Care Association also focused primarily on its members, at times exclusively. This primary focus can be expected in those organizations started by their member groups to look after their interests, such as the West Virginia Primary Care Association. For example, the Federation of Appalachian Housing Enterprises monitored legislation and policies of importance to its members and saved each member from the doing the same work. The closer the members of an organization are bonded to a single issue, such as primary health care or housing, the greater the depth of technical assistance the organization can provide them and the more likely it will focus on its primary members. A multi-issue organization or coalition, such as the Appalachian Alliance, must first determine priorities and even then may have several issue areas to cover. Some members will benefit more than others will, depending on the selection of priorities. Continued involvement of their members presents very different challenges for single- and multi-issue mediating structures.

At times, a community-based mediating structure may place urgent emphasis on its relationship with its informal or secondary members and attempt to involve them in a one-time, dramatic effort of the organization. The West Virginia Education Association, for example, attempted to mobilize students and parents in support of its strike. Bringing members of other communities into the work and advocacy efforts of a mediating structure may be an important strategy. In some cases, primary community members, such as the teachers in West Virginia, may already have visible and natural ties with others—students and their parents—who in turn may become secondary community members as a result of their collaboration. Some mediating structures, such as Brumley Gap Concerned Citizens, may reach out to very distant secondary members through the services of a person brought in to help them.

Ties to secondary community members may eventually involve mediating structures in coalitions and networks that change the forms of participation within a group. The Brumley Gap Concerned Citizens formed a coalition with other groups of consumers served by the electric power company that proposed the pumped-storage facility in its community. In Bumpass Cove, the Concerned Citizens group came into the orbit of the Vanderbilt Center for Health Services and the Highlander Research and Education Center and through that connection developed ties with two other groups dealing with toxic waste dumping—Tennesseans Against Chemical Hazards (TEACH) and the Southern Appalachian Leadership Training (SALT) Fellowship. Sometimes the bonds with these coalitions and networks are self-evident to members, as they were with the Federation of Appalachian Housing Enterprises and the state and national housing groups to which it belongs. At other times, members may have to be instructed to learn about their leaders' membership and their own common ties with other groups, as was the case in Brumley Gap and Bumpass Cove.

Marketing Appalachian Traditional Community Handcrafts (MATCH) attempted to forge communal bonds on the slender reed of market relationships. This is difficult work to start and to maintain. MATCH asked churches outside of Appalachia, as far away as Connecticut, to relate to and address needs in Appalachia. On top of that, MATCH asked those churches to take on roles that were not related to their primary mission, including marketing arts and crafts, both wholesale and retail. For a community-based mediating structure to secure and retain the participation of groups with which it has only superficial ties for the purpose of conducting a task that is a new role for them presents formidable obstacles, as the history of MATCH illustrates.

Sometimes members of an informal or secondary community of a community-based mediating structure may refuse to recognize its bond with another group and refuse efforts to support it. For example, although the ties between SWEC and its member groups were interwoven with the strands of shared problems and programs, much more so than was true for MATCH and its collaborating church groups, and even though the role of SWEC supported the work of its member groups, those ties and roles were not obvious enough to some members of some groups to make them feel even informally or secondarily members of SWEC. Without that sense of involvement, members of the affiliated groups did not support SWEC. When a sense of involvement is absent, people have less reason to participate themselves or to support the participation of others. The first rule of how to involve secondary members is to foster a good relationship with chapters or member groups. For example, the Council of Senior West Virginians focused on its relationship with its chapters, but its staff also reached out directly to the members by polling them twice a year and establishing policy priorities based on the results of the polls. This allowed members to feel involved and avoided membership apathy toward new roles of the mediating structure.

To reinforce a sense of membership, community-based mediating structures may undertake deliberate action to involve their informal or secondary members. Some measures are obvious. Membership meetings, for example, are usually open to nonmembers. Blurring the difference between members and nonmembers sometimes facilitates nonmember participation in meetings. Many groups have a newsletter to share information with their informal community. The Southern Empowerment Project advertised the availability of jobs in community organizations to the benefit of many people, not just its own formal and informal community. Often, a community-based mediating structure will undertake a program that requires a coalition effort of informal community members and their groups. The Appalachian Ohio Public Interest Center, for instance, instituted a "Rural Regeneration Strategy" that assumed the participation of members in communities beyond its own. AOPIC also included nonmembers and informal members in its training programs. The Western North Carolina Alliance made it standard practice to involve other groups in temporary and limited coalitions, such as the group that opposed clearcutting.

Human and social services also keep informal community members involved in mediating structures. Informal members participated in the child care and adult education programs of the Appalachian Communities for Children. ACC developed new services primarily for the benefit of informal community members. The Appalachian Peoples Action Coalition band played regularly at a local nursing home, which kept members of its informal community involved.

As Chapter 2 explains, the public goods and moral resources of mediating structures are not divisible. Thus, the achievements of community-based mediating structures benefit and involve their secondary as well as their primary community members. The increased access to financial capital acquired by Appalachian Center for Economic Networks, the Federation of Appalachian Housing Enterprises, and Clay Mountain Housing served the needs of other local groups as well as their own. Changes in policy and procedure that followed from APAC's court watch program and their interventions at the welfare office benefited other low-income people in addition to APAC members. Sometimes also one form of social capital develops another form to benefit the informal members of a mediating structure. For instance, APAC's bargain store served as a site for the Community Work Experience Program.

Thus, acting as social capital entrepreneurs, community-based mediating structures develop services that involve secondary community members. SafeSpace illustrates this particularly well. It provided local schools with speakers to explain sex roles, domestic violence, and nonviolent methods of settling disputes and also developed domestic violence training sessions for local police. Like SafeSpace, the Appalachian Independence Center provided speakers to various groups to explain the nature and extent of the problems of people with disabilities and the programs needed to deal with them. In addition, AIC worked with builders to retrofit buildings for better access.

Measures to forge community bonds among and between the primary and secondary communities and the formal and informal members of groups make indirect but vital contributions to community. For example, the space in which a mediating structure may conduct meetings, business, or services can provide the community an informal meeting space or a free space, as the Appalachian Peoples Action Coalition's second-hand furniture and clothing store did. Likewise, the Dungannon Depot served as a spot in the middle of town where people could gather, and illustrated the rejuvenation of social capital. The restoration of the Depot resulted from participation that in turn fostered even more community participation. It also suggests how physical space may function as a form of social capital through which people participate in the re-creation of their community. In addition to permanent spaces such as the bargain store and the Depot, community-based mediating structures may provide temporary free space. For example, the Appalachian Alliance's annual meeting enabled new forms of participation and coordination among informal community members. Roadside Theater productions created temporary free spaces for its audiences and, by using the concerns and stories of its audiences, engendered new forms of participation. The Dungannon July 4th celebration, which the Dungannon Development Commission reinstated, is another example of a temporary free space in which people expressed themselves in and as a community.

Involvement of its secondary community and informal members in programs expresses the roles of community-based mediating structures in broad forms of community development. For example, several of the mediating structures made a point of supporting local merchants and suppliers by buying building supplies, seed, equipment, and other materials locally. Some organizations fostered bonds with the local informal community through their fund-raising efforts. For example, the Ohio Valley Environment Council's "Tree Huggers Ball" was an event that was enjoyed by both formal and informal members. Clay Mountain Housing employed a local outreach worker to advertise its programs and solicit eligible participants from the community. The Kentucky Small Farms Project used volunteers from local churches in its work crews and in soliciting donations.

Involving "outsiders" as temporary members of the community may give formal members of community-based mediating structures new roles and opportunities for involvement. For example, visiting student groups provided the Dungannon Development Commission with new opportunities to involve formal members in two ways: as supervisors of the volunteer work crews in the daytime and as local interpreters in the evening programs that oriented the visitors to Dungannon and Appalachia. In a similar fashion, the Appalachian Peoples Action Coalition had its members work with service programs originating in university fraternities and sororities.

The involvement of formal members of the community can extend beyond the local area and beyond existing programs. SafeSpace brought both formal and informal members from Cocke County to the distant state capital for a grassroots lobbying day, which provided them all with training and experience in advocacy on domestic violence and related policies. Both the Appalachian Alliance and the Southeast Women's Employment Coalition made innovative use of participatory action research, which provided group members new forms of participation as well as new information useful in addressing the groups' issues of land ownership and women's economic status. Whatever the form of involvement, keeping community members— primary and secondary, formal and informal—involved is a necessary element and continuing demand of the democratic prospect of mediating structures.

Vision and Community-in-the-Making

Initially, mediating structures may have impetus and momentum. Needs, threats, or possible resources loom very visibly in front of members. Excitement occurs as people discover their potential to act for change. Over time, some efforts fail, some tasks prove time consuming and difficult, and needs, threats, and resources get resolved. Eventually, vision and imagination have to take over to sustain the mediating structure or it loses its initial vitality. This involves more than the continued involvement of members; it involves renewing the purpose of that involvement.

Despite a wide variety of organizational formats, strategies, and issues, community-based mediating structures share a common attribute: a compelling vision that starts, sustains and drives them, a vision of new forms and amounts of social capital coupled with and an urgency to preserve a community or to meet a community need.

Community within the vision of these groups almost always extends beyond formal group members to encompass everyone living in a specific area or facing a specific problem. For example, the Appalachian Independence Center intended "to foster a community environment in which persons with disabilities can achieve their maximum level of independence." Safe-Space provided shelter for women and children threatened with physical harm and worked to reduce the threats of violence against women. In Safe-Space, the latter vision evolved from the first, which suggests that as a group pursues an initial vision, new, expanded, and related awareness may emerge.

Sometimes the initial vision is the community's basic survival. The Brumley Gap Concerned Citizens, for example, faced the literal submersion of their community to the water of a pumped-storage facility. The Bumpass Cove Citizens Group initially dealt with the presence of hazardous waste in their community. However, collaboration with agencies and experts outside the community often fosters the development of broader visions. For example, experts from neighboring and distant areas—Dick Austin, Catherine Fazzina, and Rees Shearer—are credited with expanding the political imagination of the Brumley Gap Concerned Citizen's members. The Highlander

Research and Education Center gets similar credit from the Bumpass Cove group members. Such "outside" assistance can help develop a wider vision of a local problem. Local residents in Brumley Gap linked their own local efforts with a vision of helping preserve other communities like their own from "progress" linked to changed patterns of energy use. In Bumpass Cove, local leaders envisioned "the removal of hazardous waste" and developed new visions of community health education and community development. The broad vision of the West Virginia Education Association went back to the demand for public education that was part of the historical origin of the state during the Civil War. Likewise, the history and success of organized labor in the state provided the WVEA a broad vision of its role for change. The Council of Senior West Virginians also took part in the past and current strength of unions in West Virginia. It also had the assistance of national groups as did the West Virginia Education Association and the Appalachian Independence Center. Ties to a national organization stimulate and renew a broad vision of a group's mission.

Sometimes the vision of the group expands with new membership. The Ohio Valley Environmental Coalition, for example, expanded the scope of its advocacy as the membership grew beyond its initial founders. At other times, the communities of a group will fashion its vision. Roadside Theater intended "to help strengthen cultural resources at home and in the communities it visits," a vision that echoed the mission of its parent community, Appalshop, which aims "to perpetuate and strengthen the Appalachian culture." To express this vision in action, Roadside Theater shared and incorporated the visions of its audiences, and members of the ever-changing community it served, to a greater degree than other community-based mediating structures.

Expanded visions of community take new cultural forms that may express familiar values in new ways. Songs spring up time and again to express anew a community experience, just as Florence Reece expressed hers. In Bumpass Cove, the song "I'm Afraid for the Children" expressed a common concern of residents. Written by Keith and Lori Talbot and students from the Appalachian Student Health Coalition, the song has accompanied reports on Bumpass Cove on national public radio and in film.

Way up in a mountain cove
Friends listen and beware
The wastes flowing from the landfill
Allows no peace for people there.

They're afraid for the children
And the poison in the land
And they're fearful for the future
But together took a stand.

The dump was filled with toxics
And used so carelessly
Now the mountain's seeping poison
But the land's still home to me.

To the people up in Bumpass Cove
The living has been grand
Clean waters and green mountains
Good music filled the land.

Then in came the garbage trucks
Filled the hollow to the brim
Now the people's getting sick
And the fish no longer swim.

And I'm standing with you neighbor
And we'll fight it if we can
I'm afraid for the children and the land.

Some visions of community, such as the Bumpass Cove song, emphasize organizing, and other less lyrical visions emphasize development. The Appalachian Ohio Public Interest Center embraced the goal of "[creating] jobs without harming opportunity for future generations, strengthening grassroots groups, and forming public policy which gets us closer to a sustainable lifestyle." The Appalachian Peoples Action Coalition sought to assist those with low incomes "to help people like themselves." Appalachian Communities for Children combined organizing and developing in a vision that involved using local resources to improve education and services for children and their families in Jackson and Clay Counties. ACEnet worked similarly on communitywide economic revitalization through strategies of economic and leadership development.

Vision statements place emphasis on the community of place, the community of need, or the community of response regardless of the issue. Clay Mountain Housing combined both place and need in its vision of improving housing for citizens of Clay County, West Virginia. The Federation of Appalachian Housing Enterprises kept a focus on housing needs over a broader area and group, that is, low-income families in the Central Appalachian region. The Council of Senior West Virginians cast its services statewide "to gather direct evidence on the needs of seniors and provide public education on the means of meeting them." The Dungannon Development Commission mentioned numerous issues "to improve community life in Dungannon and its greater area."

The nature of an organization affects its vision. Coalitions and organizations of large mediating structures are less likely to have a local, geographic focus than are place-based groups and services. For example, the Appalachian Alliance began through the efforts of a few organizational leaders with regional perspectives and a determination "to support individuals and communities working to gain democratic control over their lives, work places, and natural resources; to help build a unified voice in Appalachia; and to change public policy through direct action." The initial organizers of the Appalachian Alliance proceeded in the belief that community, state, and regional groups could forge a regional network that would link people and issues, develop leadership, and involve community people in planning for political, economic, and social change. The leaders of the organizations that began Southeast Women's Employment Coalition also thought regionally, aiming "to improve the quality of life for women and children in the Southeast." Marketing Appalachian Traditional Community Handcrafts began with "a dream of several church groups and Appalachian craft people who wanted to find a way to work together to develop a system for marketing their beautiful Appalachian crafts." Other organizations that are member-driven and specific to a local place express more immediate concerns. As we have seen, however, these immediate concerns may develop through expanded political imagination and other political dimensions into broader concerns that are still intrinsically linked locally.

Sometimes the vision of an organization depends on the specific needs of member organizations. The Southern Empowerment Project began with the vision "to recruit and train new community organizers," a need directly related to its members. However, its member groups also asked it "to serve as a forum for strengthening ties between the groups across geographical and racial barriers." This is an example of a vision that stretches its member groups, rather than merely meeting their immediate needs. Likewise, the West Virginia Primary Care Association envisioned both a narrow role related to its members' self-interest—"to protect the interest of rural primary care"—and a broader role that went back to the original vision of its members—"to ensure that there is access to the underserved, and to advocate for primary care in West Virginia."

The expressions of vision in theory and practice come from different parts of the organization. In general, responsibility for providing and maintaining the vision of the organization is shared, like other responsibilities, according to the pattern of representation and participation of the organization. The boards of mediating structures are accountable to and for their vision statements and are responsible for seeing that their practices measure up to or exceed their vision statements. The staff is responsible for maintaining the democratic process of an organization by involving its members in activities and decision making. The vision of the organization and responsibility for it reflect the organization's vision of the community it is working to create.

The Long Haul

Maintaining a community-based mediating structure requires considerable resources. Whether such organizations continue or not depends upon many factors, including of course their members' assessment of the need for them and the willingness of members to continue to contribute their time and energy as the principal resource of the group. In general, community-based mediating structures have the best chance of continuing when they address an issue with many facets that can be improved but not entirely resolved or eliminated. Children's poverty and educational needs, for example, continue year after year. This gives a mediating structure ongoing opportunities for successful initiatives and a continuing reason for its existence. On the other hand, some problems come to an end. The cancellation of a pumped-storage dam project removed the primary target of community resistance in Brumley Gap. Conversely, the danger of removing the toxic substances from Bumpass Cove eliminated the group's primary purpose. Thus, victory as well as defeat may convince community leaders and residents that they no longer need their organization.

The Transition to New Issues

Resources influence the ability and willingness of a community-based mediating structure to make a transition from an original purpose to subsequent ones. For example, the Appalachian Peoples Action Coalition began with a furniture store and then moved on to establish a court watch program and a women's support group. These subsequent issues were well within the capacity of the group's resources to address. Other groups made transitions from their initial issues because resources were available to do so. In some cases, resources for new issues lead groups in very new directions. The Southeast Women's Employment Collective, for example, initially brought together the heads of women's organizations to develop and disseminate executive skills. Research on the economic and labor conditions of women followed from that because of the availability of funds. Federal regulations that required federal contractors to use affirmative action in hiring provided SWEC a means to provide women with jobs in construction that were not available before.

Groups evolve also because their origins contain several different purposes that find expression at different times. Roadside Theater began with the mission "to find a theatrical form and dramatic content that made sense to the rural people who live in the Appalachian mountains of east Kentucky and southwest Virginia, a people for whom there was no written body of dramatic literature or tradition of attending the theater." Another initial issue entailed providing Appalshop with an outlet for members who wanted to work on theater rather than film, video, photos, or recordings. This latter issue led Roadside Theater to take its productions to other regions of the country and eventually to other countries. This change also meant developing community residencies and workshops for stays longer than a single performance. Gradually Roadside Theater, as a part of Appalshop, took on a life and a series of issues of its own.

Addressing a new issue may entail significant organizational change. The Federation of Appalachian Housing Enterprises took on new issues separate from those of its members. FAHE developed housing programs in the African American community of Shelbyville, Kentucky, which is outside of the Appalachian region, to replicate the Nehemiah Project in Brooklyn. Similarly, FAHE organized the Mount Sterling (Kentucky) Housing Corporation to rehabilitate a historic city block for units of housing for the elderly. These projects, completed by FAHE apart from its members, permitted FAHE a direct presence in other communities, along with the opportunity to generate income separate from its members.

Some mediating structures even have their origins in the transition of previous organizations. The Appalachian Independence Center began when leaders of Handicapped Unlimited pursued federal funding for centers to provide services to people with disabilities. The Western North Carolina Alliance began with leaders' response to information about the hazards of potential oil and gas drilling discussed in the land study of the Appalachian Alliance. MATCH's leader, Ben Poage, made a personal transition from work with the Appalachian Volunteers, an OEO-funded version of VISTA within Appalachia, to his subsequent work with MATCH.

Staff may also initiate attention and transition to new issues in a community-based mediating structure. The Appalachian Center for Economic Networks began by assisting the development of worker-owned enterprises; then moved into developing the flexible manufacturing network, training programs for manufacturing, and the creation of a business incubator; and eventually created a for-profit subsidiary, AD/AS. When churches proved to be too limited an outlet for marketing Appalachian arts and crafts, MATCH opened its own retail stores, a transition that expanded directly from the primary mission of finding markets for the arts and crafts of its members. This change in MATCH led to a new name couched within the same acronym: Marketing Appalachia Through the Church became Marketing Appalachia's Traditional Community Handcrafts. In a similar manner, when the Kentucky Fair Tax Coalition was successful in revising the tax laws on unmined minerals, the organization changed its name to Kentuckians For the Commonwealth. In both these cases, new issues and a new name indicated a transition made within the framework of the group's initial purposes, rather than away from them.

Transitions occur most often and most successfully when they represent a logical extension or systematic growth of the mediating structure's original, broad purpose or issue. The services of the Appalachian Independence Center grew to include peer counseling, living skills training, information and referral, community education, transportation, support groups, advocacy, and technical assistance—all of which evolved from the single purpose of providing services to people with disabilities. Similarly, the initial work of the Dungannon Development Corporation, actions to address the community's reaction to the local sewing factory's closure, grew to encompass broad action for community development, eventually taking the form of services in prenatal and infant health care, education, literacy, housing, library services, economic development of small businesses (such as a local laundromat), recreation for youth, and crisis intervention.

Another set of logical transitions arises from efforts to address other problems of the same people served by the mediating structures. The members of the Appalachian Ohio Public Interest Center moved their organization from initial concern over the impact of the budget changes of the early Reagan administration to focus on a wide range of specific issues dealing with the economy and the environment, including rural electrical service, logging, longwall mining, and rural regeneration. Appalachian Communities for Children moved from their success with Head Start to other educational issues related to the public schools. Parents of the children served, especially the mothers, then paid attention to their own educational needs. In response to those needs, ACC began adult education services. Eventually, these evolved again into family life issues of health, day care, teen issues, and prenatal and infant care.

In addition to this logical or natural growth, the complexity and persistence of the issues that start some community-based mediating structures assist in their continuation and transitions. The Forest Service's ongoing management of the national forest provided the Western North Carolina Alliance a constant source of issues concerning higher standards for environmental quality. Because of changes in state and federal regulations, the West Virginia Primary Care Association found constant renewal for its initial issue of technical assistance for and representation of community health centers.

People continually come to mediating structures in need of services because the fundamental issues of poverty, domestic violence, and other social capital deficits have not been resolved. Women continue to be battered, and consequently SafeSpace continues to provide shelter and hotline services for abused women and their families. It also continues the social change efforts that it took on in addition to the provision of services. It conducts public education, pursues new legislation, trains police and other professionals involved in domestic violence, and attempts to have others enforce existing laws and policies.

Success with old issues and the transitions to new issues bring new challenges. SafeSpace acquired state funds for its shelter and shelters in other parts of Tennessee, which freed up some staff and member time from fundraising for other activities. The success of the shelter and its other public programs brought SafeSpace credibility, which in turn meant more clients for its programs, along with invitations to participate in other networks.

Some transitions are thrust upon community-based mediating structures by the fortunes of other groups. The Appalachian Independence Center, for example, moved into a partial vacuum left in its area when the Easter Seals regional office moved 100 miles east to Roanoke. Some of the people who in the past had called Easter Seals for information and referrals began to use the Appalachian Independence Center for that purpose. Likewise, the Appalachian Alliance found support because another regionwide organization, the Council of the Southern Mountains, reached the end of its effective operation. In these instances, new or ongoing mediating structures continued services or networks that had been disrupted.

Different mediating structures handle the transition of success and the question of continuation differently. Most are encouraged to take on new issues. For example, the Ohio Valley Environmental Coalition moved from addressing one threat to environmental quality, the BASF Chemical proposal for a toxic waste incinerator, to focusing on other potential point sources of pollution planned by Ashland Oil and a paper/pulp manufacturer. Likewise, initial success encouraged OVEC to turn its hand to other issues of pollution. Members of Brumley Gap Concerned Citizens, on the other hand, retired the group after they succeeded in canceling the dam project. In order to make their case, they had mastered a number of issues related to energy use, such as demand size management and rate reform. Having made and won their case, however, they did not continue with the alliances they had joined and fostered. After fulfilling its original goal, BGCC was left with little consensus about addressing new issues and stayed together only long enough to transfer funds and some resources into a local volunteer fire department.

A victory over a particular and local issue poses only one obstacle in a transition to other issues. The members of the Bumpass Cove Citizens Group had partial success, managing to halt continued dumping of toxic materials. The area has not been cleaned up, however, and migration of toxic materials through underground water is still possible. Some citizens received financial payments that settled their claims and removed their reason for participating in BCCG. Other members became leaders in efforts to improve roads, address community health concerns, and correct lapses by the Tennessee Department of Health, efforts that met with little success. Broad issues may be beyond the ability of local groups such as the BCCG to address from their particular base.

On the other hand, broad issues proved beyond the ability of the Appalachian Alliance to address for the opposite reason: it lacked a particular base. Its broad purpose, to foster democratic processes and create a unified voice among community organizations to change public policy, transcended particular issues. Transitions in the issues to be addressed occurred as groups with new issues arrived into the fold of the Alliance. The broad purpose and regional scope of the Appalachian Alliance meant there would be an extensive catalog of issues that dwarfed the staff's capacity to address. These issues included unemployment and other labor issues, oil and gas drilling and development, tax policies on unmined minerals, toxic waste, water pollution, health care, strip mining, and nuclear power. It would seem that a reactive, all-inclusive approach to establishing issues and direction impedes transition or any action unless clear priorities are drawn.

In the case of several of the community-based mediating structures we investigated, transitions occurred as a result of the decision-making process within the organization. The West Virginia Education Association depended upon its field staff and Delegate Assembly to elicit and decide upon issues; it also remains reactive to the initiatives of the state legislature. The Council of Senior West Virginians undertook a poll of its membership every two years to determine what positions to advocate. Far less formally, the much smaller Appalachian Peoples Action Coalition made its transitions on the basis of its membership meetings, which were used to identify needs, opportunities, and projects for the group. Group members can end the activity of a mediating structure in a number of different ways. They may decide to make a transition to a dormant state, as the Appalachian Alliance did; to end the organization altogether, as the Brumley Gap Concerned Citizens did; or to face the inability to continue because of a lack of resources, the situation that faced the Southeast Women's Employment Coalition.

Changed Involvement of Group and Community Members

As issues change, and the organization makes transitions in its work, new issues and programs may require more extensive member participation. For example, the conduct of support groups requires regularly scheduled commitments of its members. When the Kentucky Small Farms Project began its home rehabilitation program, it introduced a sweat equity requirement, a change that was not welcomed by all. Some group members drop out of organizations because they cannot adapt to a given change. In other cases, members may leave out of frustration with new processes or an unwillingness to devote additional time and resources.

Some ideas for transitions and increased participation of members come from networks that organizations enter because of their development and transitions. The practice of sweat equity, for example, was widespread and disseminated within networks. Appalachian Communities for Children used sweat equity as a quid pro quo for scholarships for children provided by the Save the Children Federation. The Ohio Valley Environmental Coalition borrowed from the Kentuckians For the Commonwealth when it moved from a staff-led, advocacy style to an organizing style, in which the staff coordinated chapters. Likewise, after training from the Southern Empowerment Project, the Western North Carolina Alliance made efforts to involve its members more, with both staff and members shifting their efforts from networking with other organizations to internal matters of chapter growth, leadership development, and outreach to communities. These changes fostered more emphasis on social justice in the group's work. The Southern Empowerment Project improved the representation and participation of its target communities when it set term limits for board participation and began rotating board members.

Staff members play a crucial role in the involvement of organization and community members during transitions. As transitions occur, the staff may make an intentional or unintentional choice to involve members to a greater or lesser degree. The staff of Appalachian Communities for Children instituted the practice of calling on board members to report on the groups they represented, a form of participation that helps educate board members for additional participation.

The size of the staff has less to do with increased participation than with the relationships that the staff, the board, and the organization's members have to each other. Naturally, when there is no staff, all responsibility falls on members of the organization. The Appalachian Alliance began without a staff, but, like the Council of Senior West Virginians, it found that without some major issue that attracted and absorbed members, such as the land study, some staff were necessary to further develop the potential of the organization's members. In cases where members and board precede staff, organizations are more likely to remain driven by member boards assisted by support staff, as in the case of the Appalachian Peoples Action Coalition. An organization with a large staff, such as the West Virginia Education Association, may drift toward less member representation and participation unless explicit mechanisms are developed for encouraging them. Even then, annual meetings and delegate selection remain a necessary but not a sufficient condition for representation and participation. Successful staff and board members are deliberate about representation and participation, especially as the organization develops and makes transitions to new issues.

At times, in order to train members for increased participation, staff and members have to begin at a fundamental stage of development, by redressing pejorative stereotypes of the group's members. The Virginia Black Lung Association attempted to build leadership and group confidence by working on the self-confidence of individual members. Marilyn Carroll, a Virginia Black Lung Association staff member, recalled hearing members preface or follow their statements in meetings with the self-deprecating assertion, "I'm just a dumb coal-miner." The group addressed this low self-esteem by giving it serious eminence. One of the members moved that there be no dumb coal miners in the organization, and the motion was seconded and approved. Thereafter, by the group's criteria, members could not be dumb coal miners. Thus, the group's criteria were used deliberately to include and promote participation, rather than to deliberately or unintentionally exclude potential members and their participation.

Ironically, some community-based mediating structures may get started and continue because of what their members *don't know*. In Brumley Gap, for example, at least one person felt that it may have been relatively easy to begin the Brumley Gap Concerned Citizens precisely because many local residents were naïve about the enormity of the task of tackling a giant utility, that is, that the scope of the problem might have defeated people early on if they had realized it. Having a clear issue and target as they moved along assisted the group in finding the morale for a continued effort at a huge task. However, the lessons they acquired about the costs and efforts required to win a battle against a utility may very well have contributed to the group's leaders' later decisions to discontinue the group after the dam project was withdrawn.

When the staff of a mediating structure does most of the labor on new issues, formal members may decrease their participation. ACEnet, for example, moved from developing worker-owned cooperatives to a flexible manufacturing network largely through the energy and drive of its staff. Formal members decreased their participation, and the thrust of the organization became development and the implementation of good ideas, rather than organizing. As a group develops, elements of member representation and participation may remain, even if at lower levels. For example, Roadside Theater ran the risk of a minimally involved audience but found that its efforts to inform teachers at its performance sites and to gain their cooperation actually *fostered* the achievement of its primary goals of cultural expression. The theater's commitment to democratic processes manifested itself also in the equal division of duties and efforts among cast members, which helped to prevent the "star syndrome." The staff of the Appalachian Ohio Public Interest Center also moved deliberately in the direction of more representation and participation and spent much of its energy on increasing member involvement. Part of an expanded staff's role would seem to be membership development, specifically facilitating increased member participation.

Organizational conditions affect participation at the time of transitions. For example, Marketing Appalachia's Traditional Community Handcrafts found it difficult to involve its board members, who were spread over a geographic area from Alabama to Pennsylvania. Participation differed for groups depending upon their need for marketing assistance; those groups that had not developed a marketing strategy or that depended exclusively on MATCH participated more than other groups. Similarly, the levels of participation in membership meetings of the Clay Mountain Housing dropped off as CMH developed. Initially, the meetings gave people information about loans and other means of acquiring or improving housing. As this information became more generally known, members had less reason to attend the meetings. In addition, once CMH acquired office space, people had a place to come to or to call for the information that had originally been given out at the group's meetings. CMH also initiated outreach work that disseminated information and thereby further detracted from attendance at meetings. In the face of these changes, CMH shifted its primary activity from community organizing to community development and service. The varied activities of the Appalachian Independence Center led to that group's having members with both temporary and ongoing participation. For example, members who led or participated in support groups had a longer involvement than those who sought technical assistance for a specific goal, such as financing for a ramp or bathroom facility. Membership involvement evolves along with the activities and success of community-based mediating structure.

Tactics play a critical role in continued participation and in some cases present substantial transition issues in themselves. Invariably, for example, lawsuits bring about less participation than does organizing people for direct action. When about 2,500 residents near Ashland Oil's facility settled their claim with the company through legal action, the Ohio Valley Environmental Coalition lost a great deal of its potential membership. Likewise, once some members of the Bumpass Cove Citizens Group settled their grievances with the offending companies, they left the organization. Legal suits often mean having to forgo direct action in order to avoid compromising the group's legal position. This leaves members with less to do, and the group's momentum becomes dependent on court dockets, lawyers, and experts from outside of the community. Continued efforts in direct, organized, collective action for common benefit elicit different responses from members in light of the litigation, including "wait and see" postures. In situations like these, the staff has a key role in dealing with the changes in participation that court action brings about.

Changes and Continuity

Not all transitions come from positive, logical, and coordinated growth of purpose. Some arise from conflict over control within the organization and the conduct of its affairs. The Council of Senior West Virginians formed a related group, the Coalition on Legislation for the Elderly, to devote attention primarily to legislation that impacted the elderly and to work with other public interest groups, such as Citizen Action. Relations between the two organizations deteriorated as leaders in the groups clashed over styles of administration and personality. Similarly, the West Virginia Primary Care Association began as the West Virginia Association of Community Health Centers, a breakaway group from a preceding organization, the West Virginia Primary Care Study Group. The groups remained separate for ten years until they merged in their current association.

The tactics and nature of other groups may raise issues of continuity and transition within and for a mediating structure. The Brumley Gap Concerned Citizens certainly faced the issue of complexity and longevity as their battle with the Appalachian Power Company dragged on. The Bumpass Cove Citizens Group faced even more discouragement. The Highlander Center's involvement in Bumpass Cove tarnished some leaders of the group with the same red-baiting that had been used against Martin Luther King Jr. twenty years before. The BCCG had developed quickly in a single year, with several outside sources in addition to Highlander. Though some of these other organizations, including the Center for Health Services at Vanderbilt University, were also implicated in this "red scare," the main alleged communist tie went to Highlander. These charges undermined the confidence of individual members and divided the group, the community, and even the families at Bumpass Cove.

Gail Story, one of BCCG's new leaders with Highlander ties, recalled her fear about these charges of communism hurled at her:

> The group [making the charges] was made up of two churches. It is real religious and strong here, so if you started calling the main workers in this group communist, that's the scariest thing on earth. This is the Bible Belt. This is mountain people. Frankly, it scared me to death, and I was the one who was supposed to be communist! It did. That was the scariest, most insulting thing that I ever had happen to me in my life. I didn't know who to fight against because everybody was calling us that and saying that . . . I was accused of infiltrating the PTA!

Story's friend, Linda Walls, found the communist scare separated her from her own mother. "I couldn't even go visit my Mama because they considered themselves our enemies. They was there all the time, two or three of them ganged up in Mom's yard all of the time." Few instances of participation in community-based mediating structures test the integrity of a member as severely as the events at Bumpass Cove. Some do, however. Organizing a relatively powerless group to redress an overt wrong may bring serious reprisals. This solidifies the resolve of some group members and dissipates the resolve of others.

Staffing problems, including turnover, may also challenge the continuity of mediating structures. The Council of Senior West Virginians lost funds and staff in 1992, but was able to keep a minimal program going. The Appalachian Ohio Public Interest Center faced a similar situation in the mid-1980s. AOPIC had rapid growth, but a lack of board oversight and an overmatched, small staff soon brought the group close to an end. The staff dwindled to one person. One founding member of AOPIC recalled how the one-person staff became

> the director, the organizer, the janitor. He was everything and he was going crazy. . . . He was trying an impossible task. He was just digging himself in deeper and deeper. No one thought about keeping track of whether or not there were canceled checks in the box, whether or not there were records of who gave money, whether or not there were mailing lists, or whether or not someone was going to answer the phone. No one cared about that. No one paid attention to that for a while, and the board, as happens with volunteer board members, they weren't keeping real notice of it. . . . That's about three major factors that can pretty well damn near kill an organization: an inactive board, no leadership staff-wise, and no order to your organization.

AOPIC survived this crisis in continuity because a founding member went back to basics and conducted four day-long membership meetings to plan the organization's future and its conduct during the crisis.

Success, as well as shortcomings, may also present substantial challenges to the continuity of a mediating structure, just as it provides problems for transition on issues. Appalachian Communities for Children provided a model for the Family Resource Centers of the Kentucky Education Reform Act. Eventually, these centers presented the possibility of competing services or a loss of control for ACC over programs it had begun. Likewise, success in finding funding may result in fundamental changes in the organization's program when the funding source changes its policies. For example, welfare reform had a major impact on the adult education programs of ACC. Students are now required to participate for a longer amount of time, a change from the voluntary program that ACC had conducted. As the program director explained:

> It used to be that all of our students were volunteers, but now a number of our students are mandated to take part in welfare reform, and we have

very little control over who gets in those slots—the JOBS program. Students in the JOBS program are mandated to go to school twenty hours a week, but the welfare office assigns those slots and then when one of those slots turns over, like when someone gets their GED, they can take any of our students out of any other slot and put them in those slots. A number of our students that might have chosen to be in other programs and might have been going to school like six hours a week can at any point be pulled into one of those twenty-hour slots. Very few people volunteer for those twenty-hour slots. It used to be that we ran one of the only programs in Kentucky where all of our students were volunteers. Now we don't do that. We are funded to teach those JOBS slots.

Problems of continuation for community-based mediating structures may come also from successful pursuit of their fundamental purpose. The Appalachian Alliance illustrates this particularly well. It brought in staff members who helped begin new community groups, such as the Kentucky Fair Tax Coalition. When an Alliance staff member left to join one of the organizations that the Alliance had started, leadership and talent went away from the Alliance and into these new organizations. This form of success meant staff turnover and increased and improved competition for funding resources. Likewise, when Marketing Appalachian Traditional Community Handcrafts helped revive Olde Towne Berea as a retail outlet for arts and crafts, it established its own competition.

Changes in their institutional environment may foster changes in mediating structures and create challenges for their continuity. The Council of Senior West Virginians, for example, has had different relationships with the staff of the state's Commission on Aging. On one hand, it worked through the state's senior centers throughout the state; on the other hand, it sued the commission over the closed-door procedure used in deciding to reduce the number of Area Agencies on Aging around the state from nine to four. The Dungannon Development Corporation has mitigated the consequences of changes in its institutional environment by filling it with numerous institutions related to its large number of programs. No set of institutions affects mediating structures so regularly and crucially as do funding sources, as the next chapter explains.

Leadership and Effort for Community

Someone has to work to create and maintain mediating structures; they do not develop spontaneously or continue effortlessly. Like all organizations, mediating structures have explicit human origins and patterns of development. At all stages of its development, a mediating structure promotes the democratic prospect successfully only if it involves the people within it and those whom it intends to serve. Members of these groups have to have some sense of ownership, some personal involvement with it, a common vision of a community-in-the-making, and the energy to continue an organization when resources dwindle and difficulties increase.

These matters of transition indicate the hard work required to create and renew the community that is the vision of mediating structures. They hint at the management abilities that seem mundane in light of the glimmer of the democratic prospect. Those mundane management matters are what make or break mediating structures, just as they make or break other forms of organizations. It is to those matters that we now turn.

CHAPTER 8

Management Matters

Just as mediating structures do not spring up and continue merely because there are human needs to address, neither do such groups have sufficient efficiency and accountability merely because their causes are just and their issues pressing. Efficient and accountable management within mediating structures develops from intentionally developed practices, just as mediating structures develop the democratic prospect by deliberate acts to forge and fashion community. This chapter examines some of the practices of efficient and accountable management and describes how mediating structures resemble other organizations in terms of their life cycles and transitions. It also examines the role of coalitions, other organizations, and funding sources in the development and vitality of mediating structures.

Efficient and Accountable Organizations with Just Causes

The glimmer of the democratic prospect may attract many people to the grassroots, but many mundane matters of management lie there. These matters are absolutely necessary for the continuation of the mediating structure, yet they lack the glamour and excitement of other aspects of the work. In its 1992 analysis of twenty-five years of community change, the Center for Community Change reported having seen countless organizations fail because they neglected to manage and administer themselves effectively (CCC 1992: 67). Poor oversight and management of finances and other resources, such as staff time, by staff or board members may jeopardize the efficiency and effectiveness of staff and programs and damage the credibility of the organization's work. As the CCC observed, it is much more stimulating to plan a demonstration than to pay payroll taxes, report publicly on the group's work, keep the books up to date, or research funding sources, but these things must be done as well (CCC 1992: 67)

Dealing with Management Problems of Continuity

Management problems seem fewest among those mediating structures that have few staff members, specific and traditional roles for them, or in which staff functions are conducted entirely by unpaid members. Only one of the community-based mediating structures we studied, the Appalachian Peoples Action Committee, reported having no management problems. This group had a continuum of volunteer staff and board members who both ran the used furniture store and undertook other programs for APAC. However, this minimal staffing pattern presents problems of its own. Some work does not get done because the low income of member-staff members often presents challenges (a car in need of repair) or opportunities (temporary paid work) that interfere with or take precedence over voluntary work. Having few staff members may diminish management problems, but it also diminishes the capacity of a group to work effectively for broad and substantial change.

Member-run groups present another management problem—a seeming inability to prioritize and act on an agenda. For example, a coalition, such as the Appalachian Alliance, has the task of establishing, prioritizing, and acting on an agenda formed by its member groups. The Alliance demonstrated the strength of openness to a wide range of issues but the inability to choose and act among them.

The management problem of handling a transition from one issue and set of tactics to another affects local, member-run community-based mediating structures as well as coalitions like the Appalachian Alliance. The Bumpass Cove residents, for example, had cohesion in their efforts to stop dumping, especially after heavy rains and swollen creeks dislodged barrels and pointed out the danger that resided near their homes. Once they succeeded in their protest, however, divisiveness replaced unity. The Bumpass Cove Citizens Group emerged as a vehicle for managing these divisions, but it never achieved the community cohesiveness of the former protests. The transition of issues and related tactics proved too difficult for BCCG to manage.

The presence of staff greatly assists mediating structures in managing the transition from one issue to another, but not without raising its own management issues for the organization. For example, in the Appalachian Center for Economic Networks (ACEnet), the switch from worker-owned cooperatives to flexible manufacturing networks caused differences among board members and the staff. Staff persistence and willingness to follow through on this change greatly affected the outcome. Dissenting board members, however, withdrew their participation. Likewise, when a husband-and-wife team took over the leadership of the Kentucky Small Farms Project, they added committees to deal with housing renovations, clothing, and furniture. These committees expanded the group's activities beyond the initial and primary issues of animal management, but the group's focus remained related to the original issue of hunger in Breathitt County. Conflicts occurred due to these changes, and some co-ops quit in protest and frustration. As we shall see, transitions such as these are a normal part of any mediating structure's development. Just as normal are the internal and external conflicts that accompany them, whether in staff-led or member-led organizations.

If continuing mediating structures presents a problem, so does ending them. The Appalachian Alliance's board declared the Alliance "dormant." Brumley Gap Concerned Citizens encountered their most difficult problems after they successfully opposed plans to flood their homes. The end of a mediating structure may be marked by reluctance to continue conflict or to expend the necessary energy to manage affairs well.

Management and Sweat Equity

Whether member staff or hired staff, people who work with mediating structures provide them sweat equity. Anne Leibig, a central actor in the early developments at Dungannon, Virginia, refers to this role as that of the "psychic guarantor." People who take on this role worry about the organization and its work and invest a portion of themselves as collateral for the community-based mediating structure. They provide the rational but non-instrumental action on behalf of community that Hirschman describes (see Chapter 2). Beginning with few resources, someone or some group must create the initial equity of the organization through their own labor. Dianne Levy explained that process in her account of the founding of SafeSpace. The staff went far beyond their job descriptions, finding motivation for extraordinary efforts in the issues and dramatic human need for physical safety that SafeSpace addressed. As organizations go through transitions, someone or some group once again provides more time and effort than an organization can reimburse. The accounts of Appalachian Communities for Economic Networks and the Appalachian Ohio Public Interest Center illustrate the continuing demand for sweat equity in mediating structures. Sweat equity exacts a great deal of work and effort from those who provide it. Nancy Robinson implied some of the personal costs those development efforts in Dungannon required of her. Lee McDaniel of Brumley Gap put it in the simpler terms of losing time for a boyfriend.

Often, the staff of one community-based mediating structure has to put sweat equity into coalitions of other similar organizations. The Southeast Women's Employment Coalition and the Appalachian Alliance both depended on the staff and board members of other groups for their membership and participation. This dependency raised problems of representation and participation among members of the groups supporting SWEC and the Alliance, because they did not feel the same degree of community membership in those two organizations as they did in their own.

The degree of sweat equity placed in another organization may present other tensions between staff and board members or the general membership. The latter may see staff time spent in other organizations, even coalitions that support the work of the group, as time taken away from the matters and management of their own group. This is especially true in instances where there are well-developed mechanisms of staff accountability to a board. Policy analysts and economists call such work an opportunity cost. The staff must make choices about the benefits to their organization from working in other groups. In general, staff members have three choices regarding the initiatives of others: support, participate, or lead. In some cases, support may mean merely a letterhead affiliation. Participation entails regular attendance at meetings and other contributions. Leadership entails taking some program responsibility for the other organization or for its genesis. The costs of the sweat equity that an organization's staff invests in other organizations may appear excessive or unnecessary to board members and other members of the organization. These different perceptions of the value of sweat equity may contribute other tensions within a community-based mediating structure.

The sweat equity that staff members invest in other organizations may well be worth the time and effort entailed. The Federation of Appalachian Housing Enterprises kept its member organizations well informed about policy and funding opportunities, which directly affected their work. Working with other organizations creates the dense networks that Robert Putnam touts (see Chapter 2) and permits ideas to travel.

Although Putnam makes clear that moral resources come from such networks, he does not explain the sweat equity that goes into establishing and maintaining them. Sweat equity also goes into coalitions that may also contribute to the success of local efforts by the networks they assemble. Coalitions also help see to it that stories of local successes travel to other places, support the democratic prospect, and overcome the particularity of any one mediating structure and its success.

Whatever their benefits and pitfalls, sweat equity and related opportunity costs are inevitable parts of any successful group's development. The success of an organization, such as that of Clay Mountain Housing, brings with it invitations to join both established groups and new ones. One staff member of Clay Mountain Housing sat on the board of West Virginia Community Works. The West Virginia Primary Care Association evolved from the efforts of a staff person to merge two other groups. In addition, staff members who join a new community-based mediating structure may have loose ends and work to conclude at an organization they left. This happens inevitably when the head of a coalition also remains in charge of a member group. Whatever its form, work with other groups suggests that social capital begins with the investment of sweat equity.

Staffing and Management

Staffs of community-based mediating structures may expand because of the severity and complexity of the issues they address. When the Southeast Women's Employment Coalition ran ads in the *Louisville Courier-Journal* and other newspapers of the region inviting inquiries from women interested in well-paying, nontraditional jobs, SWEC staff could not handle the number of women who were calling and expecting job placement. Follow-up proved difficult for the one person who was responsible for the program. Some community-based mediating structures respond to an overwhelming need by moving to the next level of organization. For example, the Appalachian Independence Center evolved from a voluntary group called Handicapped Unlimited, which provided support for its members but could not deal adequately with their personal problems or problems of transportation or access to buildings. The full-time staff of Appalachian Independence Center helped address problems that Handicapped Unlimited could not.

Management problems of community-based mediating structures increase as their staff grows. Getting and keeping good employees present obstacles, especially for an organization like the Appalachian Independence Center, which attempts to recruit from among its members. This limits the pool of potential applicants and exacerbates the ordinary disadvantages of community-based mediating structures, which include that they ordinarily offer lower pay than other organizations, lower benefits (if any), more part-time work, jobs with limited duration, and more uncertainty about continued funding for staff positions. In the face of these limits and uncertainties, community-based mediating structures often offer jobs with a wide range of responsibilities and other unique features that attract some and repel others. For example, Marketing Appalachian Traditional Community Handcrafts had difficulty hiring store managers who were also interested in scouring the countryside searching for artists and crafts people. The emphasis on democratic process, procedures, and informal roles did not suit other staff members who left.

Underqualified staff may be overwhelmed with the ordinary problems of running an organization, which include financial development and management. In at least two instances, our community-based mediating structures had to fire staff members who could not handle the administrative work of the organization. Events such as this may exacerbate the ordinary problem of staff turnover and bring the organization to an end if board members or others cannot find the time, effort, and emotional energy to find new and competent staff. Yet even an ordinary turnover of staff can be traumatic. In one instance, the entire staff left in a short time, and the one new staff person who came in had little background in the issues of the organization. Sometimes the transition of staff may benefit the group. After the steering committee of AOPIC lost a staff person, the steering committee took a more active role in the organization and placed more control in the members' hands.

In some cases, community-based mediating structures, like all other organizations, make a poor selection in staff. Their agenda of personal and political transformation encourages staff and board members to sometimes look past a lack of qualifications and hire a person whom they hope will grow into the job. Chris Weiss, a founding member of Southeast Women's Employment Coalition, recalled two instances of poor but political hiring.

> In the beginning the founders lacked administrative skills. Betty Jean Hall [Coal Employment Project director] confesses to hiring a secretary who had the correct political line but could not type; and I admit to hiring a newsletter editor who could not write, for the same reason. Each organization had to struggle through the learning phase of its founder, who knew about organizing but not about personnel policies. The lack of administrative interest and know-how eventually influenced the decision of

each of the founding executive directors to turn over the leadership of her organization to new talent. (Weiss 1993: 159)

Financial Management

Without question, financial management—including securing sufficient funding—provides mediating structures the greatest management challenge. A large organization, such as the West Virginia Education Association, may be able to handle unexpected expenses, such as replacing a heating system, by moving funds for other important but less pressing purposes to meet exigencies. Other crises occur because of changes in funding amounts and sources. Like many of our mediating structures, the Southeast Women's Employment Coalition had management problems related to funding cuts. The vagaries of funding may require staff to switch from one set of duties to another or to take on a new set of duties, for which there is funding, in addition to their regular duties, for which funding has expired. A sudden infusion of funds may also disrupt an organization that had managed on the sweat equity of its members and had not developed decision-making methods for the budgeting, allocation, and administration of funds. Early rifts among the Bumpass Cove residents occurred with the infusion of funds and support from outside. Occasionally, financial shortfalls can provide moments of almost transcendental, unselfish cooperation, as for example, when three community-based mediating structures in Athens, Ohio, cooperated in a proposal and then allocated the requested funds according to the needs of the participants.

The vast majority of community-based mediating structures put mechanisms or staff in place to assure the sound management of resources. Larger organizations may have a full-time financial manager and a part-time bookkeeper. Growth may require more and more financial management resources, including computer spreadsheet programs, as at Appalachian Communities for Children, and central cash flow systems, as at Appalshop, the parent organization of Roadside Theater. Smaller organizations may have a part-time or volunteer bookkeeper, but the burden of overall financial management usually falls upon the shoulders of another staff member, the director, or an administrative assistant. Organizations with large budgets often also arrange for externally conducted financial audits. Whatever the size of the organization and whatever the initial skills of the staff, almost all community-based mediating structures use technical assistance to establish financial management policies or to modify them in light of new funding sources or changed policies of the same ones. Some organizations rely on national organizations that do this. In other cases, one group borrows the expertise it needs from another local group. Whether they borrow policies or develop them locally or externally, community-based mediating structures face a wide range of financial and other management issues that are often unnoticed or underestimated.

Managing the Life Cycle of Mediating Structures

The development and loss of management resources are part of the organizational development of mediating structures. This development has discernible phases, which parallel the stages of human development. In any theory of development, human or organizational, the move from one stage to another entails a transition that may cause conflict as part of change. Organizational transition comes from the inevitable changes within institutional or internal environments of groups. Sometimes the changes are more than an organization can deal with. Some of our twenty-three community-based mediating structures have ceased operations. Five of the organizations folded before this study began. One of them, the Kentucky Small Farms Project, has folded since then. Sometimes mediating structures develop undemocratic styles in response to change. Michels's iron law of oligarchy (Michels 1958 [1915]) makes its appearance even at the grassroots. Analysts at the Center for Community Change saw change take its toll so often that they lamented, "Too few of the groups we worked with 20 years ago are either still alive or doing excellent work" (CCC 1992: 68). Bowing to what seems inevitable, the CCC accepted that there is a life cycle for many organizations; some organizations cease to operate, and others lose their vitality.

Most of our twenty-three community-based mediating structures have continued their work and maintain their vitality. Part of their vitality comes from good management during the transitions of organizational development.

Borrowing from a study of corporate organizations, the Management Assistance Group (MAG) devised a four-stage theory of development of nonprofit organizations (Matthieson 1984: 334–35). Phase I entails intense creativity and commitment. The management focus in this stage is the "cause," and the rewards for the large amounts of sweat equity in this phase come in the personal satisfaction derived from pursuit of the initial, compelling mission and meaning of the organization. In this phase, flexibility characterizes the management style, and roles are informal. After a time, the need for stronger management arises, and this challenges the leadership to take on management roles or to give some forms of control to other staff members with greater management skills.

Phase II brings on written and standardized procedures and a greater division of labor, all designed to help the group reach a higher level of efficiency. Communication and management become more formal and direct. This phase challenges members and staff because it suggests to them less ownership of the group. They may feel restricted in their new, formally defined, less flexible roles.

Phase III is marked by expansion of the organization's programs or extension into new communities. Management becomes more decentralized as top-level staff members assume primary responsibility for preventing problems or intervening when problems occur. The increased influence of staff over responsibilities delegated to them introduces the risk of project goals being emphasized over overall organizational goals; the forest is lost to the sight of the trees. Internal communication and coordination present challenges to the organization. Leadership faces the challenge of renewing an overall sense of direction for the organization. The challenges of phase III include formal and time-consuming planning to give the organization greater coherence, consolidation, and coordination.

During phase IV, top staff members implement new reporting procedures to achieve new levels of coordination. Emphasis on coordination through planning can make a crisis of red tape, and there is the danger that process may take precedence over purpose. The Center for Community Change described this crisis in terms of institutionalization or bureaucratization, an unwillingness to change, and a focus on survival.

Applying these phases and their characteristics to community-based mediating structures provides several difficulties. Most vibrant community-based mediating structures, regardless of what phase they are in, maintain the phase I characteristics of emphasis on mission, a style of frequent and informal communication, and rewards from mission and meaning. Groups may take some characteristics from their early development into new phases, much as adults retain characteristics from their childhood and adolescence. Transitions typically are not marked by a total change and a distinct set of characteristics from one phase or another but rather by new emphasis on practices that were absent or less developed before. In addition, it is easier to identify the phase of each group in terms of its positive characteristics rather than by the crisis that supposedly identifies the transition to that phase. Some of our groups made relatively crisis-free transitions, simply evolving through the gradual development of skills among staff and members.

Despite these difficulties in applying MAG's framework of organizational development, it helps to identify management issues that face community-based mediating structures and the hard work entailed in building an effective, efficient, and accountable group. The Bumpass Cove Citizens Group probably best portrays the "crisis in leadership" described by the Management Assistance Group. This group had an initial period of intense creativity and commitment in its protest of local toxic material dumping; its direct action halted new dumping and induced a settlement. Later, BCCG had an equally intense leadership crisis over a red scare, the inadequacy of its management structure for handling new resources, and the inability to achieve its original mission—the removal of the toxic substances.

Many times, group members have no intention of developing and evolving into other phases. The Brumley Gap Concerned Citizens spent its time, intense creativity, and commitment to save their valley from a dam project of Appalachian Power. The crisis of leadership for this group boiled down to a group decision as to whether or not to continue their battle against utility company policies after their initial victory. The group decided not to do so. The development of the Southern Empowerment Project, which trains staff and board members for community-based organizations, also illustrates a deliberate choice about its evolution. It had a crisis of leadership when the board decided to rotate its membership, causing many of the original members to face leaving the board. This crisis meant integrating people who had not been part of the founding of SEP and who had little knowledge of its history. Apart from this organizational change, however, SEP had few characteristics of more formal communication (phase II), although it has expanded its program and entered new areas (phase III). SEP intended to maintain the elements of commitment and creativity of phase I even as other changes brought on new management challenges.

Other organizations move from their initial forms of management simply because of the success they have. For example, the technical nature of eligibility for housing loans and the success Clay Mountain Housing has had in enrolling and housing people meant that it had less group participation and more of the characteristics of phase II management in its later operations. The acquisition of a permanent office helped change the emphasis of the group from fieldwork to office work. The founding leaders of Clay Mountain Housing changed their own roles in order to deal with the increased administrative work their success had generated, hiring new staff through VISTA to continue some of the outreach-oriented fieldwork that they had formerly performed themselves. Similarly, because of its success in supporting victims, the Virginia Black Lung Association expanded its purpose from victim support to legislative advocacy.

The Ohio Valley Environmental Coalition represents the clearest transition from phase I to phase II. The OVEC transition included shifts from an all-volunteer staff to a paid one and from the advocacy and protest of a few individuals to the establishment of chapters focused on advocacy and protest. Consequently, it would seem that a change in management style succeeds when it comes as an appropriate response to increased size and expanded or changed activities.

Evolution may take reverse as well as forward direction. For example, the Council of Senior West Virginians experienced two events that moved it from phase II back to phase I. The split with its daughter organization, the Coalition on Legislation for the Elderly, and a 100 percent turnover in staff led to an organizational crisis that required intense creativity and commitment just to keep the organization going. CSWV preserved the informal, mission-driven management style of phase I within phase II to recreate itself when it had to do so.

Most of our community-based mediating structures have expanded rather than contracted their programs and have entered into new issues or new geographic areas with their work, all actions characteristic of phase III. For Appalachian Communities for Children, a program for low-income families in Eastern Kentucky, this change was marked by the expansion from one county to another. ACC managed this transition without crisis because of the ability of its leaders to take on new roles while sharing power with an expanding staff and because its members maintained the informal and frequent communication style of phase I. On the other hand, Appalachian Communities for Economic Networks moved to phase III by using a more formal communication style. After the organizational strife entailed in moving from worker-owned networks to flexible manufacturing networks, the staff of this economic development effort in southeastern Ohio emerged with greater autonomy and influence within the organization. When SafeSpace, a domestic violence prevention program, expanded its programs to include a nonviolence curriculum in the schools and training of law enforcement officers and officials, the founder and leader of Safe-Space spared the group conflict by sharing power with new staff and supporting expanded roles for board members. She thereby averted the risks inherent in the transitions from phase I to II and from II to III.

New arrangements for sharing power and coordinating efforts among staff, board, and members constitute parts of the effective management of organizational transitions into phase III. The merger with another primary health care group marked a major transition for the West Virginia Primary Care Association. Ironically, this merger represented another stage in a crisis of leadership that led some members of the Primary Care Study Group to split off and start the West Virginia Association of Community Health Centers. The eventual merger of these two groups meant a move into phase III with an expansion of programs and a new issue area—nonfederally funded programs.

The Appalachian Peoples Action Coalition defies categorization by phases. Clearly, when it began the used furniture store, APAC took on formal roles for staff and a need for efficiency. In this sense, elements of phase II and III are very visible. On the other hand, it maintained its original focus during monthly membership meetings and in support groups it sponsored. Continuity of leadership (it had the same president for six years) and the tight integration of staff and board has spared it the risks of autonomous roles developing that hinder coordination.

The Appalachian Independence Center, a program serving persons with disabilities in southwestern Virginia, had job descriptions, differentiation of staff roles, and movement into new programs—all of which are elements of phases II and III. The action of the Appalachian Independence Center to fire a staff person implied the development and enforcement of employee evaluation standards. As in some of our other mediating structures, the organizational development of the Appalachian Independence Center eventually included an effort to instill in its members and other people with disabilities some of the intensity of its initial stages, through its program to develop leaders through ACTION (Advocates Committee to Independence and Opportunities Now).

The transition into any new organizational phase sometimes takes its toll. We have examined organizations that managed changes with some degree of success. Others failed or declined to try. The Appalachian Alliance, for example, foundered in part on a crisis in control, demonstrated by its inability to form a cohesive new project after the completion of its study of land ownership in Appalachia. Hiring a director who became ill exacerbated the risks to the Alliance, especially because it faced a crisis of member autonomy and competition among its members and between it and some of its member groups. The members of the Alliance preferred its openness and informality to efficiency and efficacy. The delegation of authority was so complete that the Alliance had difficulty in finding and keeping direction. In the face of these problems, members asked the leadership explicitly to provide greater coordination and a renewed sense of overall direction. When the Alliance could not achieve these goals, its members put it to rest.

Marketing Appalachian Traditional Community Handcrafts also succumbed to some of the risks of transitions. Its success required moving from phase I to phase III, almost skipping phase II. It began retail outlets and offered long-term planning services for its members, both typically phase III and phase IV functions. From the beginning, however, MATCH faced a crisis of control. It simply could not both master market forces and the response of its members to the demands that market forces made. Member craftspeople had a wide choice of retail outlets, even if none of them were satisfactory. Thus, MATCH had to compete for its members' allegiance while simultaneously competing for a niche in a crowded market; effectively, it competed for both supply and demand. Communication between and coordination of producers, consumers, and sales outlets were not strong enough to allow MATCH to survive the transitions from phase I to phase III.

A few of our groups have made it to phase IV. "Time-consuming planning procedures to provide the organization with greater coherence, consolidation, and coordination" are a hallmark of phase IV and of the work of the Federation of Appalachian Housing Enterprises. The autonomy of its member groups as well as the skills of the leaders of FAHE have helped it avert the red-tape crisis that often characterizes phase IV. The size of the West Virginia Education Association, 17,000 members, requires the administrative characteristics of a phase IV group, which also placed it at inherent risk for the paralysis of institutionalization that the Center for Community Change described. The statewide teachers' strike that it led rekindled the intense creativity and commitment typical of phase I organizations and thereby averted some of the risks of phase IV.

New programs may help an established organization avert the risks of institutionalization by restoring elements of an earlier, goal-centered phase of development. Appalshop, for example, the home and origin of Roadside Theater, entered into a new program (phase III) after being ensconced in phase IV because of its longevity and success with previous programs. Roadside Theater itself maintains predominant characteristics of phases I and II. FAHE, despite its very advanced organizational development, also reverted to earlier phases when it began two programs separately from its members. Implementing programs within the organization that are at earlier stages of development may help a well-developed organization avert risks of phase IV bureaucratization, an unwillingness to change, and a focus on survival.

The analytical framework of the Management Assistance Group rounds out the insight of the Center for Community Change that grassroots groups have a life cycle. There are phases in the development of organizations, and there are risks entailed in the transition from one phase to another. Generally, the normal consequences of continued operation and success will bring the challenges of adding or changing staff, initiating new programs, extending current programs, and other challenges that invite organizations to formalize staff roles and further develop other aspects of its management abilities. The possibility that these challenges will provoke crisis is real, yet turmoil may be creative and constructive, as many of our groups have showed.

Leadership skill, tackling new tasks, and delegation and decentralization of old tasks seem key elements in moving successfully through the life cycle phases of an organization and the conflicts entailed in those transitions. Our successful groups also demonstrated the capacity to retain valuable elements of earlier phases of development as they evolved. In some instances, later stages of development provide the capacity to try deliberate efforts to regain the energy and personal transformation found in the initial stages of the organization. The ACTION program of the Appalachian Independence Center exemplified efforts at leadership development and member involvement that come late in an organization's development yet take it back to its origins. The experience of our groups suggests that the life cycle of organizations does not always result in termination of the vitality or operation of a group. Groups may revitalize themselves through the intentional effort to preserve elements of their creative, committed, and mission-driven initial phase of development.

A group's sense of longevity affects its development and its way of managing crisis in the phases of its development cycle. Some groups may not view longevity as a goal and have only short-term, limited goals, such as stopping a dam or toxic dumping in their community. For groups that see beyond one achievable goal, such as the Appalachian Ohio Public Interest Center, the ability to survive a management crisis imparts optimism for the future. New programs also bring optimism about the continuation of an organization, especially when those programs entail physical space and monetary investment, such as the used furniture store of the Appalachian Peoples Action Coalition. Sometimes a crisis entails losing or dismissing staff and reassigning responsibility to members of the group, as happened in the Western North Carolina Alliance. Within those events, there are times when the future of the organization may seem tenuous. Not all of the organizations survive, as seen in the case of the Appalachian Alliance.

Other unique elements of a program may affect its sense of longevity. The Federation of Appalachian Housing Enterprises finances mortgages for twenty years and longer, which expands its time horizon. The 125-year history of the West Virginia Education Association, the large size of its member base, and the permanence of public schools give it optimism for longevity. Groups with twenty or more years of operation share the same optimism, which is rooted in a sense of their successful past.

Most often, the expressed optimism about longevity has roots in a determination to address a problem that will not go away. The need to address the problems of inadequate housing, violence, poverty, environmental degradation, serving those with disabilities, and meeting gaps in healthy child development—all of which are the products of deficits of social capital—are so great that they temper the resolve of some leaders. A focus on the ongoing problem that the group addresses may renew a sense of mission and meaning. This permits a sustained level of intensity that best guarantees longevity and avoidance of the risks of institutionalization and other risks in the transitions and stages of organizational development.

Ideas Need to Travel at the Grassroots

Some advocates of the democratic prospect view community-based mediating structures suspiciously partially because of their particularity (Barber 1984: 235; Berry, Portney, and Thomson 1993: 213). The specific leadership, culture, issues, history, and unfolding events may make one community's lessons inapplicable to another. Nonetheless, members of a mediating structure acquire a great deal when they learn about the lessons of similar groups. They are then in a position to adopt, adapt, or ignore those lessons, which include how to handle management issues.

Finding time and the resources to spend in settings where one can share and acquire lessons of local change efforts presents a management issue in itself. Many factors militate against sharing ideas at the grassroots and thus foster particularity. For example, some community-based mediating structures may work in areas far from media markets and interstate highways. They are not isolated, but they do not have ready access to other organizations like their own unless they create or join networks and actively seek out other groups. Likewise, as much as we extol the efforts of community-based mediating structures, most of their histories do not find their way into formal accounts that are widely disseminated. Consequently, local leaders find themselves cut off from the experience of others like themselves. Sometimes local leaders lack an awareness of even their own history. The

Dungannon Development Corporation deliberately remedied this by making local history one of its first projects. Sharing ideas helps members of different groups find the common elements in their groups' experiences, thereby reducing their particularity, and increases the potential for good management by increasing the ideas and experiences upon which all groups can draw and build.

Gary Delgado points out the important role that training intermediaries play in helping ideas to travel. Delgado worked with and studied ACORN (Association of Community Organizations for Reform Now), a successful, multistate, multi-issues grassroots organization. He surveyed community organizing in the 1990s (Delgado 1993) and found a significant development of community organizing training intermediaries, which he grouped into four categories. The Southern Empowerment Project, which served as a vehicle to disseminate the experience and history of grassroots efforts, illustrated the first type, one that was specific to a network of community-based mediating structures.

Other community organizing training intermediaries have a regional focus but no membership network. Highlander Research and Education Center, for example, ran the Southern Appalachian Leadership Training (SALT), which played a major role in leadership training for both the Appalachian Ohio Public Interest Center and Bumpass Cove Citizens Group. Highlander also initiated and sponsored the Appalachian Alliance. Members of several other of our mediating structures received training from Kentuckians for the Commonwealth. KFTC had roots in the Appalachian Alliance and a talented staff that brought the group success and the opportunity to disseminate its experience and ideas on community organizing to groups such as the Ohio Valley Environmental Coalition. KFTC, like SALT, represented this second type of community organization training intermediary, one that was regional but not membership based.

Delgado identified a third type of training intermediary, one that focuses on specific issues or constituencies and provides training and technical assistance to groups within them. The Federation of Appalachian Housing Enterprise functioned as this type of intermediary on housing issues for its members and itself holds membership in a considerable array of other such intermediaries, including the National Low-Income Association, National Rural Housing Coalition, Housing Assistance Council, and National Community Association Load Funds. Naturally, community-based mediating structures that are involved in several projects take on some of the characteristics of this type of intermediary training organization. Appalachian Communities for Children provided technical assistance and training for the staff of its family of projects. To develop this capacity, it received support from the Association of Community-Based Education.

The fourth and final type of training intermediaries, according to Delgado, are ones that intend to create dense and formidable networks of organizations precisely to transcend local focus and to leverage political change. The Appalachian Alliance best resembled the intermediaries in this category, although its focus was regional rather than national and it never succeeded in rising above local and organizational particularities after it completed the land study. The Southern Empowerment Project borrows from the work of the Midwest Academy, another example of this fourth type of training intermediary, to conduct its work as a network-based intermediary.

Clearly, community-based mediating structures with member groups or chapters served some of the dissemination roles of training intermediaries. These roles may be direct. The training of the Southern Empowerment Project and the technical assistance of the Federation of Appalachian Housing Enterprises and the West Virginia Primary Care Association illustrate direct dissemination roles. At other times, the dissemination of ideas is indirect and secondary to instruction about project management, as in the case of the Appalachian Communities for Children or in the research and referral that a community-based mediating structure may do for its members, like the work of the West Virginia Education Association and the Western North Carolina Alliance. Finally, ideas are disseminated in the exchange of information and support that goes on in meetings such as those of the Southeast Women's Employment Coalition and the potluck dinners of the Appalachian Peoples Action Coalition.

In some cases, mediating structures may create the appropriate training and dissemination intermediary they need and cannot find. SafeSpace leaders played a major role in bringing many domestic violence shelters across the state into a single organization, the Tennessee Task Force Against Domestic Violence, which coordinated efforts of advocacy on their behalf and monitored and educated state legislators about policies related to domestic violence. The consequence was that SafeSpace received better information about state and national policies and spent less staff time to acquire them. Less formally, the Virginia Black Lung Association, due to its solid staff and its achievements, functioned as the ad hoc national black lung association. In this role, it devoted time to coordinating efforts of other state associations and disseminating information to them through reports on federal policies and at annual meetings. When staff members of the Dungannon Development Commission perceived a need for training in alternative styles of leadership of and for women, they established a training intermediary, called

Appalachian Women Empowered. Local groups may develop intermediaries to meet their own needs or may themselves develop into intermediaries that disseminate successful strategies to other groups.

Most often, however, mediating structures find an array of state and national organizations and construct a pyramid of intermediary organizations among them through which to acquire and disseminate lessons. For example, the Council of Senior West Virginians related directly to the National Council of Senior Citizens, but it also depended on coalitions for information on specific issues in which it had a stake. The Long Term Care Coalition and the Universal Health Care Action Network provided ideas on health care, and a state tax reform coalition provided ideas on tax issues. SafeSpace found itself at the base of an information pyramid of groups working against domestic violence at a state and national level. The National Education Association provided a national counterpart to the West Virginia Education Association. The West Virginia Primary Care Association provided a layer of information and technical assistance between its members and the National Association of Community Health Centers, of which it is a charter organizational member.

These state and national networks develop partially because even community-based mediating structures depend on state and national policy to sustain both local services and supportive networks. Their dense vertical networks obviously reflect the federal organization of policy and politics and replicate a local, state, and national structure of policy origins and political activity. Community-based mediating structures may also participate in national efforts to replicate and sustain the process of change of which they are a part. For example, the Appalachian Communities for Children and the Dungannon Development Commission both participated in the Association for Community-Based Education.

Grantors also serve as intermediaries for information exchange and technical assistance. All our groups were members of the Appalachian Development Projects Committee and were required by terms of their funding from the Commission on Religion in Appalachia to attend an annual meeting. Similarly, the director of the Appalachian Independence Center attended quarterly meetings with other directors of similar centers also funded by the Virginia Department of Rehabilitative Services. Staff of a particular program may also receive training and information through meetings required by a program grantor. The Maternal and Infant Health Outreach Worker program of the Dungannon Development Commission required lengthy quarterly meetings that provided each project staff member with training, technical assistance, information, and support in the innovative areas of prenatal care and early child development. VISTA provided training for its members as well. Mediating structures may turn to funding sources for technical assistance as well as training. The Kentucky Small Farms Project, for instance, drew upon the Heifer Project International and Habitat for Humanity for such assistance.

Ideas come from sources close to home as well as those at a distance. Small groups with modest budgets depend heavily on other mediating structures in their immediate area for ideas on management and programs. For example, the Appalachian Peoples Action Coalition relied on two other of our community-based mediating structures that are also based in the Athens, Ohio, area. Its members also participated in the meetings of boards, committees, and members of other groups such as Have a Heart Ohio, Tri-County Community Action, Habitat for Humanity, and the Human Needs Council. APAC also depends on the Ohio Legal Services program for ideas and technical assistance. The Ohio Valley Environment Center went to the staff of Kentuckians for the Commonwealth for ideas to improve their organizing capacity.

Ideas may also come to community-based mediating structures from agencies that work on the same or similar issues in other places. For example, Appalachian Communities for Economic Networks developed close relationships with the Ohio Department of Economic Development. The Appalachian Ohio Public Interest Center members attended meetings of Highlander and the Ohio Environmental Council. Clay Mountain Housing staff depended on the Housing Assistance Council and the West Virginia Housing Development Fund in addition to other member groups in the Federation of Appalachian Housing Enterprises. To connect with people from other communities engaged in work similar to its own, Roadside Theater participated in the American Festival and in the biannual conference, "Cultural Grounding," which was held by the Caribbean Cultural Center in New York City. The Virginia Black Lung Association depended upon a local health care clinic in West Virginia for black lung examinations and medical support for claims. The West Virginia Bureau of Public Health was important to the work of the West Virginia Primary Care Association. Through the work of Dick Austin, the Brumley Gap Concerned Citizens acquired training in nonviolent protest from the American Friends Service Committee and legal services from the Sierra Club Legal Defense Fund.

Ideas also come from other local community-based mediating structures working on different issues. Sometimes there are formal associations, such as the Bristol Inter-Agency Council that the Appalachian Independence Center joined. Other times, the exchange comes from regular but informal interaction. The Kentucky Small Farms Project found the Christian Appalachian Project, Jackson Ministries, the Brethren Church, the Methodist Mountain Mission, and the Interfaith Council of Breathitt County all to be important sources for information and ideas.

In addition to these horizontal and vertical networks, mediating structures have other resources from which to draw ideas. Staff development provides a source of ideas. This development comes from reading specialized information, such as newsletters of similar organizations or the literature on the issue area. The Appalachian Communities for Economic Networks pored through the flexible manufacturing network literature of Europe for ideas on successful economic development in southeast Ohio. Training for individual staff members brings to the organization ideas and resources for other staff members to share, if time is provided for it, as did the Dungannon Development Commission and the Appalachian Communities for Children. The experience of staff members is another important and obvious source of ideas that is especially valuable when there are multiple staffs, as in the case of the Southern Empowerment Project.

Participation in meetings of other organizations may also provide staff members with ideas for management and programs. Meetings of kindred members of other community-based mediating structures serve their staffs particularly well. The quarterly meetings of the Tennessee Task Force Against Domestic Violence provided SafeSpace staff with information and ideas. The Western North Carolina Alliance was served well by the annual National Forest Reform Pow-Wow. Similarly, a meeting of its own members may serve a group as a learning and listening device. Like the Federation of Appalachian Housing Enterprises, the Southern Empowerment Project depended on its quarterly board meetings to gain as well as disseminate ideas about the conduct of its business. The Appalachian Alliance depended on its annual meeting to acquire ideas from its members while sharing ideas as well. Alliance members also found the meetings to be a forum for the informal exchange of ideas. The occasions became so valuable that when budget restrictions limited the capacity of staff to travel to them, staff members felt very isolated.

Even at times of restricted budgets and restricted access to outside ideas, community-based mediating structures still have a ready supply of ideas and information within themselves. New forms of participation may uncover this supply. The Appalachian Ohio Public Interest Center looked inward to develop a set of priorities and the determination to continue its operation. Training intermediaries and organizations of community-based mediating structures used board meetings and other forms of communication with member groups for gleaning ideas on management. Their actions also supported accountability of the staff to the organization's member groups. Similarly, board members may be selected for their ability to contribute resources, especially ideas, to the group. Regular board meetings provide for contributions in addition to consultations in the interim between meetings and participation on committees and ad hoc groups. SafeSpace and Virginia Black Lung Association exemplified mediating structures that relied on the people they served as a source of ideas for management and programs. The Tennessee Task Force Against Domestic Violence had a caucus for battered women that provided a continuing forum for the exchange and dissemination of ideas to shelters. Black lung victims who had problems in dealing with the Social Security Administration over claims and benefits continually kept the VBLA informed of changes in policy and administration.

Ideas for the form and content of their work also come to communitybased mediating structures from the people of the communities in which they work and reside. Perhaps due to the nature of its dramatic performances and the role of audiences in providing feedback, Roadside Theater was clearest about the role of the cultural experiences of people "at home" in informing their work.

Successful mediating structures generally use some combination of all of the sources just discussed to keep up with good ideas. Each group's community, issue, size, and organizational development affect how many and what forms of information sources it can reach. This network of ideas is part and parcel of the dense horizontal and vertical networks that support and constitute the entrepreneurial social capital work of community-based mediating structures.

Coalitions Are Crucial

The Center for Community Change's reflections include the essential role of coalitions in the vitality of community-based mediating structures and their creation or preservation of social capital. CCC acknowledges the difficulty of building coalitions but chides mediating structures for their particularity, just as some theorists of the democratic prospect have done, concluding, "Many groups are oriented toward themselves. They don't see a broad view of the world. They don't see their role as helping others. They worry they'll lose their funding. We've got to overcome this pettiness and lack of vision" (CCC 1992: 68).

The emphasis on coalitions grew in the 1980s. Coalitions seemed better able to address and perhaps redress shortages of social capital resources and to increase efficiency and effectiveness in the uses of existing social capital. Foundations and government funding programs often made coalitions a necessary condition or element of programs they funded or initiated. Some advocates of community-based coalitions expressed disappointment in them because they functioned in a limited, means-oriented, and temporary manner. Even so, the attention accorded them underscored the role of coalitions, their growth and development (Speer and Chavis 1995).

Numerous problems impede the formation and continuation of coalitions of community-based mediating structures. Patterns of representation and participation and management styles distinguish some organizations. Issues create different areas of focus. Different levels of organizational development make coalition participation easier for more developed groups and difficult for newer and smaller organizations. Mediating structures that provide services may have problems working with mediating structures that organize and advocate or vice versa (Couto 1998).

Despite these problems, coalitions occur deliberately and intentionally. Some of the mediating structures discussed in this book are coalitions of groups with some common elements. Southeast Women's Employment Coalition formed to give executive directors of women's groups more opportunities to learn the management and leadership of mediating structures. It also gave these groups the capacity to initiate programs such as the regionwide highway project, a program they could not have tackled individually or even collectively without additional staff. The Appalachian Alliance began to coordinate a regional response to the 1977 floods in Appalachia. The land study demonstrated the unique capacity of a coalition but also its limits. The coalition attracted funds and resources to conduct the study, but it managed only disparate efforts for follow-up and limited commitment and energy to undertake successive issues. Both SWEC and the Alliance eventually ended operations. A third coalition among our mediating structures, Marketing Appalachian Traditional Community Handcrafts, also ended. Coalitions, exemplifying entropic laws of nature, tend to fall apart.

Some coalitions continue. The Federation of Appalachian Housing Enterprises had a specific issue focus and a major role of information gathering and technical assistance for its member groups. By 1990, FAHE had become a regional intermediary for funding sources. FAHE and its member groups would decide together which proposals for public or private funding would be stronger if prepared by FAHE and which would be stronger if prepared by individual member groups. The Southern Empowerment Project began in response to its members' needs for staff recruitment and training. The Ohio Valley Environmental Coalition and the Western North Carolina Alliance both worked to develop the potential of coalitions. Appalachian Center for Economic Networks functioned as a coalition of networks, which included the Flexible Manufacturing Network, the Coop Council, the Microenterprise Network, Creative Employment Opportunities, and Appalachian Networks. A specific issue focus, a set of common needs among member groups, dealing directly and effectively with them, and a common point of policy leverage, most often state government, are some necessary but not sufficient elements for successful and continuing coalitions.

Many of our groups joined or formed coalitions in order to acquire information or to achieve more leverage in policy making. Some of their efforts took on considerable influence and lives of their own. SafeSpace provided some of the impetus for the formation of the successful Tennessee Task Force Against Domestic Violence. The West Virginia Primary Care Association and the Council of Senior West Virginians were both charter members of their national counterparts. Roadside Theater participated in the formation of collaborative projects such as the American Festival projects, Alternate ROOTS, and the Alliance for Cultural Diversity, which functioned as coalitions to support art and theater at the grassroots. Marketing Appalachian Traditional Community Handcrafts blended its work with Human Economic/Appalachian Development Corporation (HEAD) largely because of common staff.

Other coalition efforts with more limited and immediate purposes did not fare well. Brumley Gap Concerned Citizens helped to fashion the Coalition of American Electric Consumers and provided the coalition with an initial focus, but BGCC's participation did not extend much beyond their successful protest of the pump storage project. The Bumpass Cove Citizens Group was a charter member of TEACH (Tennesseans Against Chemical Hazards), a statewide coalition of similar local environmental groups. TEACH eventually joined forces with the Tennessee Environmental Council on toxic dumping. By that time, the Bumpass Cove group had ceased to function.

With time, organizational development, and a great deal of credible experience from which to draw, mediating structures may shape the agendas of the coalitions that they join and may join them for that precise purpose. For example, the Federation of Appalachian Housing Enterprises worked with a number of national coalitions to instill a rural element in the consideration given to housing and the needs of low-income groups. Similarly, Roadside Theater contributed to the diversity celebrated in some of its collaborative projects by presenting programs rooted in Appalachian culture.

Coalitions provide numerous advantages to member groups, including increased moral resources of social capital. Members and staffs of mediating structures find encouragement and inspiration for their own efforts by discovering a capacity to extend their influence. The collective efforts validate local efforts and experience and also provide local groups increased credibility. Coalitions also disseminate information and ideas for management and programs.

Sometimes there are tangible, monetary benefits to coalition participation. Some national associations share a portion of their members' dues with their state affiliates, such as the West Virginia Education Association and the Council of Senior West Virginians. The Tennessee Task Force Against Domestic Violence successfully lobbied for increased marriage license fees as state revenue to provide funds to initiate and operate domestic violence shelters.

There are costs as well as benefits to coalition participation. Coalitions survive on sweat equity no less than grassroots groups and services. Time put into coalition formation and functions is an opportunity cost that needs to return a benefit, as we discussed in the section on management and sweat equity. An irrelevant meeting that requires a day of travel will occasionally mar even a satisfactory coalition experience. The West Virginia Primary Care Association distributed the responsibility for participating in meetings of other groups and coalitions among its staff, board, and members. This responsibility spread and lowered the opportunity costs. Not surprisingly, the greater the leverage of a coalition, the more competition there is for influence within it, and consequently the higher the requirement for participation. The Federation of Appalachian Housing Enterprises found that gaining and maintaining influence in national and several different state coalitions required lots of traveling, which entailed considerable time and monetary costs.

The Appalachian Ohio Public Interest Center found that the statewide platform of the Ohio Public Interest Center had too many planks for them to carry. The commitment of staff time without financial assistance made membership in OPIC a burden for AOPIC. Membership dues may also deter coalition membership of small mediating structures. Smaller groups also have the problem of limited budgets, which may restrict travel funds. This is a serious impediment for rural groups spread out over a wide area. Despite this, the Virginia Black Lung Association had chapters in contiguous counties of southwest Virginia and spread into Illinois and Indiana as well. Competing agendas, financial costs, time, and distance all work against strong and enduring coalitions.

Sometimes, member groups may find themselves competing with coalitions of which they are a part for limited funds from the same few funding sources. The Appalachian Alliance proved particularly susceptible to the reluctance of member groups to risk funding lines for its sake. The close association of Marketing Appalachian Traditional Community Handcrafts and Human Economic/Appalachian Development Corporation—the director of one was married to the director of the other—also meant smaller slices of a declining pie. Compounding this problem for MATCH, its own member groups began competing with it for funds from the same sources. Coalitions may find it difficult to acquire support from funders who do not recognize their format, such as flexible manufacturing networks, or who shy away from the advocacy often implied by coalition formation and even more likely in its operation.

Generating Financial Support

The incredible array of coalitions among our community-based mediating structures pales in comparison with the plethora of funding sources tapped to find social capital for their work. Our groups made mention of the following specific sources of support: individual donors, local churches, dioceses of various religions and denominations, local health departments, local economic development districts, local United Way campaigns, fees for services, membership dues, profits from conferences, Adrian Dominican Fund, Alexander Fund, Alternate ROOTS, American Festival New Work Fund, Andrew W. Mellon Foundation, Appalachian Community Fund, Appalachian Regional Commission, Aspen Institute Rural Economic Policy Program, Ben and Jerry's Foundation, Benedum Foundation, Campaign for Human Development, Charles Stewart Mott Foundation, Church Women United, Clear Water Fund, Cleveland Sisters of St. Joseph, Coalition on Human Needs, Commission on Religion in Appalachia, Common Wealth Inc., Community Development Block Grants, Community Shares, Cooperative Development Foundation, Deer Creek Foundation, Department of Rehabilitative Services, E. O. Robinson Mountain Fund, Economic Development Administration of the U.S. Department of Commerce, Edward Hazen Foundation, Farmers Home Administration, Finlandia Foundation, Ford Foundation, Heifer Project International, Janirve Foundation, Job Training Partnership Administration, Joe and Emily Lowe Foundation, Joyce Foundation, Kellogg Foundation, Kentucky Arts Council, Kentucky Foundation for Women, Lila Wallace–Readers Digest Arts Partners Program, Lutheran Church-Missouri Synod, Lyndhurst Foundation, Mary Reynolds Babcock

Foundation, McKinney Act (housing), Nathan Cummings Foundation, National Cooperative Development Corporation, National Endowment for the Arts, Needmor Fund, New World Foundation, New York Community Trust, Office of Vocational Education, Ohio Department of Development, Ohio University, Partners for the Common Good, Pettus Crowe Foundation, Pew Charitable Trusts, Points of Light Foundation, Presbyterian Committee on the Self-Development of People, Presbyterian Hunger Fund, Proctor Fund, Public Welfare Foundation, Rockefeller Foundation, Save the Children Foundation, Schumann Foundation, Sisters of Mercy, Sunflower Foundation, Tennessee Valley Authority, Theaters for New Audiences Program, Threshold Foundation, Town Creek Foundation, Van Leer Foundation (Netherlands), Vanderbilt University Center for Health Services, Veatch Foundation, Virginia Foundation for the Humanities, W. Alton Jones Foundation, and Z. Smith Reynolds Foundation.

These sources, though numerous, are spigots of limited funding, trickles in relation to the needs that mediating structures address and the costs of their work. This does not negate their importance; the work of mediating structures is not possible without public and philanthropic funding sources. However, the number of sources does not imply a cornucopia for community-based mediating structures, nor does it suggest sufficient funding. The size and diversity of the list of contributors testify to the ability of the directors of community-based mediating structures, as social capital entrepreneurs, to strike the tambourine, shake the money tree, beat the bushes, and do everything else it takes to locate sources and acquire funding. Not even college presidents outdo the directors of successful community-based mediating structures in this skill and capacity.

The need for more generous and general support for mediating structures concludes the list of management lessons that the Center for Community Change learned. Without general support, mediating structures may lack the money to support the management practices extolled in this chapter. How do ideas travel without funds and time for staff training, development, and participation in coalitions and meetings of other organizations? How do organizations meet opportunity costs without some general support? How do organizations pay their directors without funds for administration and management and not merely for the conduct of programs? As important as coalitions are to the success of mediating structures, they are difficult to "sell" to funding sources for an extended period of time. The Federation of Appalachian Housing Enterprises had a particularly difficult time winning support for its overhead functions for other groups in particular.

In addition to this twofold need for support, our community-based mediating structures identified other management issues related to funding. Very few funding sources maintained support over an extended period of time. A three-year grant with a possible renewal for an additional three years was an eternity in the foundation world. The Commission on Religion in Appalachia was one of the few funding sources, if not the only one, that considered annual requests regardless of the number of years an applicant had previously been funded. However, even with CORA, the period of support affected the amount funded; it declined over time. Save the Children Foundation provided Appalachian Communities for Children with stable support from its beginning. This proved invaluable. It provided ACC with a "down payment," which is matching funds for other grants. Some funding sources have a geographic focus, which also fosters longer relationships and funding, such as the Z. Smith Reynolds Foundation's support of the Western North Carolina Alliance.

State and federal agencies have many programs and more funds than foundations, but they present a different set of vagaries. Funding availability from public sources comes and goes quickly. Interparty and intraparty conflicts at the national and state level may suddenly begin, end, and interrupt the flow of funds to groups and organizations many hundreds of miles away. The Reagan administration brought a new emphasis on teenage sexual abstinence, and suddenly millions of dollars became available in thousands of $100,000 grants to agencies conducting sexual abstinence programs. Most often, agencies of state and local government are better prepared to draw from these gushes of funding than are community-based mediating structures. Organizations of mediating structures, such as the Federation of Appalachian Housing Enterprises, provide their member groups the best opportunity to stay apprised of and attuned to government funding opportunities. They also provide adequate administrative capacity and a sufficient membership size to handle the large grants that federal and state governments are inclined to make. They also have more time and more avenues for disseminating the results of one group's success in deciphering complicated processes and forms, such as the Farmers Home Administration loans, than the successful group does.

Funding from government sources also comes with more strings attached than does that from philanthropic sources. Some of these strings promote accountability and, though onerous, are understandable. Regular reporting may require counts of the number of people served and the forms of services provided to them. Some of the informal strings draw on political considerations. For example, as it approached its conclusion, the Appalachian

Alliance's land study drew very nervous attention from the Appalachian Regional Commission The land study's final product (Appalachian Land Ownership Task Force 1983) included an introduction that placed a curious distance between the Appalachian Regional Commission and the study that it supported. The introduction went beyond the usual disclaimer about which views belonged to whom; it raised questions about the study's methods and findings. It is a tribute to the leadership of the Appalachian Alliance that the study was released and circulated at all. The public never sees many other government-supported studies with controversial conclusions.

Mediating structures with funding from public sources are more likely to be circumspect in their protest of current policies or advocacy of alternative policies. This hesitancy increases with the proportion of an agency's budget that comes from a government program. An agency depending on a state agency for 75 percent of its budget will be less likely to criticize that agency publicly than an agency deriving only 10 percent of its budget from the agency. On the other hand, high levels of funding also indicate that state agencies are dependent on that mediating structure to carry out significant programs and policies. This other form of dependence may permit a government-funded mediating structure to evaluate and change some government policies and programs. The West Virginia Primary Care Association and the Appalachian Independence Center represent two mediating structures of important policy makers and implementers that operate with state funding and its concomitant political restrictions and opportunities.

Finding and pursuing public and philanthropic funding sources demands time and effort. Those mediating structures closest to the local community have the least time and expertise to devote this effort. Consequently, some community-based mediating structures, such as Appalachian Peoples Action Coalition, depend on other organizations, such as the Appalachian Center for Economic Networks, in which funding skills are more developed to assist them in fund-raising. The most common observation of our groups involved the dilemma of balancing fund-raising and the conduct of programs. Each set of necessary tasks levies an opportunity cost on the other, and each requires the other. A group cannot conduct programs without funding, but finding funds is much easier if an organization has successful programs.

Time constraints may bring a sense of frustration in dealing with funding sources. The requirements posed by federal and state agencies appear laborious: long and detailed forms, assurances regarding a drug-free environment and other practices and policies, numerous clearances among local and state agencies, etc. The number of forms and the formality of the governmental funding process construct paper walls that hide supportive people in the funding agencies. Philanthropic sources may offer more direct communication, but the processes are more informal. Priorities shift among these sources, and issues come and go. Buzzwords, such as "empowerment" or "cultural diversity," are suddenly in fashion and then, just as suddenly, out of fashion. This direct but informal process expresses little accountability to funded programs and prompted some of our groups' staff members to complain about the difficulty of getting "straight answers" from staff at philanthropic funding sources.

Funding needs change with the size of the budgets of mediating structures. Among the organizations we studied, annual budgets varied from a few thousand dollars to $500,000. Naturally, the budget reflects the scope of activity. Appalachian Peoples Action Coalition required few funds, for much of its work had a volunteer and member emphasis. The Dungannon Development Corporation required many more sources and a larger amount of funds for its many programs, which included water projects, a community center, literacy and education programs, and a maternal and infant health program.

Budgets, and consequently management matters, vary among groups and within the same group over time. APAC expanded its budget when it took on the Bargain Furniture Store. The Dungannon Development Commission began small, growing over its almost twenty-year history as new funding sources and programs came on line and others ended. Appalachian Communities for Economic Networks underwent the greatest metamorphosis, growing from an initial budget of $10,000 to $500,000 a year. Foundation funds changed the Ohio Valley Environmental Coalition from a volunteer organization to one with a staff of three, growth that brought on a complex set of organizational development issues, as we have seen. A sudden infusion of funds can be a mixed blessing, because it requires an organization to develop the capacity to allocate and administer the new money. This problem disrupted the Bumpass Cove Citizens Group early and the Brumley Gap Concerned Citizens late in their work.

Growth, such as ACEnet's, generally suggests a change in the sources of funding. ACEnet began with small church grants, moved to foundation funds, and then to funding from state and federal agencies. Some progression in sources and amounts of funding is common. The Federation of Appalachian Housing Enterprise began with a large infusion of federal CETA (Comprehensive Employment Training Assistance) funds and then moved to foundations, other government programs, and eventually financial lending institutions for loans. Roadside Theater also started with a federal grant to Appalshop from the National Endowment for the Arts (NEA) and its Expanding Arts Program. It continued to draw from the NEA and its state counterpart but added private foundations to its funding stream as well. Roadside Theater's affiliation with Appalshop's long and distinguished track record helped it immensely in the search and pursuit of funds.

Large budgets also imply several different funding sources. The long list at the beginning of this section suggests how many sources have been tapped by our twenty-three community-based mediating structures. Diverse funding alleviates dependence on one funding source, which makes the continuation of an organization precarious, since funding sources come and go and change their priorities. In addition to diversity in external support, mediating structures diversify by developing internal support such as membership dues. Even the modest budget of the Kentucky Small Farms Project required internal as well as external fund-raising. Requiring members to pay back in-kind for what they receive—a heifer for a heifer or sweat equity in the construction of someone else's home in exchange for the sweat equity put into one's own home—creates revolving funds that have a claim on new resources even as they yield existing ones. In restructuring itself, the Appalachian Ohio Public Interest Center included developing a membership, dues-paying base to reduce its dependence on external support. Small groups, such as AOPIC, seldom generated sufficient funds for staff and operations from membership dues. Large groups, like the West Virginia Education Association, did. The West Virginia Primary Care Association also derived a good part of its budget from its member clinics and health centers. In addition, WVPCA generated revenues from the annual meetings, conferences, and workshops that it conducted.

A few mediating structures can conduct fee-generating activities. When they do, the revenues are important streams into the cash flow of an organization. Clay Mountain Housing eventually reached the point where it could administer its own revolving fund for home loans. Roadside Theater had paying audiences or sponsors for most of its performances. Virginia Black Lung Association charged fees for successful cases of litigation; in other cases, the attorney services were free.

Developing revenue-generating services, developing and maintaining internal funding sources through membership dues and fund-raising and benefit events, and successfully gliding from one external funding source to another requires effort, luck, and experience. The challenges that these tasks present create instability for most community-based mediating structures. Some, like the Council of Senior West Virginians, reached points of decline, and others succumbed to revenue roulette. Southeast Women's Employment Coalition ended after six years of Ford Foundation funding. The Appalachian Alliance remained a part of Highlander, mixed its fund-raising efforts with it and with numerous groups in the region, and never did acquire a solid, independent financial foothold. The vagaries of financing can be fatal.

Insufficient forms and amounts of funding for mediating structures require such groups to pay consistent attention to finances. Success comes from competition with numerous similar and worthwhile programs. Failure, decline, and perhaps even the end of a program or mediating structure come from the same competition. Its own observations led the Center for Community Change to conclude: "Community-based organizations are essential to solving this country's most pressing social problem[s]. They need and deserve far more support than they receive" (CCC 1992: 69).

Money, Management, and Mission

More efforts in support of the democratic prospect and continuation of the ones that we have depend on how well we heed the management lessons of community-based mediating structures. First and foremost, we know that funds for the creation and operation of mediating structures are less available in the areas where they are most needed to promote the democratic prospect. Second, the most obvious management lesson entails the need for more support for mediating structures. Relatedly, there is a need for support of the general operating costs of community-based mediating structures as well as their programs. These funds would cover the costs of travel to meetings and training for the dissemination and sharing of ideas on program and management. Ideas can travel without lavish travel accounts, but general operating funds make their travel more likely.

Third, we know that philanthropic grantors and government programs assist the vitality of the democratic prospect when they support intermediaries and coalitions of mediating structures. Obviously, a balance must be struck among grantors. Mediating structures need intermediaries, such as the Southern Empowerment Project, for training, recruitment, and retention of staff and for other services, such as the technical assistance that the Federation of Appalachian Housing Enterprises provided its member groups. However, the significance of the function of these intermediaries comes from the set of vital and stable groups that they serve. External funds are necessary for that vitality and stability, just as they are necessary for the full-scale implementation of the services provided by intermediaries. In choosing between funding intermediaries or local programs, funding sources risk neglecting the one for the other. While no funding source can meet every need, they can initiate and participate in efforts to survey and coordinate the resources of other grantors to see that some balance is struck among them.

Fourth, the responsibility for nurturing a vital network of mediating structures also falls upon the members of that network. Organization and efficient administration express the accountability expected of them for the resources, including the communal trust and democratic hope, that their members and others invest in them. Their membership and staff meetings, if managed properly, provide a source for new ideas and vitality. Similarly, staff members in mediating structures often must pay in sweat equity up front in order to begin and sustain coalitions and networks for the dissemination of ideas on program and management. At the same time, the staff members of each mediating structure need to renew the vision of the human need that their organization addresses. No matter the level of organizational development, mission must drive the organization and fashion its management. Mediating structures preserve the democratic prospect of their work as long as they renew their early "cause-driven" nature and their mission to increase the amounts and improve the forms of social capital. It is to explicit considerations of the democratic prospect that we now turn.

CHAPTER 9

Community Change

The myriad of management matters and the problems of dealing with them, which we discussed in Chapter 8, present practical obstacles to community-based mediating structures and their pursuits of the democratic prospect. The inclusive, active, efficacious, and sharing community sustained by community-based mediating structures, which we discussed in Chapter 7, provides a glimmer of the democratic prospect. In this chapter, we probe beyond the glimmer for explicit lessons about the democratic prospect that community-based mediating structures provide. Three lessons stand out:

- community organizing and development, like service and advocacy, are distinct but related realms of action;
- community change to promote increased social and economic equality is a long-term and difficult process; and
- prevailing in that process requires a combination of human and financial resources and leadership from within and outside of the local community.

Organizing and Development Are Compatible

Community organizing and community development are distinct and similar. Community organizing mobilizes resources to acquire new or improved services from others or to require that some other group stops harmful action. The Brumley Gap Concerned Citizens, the Ohio Valley Environmental Coalition, and the Bumpass Cove Citizens Group organized to require that corporations halt plans or practices destructive to their communities. The West Virginia Education Association and the Western North Carolina Alliance organized to require a corporation, federal agency, or their state legislatures to take action. Organizing may address power initially and directly by demanding someone else to do or not to do something. Organizing incurs the risk of conflict with those on whom demands are made. Organizing prefers the collective action of members and supporters over individual action. People are empowered individually and as a group by their collective efforts to change a condition that increases social capital—both in the form of services and goods, such as education and clean environments, and in the form of moral resources, such as trust, esteem, and self-confidence. Personal transformation occurs in the process of organizing and not merely in the accomplishment of results. In this manner, organizing for collective action to achieve some form of social capital resembles the moral resources that Hirschman describes (see Chapter 2).

Community development differs from organizing in that development entails the mobilization of resources for the provision of a service by the group mobilizing the resources, not by someone else. Appalachian Communities for Children and SafeSpace mobilized to acquire resources, voluntarily, from others to meet the needs of children and battered women through services that their programs would provide. Community development aims to empower clients and staff. It depends on mutual agreement, not conflict, with agencies and officials about the nature and amount of a voluntary transfer of resources to support the services of a group. Clearly, however, community organizing and community development blend at points, conceptually and certainly within the experience of each of our community-based mediating structures.

Advocacy is a middle ground between organizing and development. Successful advocacy comes from the capacity of a community-based mediating structure to pursue community organizing and community development simultaneously, at least to some degree. Obviously, every group will vary in the amount of emphasis and the point from which they start—organizing or development—but eventually, a group's path comes to advocacy. When groups disavow advocacy, as Lester Salamon reminded us in Chapter 2, they "can become largely irrelevant to democracy." At times, a community-based mediating structure may advocate for increased or improved forms of social capital, without conflict, within groups that support it or before public agencies that oppose it. The Brumley Gap Concerned Citizens advocated before the Federal Energy Regulatory Commission. Although its style was primarily organizing, it also raised funds through community development efforts, such as the "Save Brumley Gap Festival." Conversely, Dianne Levy determined that SafeSpace would not be, in her words, "a social services organization." SafeSpace's development of the community service of offering shelter from violence extended to include advocacy and organizing at the state level to acquire legislation to prevent domestic violence and tax revenues to support domestic shelters. Neither the legislation nor the revenues would have come from the legislature voluntarily without the actions of organized advocates.

The specious debate over whether community-based mediating structures should focus on organizing or development overlooks the fact that they do both if they succeed. Without organizing, community services cannot find the resources to do their work. Without a strategy for development, community organizing efforts are likely to forfeit resources for their communities. For the moral resources in social capital, such as community and trust, to be clearly expressed, community development is frequently required. In literally concrete terms, development may provide a community center or some other space or service where moral resources and civic pride can be expressed clearly (CCC 1992: 67). Tangible services and spaces indicate the specific differences a community may make by organizing its own resources. They may instill confidence in the community's ability to achieve additional change by organizing to acquire resources from others. The community center at Bumpass Cove illustrated the connection of development that came from and after community organizing. Whatever the order, community organizing and community development merge conceptually and in the experience of groups.

Like all other matters of community-based mediating structures, the pursuits of community organizing and development do not follow an easy course according to a set of directions leading to a predictable result. Some community development clashes with community organizing, but not because the two are inherently incompatible. For example, when the Brumley Gap Concerned Citizens decided to end their organizing efforts against electric utilities, they put their remaining funds into a community center and fire department. This expressed, first and foremost, an emphasis on local matters and needs. On the other hand, the Bumpass Cove Citizens Group began a community center as part of their organizing effort. The center marked a new development stage for the group, and there ensued a factional conflict that disrupted its organizing efforts.

In most cases, the pursuit of community development entails forms of organizing. For instance, Roadside Theater involved as many groups as possible within the communities where it conducted residencies. By assembling together representatives from the local arts council, teachers, students, parents, local officials, and others to make decisions about their residency, Roadside intended to develop a group that would continue to advocate and develop its own theater or other forms of artistic expression.

In other cases, organizing follows development unintentionally. For example, Marketing Appalachian Traditional Community Handcrafts pursued primarily economic development, organizing craft groups sufficiently to meet those aims. Some of the groups in MATCH also organized support networks for low-income women, which addressed issues such as school lunch programs or family conflicts stemming from the new and independent income of women. In addition, the MATCH board meetings, like those of the Southeast Women's Employment Coalition, provided women a unique opportunity to raise and address issues of importance to them. Thus, even in what are primarily development efforts, some characteristics and instances of organizing will emerge.

Finally, several of our community-based mediating structures helped other groups develop their organizing focus. The Southern Empowerment Project did this exclusively. It placed the greatest emphasis of any of our groups on community organizing but did not have its own program of organizing. The Appalachian Ohio Public Interest Center trained members of other groups in organizing in addition to conducting its own organizing.

This mistaken distinction between organizing and development comes in part from not understanding that changes that occur within a community-based mediating structure are interrelated, whether its focus is on organizing or development, advocacy or service. Advocacy *of* people with disabilities *by* people with disabilities began with the services provided *for* people with disabilities within the activities of the Appalachian Independence Center. Disabled people working with AIC, especially people disabled at birth, often required training in interpersonal skills before they could take on lobbying efforts for funds and legislation on behalf of other people with disabilities. Personal support and support groups, which are services, helped uncover the political relevance and utility of AIC's advocacy and organizing efforts. Other groups developed their organizing efforts by branching out to more people. For example, the Ohio Valley Environmental Coalition attempted to move toward more member-based direct action and self-advocacy and away from its initial advocacy work by a few experts; the Western North Carolina Alliance attempted to move in the same direction, away from advocacy that was limited primarily to only one set of local residents. Both OVEC and WNCA received training for their membership and chapter development efforts from Kentuckians for the Commonwealth.

KFTC's work suggests how groups can help one another find the right mix of organizing, advocacy, development, and service. This, of course, is one avenue along which ideas travel, which we discussed in Chapter 8. The Appalachian Alliance had the explicit purpose of developing a regional strategy with and among community organizations of the region. Its work brought member groups together in a voluntary exchange of resources, information primarily. The voluntary nature of this exchange displayed elements of development, but the limited fiscal, physical, and human resources that Alliance group members had available to transfer showed the limited capacity for development that the Alliance had.

Sometimes this developmental exchange of resources takes place within an organization, from one program to another. Within Appalachian Communities for Economic Networks, for example, leaders brought lessons from the worker-owned cooperative past of the organization to help resolve the conflicts over shop floor issues in its later operation with flexible manufacturing. This development represented more of an exchange between more and less democratic forms of economic organization rather than between community organizing and development.

ACEnet combined advocacy and community development, but leaders of ACEnet remained acutely aware of their roles as change agents. ACEnet emphasized economic development as much as the Southern Empowerment Project emphasized organizing. Its leaders worked individually or with a few others to make recommendations to state and local agencies regarding economic development and funding. This advocacy did not include collective action or protest. ACEnet's capacity for change came from its role as a social capital entrepreneur, providing partially tested ideas for social capital.

Both the Federation of Appalachian Housing Enterprises and the West Virginia Primary Care Association also put forward new ideas for social capital. Leaders within both organizations had influence over state and national policies through other organizations. They acquired this influence by presenting the experience of their members to address human needs through innovative programs. By supporting housing and health care efforts, FAHE and WVPCA did not empower groups directly or involve groups in direct, collective action. Yet they were effective in acquiring resources from others that would not have been there without their efforts. In this manner, social capital entrepreneurism shares the hallmarks of organizing, developing, and mobilizing resources.

This advocacy on behalf of others in need carries with it the risks of paternalism, self-aggrandizement, and a debilitating sense of institutional self-importance. These risks also accompany an overly narrow focus on service or development. Maintaining some elements of community organizing provides one antidote to these risks of advocacy. On a small scale, the Appalachian Peoples Action Coalition balanced the service and development of its Bargain Furniture store with a continued emphasis on organizing through monthly membership meetings. The Kentucky Small Farms Project undertook to move more responsibilities for meetings, committees, and planning to its members. Both the Virginia Black Lung Association and the West Virginia Education Association ran substantial risks of unaccountable advocacy because of legal expertise or sheer size, respectively, but both organizations managed to dodge the risk. VBLA worked through chapters and members in its organizational focus, which was primarily organizing. Its success depended on successfully providing services for black lung victims and their dependents, but these accomplishments were interpreted as coming from the action of members and not the skills of staff. The West Virginia Education Association renewed its organizing focus with the statewide strike that it conducted. Both VBLA and WVEA have been assisted in preserving an organizing focus in the provision of services by the activities of the United Mine Workers in their areas, which provided a rich history of solidarity and collective action in the face of adversity.

Three essential points about the combination of organizing and development appear in the experiences of our community-based mediating structures. The points confirm the findings of the Center for Community Change and our earlier discussions about social capital in Chapter 2.

- *Community development requires new resources, and these resources come only with some form of advocacy for them.* Although Clay Mountain Housing emphasized that it developed housing, it was heralded in the region for its success in acquiring the cooperation of the Farmers Home Administration in its work. Similarly, the Dungannon Development Corporation did development only because of its incredible capacity to attract resources from a broad array of sources and agencies, many of which had to be talked into their support.
- *Organizing often entails looking at how current resources are utilized.* The Council of Senior West Virginians, proud of its working-class char-

acter, monitored public programs from health care to energy rates for their impact on its members and other elderly residents of the state. CSWV spent time assessing the function and utilization of senior citizen centers as well.

- *Finally, dense horizontal and vertical networks of community-based mediating structures require a repertoire of strategies and tactics that encompass organizing and development, advocacy and services.* Appalachian Communities for Children, like SafeSpace and other apparent service programs, provided personal development and informal support groups for people who needed them. This individual empowerment precedes group empowerment; the latter does not occur without the former. Within service programs, dense horizontal networks of clients and staff may increase the social capital of the community. Their successes with clients and programs inevitably bring changes in practices and some collaboration with other institutions in the area, such as schools, health centers, and police departments. This network also increases the social capital of the community as a whole.

A Long Process without Shortcuts

Each group has major accomplishments rooted in the lives of the people with whom they work and who work with and for them. Ironically, the only safe generalization to make about successful community-based mediating structures is that they respond effectively to particular and unique local conditions. What is possible for a group to accomplish most often depends on the local context, as the Center for Community Change observed: "The context determines everything. . . . You have to assess the local context. The leadership. The politics. The environment. Something that works in one place won't have a chance in another" (CCC 1992: 68).

Emphasis on the local context raises the risk of all mediating structures and democratic prospects being local, which is to say, irreplicable in other places or in regional, statewide, and national efforts to improve upon the democratic prospect for everyone. In part, the local emphasis finds its counterpoints in the ubiquitous development of leadership within each group and training and development of staff and board member for leadership. These measures do not transform local community-based mediating structures into a national democratic movement, but they go a long way toward producing an informed and active citizenry that provides the foundation for the democratic prospect. As the experience of our groups indicate, a myriad of local efforts for the democratic prospect constitutes a long process without what the Center for Community Change calls, "cookie-cutter solutions."

Major Accomplishments

An increase in local social capital goods and services and moral resources appears first and foremost on the list of successes of community-based mediating structures. Appalachian Ohio Public Interest Center led the effort to bring electric line extensions into rural areas for low-income residents. AOPIC later developed ideas for rural regeneration and thus continued its role of testing partial ideas and risk social capital. The Appalachian Independence Center brought people with disabilities into the community through architectural modification, transportation, counseling, and skill training. It thereby added human resources to the community and expanded the imaginations of those who had been isolated from people with disabilities. The Federation of Appalachian Housing Enterprises provided housing to families by pushing, pulling, and prodding public policy to shake loose resources and procedures that provided capital to individuals and areas that previously had had too little social overhead. The Ohio Valley Environmental Coalition and the Bumpass Cove Citizens Group stopped further degradation of their immediate environment. The Western North Carolina Alliance preserved environmental quality from the practice of clearcutting in the national forest. SafeSpace extended recognition to the battered women and children of its community by giving the community a heightened awareness of their problems. In turn, it gained resources from the community to extend to battered women and children, which provided them increased freedom from physical harm and thus the opportunity for fuller community participation. The Virginia Black Lung Association attempted to gain increased compensation for working people and their dependents for the costs of work on their health. Illness, VBLA maintained, was not to continue as a subsidy to employers, like some cruel Faustian bargain with savage capitalism. The West Virginia Education Association brought educational investment levels to the public's awareness in its 1990 strike and thereby created new and higher forms of social capital. Community-based mediating structures not only attract funds to their community that would not have come otherwise, but they provide models of social capital investment, such as literacy and maternal and infant health programs. Increases in social capital cannot be taken for granted, as the arduous efforts of community-based mediating structures show.

This conspicuous relationship between community-based mediating structures and social capital binds both of them to the democratic prospect by new forms of participation and trust in networks of influence and resources. For example, the West Virginia Primary Care Association developed a unified voice for health centers that joined a network of other organization actors in the health care field. Similarly, Clay Mountain Housing filled in a gap of the network of housing resources between the state and federal level and the needs of residents in its county. CMH achieved credibility or trust among local residents and among state and federal sources. That trust extended to recognition of the role and capability of women to run an organization, to master complex lending regulations and housing codes, and to supervise the construction of well-built, low-cost houses. One leader in the Dungannon Development Corporation explained that group's new place in the network of social capital as its major achievement, especially in the face of opposition of some people who did not want them to be there.

This subtle social capital of network infiltration means increased political participation. For example, the Council of Senior West Virginians provided a space for political activism for seniors. This space extended and continued the political activism of some of its members from the labor movement, in particular. This political activism, along with others' activism and other factors, produced an ombudsman program for people in nursing homes and for their families. Similarly, the Virginia Black Lung Association pursued legislation successfully. In some cases, increased political activism transforms political practice. Naturally, this transformation includes conflict sometimes, as in the strike of the West Virginia Education Association and the protests of the Bumpass Cove Citizens Group.

The Appalachian Alliance transformed politics by network building. It brought new forms of familiar information into the political discussion of social capital and human services in Appalachian states. The land ownership study documented in detail, county by county, inequities of corporate wealth and corporate tax responsibilities. This work provided some of the sparks for the West Virginia teachers' strike in 1990. In addition, the Alliance played a direct role in the creation of the Kentucky Far Tax Coalition and the Western North Carolina Alliance. KFTC became a major new actor in the network of community-based mediating structures in the state and region.

The social capital and democratic achievements of community-based mediating structures include improved and increased human capital. One leader of the Appalachian Communities for Children pointed to leadership development, one form of human capital, as ACC's major accomplishment.

Similarly, increased control over their own lives struck a leader of the Appalachian Independence Center as its major accomplishment among its members. The new directors of the Kentucky Small Farms Project set as their goal increasing human capital within KSFP. The Southern Empowerment Project began with a similar goal. Through its work, SEP improved the qualifications of staff of their member groups and increased the overall number of qualified staff. SEP's workshops also provided the leaders among their member groups opportunities to practice and share their skills. Southeast Women's Employment Coalition contributed to the human capital of its member groups in similar fashion.

This development of human capital forms another of the lessons that the Center for Community Change drew from its twenty-five-year history:

> Community groups . . . need a constant stream of new people as well as a plan to hang on to experienced people. Just as new organizations are often the most energetic and creative, new people can add a dynamic that organizations need. Plus, the supply of good organizers is perilously low. We know of groups that have spent well over a year trying to fill a key staff position. This can be fatal, given the strong correlation we have found between the quality of key staff and the success of the organization. (CCC 1992: 69)

Our community-based mediating structures also increase and improve other forms of capital. Appalachian Peoples Action Coalition provided an entry for low-income consumers into the home furnishings market. On the supplier side, Marketing Appalachian Traditional Community Handcrafts did just as its name implied. MATCH helped revitalize a section of Berea, Kentucky, into a crafts outlet and provided a link between groups and individuals, especially women, from their own production to a market.

At the core of these achievements and providing a foundation for them all, we find changes in the way people work together. The Appalachian Center for Economic Networks fostered satisfaction and efficacious collaboration among the people with whom it worked. Working together supported the major accomplishment of Roadside Theater, which maintained an ensemble company for almost twenty years. One leader attributed this success to the democratic process within Roadside and Appalshop, its parent organization. A bottom-line commitment to the "cause" of perpetuating and strengthening Appalachian culture also played a part. Thus, we come almost to a circle. The achievements of community-based mediating structures in pursuit of the democratic prospect stem, in part, from their commitment to it. Success in developing social capital and furthering the democratic prospect, over the long haul and despite obstacles, comes from deliberate action and the commitment of specific local leaders to these goals. It does not come as an externality guided by an invisible hand.

Major Disappointments

The long process of community change entails disappointments. There are times when groups fail. The West Virginia Education Association failed in 1988 to get legislation to provide uniform school funding and to reduce some of the inequities among districts. The merger of the Primary Care Study Group and the West Virginia Association of Community Health Centers took a long time, during which the groups' combined efforts were less effective than they had been either before or after their split. Some members of the Brumley Gap Concerned Citizens expressed dismay that the group did not stay active after they won their fight.

Inadequacy disappoints ongoing, successful, vibrant community-based mediating structures more often than outright failure. The deficits in social capital and consequent human needs simply exceed the capacity of most groups to meet. In some cases, such as the Appalachian Ohio Public Interest Center, the staff and board simply did not have the capacity to match the ideas that come from AOPIC's committees for action. The Ohio Valley Environmental Coalition also had more issues than it could deal with. The Appalachian Peoples Action Coalition, which depended on volunteers, had constraints on its capacity for action that came from the limited resources of its members, who were mostly low-income people. Their daily lives have interruptions—from having to attend to bills, to taking advantage of offers of free help, to needing to repair a septic tank, to having too little money to repair a car—that limit their capacity to volunteer. This mismatch of issues and capacity led some group leaders to disappointment mixed with frustration that more people could not be served.

Underutilization contributes to frustration as well. Some members used the Appalachian Independence Center only for the limited purpose of acquiring funding for a single accessory and did not become further involved. Sometimes even member groups "don't get" the whole picture of organizing, advocacy, development, and services. One of the major disappointments of the Southern Empowerment Project staff was to see member groups not use the resources SEP offered. Seeing member groups decline and cease operation presented another major disappointment, which was probably beyond the resources or power of SEP to prevent.

Delays and the lengthy process of change also provide frustration and disappointment. Clay Mountain Housing often had to wait long periods of time to obtain funds for an eligible family. This extended the need of the family for improved housing while dampening the enthusiasm of the promise that something could be done to address their need. Working with a bureaucracy such as Farmers Home Administration may seem long by a calendar, but working to change the policies of a bureaucracy such as the Forest Service sometimes seems beyond human-made measurement. Western North Carolina Alliance had to deal with the wish that they could have gotten "more done quicker," as the growth of the organization was slow, especially relative to the enormity of their issues. The slow fulfillment of big expectations can temper the pride of achievement with disappointment.

Sometimes disappointment comes from the disembodied "market" rather than bureaucracy. The Appalachian Center for Economic Networks found the market for their products difficult to break into. The Dungannon Development Commission found itself competing unsuccessfully in the market for ladies' garments with other sewing factories around the world. Even local enterprises, such as the cannery and laundromat, failed financially. Marketing Appalachian Traditional Community Handcrafts could not maintain profitable retail stores and found itself competing in the same markets with its own members.

Some disappointments are internal rather than external. The Appalachian Communities for Children did not succeed in developing the necessary strong board structure and staff communication between the two counties that ACC serves. Efforts to address some of these issues within the Kentucky Small Farms Project brought about the departure of one of its co-ops, which left in frustration and disagreement over the changes.

The unyielding context in which they work also disappoints community-based mediating structures and tarnishes the glimmer of the democratic prospect for them. Raising overhead costs and winning respect as a non-profit organization plagued the Federation of Appalachian Housing Enterprises after a decade of operation. The multiple demands of an overload of work, keeping up with funding, creating and maintaining the group's cohesion internally and identity externally, and internal and external conflict contributed to the burnout of staff. Even SafeSpace found the continued and growing expectation that it could operate on the sweat equity of volunteers and underpaid staff to be a burden. The slow and uncertain process of passing legislation disappointed the Virginia Black Lung Association. A leader of the Bumpass Cove Citizens Group lamented, "We lost our innocence," in the face of the stubborn opposition that group faced, even from public officials. Eventually, BCCG lost both its group and any hope of having the toxic materials in the area removed.

Not surprisingly, some of our community-based mediating structures expressed disappointment with the politics of the 1980s, despite its new emphasis on mediating structures. The Southeast Women's Employment Coalition lost funding in the 1980s as foundation funds shifted to make up for deficits created by changes in funding within the Reagan administration. Despite its ability to survive the 1980s, one leader at Roadside Theater still found the decade "pretty dark political times when cultural equity has not been a priority of the government."

The disappointments of our community-based mediating structures with the 1980s are well founded. Poverty increased dramatically, income declined, and social capital was depleted further, as we have seen in Chapter 1. Tarnish fell on the democratic prospect in Appalachia from the smoke of burnt offerings to limited government and marketplace politics. However diminished the democratic prospect, though, community-based mediating structures still provide a safe and sure road to it, despite their shortcomings and disappointments.

Developing Leadership

The long process of community change includes the development of local leadership. Clearly, most of our community-based mediating structures deliberately attended to this form of human capital development through organizational arrangements. Appalachian Peoples Action Coalition limited its board positions to two years and thus rotated opportunities for decision making among members. The Western North Carolina Alliance limited positions on its steering committee to two years as well. Committee participation provided the staff of the Appalachian Ohio Public Interest Center the opportunity to share responsibility with members and to develop or utilize their leadership skills. Group facilitation offered a particular focus for development. A large effort, such as the protest of the Brumley Gap Concerned Citizens, provided a wide range of opportunities for leadership development. The "expert" from outside the group deliberately arranged for "experts" from within the group to testify, conduct research, and raise funds. A large organization may also be deliberate in its own renewal through leadership development. The West Virginia Education Association had field workers who went to individual schools and chapters to find, recruit, and develop potential new leaders. Conferences and workshops provided formal training opportunities in leadership skills. Members elected to the Delegate Assembly had additional opportunities to attend workshops on leadership skills, including lobbying. Although the methods vary from organization to organization, based on size and other factors, all serious efforts at community change include some form of leadership development.

Some leadership development comes from the conduct of ordinary business of community-based mediating structures. The plethora of programs of the Dungannon Development Corporation required members and local residents to get personal training and background in areas such as child care, economic development, the conduct of high school and college classes, maternal and infant health, water utilities, and the like; to seek funding for such programs; and to implement them. The Kentucky Small Farms Project created new leadership roles for members: conducting programs of animal management and supervising the work crews that visited their communities. The Ohio Valley Environmental Coalition provided members who showed promise for expanded participation and leadership roles challenges such as running a meeting or new forms of involvement such as participating in grassroots lobby day. Members of the Bumpass Cove Citizens Group had to become researchers in order to produce the information on the toxic effects of chemicals in the landfill that they wanted and could trust. The quality of their work surprised, but did not please, state officials.

Some leadership development entails undoing years of socialization to poor self-images. For example, SafeSpace had a wonderful record of developing volunteers and staff from among its clients. This work began with counseling and support groups to inform individual women of the public nature of their problem and to remove a sense of their responsibility for the violence toward them. The ability to get people to tell their own story and to share it with others within the free space of a community-based mediating structure validates the storytellers' experience, grievance, and courage and competence to deal with them. Narratives have always played a major, although often unobserved, role in social movements and other forms of collective action for social and political transformation (Couto 1993). Roadside Theater directly addressed the form of leadership development that promotes self-worth and pride by the importance they placed on telling one's history. The narratives of leadership development extend to current events in local communities and not just to past history. The ability of some of the Bumpass Cove Citizens Group's members to deal with state officials as peers improved the level of their participation and did much to eradicate the "I'm just a housewife" syndrome.

Some community-based mediating structures are intermediaries that have the specific task of assisting member groups with leadership development. BCCG members acquired their skills to research toxic materials from

Highlander Research and Education Center. Marketing Appalachian Traditional Community Handcrafts gave workshops for its groups on long-term planning, financial management, board structure, grant writing, and marketing. The success of this effort marked the increased independence of the member groups and their capacity to compete with MATCH for funding for the same sources. The Federation of Appalachian Housing Enterprises considered one of its major responsibilities to be the development of its own internal leadership from among its member groups. Sharing the experience of other groups, especially during the time of start-up, gave groups such as Clay Mountain Housing a boost in developing its leaders. The Southern Empowerment Project specifically emphasized the development of local leaders. In member-run and member-controlled mediating structures, SEP trained people in the development of local leadership, rather than in service provision or expert advocacy. The Tennessee Task Force Against Domestic Violence also functioned as a training intermediary for leadership development. Like SEP, the task force grew from the expressed intention of its members, such as SafeSpace, to contribute to its leadership development needs.

Other community-based mediating structures provide more general support for leadership development to their member groups. Southeast Women's Employment Coalition began to support women as directors of community-based mediating structures and followed its members' needs into other areas of training. Its work involved the further development of current leaders rather than developing new leadership. Similarly, the West Virginia Primary Care Association worked to increase the influence of its members—health professionals, doctors, and administrators—who were already leaders in the state's health care field. The Appalachian Alliance also worked with current leaders rather than working to develop new ones. It lacked a specific focus such as gender or a specific issue such as health. It did not contribute to leadership development as much as it did contribute leaders to new groups, such as the Kentucky Fair Tax Coalition and the Western North Carolina Alliance.

When management matters pile up, a community-based mediating structure unfortunately may neglect leadership development, at least temporarily. For example, the funding problems and staff turnover at the Council of Senior West Virginians meant that staff depended on established leaders of the organization, supported the visible, "natural" leaders in the community, and put less effort into the development of new leadership.

People served by a community-based mediating structure who are not its members offer additional opportunities for leadership development. The Appalachian Independence Center's ACTION program (Advocates Committed to Independence and Opportunities Now) intended to develop leaders among people with disabilities. Appalachian Communities for Children made leadership development part of every program rather than the focus of one. All of the work of ACC related to leadership. Over half of ACC's staff members were former students. ACC encouraged parents, in groups of ten, to form their own councils and create their own projects. If a council could present a need and propose a program to address it, ACC would provide a small amount of seed money, $100, to develop the idea. ACC's small grants were significant in the capital-starved area in which ACC worked.

Thus, we come back to a fundamental of leadership development—the provision of social capital. Community-based mediating structures develop leadership by investing moral resources and increased and improved human goods and services in people as community members and in their roles in continuing and improving their communities. The Appalachian Center for Economic Networks did this by providing relevant work skills, which allowed people to find income-producing jobs. Clay Mountain Housing dealt directly with the fundamental human need for shelter and indirectly with leadership development. Better housing improved not only the self-esteem of parents and children but also the prospect that they would set other development goals for themselves. Directly and indirectly, community-based mediating structures make a fundamental contribution to social capital through their efforts to develop leadership among their members and also the people they serve.

Finding Help in Their Efforts of Change

In Chapter 8, we recounted the forms of help that our community-based mediating structures acquired to deal with their management matters. Our groups also use these forms of assistance to deal with the long and unsure process of community change. Not surprisingly, dense horizontal and vertical networks of many of the same groups play a part in finding help in the process of change. This extends beyond sharing ideas to sharing resources.

Locally, our community-based mediating structures depended on common funding sources, such as the Commission on Religion in Appalachia and the Appalachian Development Projects Committee (ADPC), for general assistance in dealing with the challenges and long process of community change. Exchanges at meetings of ADPC provided a foundation for additional formal and informal exchanges among the groups. For example, the Ohio Valley Environmental Coalition utilized staff from Kentuckians for the Commonwealth for training. These exchanges also validated the individual experiences of staff and members of organizations in dealing with the ups and downs of community change efforts. Other funding sources brought community-based mediating structures into vertical networks with organizations dealing with the same issues of the disabled, health care, housing, etc. Some of these funding sources were national, such as the federal government, and thereby provided local groups with a national array of experiences from which to draw.

Some groups entered vertical national networks because of their institutional make-up or the issues that they addressed. The West Virginia Educational Association, the West Virginia Primary Care Association, and the Council of Senior West Virginians all had national counterparts that helped with broad social change issues as well as management matters. Local environmental groups may be independent, but they still may relate to a variety of national environmental groups, such as the Environmental Support Center and the Citizens Clearinghouse on Chemical Waste, for direction in their efforts. These national groups distill lessons from thousands of local efforts, and disseminate them through horizontal and vertical networks.

Experience also brings some groups into the network of training intermediaries that may themselves be in the network of other training intermediaries. For example, the Southern Empowerment Project provided a network for its members and placed them in touch with the Midwest Academy because of the reliance that SEP placed on it. Highlander played a similar role in providing some direction for community change efforts and introducing groups to additional resources, including training intermediaries.

Sometimes, groups may look afield for the assistance they need. For example, the Brumley Gap Concerned Citizens gained training in nonviolent protest from the American Friends Service Committee. Roadside Theater brought in guest directors to renew its creative energies. The Appalachian Ohio Public Interest Center utilized the services of the Peace Development Fund to deal with its difficult transition.

Community-based mediating structures create their own resources to add to the horizontal and vertical networks of which they are a part if the networks are insufficient. SafeSpace developed the Tennessee Task Force Against Domestic Violence to assist in broad change efforts as well as other matters. The Dungannon Development Council developed staff members with new management styles, who formed Appalachian Women Empowered (AWE). AWE trained other community groups in decision making within circles rather than within the traditional pyramids and networks of bureaucratic lines. As in the matters of management, these networks support local efforts and, reciprocally, provide the vitality of intermediary training and the accountability of funding organizations.

Reflecting on What Works

As we saw in Chapter 2, political democratic theorists generally despair of replicating and extending the success of particular local groups and their leadership into some transforming political movement. The long and difficult process of community change includes the problem of generalizing from local experience and finding hope for the democratic prospect in scores of modest and out-of-way examples. Yet, there are general lessons that can be drawn from local experiences with the democratic prospect—both those that succeeded and those that failed.

The Factors of Success

Community-based mediating structures promote the democratic prospect when they successfully defend their communities against grave threats to their very existence. The Brumley Gap Concerned Citizens provided the clearest example of a total victory and the achievement of a group's goals and objectives. Four elements suggest what works in these successful efforts. First, the people of Brumley Gap had a *clear and cohesive identity*. Second, *the threat was clear*. Two mountain ridges and a valley left no doubt as to who would be left under water by the flood of a reservoir. Third, BGCC *had excellent leadership and expert advice* from Dick Austin, who did not live in Brumley Gap but functioned as staff to BGCC. Fourth, BGCC joined *horizontal and vertical networks to influence decision makers*. This included forming the Coalition of American Electric Consumers. The story of Brumley Gap sharpens the disappointment of some political theorists with local victories, because the group disbanded after its victory. They developed a systematic critique of the political economy of energy policy and use, just as Fisher hoped transformative democratic groups would. However, they also chose not to use this critique once the dam project was canceled. For some observers, this detracts from the victory at Brumley Gap. Nonetheless, Brumley Gap illustrates that local people can organize and successfully preserve community if they have a clear identity, a clear threat, excellent leadership, and leverage points in horizontal and vertical networks of organizations.

The story of the Bumpass Cove Citizens Group suggests what happens when a group has only a few of these elements. Its organized protest was partially successful; dumping stopped but the toxic materials were not removed. The group had excellent leaders, but their differences and quarrels reduced their effectiveness. The use of leverage points in vertical networks—for example, assistance from outside groups such as Highlander—

became divisive. One leader who had married into the community attempted to save the community from other longtime residents, who had supposedly fallen under the influence of alleged communists. Too many external threats may overwhelm and divide a group, increase the parochial nature of the conflict, and permit racism and other forms of social divisions to emerge. Events such as those at Bumpass Cove give political theorists of the democratic prospect reasons for skepticism about the transforming power of local change efforts.

Despite its problems, there are reasons to extol and celebrate the Bumpass Cove Citizens Group's contribution to the democratic prospect. Internally, local residents acquired leadership skills. Women especially increased their self-esteem and their competencies for political participation. Externally, other groups learned lessons from BCCG. In particular, the Yellow Creek Concerned Citizens (YCCC) group in Middlesboro, Kentucky, acquired lessons on internal cohesion and control over outside assistance. Coupled with a clear focus on a real threat and excellent leadership, YCCC replicated all four elements of successful efforts evident at Brumley Gap. Its local success has been complete: a halt to the pollution, clean-up, and a court victory establishing funds for medical care of residents in Yellow Creek and health screening for people exposed to environmental toxic materials in other parts of the state (L. Wilson 1989; Couto 1986; Staub 1983; and Cable 1993). National television networks broadcast segments on YCCC efforts, and two leaders from YCCC served on the staff of Highlander's environmental program. This transformative democratic achievement took place in part because of the lessons on the limits and problems of local organizing provided by the Bumpass Cove Citizens Group.

Likewise, successful efforts of community-based mediating structures to promote the democratic prospect also contain tensions. Group cohesion may be threatened by attempts to find leverage in vertical and horizontal networks or by attempts to select one or a few clear threats on which to focus. Excellent leadership by staff or group members can enable a group to navigate through these shoals that can wreck a community-based mediating structure or can leave it grounded and unable to move. In some cases, such as the Appalachian Alliance, excellent leadership is not enough. Successful as they were in some ways, the Alliance's leaders were not able to forge a sense of cohesion and a single purpose among the Alliance's members.

In other cases, leadership successfully created networks through chapters of its community-based mediating structures or among groups with common programs or problems. The Virginia Black Lung Association, the West Virginia Education Association, and the Western North Carolina Alliance were chapter organizations. The Federation of Appalachian Housing Enterprises, the Southern Empowerment Project, and the West Virginia Primary Care Association had organization members. The Appalachian Alliance, Marketing Appalachian Traditional Community Handcrafts, and the Southeast Women's Employment Coalition were organizations of member organizations. These umbrella organizations provided their member organizations additional leverage in their efforts to produce change or to acquire needed resources, including influence. Community-based coalitions and associations may reduce the tensions within community-based mediating structures between internal cohesion and external linkages.

Local and personal prejudices construct more tensions for successful community-based mediating structures to address. Most of our community-based mediating structures used the low number of African Americans in Central Appalachia to distance themselves from deliberate policies of racial inclusion. A few of them, such as the Southern Empowerment Project and the Southeast Women's Employment Coalition, adopted explicit policies of inclusive membership of groups or board members and programs on race. In addition, many community-based mediating structures utilized other means to break down barriers of race, gender, and class. Hiring and recruiting personnel, whether full-time or part-time, provides organizations with opportunities to diversify and address issues of human value and worth within the group. Leadership and staff exchanges, as in the case of the Appalachian Communities for Children, and program exchanges provided opportunities for personal contact between people of different races and backgrounds. An array of chapters and member groups also provided some guarantees against a strictly local focus and narrow constituency. Coalitions provided a broad context for the problem each member group or chapter addresses. Meetings of all chapters and member groups were more likely to be diverse than those of local groups, and they also provided more opportunities to address racism, sexism, homophobia, and other socially divisive prejudices while still maintaining group cohesion.

Our community-based mediating structures also showed what works to challenge institutional stagnation. Forms of representation and participation, such as member polls; organizational structure, such as chapters; and renewing and developing leadership by rotating board members and requiring extensive committee work all provide democratic processes within management matters. These processes play a role in providing excellent leadership, which along with group cohesion, a clear threat, and participation in horizontal and vertical networks, is part of the process of the democratic prospect at the community level. Obviously, these elements are not sequential, nor are they separable. Group cohesion arises from and supports excellent leadership. Participation in horizontal and vertical networks to remove a threat makes those networks all the more valuable.

Even when they succeed, our community-based groups are only part of a process of the democratic prospect, not the achievements of its goals. The most successful efforts of community-based mediating structures to promote the democratic prospect contain lessons, which need dissemination, about avoiding problems and pitfalls. The less successful efforts of community-based mediating structures make clear that progress toward the democratic prospect will not come as a series of uninterrupted successes. However, even the shortcomings of some groups, such as the Bumpass Cove Citizens Group, prepare other groups, such as the Yellow Creek Concerned Citizens, for great efficacy as long as there is a vehicle, such as the Highlander Center, to impart from one group to another the lessons of what works to further the democratic prospect.

The Content of the Democratic Prospect

The networks of community-based mediating structures within the democratic prospect introduce, once again, the concept of social capital into considerations of the democratic prospect. Robert Putnam, Robert Nisbet, and other commentators emphasize the moral resources of trust and cooperation as social capital and the formation and maintenance of dense horizontal networks. The input of members and the work of volunteers portray the sweat equity that community-based mediating structures locate and accrue. Underlying the sweat equity are trust and belief in cooperation, which are the moral resources of social capital. The support that community-based mediating structures provide to one another within horizontal networks is also a moral resource. Networks of social capital have origins that precede community-based mediating structures. Most apparently, Appalshop preceded Roadside Theater, and labor union participation provided leadership training and membership development for the Virginia Black Lung Association. Vertical networks are also related to collaborative efforts at social change. They serve as intermediary organizations for training, technical assistance, fund-raising, and meeting other needs of chapters or members at the local level. Not surprisingly, pursuit of the democratic prospect uses and increases the various forms of social capital.

Exclusive emphasis on the moral resources of social capital ignores the "cause" that contributes to the continuation of community-based mediating structures: the real social, human, economic, and community needs that community-based mediating structures address. These needs have roots in the paucity of public goods in the American formulation of social capital and the related narrow focus on the market as the primary arbitrator of social relations and provider of housing, health care, culture, environmental quality, and the other human goods and services of social capital. In addition to their development and use of moral resources, the West Virginia Education Association and the West Virginia Primary Care Association were rooted in and drew sustenance from real human needs and the urgent necessity to respond to them.

As social capital entrepreneurs, community-based mediating structures treat some market goods as public goods. Inasmuch as they can, they approach human needs and services as a right, not a commodity. Community-based mediating structures seem most successful in those areas of social capital that are mixed between market and public goods, such as housing, health care, and culture. They are least effective in the more market-driven domains of jobs and incomes. For example, the large-scale unemployment of coal miners in the early 1980s stymied the Appalachian Alliance as a problem beyond its capacity to respond. Social capital entrepreneurs have the same problems as other small capital entrepreneurs in the production and sale of market goods. ACEnet, MATCH, and DDC, which took on these tasks directly, found their greatest disappointment was lack of success in these areas. Obviously, the market provides a giant background and context for the social capital efforts of community-based mediating structures, efforts that have shown very little capacity to transform markets.

On the other hand, community-based mediating structures have a great deal of success in meeting the unique market demands of other community-based mediating structures. Southern Empowerment Project and Southeast Women's Employment Coalition responded to the "market" for training of one set of community-based mediating structures. The capacity to continue in this market depends upon a group's initial success, its ability to maintain and expand the community-based mediating structures they serve, and its ability to attract funds to support its work in this market. When SWEC's primary source of support withdrew, its capacity to work in this training market faded and then ended. SEP, however, continued to find foundation funds to support its work, supplementing the income it derived from tuition for its training and from membership dues.

Community-based mediating structures play their most effective roles in social capital by dealing with market failures. They draw attention to externalities, the consequences of market transactions that are subsidized at the expense of limiting community to market relations. The search for inexpensive handling of toxic wastes, for example, leads eventually to dumping them in the communities that have little political power and income. The toxic wastes in turn subtract from the environmental quality required to sustain community. Dumping these materials in places like Bumpass Cove subsidized an externality of the market at the cost of social capital. The public often learns of these subsidies through the protests of community-based mediating structures. Community-based mediating structures also challenge the internal, self-serving logic of market-driven resource development. Community-based mediating structures also enter into the cooperative arrangements of public agencies and corporate practices to challenge the management or provision of public goods. For example, the Western North Carolina Alliance challenged state and federal agencies, including the U.S. Forest Service, in its efforts to preserve environmental quality. Community-based mediating structures offer an early warning system of the depletion of social capital.

They may also warn of important omissions in the provision of social capital. Security from physical harm, for example, seems a primary prerequisite to community, yet many women and their children do not have this security. SafeSpace pointed this out locally, statewide, and nationally through its shelter program and its advocacy through the vertical networks that it helped to construct.

Community-based mediating structures play a central role in the provision of social capital, and not merely its defense. Appalachian Communities for Children introduced social capital programs of adult education in Clay County, where they were needed but absent. The Virginia Black Lung Association's experience also suggests how community-based mediating structures provide an important source of social capital not to an area but to people with a common problem. Roadside Theater brought social capital to the region in its cultural work. In addition, Roadside conducted its work in an alternative fashion, tailored to meet the political and cultural needs of its audience. ACC also introduced alternative approaches in the education that it provided, emphasizing "hands-on" approaches and the use of paraprofessionals recruited from among the ranks of successful students. The Ohio Valley Environmental Coalition took on the role of generating alternative plans to existing practices that depleted the social capital of environmental quality. Thus, community-based mediating structures may be both alternative sources of social capital and sources of alternative forms of social capital.

In this capacity, community-based mediating structures test new ideas and provide new forms of social capital. Their success means increased credibility for new approaches to human needs and services. Clay Mountain

Housing, reflecting the success and influence of the Federation of Appalachian Housing Enterprises, established credibility with government and banking officials for community-based mediating structures in a field crowded with lending regulations and housing codes. At the other end of their intermediary work, they also established credibility for people in need of housing. CMH and FAHE approached housing as a social capital investment in human capital and community rather than as the output of their programs.

Democratic Process and Democratic Prospects

The surest progress toward the democratic prospect is the provision of new forms and larger amounts of social capital. This entails organizing, advocacy, development, and services at the local level as well as the regional, state, and federal level. Improvement in the democratic prospect does not come easily, quickly, or irrevocably. There are no shortcuts and many disappointments. Large networks, both horizontal and vertical, sustain groups and individuals in their efforts to bring about change. Similarly, the process of promoting the democratic prospect entails developing new leaders and creating spaces in which people share their stories and find encouragement to develop their abilities and resources, individually and together.

CONCLUSION

They say they cannot pay us
To educate our child.
Their children live in luxury
Our children almost wild.

Which side are you on?
Which side are you on?
—Florence Reece,
   "Which Side Are You On?"

In 1944, Gunnar Myrdal completed ten years of exhaustive study on American race relations with the publication of the two-volume work, *An American Dilemma: The Negro Problem and American Democracy*. Few works in social science equal its breadth and the quality of its analysis. One hundred years after Alexis de Tocqueville's commentaries on America, Myrdal offered another international visitor's "outsider's" insight into American life. Unfortunately, Myrdal's views do not receive the same amount of attention as Tocqueville's.

Myrdal was concerned primarily with the central dilemma of American life: Americans do not live up to their beliefs. We believe that no group in America should be allowed to fall under a certain minimum level of living, the famous safety net that we heard so much about in the 1980s. We believe also that economic equality, in itself, is not wrong. Finally, according to Myrdal, the third element of the American Creed professes that groups and individuals should have equal opportunity. Despite these avowed beliefs, Myrdal found an America where Jim Crow and less formal racist arrangements denied opportunities to African Americans and tolerated social and political inequality that reinforced a degree of economic inequality so serious that the income of many Americans fell below subsistence level. The facts of everyday life contradicted the high moral plane that Americans professed to believe in and even died for. Our efforts to remedy some of the most egregious elements of that dilemma resulted in the civil rights movement. The legislation and court decisions of the 1950s through the 1970s brought about some progress, but it also made us more aware of how far we have to travel to bring national conditions and practices into line with our beliefs.

Our beliefs about equality have a continuing tension, if not an outright contradiction, with the enduring facts of inequality in American life. There are many Americans, including 20 percent of our children, who live in poverty and whose conditions challenge the American Creed. Some of us piece together this poverty with fragments of liberty, opportunity, and equality and promote social change as a defense of the American Creed against its shortcomings in practice. Others turn the kaleidoscope of the fragments of the American Creed and see the same groups of Americans in poverty and need but instead hold them responsible for their own conditions. This view defends the American Creed from its shortcomings by denying them and the consequent need to promote social change.

Myrdal brilliantly described the social practice he observed of defending the American Creed from the conditions of people in need even though these conditions contradicted the Creed's tenets of equality and acceptable minimal standards. He extrapolated this practice to the role of social science in America. In his estimation, American social science overstated its objective neutrality and defended the American Creed against its apparent contradictions by attributing the cause of inequality to some group, individual, or genetic condition. Social and economic inequalities were viewed as arising from individual and group differences rooted in culture. Social and economic inequalities could be amended by the choices of group members or could not be amended because of genetics. In either case, inequalities and their remedies were not the products of social relationships and thus were not subjects for social or public remedy (Myrdal 1944: 1035–64).

Myrdal found a parallel in the problems of race in America with the status, history, and problems of women and children (Myrdal 1944: 1073–78). He examined the history of abolition and race relations for parallels with women's conditions. It is not surprising, then, that the 1980s, which found new evidence that racial inequality continued in American society, also brought new social tolerance for increased numbers of women and children in poverty. The 1980s produced new social scientific defenses of inequality with new evidence of the origins of social and economic inequality in the culture and characteristics of the disadvantaged (Katz 1995). Myrdal would have recognized much of the social science of the 1980s as a thinly disguised effort to deny the social origins of social problems and the moral and social responsibilities that we as a community share for them. By the end of the decade, the United States could sadly claim first place among industrial nations in the percentage of children who grow up in poverty and last place in social policies to deal with the basic needs of poor children and families. The 1990s pushed us further into our sad status and denial. The welfare reform measures of 1996 rested solidly on our assumptions of personal responsibility for poverty and the adequacy of market mechanisms to promote social and economic equality.

This book began with a dilemma comparable to Myrdal's—the enduring poverty of the Central Appalachian region. Indeed, Florence Reece wrote "Which Side Are You On?" in 1935, just as Myrdal began his study. Our findings parallel Myrdal's observations. We have portrayed the dilemma that Myrdal found in American beliefs in terms of James Morone's concept of the democratic wish. Like the American Creed, we fashion the democratic wish from related but distinct parts. The democratic promise of limited government and market efficiencies fits well within the American Creed, as does the democratic prospect of community and increased social and economic equality.

We found a social conservative bias, just as Myrdal did. The democratic promise not only fashions the democratic wish, it also defends American social policy from the public and social sacrifices that the democratic prospect requires. Even social capital may be put to the service of the democratic promise rather than the democratic prospect. Robert Putnam's work on social capital permits those inclined to deny social responsibility for social problems to point to a deficit of social capital within a group as the origin and cause of their condition of need. We have examined how some analysts envision the role of mediating structures in relation to the democratic promise of the market rather than the democratic prospect of community. We have spent the brunt of these pages making the case for mediating structures and social capital in terms of the democratic prospect, or an expansive American Creed. This case assumes the need to change the social conditions that contradict the American Creed of some basic minimum level of welfare, equal opportunity, and a higher middle ground to mitigate the extremes of socioeconomic inequality. These pages interpret social conditions in terms of social capital, which ultimately is a form of social responsibility.

New Prospects for Democracy

Our primary concern has been to explain how mediating structures can promote the democratic prospect. We have explained that mediating structures have several conflicting roles in democratic theory. As Salamon pointed out, they may promote, hinder, or be irrelevant to democracy. Most of the social theorists of mediating structures extol them as a defense of limited government. Political theorists, if they deal with mediating structures at all, find them irrelevant and a possible hindrance to the democratic prospect. We have made the case that mediating structures may promote the democratic prospect and have pointed to when and how they do so.

Myrdal commented briefly on Tocqueville's observation about voluntary associations. He agreed with Tocqueville that voluntary associations manifest the generosity and helpfulness of Americans. Myrdal suggested that this temperament is "part and parcel of the American Creed." He elaborated, "It shows up in the Americans' readiness to make financial sacrifices for charitable purposes. No country has so many cheerful givers as America. It was not only rugged 'individualism,' nor a relatively continuous prosperity that made it possible for America to get along without a publicly organized welfare policy almost up to the Great Depression in the thirties, it was also the world's most generous private charity" (Myrdal 1944: 11–12).

Ironically, in the 1980s, the ascendancy of the democratic promise of limited government and market economics invoked mediating structures as being illustrative of American charity and as evidence that we could revert to the reduced policies of welfare that characterized America before the New Deal. Somehow, the rugged individualism of unadaptive capitalism, modestly mitigated by "kinder and gentler" mediating structures, would permit Americans to dismantle the social welfare policy programs in place since the New Deal and dismiss the sense of social responsibility and cohesion that prompted those policies.

The evidence that we have provided here suggests that such a reversion would be both a false democratic promise and a detriment to the democratic prospect. First, a portion of the human needs in American society are tied to market capitalism, especially the labor force knot that binds social capital and the market. Second, the "generosity and helpfulness" of the tradition of voluntary associations, which Tocqueville commented upon and Myrdal also found later, are inversely distributed. They are more closely associated with the places and wealth of their origins than with the places and people who need them. The facile reliance on mediating structures for social welfare policies by advocates of limited government and market economics ignores the narratives and lessons of mediating structures. Community-based mediating structures spend a considerable portion of their effort mitigating the worst consequences of a market economy predicated on rugged individualism or unadaptive capitalism. Community-based mediating structures promote the democratic prospect in places where public social welfare policies are most desperately needed. They are a redistributive element of the generosity and resources of voluntary associations as well.

The narratives of these community-based organizations suggest that they have complex political, social, and economic roles. Their political roles involve providing groups and individuals space to trace their conditions to their historical, social, and economic origins and to create imaginative alternative practices to redress their condition and to better express the American Creed. Their social role entails the networks that Putnam and others suggested that we look for, but they weave government programs into these networks far more than limited-government advocates understand. Far from being only a protective shield from government intrusion, as many social theorists portray them, community-based mediating structures leverage government funds for needed services and invoke government regulations to protect their members from incursions of the corporate champions of market capitalism.

These political roles express themselves differently from group to group and from time to time in the same group. Some community-based mediating structures—Appalachian Center for Economic Networks, Appalachian Communities for Children, and the Appalachian Independence Center, for example—received government funds and other forms of assistance to carry out their work of increasing and improving social capital. Other community-based mediating structures—Brumley Gap Concerned Citizens and the West Virginia Education Association, for example—demanded from public officials a higher standard for their protection and provision of social capital. The Council of Senior West Virginians did both at different times. The people of the Bumpass Cove Citizens Group increased their networks of moral resources when they learned not to trust government and to trust themselves more. This action did not endorse the neoconservative premise of the untrustworthiness of government but rather a citizens' critique that government and public decision making should be less influenced by the interests of private capital and corporations than they are. The democratic prospect does not attempt to turn public responsibility over to government but sees government as one expression of community. The relationship of community-based mediating structures and government retells the story told by Abraham Lincoln at Gettysburg, "government of the people, by the people, and for the people."

Naturally, these political and social roles have economic implications. The narratives of our community-based organizations suggest that mediating structures only supplement efforts to redress market failures rather than reduce or eliminate the need for such public efforts. They mitigate market externalities such as workers' injury and environmental degradation. They also attract a portion of the small supply of social capital to supplement a dearth of public goods such as education and housing. The roles expressed in the narratives of our community-based mediating structures indicate that they give much more attention to the democratic prospect than to the democratic promise of limited government and market economics.

The facile reliance on mediating structures within the democratic promise also ignores the lessons we have acquired about leadership within community-based mediating structures. Leadership provides such mediating structures the capacity for empowerment and change by expressing the value and dignity of individual members of a community. In addition, leadership is responsible for complex management matters at the local level. The origins of this leadership cannot be taken for granted, as if it arises from needs. It does not. It rises from hope in the midst of needs—hope that organized efforts can change adverse conditions and that people can be effective change agents. That hope is rooted in the belief that public officials and the general public abide by an American Creed of opportunity, equality, and basic decency. It is kept alive by public and political leaders who show that they too abide by those beliefs and accept social responsibility for addressing and redressing the conditions of others.

The lessons of community-based mediating structures also suggest that the continuation of their leadership, like their origins, cannot be taken for granted. Time after time, the narratives instruct us about discouragement and the demands of renewal. These are not merely personal and private troubles. Leaders borrow from each other and support each other in loose networks and formal organizations. Funding provides an important context for the continuation of leadership. Leadership among community-based mediating structures amounts to social capital entrepreneurship. It is made possible by philanthropic foundations and public funds of local, state, and federal programs. It is made difficult by the inadequacy of these funds at all times and by their decline at other times, such as in the 1980s.

Which Side Are You On?

Eventually, the success of community-based organizations in promoting the democratic prospect depends upon a broader, national willingness to provide increased amounts and improved forms of social capital, the moral resources and human goods and services that we invest in each other to produce and maintain ourselves in a community that extends beyond market relations of the workplace. We have focused on one decade, the 1980s, and portrayed its policies as part of a continuum of politics that extends from the New Deal to the present and that will continue into a new century. This segment of politics expressed our difficult efforts to fashion the democratic wish from individual liberty and community bonds.

The lyrical question, "Which Side Are You On?" reaches us across time from a miner's cabin in Harlan County. The sides may have changed since Harlan County and the 1930s, but our own time has its own challenges to meet in combining the economic differences that come with individual liberty and the social equality implied in community bonds—the democratic promise and the democratic prospect. The politics and policies of the 1980s betrayed the democratic promise and promoted market democracy as a surrogate for liberty and limited government. The democratic prospect needs new attention. Community-based mediating structures carry our hopes for that renewed attention. They will realize our hopes, however modestly, under the conditions we have explained. Those conditions include the deliberate action of local leadership supported by public and philanthropic resources to increase the amounts of social capital and to improve its forms. However their roles may have changed since Florence Reece's question, mediating structures still play a vital part in the expression and pursuit of the democratic prospect, with stakes for the American Creed that remain just as high.

Community-Based Mediating Structures by Area of Focus

Culture and the Arts

Roadside Theater, Whitesburg, Kentucky
Repertory theater dealing with political events and cultural aspects of Central
 Appalachia; part of a media collective called Appalshop.

Economic Development

Appalachian Center for Economic Networks (ACEnet), Athens, Ohio
Formation and support of small enterprise.

Dungannon Development Commission (DDC), Dungannon, Virginia
Development of services, infrastructure, and small manufacturing.

Marketing Appalachian Traditional Community Handcrafts (MATCH), Berea,
 Kentucky
Support and marketing of arts and crafts.

Southeast Women's Employment Coalition (SWEC), Atlanta, Georgia
Coordination of groups and efforts to gain increased and better paying employment
 opportunities for women.

Education

West Virginia Education Association (WVEA), Charleston, West Virginia
Led a strike in 1990 to increase state funding for education.

Environment

Brumley Gap Concerned Citizens (BGCC), Washington County, Virginia
Protested and stopped plans of the American Electric Power Company to build a
  pumped-storage dam and reservoir.

Bumpass Cove Citizens Group (BCCG), Washington County, Tennessee
Protested and halted dumping of hazardous waste in former zinc mines in the area.

Ohio Valley Environmental Coalition (OVEC), Proctorville, Ohio
Monitors threats to air and water quality in the tri-state area of Kentucky, Ohio, and
  West Virginia.

Western North Carolina Alliance (WNCA), Asheville, North Carolina
Monitors and participates in plans of the U.S. Forest Service in the region.

Families and Children

Appalachian Communities for Children (ACC), Annville, Kentucky
Educational service from preschool to adult; family support services and leadership
  development.

SafeSpace, Newport, Tennessee
Domestic violence shelter and advocacy to prevent family violence.

Housing

Clay Mountain Housing, Inc. (CMH), Clay County, West Virginia
Local development of affordable housing.

Federation of Appalachian Housing Enterprises (FAHE), Berea, Kentucky
Coordination of housing development efforts in the Central Appalachian region; public
  interest advocacy.

Human Resources

Appalachian Peoples Action Coalition (APAC), Athens, Ohio
General advocacy and service for low-income residents of the area.

Appalachian Independence Center (AIC), Abingdon, Virginia
Provides services for persons with disabilities and advocacy for policies that permit
  independent living.

Council of Senior West Virginians (CSWV), Charleston, West Virginia
Policy advocacy on behalf of seniors.

Kentucky Small Farms Project (KSFP), Jackson, Kentucky
Confederation of small-garden and livestock cooperatives.

Virginia Black Lung Association (VBLA), Richlands, Virginia
Advocacy for the prevention of black lung and compensation for its victims.

Organizational and Leadership Development

Southern Empowerment Project (SEP), Maryville, Tennessee
Provides training for staff and members of community organizations in the region.

Public Policy

Appalachian Alliance, Knoxville, Tennessee
Public interest advocacy, including major study of landownership and taxation.

Appalachian Ohio Public Interest Campaign (AOPIC), Athens, Ohio
Public interest research, training of community leaders.

West Virginia Primary Care Association, Charleston, West Virginia
Advocacy and monitoring of policies dealing with primary care and technical assistance to primary care centers serving low-income residents.

APPENDIX B

Methodology

Selection Criteria

The twenty-three community-based mediating structures selected for this study are or were based in the Central Appalachian region or immediately surrounding areas. Eighteen of the groups were active when interviewed and studied; the five others had ended activity after significant achievement over at least three years. All of the groups received grants from the Appalachian Development Projects Committee (ADPC) of the Commission on Religion in Appalachia (CORA). ADPC provided grants to community-based mediating structures and required that they have representation of the people they served and that the groups use organized action of local residents to improve the conditions they addressed. The grants of ADPC were small (generally $5,000 to $20,000), came from mainline Protestant denominations, and were limited geographically to Appalachia.

In selecting among the ADPC projects to be included, we chose groups that satisfied the following overall criteria:

- geographic dispersion (groups from different places within Central Appalachia and nearby areas);
- groups with some clear link to social capital formation (groups involved in the organization and delivery of human services, advocacy for low-income and disfranchised groups, the development of alternative economic opportunities, etc.);
- groups with successful track records (ones that had operated for at least two years with clear victories or successful programs);
- groups with various organizational patterns in terms of staff size, funding level, membership based on residence, workplace, or other factors; and
- groups with different orientations to change, including organizing, advocacy, development, service provision, self-help, or some combination.

Several sources provided information on the groups selected. In addition to proposals and reports filed with CORA, we conducted and transcribed on-site interviews with staff, residents, board members, and formal members of each group. Finally, each group graciously provided reports and other written information about themselves.

Another criterion for selection was a lack of published material about the group. Several other excellent and important community-based mediating structures and their efforts are not included in our study because their efforts have made it into print already. Save Our Cumberland Mountains (SOCM) is one of the most successful and longest operating grassroots citizens' organizations in the nation. Staff and members of SOCM instructed Paul Wellstone in rural organizing as he wrote his book *How the Rural Poor Got Power* (1978) and provided Harry Boyte an example of a backyard revolution for his book *The Backyard Revolution: Understanding the New Citizen Movement* (1980). Kentuckians for the Commonwealth, in an expression of their own power to define themselves, conducted and published their own history of grassroots organizing on several issues, including the broad form deed, which permitted coal companies legal justification for environmental havoc, taxation of unmined minerals, and environmental quality. In ten years, this exemplary grassroots organization had established eleven chapters with almost 2,500 members (Zuercher 1991; Szakos 1993). Two other nationally significant worker- or citizen-led efforts deserve to be mentioned and studied further: the worker buyout of Wierton Steel (Harvard Business School 1983) and the Tri-State Environmental Council (Clorefene-Casten 1993). Community organizing and leadership in Ivanhoe, Virginia, received extraordinary attention in the book *It Comes from the People*, by Hinsdale, Lewis, and Waller (1995), which combines participatory action research, liberation theology, and in-depth reflections on leadership and the process of change. Prior to this study, the people of Ivanhoe wrote their own two-volume history, *Remembering Our Past, Building Our Future* and *Telling Our Stories, Sharing Our Lives* (Lewis and O'Donnell 1990). Alex Haley, author of *Roots*, took note of the study and invited the contributing authors to his farm in East Tennessee to read from it to other writers in the region. The book also received the annual W. D. Weatherford Award of Berea College, which goes to the book best portraying Appalachian people and issues.

Though not included in the twenty-three groups we studied, the Highlander Research and Education Center deserves special mention for the role it played in educating and developing the leadership qualities of many of the leaders of those groups. Begun in the 1930s, Highlander trained union leaders and organizers throughout the South initially; civil rights workers in the 1940s and 1950s; and, since the mid-1960s, has worked with a wide variety of community organizations and organizing efforts in Appalachia (Adams 1975; Glen 1988; Glen 1993; Horton and Freire 1990). Indeed, one of the outstanding lessons that the experiences of successful community-based mediating structures impart is the importance of the analytical perspective and horizontal and vertical linkages with other groups and resources that they acquire through the work of organizations such as Highlander.

Since at least the New Deal, Appalachia has been center stage in the drama of mediating structures in American democratic life. Highlander is part of that drama. There are other important actors that make cameo appearances in the events that this book depicts. The United Mine Workers of America, in the time from the Wagner Act of the early New Deal until the late 1940s, grew into the most powerful labor union in America. Its agreement with the Bituminous Coal Operators of America in the 1950s marked its extensive power in the industry (Couto 1987). Eventually, that power led to corruption and, in turn, to reform movements. Miners, their families, and their supporters organized roving pickets to protest changes in the coal industry, including new UMWA policies, despite the opposition of the union. Inspired in part by the civil rights movement, miners, their families, and supporters organized the black lung movement and the Miners for Democracy. The first achieved an unprecedented policy to compensate for occupational illness and to regulate the conditions that brought it on. The Miners for Democracy achieved one of the most complete reforms of a labor union in recent history. Both of these achievements had their vagaries and subsequent ups and downs, which simply illustrate that reform is not a one-time effort and that the work of mediating structures may change over time but does not end. The cotton industry produced an occupational illness just as the coal industry did. Workers in that industry also organized to compensate victims of byssinosis or brown lung and to reduce its occurrence (Botsch 1993). The published scholarship on these events is extensive (B. E. Smith 1987; Seltzer 1985; Couto 1993a: 165–241) and consequently not repeated here. Part II brings new attention to less visible and less familiar cases of community-based mediating structures in Appalachia.

The Use of Narrative

The 1980s brought renewed attention to stories or narratives, which we use extensively in Part II. Narratives became important elements of methodology in the social sciences (Couto 1993b). In their major and popular study of the 1980s, *Habits of the Hearts*, Robert Bellah and his colleagues depended primarily on stories to examine American social and political life. Alasdair MacIntyre (1981), the preeminent philosopher, distinguishes human beings by their ability to tell stories. In his *The Call of Stories: Teaching and the Moral Imagination* (1989), Robert Coles expresses the value of grounding large social and human dramas in the stories of individual human beings (Coles 1989: 23). I have been more pedantic than Coles and have rendered very concrete, human stories in abstract, impersonal, social science terms.

I took my analytical direction with the encouragement of Howard Gardner's work, *Leading Minds: An Anatomy of Leadership* (1994). Gardner distinguishes leadership by the ability of a person to relate a story of a group or organization. Relating a story, he argues, involves embodying it more than merely telling it. The nature of the story that leaders relate distinguishes them. For Gardner, an ordinary leader "relates the traditional story of his or her group as effectively as possible"; an innovative leader brings new attention or a "fresh twist" to a familiar but ignored story; a visionary leader relates a new story or one that is familiar to only a few. Gardner cites great religious leaders of the past—Moses, Confucius, Jesus, Buddha, Mohammed—and more contemporary leaders, such as Gandhi and Jean Monnet (Gardner 1994: 9–11), as visionary leaders who improve and increase social capital. Such leaders relate stories of common bonds among people that imply new forms of association and larger amounts of social responsibility, that envision "potential life experiences" of groups marginalized by the current distribution of social, economic, and political resources (Gardner 1994: 223). In the terms of James MacGregor Burns (1978), the stories that visionary leaders embody are ones that relate transforming values. Gardner continues, "The formidable challenge confronting the visionary leader is to offer a story, and an embodiment, that builds on the most credible of past syntheses, revisits them in the light of present concerns, leaves open a place for future events, and allows individual contributions by the persons in the group" (Gardner 1994: 56).

The 1980s spilled over with innovative leadership. Ronald Reagan, Margaret Thatcher, and others brought old stories and values of the limited government and free markets to new prominence. However charismatic, these innovative leaders championed old forms of association and smaller amounts of social responsibility. These are the opposite of the elements of visionary leadership. Reagan, Thatcher, and their fellow conservatives presented innovative leadership for the traditional story of their groups. The stories of the community-based mediating structures we present here offer other, less known, and very different innovative stories, stories of social and political intervention to redress inequality, human need, and human suffering. The stories of the social and political interventions of these community-based mediating structures in many instances suggest transforming values and social bonds that imply expanded responsibilities that people have for one another. Their innovative stories have many more elements of the stories of visionary leaders.

Several sources contributed to the narratives of each of the organizations. Two to six people in each group were interviewed. In general, they were staff, members, and board members of the organizations. All of the people interviewed are listed in the references. In some cases, I have used quotes without attribution. I have done this when I thought it best to protect the privacy of the source. In telling the story, I have done my best to provide the place and context of the quote. All of the organizations had records and clippings of their activities, which we consulted. All of them had received funding from the Commission on Religion in Appalachia and had proposals and reports on file with CORA, which we consulted. In one or two cases, the organizations had compiled such extensive records that they had been turned over to university archives, which we also consulted. Hopefully, the stories we have used validate the claims that social and human analysts, philosophers, and scholars have made about narrative as method.

Protocol for Research

The work of the Center for Community Change reflected on the lessons it acquired during twenty-five years of work with community-based mediating structures (CCC 1992). Ten of those lessons went into the following interview protocol, which was used in conducting the interviews and other investigations of the community-based mediating structures we studied.

1. The community must feel it "owns" the organization.
What is the community of this group?
What forms of representation and participation do community members have?
How do the organization's leaders maintain extensive involvement of community members?
What is the current vision of the organization, and who provides it?

2. A community-based organization must continue to organize and involve community people.
What initial issues brought the group together?
Has the group taken on other issues? If so, how did that transition occur?
Has the group continued to involve members and board members in organizing efforts? What is the level of participation of members in the actions and activities of the organization?
What effect has the continued or decreased involvement of community members had on the vitality and creativity of the group?

Has the group been inclusive or exclusive of people based on race, gender, or any other factor?

What changes, if any, have occurred over time to make it easier or more difficult to organize people?

Have there been changes within the community—for example, decline or change of other organizations?

3. A community group needs efficient, accountable organization as well as a cause.

How did the group acquire the skills to manage finances and make reports?

Has the group had management problems? If so, what were they, and how did the group deal with them?

4. Development and organizing are not incompatible.

Is the group's main focus organizing or development?

In what ways has the group combined its main focus with the other?

How and why did the group move from one focus to another?

5. There is a life cycle to many community organizations.

Where is this group in organizational development according to stage theory for nonprofit organizations that the work of Management Assistance Group provides?

How has the group dealt with any transitions in its development?

If it is still operating, what is the feeling for longevity?

If it is defunct, what were the causes of cessation? Was its purpose completed?

6. Community change is a long-term process for which there are no cookie-cutter solutions.

What are the accomplishments of the group?

What are its major disappointments?

To what may success and disappointment be ascribed?

What are the unique aspects of the specific context of the group?

What has the group done to develop new leadership within the organization and the community?

Who does the group depend on for staff and board training and development?

7. Ideas need to travel.

On whom do the group's staff, board, and members depend for information on the broad nature of its issues, strategies, and resources?

What meetings, associations, and forms of information are most useful about community-based change efforts?

8. Coalitions are crucial.

What coalitions has the group formed, joined, or avoided?

Why did they take this action?

What are the advantages of coalition membership?

What are the difficulties in constructing, maintaining, and participating in coalitions?

9. We need to generate more financial support for the movement of community groups.
What has been the financial history of the group? How have its size and sources
  changed?
Who has provided funding?
What practices of funding agencies hinder and aid the group?

10. We need to reflect more on what works.
What "works" for this group in community-based change?
What do staff and board members single out as the most important reason for the suc-
  cess of the group and the most important problem for the group?

REFERENCES

Archives

Johnson City, Tennessee
　　Archives of Appalachia, East Tennessee State University
　　　　Appalachian Alliance
　　　　Bumpass Cove–Embreeville Collection
　　　　Tennessee Department of Health Collection
Knoxville, Tennessee
　　Commission on Religion in Appalachia
　　　　Records of annual reports and proposals on all of the community-based
　　　　　　organizations (see Appendix A for list of organizations)
New Market, Tennessee
　　Highlander Research and Education Center Library

Interviews

Interviews by Richard A. Couto
West Virginia Education Association: Jackie Goodwin, Charleston, W.Va.,
　　October 1992
West Virginia Primary Care Association: Jill Hutchinson, Charleston, W.Va.,
　　October 1992

Interviews by Catherine S. Guthrie
Appalachian Alliance and Southeast Women's Employment Coalition: Betty Jean Hall,
　　Washington, D.C., March 29, 1993
Appalachian Alliance and Southern Empowerment Project: June Rostan, Maryville,
　　Tenn., June 28, 1993
Appalachian Communities for Children: Judy Martin, Judy Sizemore, and Carolene
　　Turner, Annville, Ky., April 2, 1993; Judy Martin, telephone, December 7, 1993

Appalachian Communities for Economic Networks: Kathryn Lad and Marty Zinn, telephone, October 15, 1993

Appalachian Independence Center: Greg Morrell, telephone, April 30, 1993; Greg Morrell and Jeannette Seitz, Abingdon, Va., April 30, 1993

Appalachian Ohio Public Interest Center: Bob Garbo and Carol Kuhre, Athens, Ohio, April 4, 1993; Carol Kuhre, telephone, October 27, 1993

Appalachian Peoples Action Coalition: Dean Ferrell, Kathryn Lad, Paul Rutter, and Peg Winkler, Athens, Ohio, April 13, 1993

Brumley Gap Concerned Citizens: Levonda McDaniel, Yvonne and Mark Pratt, Jim Vickers, Brumley Gap, Va., April 28, 1993; Catherine and Sam Dickinson, Shirley Lee, Cletis Leonard, Audrey and Jay Mitchell, and Cricket and Jim Woods, Brumley Gap, Va., April 29, 1993

Bumpass Cove Citizens Group: Mary Lee Rogers, Gail Story Sams, Linda Walls, and Roxy Wilson, Bumpass Cove, Va., April 28, 1993

Clay Mountain Housing, Inc.: Kathy Britt and Clara Deyton, Clay, W.Va., March 4, 1993; Kathy Britt, telephone, November 2, 1993

Council of Senior West Virginians: Mike Harmon, Charleston, W.Va., March 5, 1993; Maggie Meehan, Charleston, W.Va., March 5, 1993; Maggie Meehan, telephone, November 4, 1993

Dungannon Development Corporation: Wanda Duncan and Nancy Robinson, Dungannon, Va., May 6, 1993; Anne Leibig, Dungannon, Va., May 7, 1993; Nancy Robinson, telephone, August 8, 1993

Federation of Appalachian Housing Enterprises: David Lollis, Berea, Ky., March 23, 1993

Kentucky Small Farms Project: Pat and Bill Stoughton, Jackson, Ky., January 28, 1993; Pat Stoughton, telephone, December 9, 1993; Steve Muntz, field representative for the Heifer Project International, telephone, December 10, 1993

Marketing Appalachian Traditional Community Handcrafts: Ben and Nina Poage, Berea, Ky., May 10, 1993

Ohio Valley Environmental Coalition: Dianne Bady and Kim Baker, Proctorville, Ohio, March 5, 1993

Roadside Theater: Donna Porterfield, telephone, November 8, 1993

SafeSpace: Dianne Levy, Newport, Tenn., April 22, 1993; telephone, October 26, 1993

Urban Appalachian Council: Pauletta Hansel and Bob Moore, Cincinnati, Ohio, October 19, 1993

Virginia Black Lung Association: Marilyn Carroll and Calvin Dunford, Richlands, Va., May 5, 1993; Vince Carroll, telephone, December 10, 1993; Marilyn Carroll, telephone, December 13, 1993

Western North Carolina Alliance: Elmer Hall, Hot Springs, N.C., April 23, 1993; Ron Lamm, telephone, October 26, 1993

West Virginia Primary Care Association: Jill Hutchinson, telephone, November 3, 1993

Books and Articles

Adams, Frank. 1975. *Unearthing Seeds of Fire: The Idea of Highlander*. Winston-Salem, N.C.: J. F. Blair.

Alexander, Dawn. 1993. "David and Goliath Revisited: Lessons from the Brumley Gap Concerned Citizens' Struggle to Save Their Valley." Honors thesis, Department of Political Science, Emory and Henry College.

Ansley, Fran, and Jim Sessions. 1992. "Singing Across Dark Spaces: The Union/Community Takeover of Pittston's Moss 3 Plant." In *Fighting Back in Appalachia*, ed. Stephen L. Fisher, 195–224. Philadelphia: Temple University Press.

Appalachian Land Ownership Task Force. 1983. *Who Owns Appalachia? Landownership and Its Impact*. Lexington: University Press of Kentucky.

"Ashland Oil Forced to Pay." 1993. *The (Banner, Ky.) Appalachian Reader* 6, no. 1 (Spring): 1, 3.

Austin, Richard Cartwright. 1984. "The Battle for Brumley Gap." *Sierra* 69, no. 1 (January/February): 120–24.

Barber, Benjamin. 1984. *Strong Democracy: Participatory Politics for a New Age*. Berkeley: University of California Press.

Batteau, Allen W. 1990. *The Invention of Appalachia*. Tucson: University Press of Arizona.

Bellah, Robert N., Richard Madsen, William M. Sullivan, Ann Swidler, and Steven M. Tipton. 1985. *Habits of the Heart: Individualism and Commitment in American Life*. Berkeley: University of California Press.

———. 1992. *The Good Society*. New York: Vintage.

Berger, Peter, and Richard J. Neuhaus. 1977. *To Empower People: The Role of Mediating Structures in Public Policy*. Washington, D.C.: American Enterprise Institute for Public Policy Research.

Berry, Jeffrey M., Kent E. Portney, and Ken Thomson. 1993. *The Rebirth of Urban Democracy*. Washington, D.C.: Brookings Institution.

Bienko, John. 1992. *Appalshop*. Boston: Harvard Business School Case Services.

Blanton, Bill. 1979. "Not by a Dam Site: Brumley Gap, Virginia—How One Community Fought Back." *Southern Exposure* 7 (Winter): 98–106.

Bluestone, Barry, and Bennett Harrison. 1982. *The Deindustrializing of America: Plant Closings, Community Abandonment and the Dismantling of Basic Industries*. New York: Basic.

———. 1988. *The Great U-Turn: Corporate Restructuring and the Polarizing of America*. New York: Basic.

Botsch, Robert E. 1993. *Organizing the Breathless: Cotton Dust, Southern Politics, and the Brown Lung Association*. Lexington: University Press of Kentucky.

Bourdieu, Pierre. 1986. "The Forms of Capital." In *Handbook of Theory and Research for the Sociology of Education*, ed. John G. Richardson, 241–58. New York: Greenwood.

Bowles, Samuel, David M. Gordon, and Thomas E. Weisskopf. 1990. *After the Waste Land: A Democratic Economics for the Year 2000*. Armonk, N.Y.: M. E. Sharpe.

Boyte, Harry C. 1980. *The Backyard Revolution: Understanding the New Citizen Movement*. Philadelphia: Temple University Press.

Breed, Allen G. 1993. "Case Reflects Woes of Black Lung Program." *The (Whitesburg, Ky.) Mountain Eagle* (May 19).

Burkett, Gary. 1994. "Status of Health in Appalachia." In *Sowing Seeds in the Mountains: Community-Based Coalition for Cancer Prevention and Control*, ed. Richard A. Couto, 43–60. Washington, D.C.: National Cancer Institute.

Burns, James MacGregor. 1978. *Leadership*. New York: Harper & Row.

Cable, Sherry. 1993. "From Fussin' to Organizing: Individual and Collective Resistance at Yellow Creek." In *Fighting Back in Appalachia*, ed. Stephen L. Fisher, 69–83. Philadelphia: Temple University Press.

Campbell, John C. 1921. *The Southern Highlander and His Homeland*. New York: Russell Sage Foundation.

Carawan, Guy, and Candie Carawan. 1982. *Voices from the Mountains*. Urbana: University of Illinois Press.

Caudill, Harry M. 1962. *Night Comes to the Cumberlands: A Biography of a Depressed Area*. Boston: Little, Brown.

Center for Community Change (CCC). 1992. *25 Years of Community Change*. Washington, D.C.: Center for Community Change.

Center on Budget and Policy Priorities. 1989. *Poverty Rates and Household Income Stagnate as Rich-Poor Gap Hits Post-War High* (October 20 report). Washington, D.C.: Center on Budget and Policy Priorities.

———. 1996. *Poverty and Income Trends: 1995*. Washington, D.C.: Center on Budget and Policy Priorities.

Clorefene-Casten, Liane. 1993. "Politics and Pollution: E.P.A. Fiddles While W.T.I. Burns." *Nation* 257, no. 9 (September 27): 307–10.

Coe, Pam, and Craig B. Howley. 1989. *The Condition of Rural Education in West Virginia: A Profile*. Charleston, W.Va.: Appalachian Educational Laboratory.

Cohen, Joshua, and Joel Rogers. 1995a. "Secondary Associations and Democratic Governance." In *Associations and Democracy: The Real Utopias Project*, ed. Erik Olin Wright, 7–98. London: Verso.

———. 1995b. "Solidarity, Democracy, Association." In *Associations and Democracy: The Real Utopias Project*, ed. Erik Olin Wright, 236–67. London: Verso.

Coleman, James S. 1990. *Foundations of Social Theory*. Cambridge, Mass.: Belknap Press of Harvard University Press.

———. 1993. "The Rational Reconstruction of Society." *American Sociological Review* 58, no. 1: 1–15.

Coles, Robert. 1989. *The Call of Stories: Teaching and the Moral Imagination*. Boston: Houghton Mifflin.

Couto, Richard A. 1982. *Streams of Idealism and Health Care Innovation: An Assessment of Service-Learning and Community Mobilization*. New York: Teachers College Press.

———. 1986. "Failing Health and New Prescriptions: Community-Based Approaches to Environmental Health Risks." In *Contemporary Health Policy Issues and Alternatives: An Applied Social Science Perspective*, ed. Carole E. Hill, 53–70. Athens: University of Georgia Press.

———. 1987. "Changing Technologies and Consequences for Labor in Coal Mining." In *Workers, Managers and Technological Change*, ed. Daniel B. Cornfield, 175–202. New York: Plenum.

———. 1991a. *Ain't Gonna Let Nobody Turn Me Round: The Pursuit of Racial Justice in the Rural South*. Philadelphia: Temple University Press.

———. 1991b. "Heroic Bureaucracies." *Administration & Society* 23, no. 1 (May): 28–43.

———. 1991c. "Toward a Human Service Economy." In *Communities in Economic Crisis: Appalachia and the South*, ed. John Gaventa, Barbara Ellen Smith, and Alex Willingham, 251–62. Philadelphia: Temple University Press.

———. 1993a. "The Memory of Miners and the Conscience of Capital." In *Fighting Back in Appalachia: Traditions of Resistance and Change*, ed. Stephen L. Fisher, 264–94. Philadelphia: Temple University Press.

———. 1993b. "Narrative, Free Space, and Political Leadership in Social Movements." *Journal of Politics* 55, no. 1 (February): 57–79.

———. 1994. *An American Challenge: A Report on Economic Trends and Social Issues.* Dubuque, Iowa: Kendall/Hunt Publishing.

———. 1998. "Community Coalitions and Grassroots Policies of Empowerment." *Administration & Society* 30, no. 5 (November): 569–602.

Delgado, Gary. 1993. *Beyond the Politics of Place: New Directions for Community Organizing in the 1990s.* Oakland, Calif.: Applied Research Center.

Dionne, E. J., Jr. 1996. *They Only Look Dead: Why Progressives Will Dominate the Next Political Era.* New York: Simon and Schuster.

"Disabled Miners Lose Benefits: Virginia Black Lung Association Re-Organizes." 1988. *Mountain Life and Work* 64, no. 3 (July–September): 3–6.

Douglas, James. 1987. "Economic Theories of Nonprofit Organizations." In *The Nonprofit Sector: A Research Handbook,* ed. Walter W. Powell, 43–54. New Haven: Yale University Press.

Dryzek, John. 1990. *Discursive Democracy: Politics, Policy, and Political Science.* Cambridge, U.K.: Cambridge University Press.

DuBois, Tom. 1983. "Steel: Past the Crossroads." *Labor Research Review* (Winter): 5–25.

Education Week. 1998. "Quality Counts '98." http://www.edweek.org/sreports/qc98/.

Ekberg, John. 1993. "Theater Troupe Jars Memories of Appalachia." *Cincinnati Enquirer,* October 17.

Eller, Ronald D. 1982. *Miners, Millhands, and Mountaineers: Industrialization of the Appalachian South, 1880–1930.* Knoxville: University of Tennessee Press.

Evans, Sara M., and Harry C. Boyte. 1986. *Free Spaces: The Sources of Democratic Change in America.* New York: Harper & Row.

Fisher, Stephen L. 1990. "National Economic Renewal Programs and Their Implications for Appalachia and the South." In *Communities in Economic Crisis: Appalachia and the South,* ed. John Gaventa, Barbara Smith, and Alex Willingham, 263–78. Philadelphia: Temple University Press.

———, ed. 1993. *Fighting Back in Appalachia: Traditions of Resistance and Change.* Philadelphia: Temple University Press.

Ford, Thomas R. 1962. *The Southern Appalachian Region: A Survey.* Lexington: University of Kentucky Press.

Galbraith, John Kenneth. 1958. *The Affluent Society.* New York: New American Library.

———. 1992. *The Culture of Contentment.* Boston: Houghton Mifflin.

Gardner, Howard. 1994. *Leading Minds: An Anatomy of Leadership.* New York: Basic.

Gaventa, John. 1980. *Power and Powerlessness: Quiescence and Rebellion in an Appalachian Valley.* Urbana: University of Illinois Press.

Gaventa, John, Helen Lewis, and Susan Williams. 1992. "Disposable Communities: Picking Up the Pieces After the Company Leaves Town." *Dollars & Sense* (May): 12–14, 22.

Gaventa, John, Barbara Ellen Smith, and Alex Willingham, eds. 1990. *Communities in Economic Crisis: Appalachia and the South.* Philadelphia: Temple University Press.

Geertz, Clifford. 1983. *Local Knowledge: Further Essays in Interpretative Anthropology.* New York: Basic.

Gilder, George. 1981. *Wealth and Poverty.* New York: Basic.

Glen, John M. 1988. *Highlander: No Ordinary School, 1932–1962*. Lexington: University Press of Kentucky.

———. 1993. "Like a Flower Slowly Blooming: Highlander and the Nurturing of an Appalachian Movement." In *Fighting Back in Appalachia: Traditions of Resistance and Change*, ed. Stephen L. Fisher, 31–56. Philadelphia: Temple University Press.

Greider, William. 1992. *Who Will Tell the People: The Betrayal of American Democracy*. New York: Simon & Schuster.

Hall, V. Aileen. 1984. *Poverty and Women in West Virginia*. Charleston, W.Va.: Women and Employment, Inc.

Hansmann, Henry. 1987. "Political Theories of Nonprofit Organizations." In *The Nonprofit Sector: A Research Handbook*, ed. Walter W. Powell, 27–42. New Haven: Yale University Press.

Harrington, Michael. 1962. *The Other America: Poverty in the United States*. New York: Macmillan.

Harvard Business School. 1983. "Wierton Division National Steel." Boston: Harvard Business School Case Services.

Heilbroner, Robert L. 1986. *The Essential Adam Smith*. New York: W. W. Norton.

———. 1993. *21st Century Capitalism*. New York: W. W. Norton.

Heilbroner, Robert L., and Lester Thurow. 1994. *Economics Explained: Everything You Need to Know About How the Economy Works and Where It's Going*. Rev. ed. New York: Touchstone.

Hinsdale, Mary Ann, Helen M. Lewis, and S. Maxine Waller. 1995. *It Comes from the People: Community Development and Local Theology*. Philadelphia: Temple University Press.

Hirschman, Albert O. 1984. "Against Parsimony: Three Easy Ways of Complicating Some Categories of Economic Discourse." *American Economic Association Papers and Proceedings* 74, no. 2: 89–96.

Horton, Myles. 1991. *The Long Haul: An Autobiography*. With Judith and Herbert R. Kohl. New York: Doubleday.

Horton, Myles, and Paulo Freire. 1990. *We Make the Road by Walking*. Philadelphia: Temple University Press.

Judkins, Bennett. 1993. "Quality Counts Respirator: Coalition Building and the Black Lung Association." In *Fighting Back in Appalachia*, ed. Stephen L. Fisher, 225–41. Philadelphia: Temple University Press.

Katz, Michael B. 1995. *Improving Poor People: The Welfare State, The "Underclass," and Urban Schools as History*. Princeton, N.J.: Princeton University Press.

Kephart, Horace. 1913. *Our Southern Highlanders: A Narrative of Adventure in the Southern Appalachians and a Study of Life Among the Mountaineers*. New York: Macmillan.

Kerrine, Theodore M. 1980. "Mediating Structures: A Paradigm for Public Policy." *Soundings* 62, no. 3 (Winter): 331–37.

Krajcinovic, Ivana. 1997. *From Company Doctors to Managed Care: The United Mine Workers' Noble Experiment*. Ithaca, N.Y.: Cornell University Press.

Kuttner, Robert. 1991. *The End of Laissez-Faire: National Purpose and the Global Economy After the Cold War*. New York: Alfred A. Knopf.

Lewis, Helen, Linda Johnson, and Donald Askins, eds. 1978. *Colonialism in Modern America: The Appalachian Case*. Boone, N.C.: Appalachian Consortium Press.

Lewis, Helen M., and Suzanna O'Donnell, eds. 1990. *Ivanhoe, Virginia*. Vol. 1, *Remembering Our Past, Building Our Future*; Vol. 2, *Telling Our Stories, Sharing Our Lives*. Ivanhoe, Va.: Ivanhoe Civic League.

Loury, Glenn C. 1987. "Why Should We Care About Group Inequality?" *Social Philosophy & Policy* 5, no. 1: 251–71.

McFate, Katherine, Roger Lawson, and William Julius Wilson, eds. 1995. *Poverty, Inequality, and the Future of Social Policy*. New York: Russell Sage Foundation.

McFate, Katherine, Timothy Smeeding, and Lee Rainwater. 1995. "Markets and States." In *Poverty, Inequality, and the Future of Social Policy*, ed. Katherine McFate, Roger Lawson, and William Julius Wilson, 29–45. New York: Russell Sage Foundation.

MacIntyre, Alasdair. 1984. *After Virtue: A Study in Moral Theory*, 2d ed. Notre Dame, Ind.: University of Notre Dame.

Marshall, Will, and Martin Schram. 1993. *Mandate for Change*. New York: Berkeley.

Matthieson, Karl. 1984. "Passages: Changing Organizations and Boards." In *Steering Nonprofits*, comp. Management Assistance Group, 334–35. Washington, D.C.: Management Assistance Group.

Meadows, Kayetta. 1992. "Advancing the Agenda." *West Virginia School Journal* 120, no. 11 (May): 2.

Metzgar, Jack. 1983. "Would Wage Concessions Help the Steel Industry?" *Labor Research Review* (Winter): 26–37.

Michels, Robert. 1958 [1915]. *Political Parties: A Sociological Study of the Oligarchical Tendencies of Modern Democracy*. Reprint, Glencoe, Ill.: Free Press.

Morone, James A. 1990. *The Democratic Wish: Popular Participation and the Limits of American Government*. New York: Basic.

Murray, Charles. 1984. *Losing Ground: American Social Policy 1950–1980*. New York: Basic.

Myrdal, Gunnar. 1944. *An American Dilemma: The Negro Problem and Modern Democracy*. New York: Harper & Row.

Neuhaus, Richard J. 1980. "Response to Mecling and Price." *Soundings* 62, no. 4 (Winter 1980): 401–16.

Newman, Katherine S. 1988. *Falling from Grace: The Experience of Downward Mobility in the American Middle Class*. New York: Vintage.

Nisbet, Robert A. 1962. *Community and Power*. New York: Oxford University Press.

Park, Peter, Mary Brydon-Miller, Bud Hall, and Ted Jackson, eds. 1993. *Voices of Change: Participatory Research in the United States and Canada*. Toronto: Ontario Institute for Studies in Education.

Phillips, Kevin. 1990. *The Politics of the Rich and Poor: Wealth and the American Electorate in the Reagan Aftermath*. New York: Harper Perennial.

Piven, Frances Fox, and Richard A. Cloward. 1979. *Poor People's Movements: Why They Succeed and How They Fail*. New York: Vintage.

Poage, Ben. 1973. "The Cooperative Movement among the Southern Rural Poor." In *The Church and the Rural Poor*, ed. James Cogswell, 27–46. Atlanta, Ga.: John Knox Press.

———, ed. 1996. *"We Never Started to Quit": Celebrating 20 Years of Community Economic Development in Appalachia*. Berea, Ky.: Human/Economic Appalachian Development Corporation.

Price, David E. 1980. "Community, 'Mediating Structures,' and Public Policy." *Soundings* 62, no. 4 (Winter): 369–94.

Putnam, Robert D. 1993. *Making Democracy Work: Civic Traditions in Modern Italy*. Princeton, N.J.: Princeton University Press.

———. 1995. "'Tuning In, Tuning Out': The Strange Disappearance of Social Capital in America." *PS: Political Science & Politics* 28, no. 4 (December): 664–83.

Reich, Robert B. 1992. "On the Slag Heap of History: Review of *Homestead*." *New York Times Book Review* (November): 15–16.

The Rural Homelessness Project. 1990. "'It Ain't Much, But It's All I Got': A Study of Living Conditions in Three Rural West Virginia Counties." Charleston, W.Va.: Covenant House.

Salamon, Lester M. 1987. "Partners in Public Service: The Scope and Theory of Government-Nonprofit Relations" In *The Nonprofit Sector: A Research Handbook*, ed. Walter W. Powell, 99–117. New Haven: Yale University Press.

———. 1993. "The Nonprofit Sector and Democracy: Prerequisite, Impediment, or Irrelevance?" Paper presented at the symposium "Democracy and the Nonprofit Sector," sponsored by Aspen Institute Nonprofit Sector Research Fund, Washington, D.C.

Salmons-Rue, Janet. 1994. *Storytelling Theater: Culture, Communication and Community*. Ithaca, N.Y.: The Community-Based Arts Project, Cornell University Center for Theater Arts and Roadside Theater.

Salsbury, Karen, ed. 1990. *The Senior Community Service Employment Program: The First 25 Years*. Arlington, Va.: Green Thumb, Inc.

Sanders, Linda. 1980. "Hobert Story: He Devoted His Life to Preserving Bumpass Cove." *Johnson City Press-Chronicle* (September 9): 7.

Schumacher, E. F. 1973. *Small is Beautiful: Economics As If People Mattered*. New York: Harper & Row.

Seltzer, Curtis. 1985. *Fire in the Hole: Miners and Managers in the American Coal Industry*. Lexington: University Press of Kentucky.

Serrin, William. 1992. *Homestead: The Glory and Tragedy of an American Steel Town*. New York: Vintage.

Sevison, A. 1952. "Give Me Oil for My Lamp." In *Action Songs for Boys and Girls*, Vol. 3, comp. A. B. Smith. Grand Rapids, Mich.: Zondervan.

Shapiro, Henry D. 1978. *Appalachia on Our Mind: The Southern Mountains and Mountaineer in the American Consciousness, 1870–1920*. Chapel Hill: University of North Carolina Press.

Shifflett, Crandall A. 1991. *Coal Towns: Life, Work, and Culture in Company Towns of Southern Appalachia, 1880–1960*. Knoxville: University of Tennessee Press.

Sills, David L. 1967. "Voluntary Associations: Sociological Aspects." In *International Encyclopedia of the Social Sciences*, 16: 362–79. New York: Macmillan/Free Press.

Silverstein, Leonard L. 1983. "The Third Sector: Commission on Private Philanthropy and Public Needs." In *America's Voluntary Spirit: A Book of Readings*, ed. Brian O'Connell, 299–314. New York: The Foundation Center.

Sizemore, Judy. 1990. "Partnership for Change." Westport, Conn.: Save the Children.

Smith, Adam. 1937 [1776]. *An Inquiry into the Nature and Causes of the Wealth of Nations*. Modern Library edition. Reprint, New York: Random House.

Smith, Barbara E. 1986. *Women of the Rural South: Economic Status and Prospects*. Atlanta, Ga.: Southeast Women's Employment Coalition.

———. 1987. *Digging Our Own Graves: Coal Miners and the Struggle Over Black Lung Disease*. Philadelphia: Temple University Press.

Smith, David Horton. 1983. "The Impact of the Volunteer Sector on Society." In *America's Voluntary Spirit: A Book of Readings*, ed. Brian O'Connell, 331–44. New York: The Foundation Center.

Smith, Stephen R., and Michael Lipsky. 1993. *Nonprofits for Hire: The Welfare State in the Age of Contracting*. Cambridge, Mass.: Harvard University Press.

Sowell, Thomas. 1994. *Race and Culture: A World View*. New York: Basic.

Speer, Paul W., and David Chavis. 1995. "Community Coalition Theory and Rural Practice."In *Sowing Seeds in the Mountains: Community-Based Coalitions for Cancer Prevention and Control*, ed. Richard A. Couto, Nancy K. Simpson, and Gale Harris, 138–55. Washington, D.C.: National Cancer Institute.

Staub, Michael. 1983. "'We'll Never Quit': Yellow Creek Concerned Citizens Combat Creekbed Catastrophe." *Southern Exposure* 11 (January–February): 43–52.

Stokey, Edith, and Richard Zeckhauser. 1978. *A Primer for Policy Analysis*. New York: W. W. Norton.

Szakos, Joe. 1993. "Practical Lessons in Community Organizing in Appalachia: What We've Learned at Kentuckians for the Commonwealth." In *Fighting Back in Appalachia: Traditions of Resistance and Change*, ed. Steve Fisher, 101–22. Philadelphia: Temple University Press.

Toffler, Alvin. 1970. *Future Shock*. New York: Vintage.

Town, Stephen W. 1978. *After the Mines: Changing Employment Opportunities in a South Wales Valley*. Cardiff: University of Wales Press.

Uzawa, Hirofumi. 1988. "On the Economics of Social Overhead Capital." In *Preference, Production, and Capital: Selected Papers of Hirofumi Uzawa*, 340–62. New York: Cambridge University Press.

Vahrian, Scott. 1981. "TEACH Links Health Problems to Chemical Dumping." *Mountain Life and Work* (May): 35.

Verba, Sidney, Kay Lehman Schlozman, and Henry E. Brady. 1995. *Voice and Equality: Civic Voluntarism in American Politics*. Cambridge, Mass.: Harvard University Press.

Waller, Altina A. 1988. *Feud: Hatfields, McCoys, and Social Change in Appalachia, 1860–1900*. Chapel Hill: University of North Carolina Press.

Walls, David. 1978. "Internal Colony or Internal Periphery? A Critique of Current Models and an Alternative Formulation." In *Colonialism in Modern America: The Appalachian Case*, ed. Helen Lewis, Linda Johnson, and Donald Askins, 319–49. Boone, N.C.: Appalachian Consortium Press.

Ware, Alan. 1989. *Between Profit and State: Intermediate Organizations in Britain and the United States*. Princeton, N.J.: Princeton University Press.

Weimer, David L., and Aidan R. Vining. 1989. *Policy Analysis: Concepts and Practice*. Englewood Cliffs, N.J.: Prentice Hall.

Weiss, Chris. 1993. "Appalachian Women Fight Back." In *Fighting Back in Appalachia: Traditions of Resistance and Change*, ed. Stephen L. Fisher, 151–64. Philadelphia: Temple University Press.

Wellstone, Paul. 1978. *How the Rural Poor Got Power: Narrative of a Grass-Roots Organizer*. Amherst: University of Massachusetts Press.

Whisnant, David E. 1983. *All That is Native and Fine: The Politics of Culture in An American Region*. Chapel Hill: University of North Carolina Press

Wilson, Larry. 1989. "Moving towards a Movement." *Social Policy* 20, no. 1 (Summer): 53–58.

———. 1994. "Environmental Destruction is Hazardous to Your Health." *Social Policy* 24, no. 4 (Summer): 16–25.

Wilson, William Julius. 1987. *The Truly Disadvantaged: The Inner City, the Underclass and Public Policy.* Chicago: University of Chicago Press.

Wolpert, Julian. 1993. *Patterns of Generosity in America: Who's Holding the Safety Net?* New York: Twentieth Century Fund Press.

———. 1994. *Fragmentation in America's Nonprofit Sector.* Washington, D.C.: Aspen Institute Nonprofit Sector Research Fund.

World Bank. 1991. *World Development Report 1991.* New York: Oxford University Press.

Young, Iris Marion. 1995. "Social Groups in Associative Democracy." In *Associations and Democracy: The Real Utopias Project,* ed. Erik Olin Wright, 207–13. London: Verso.

Zuercher, Melanie A. 1991. *Making History: The First Ten Years of KFTC.* Prestonsburg, Ky.: Kentuckians for the Commonwealth.

Abingdon, Va., 72, 97, 209
Accountability, 101, 109, 110, 118, 126, 135, 137; management and, 239–46
ACTION (Advocates Committed to Independence and Opportunities Now), 99–100, 250, 252; and leadership development, 285–86
Advocacy, 99, 135, 164, 190–91, 201, 202–3, 222, 249, 255; and community organizing and development, 94, 217, 272–77; defined, 272–73; and funding issues, 266; limits of, 154, 156, 214; limits on, 188–89; preparation for, 99; and public policy, 101, 106–9, 125, 127; and service provision, 228, 249, 274
Alexander, Dawn, 87
Alliance for Cultural Diversity, 261
Alternate Roots, 261
American Creed, 295–97, 300, 301
American Electrical Power (AEP), 85–87, 122
American Enterprise Institute, 43. *See also* Mediating Structures Project
American Festival, 261
American Friends Service Committee, 257, 287
Americans with Disabilities Act, 98, 104
Anderson, Homer, 161

Ansley, Fran, 142
Appalachia, xv, 3; and community organizations, 50–51; definitions and explanations of, 10–14; and economic conditions, 7–8, 9, 12, 15–19, 27–29, 35–36, 62–63, 71, 102; and labor force participation, 25–27; and population changes, 26–27; and social capital, 10, 15, 23–33, 71, 283
Appalachian Alliance, 73, 126, 305; achievements of, 278, 279; and coalitions, 260, 263; and community, 210, 213–14; and community organizing and development, 275; and continuity, 236; and funding issues, 269; and issue selection, 140–41, 217, 226, 229, 230, 240; and leadership development, 285; lessons from, 289, 290, 292; and management, 240, 241, 242; and members, 217, 220, 231; and networks of ideas, 254, 255, 258; and organizational development, 250–51, 252; and role in transformative politics, 137–42; vision of community, 224
Appalachian Center for Economic Networks (ACEnet), 72–73, 121, 305; achievements of, 280; and coalitions, 261; and community, 209, 215; and community organizing and develop-

ment, 275; disappointments of, 282; and funding issues, 266, 267; and issue selection, 227; and leadership development, 286; lessons from, 292, 299; and management, 241, 242; and members, 219, 232; and networks of ideas, 257, 258; and organizational development, 249; role in the promotion of ideas, 102–5; vision of community, 223

Appalachian Communities for Children (ACC), 73, 177–86, 304; achievements of, 279; and community, 208, 212, 213; and community organizing and development, 272, 277; and continuity, 235; disappointments of, 282; and funding issues, 265; and issue selection, 227–28; and leadership development, 286; lessons from, 293, 299; and management, 245; and members, 219, 230, 231; and networks of ideas, 254–55, 256; and organizational development, 249; vision of community, 223

Appalachian Community Development Association, 144, 286

Appalachian Community Foundation, 155

Appalachian Development Projects Committee, 256, 307

Appalachian Education Laboratory (AEL), 168–69

Appalachian Identity Center, 134

Appalachian Independence Center, 72, 304; achievements of, 278, 280; and community, 209, 211, 212; and community organizing and development, 274; disappointments of, 281; and funding issues, 266; and issue selection, 226, 227, 228; and leadership development, 285–86; lessons from, 299; and management, 243–44; and members, 219, 233; and networks of ideas, 256, 257; and organizational development, 250, 252; role of liberation and self-actualization, 97–102; vision of community, 221, 222

Appalachian land ownership study, 126, 266, 279; aftermath, 138–40, 169, 226, 231, 250, 279

Appalachian Ohio Public Interest Center (AOPIC), 73, 129, 305; and coalitions, 262; and community, 209; and community organizing and development, 274; and continuity, 235; disappointments of, 281; and funding issues, 268; and issue selection, 227; and leadership development, 283; and management, 241, 244; and members, 218, 232; and networks of ideas, 254, 257, 258; and networks of resources, 287; and organizational development, 252; role of discursive democracy, 121–26; vision of community, 223

Appalachian Peoples Action Coalition (APAC), 73, 121, 129, 142, 304; achievements of, 280; and community, 208, 214; and community organizing and development, 276; disappointments of, 281; and funding issues, 266, 267; and issue selection, 225, 230; and leadership development, 283; and management, 240; and members, 219–20, 231; and networks of ideas, 255, 257; and organizational development, 250, 252; role as free space, 133–34; vision of community, 223

Appalachian Power Company (APCO), 85–86, 89–90, 234, 248

Appalachian Regional Commission, 10, 79, 138, 140, 198, 266

Appalachian Student Health Coalition, 222

Appalachian Volunteers, 226

Appalachian Women Empowered, 256, 287

Appalshop, 142–43, 210, 222, 226, 245, 251, 268, 280, 291

Aristech, 153, 154

Ashland Oil, 154–55, 229, 233

Aspen Nonprofit Sector Research Fund, xviii

Association of Community-Based Education, 255, 256

Association of Community Organizations for Reform Now (ACORN), 254

Athens, Ohio, 102, 121, 129, 135, 208, 257

Austin, Richard (Dick) C., 85–90, 221, 257, 288

Bady, Dianne, 153–56
Baker, Kim, 155, 156
Barber, Benjamin, 48, 49, 50, 114, 211
Bargain Furniture Store, 135–37, 267, 276. *See also* Appalachian Peoples Action Coalition
BASF, 153, 154, 229
Beach, Doris, 90
Bellah, Robert, 173–74, 187, 309
Berea, Ky., 163, 193, 198, 236, 280
Berger, Peter L., 43, 45, 53, 63, 187
Berry, Jeffrey M., 49
Bituminous Coal Operators Association (BCOA), 16, 308
Black lung: disease, 148, 157–63, 259; movement, 309
Bluestone, Barry, 15
Boards of directors, 94, 95, 98, 106, 156, 187, 200, 241–42; and networks of ideas, 258–59
Bourdieu, Pierre, 60–62, 65, 71, 199
Boyte, Harry, 49, 96, 129, 137, 308
Brady, Henry E., 47
Brink, Carolyn, 182
Britt, Kathy, 174, 183
Brown lung disease, 309
Brumley Gap, Va., 92, 135; "Ballad of Brumley Gap," 90–91
Brumley Gap Concerned Citizens, 72, 98, 108, 304; and coalitions, 261; and community, 208, 212, 216; and community organizing and development, 272, 273; and continuity, 225, 234; disappointments of, 281; and funding issues, 267; and issue selection, 229, 230; and leadership development, 283; lessons from, 288, 299; and management, 241; and members, 217, 232; and networks of ideas, 257; and networks of resources, 287; and organizational development, 248; and post-victory activities, 91, 229, 248; role of support and trust, 84–92; and strategies, 87; vision of community, 221–22. *See also* Brumley Gap, Va.

Bumpass Cove, Tenn., 114–20, 126, 142, 293
Bumpass Cove Citizens Group, 73, 114, 304; achievements of, 278, 279; and coalitions, 261; and community, 208, 209, 211, 212, 216; and community organizing and development, 272, 273; and continuity, 225, 234; disappointments of, 282–83; and funding issues, 267; impact of, 120; and issue selection, 229; and leadership development, 283, 284; lessons from, 288–89, 291, 299–300; and management, 241, 245; and members, 217, 233; and networks of ideas, 254; and organizational development, 248; role in expanding imagination, 116–20; vision of community, 221–23
Burkett, Gary L., 157
Burns, James MacGregor, 66, 309

Campbell, John C., 10
Camp Solidarity, 142
Carroll, Marilyn, 159–63, 182, 231
Carroll, Vince, 162
Carter, Jimmy, 199
Caudill, Harry, 11
Center for Community Change, 200, 205; and coalitions, 259; and community involvement, 207; and community organizing and development, 276–77; and democratic practice, 216; and funding, 264, 269; and human capital, 280; and management, 239–40; and organizational development, 246, 251, 252; and recruiting organizers, 93; and research protocol, 310–12; and success of community groups, 277–78
Champion International Paper Company, 126, 127
Children, 29–31, 178–79, 225; and development, 78, 253
Christian Appalachian Project, 187, 258
Churches: role in community development, 194, 196–97
Citizen Action Group, 108, 110, 122, 234
Citizens Clearinghouse on Chemical Waste, 287

Citizens Organized Against Longwalling (COAL), 122

Civic associations, 3; and public policy, 3, 4, 76

Civil society, xiv, 51–52, 64, 68

Class and class structure, 127, 180, 215, 290. *See also* Economic inequality; Equality

Clay County, Ky., 73, 177–78, 181, 213, 223, 293

Clay Mountain Housing (CMH), 73, 202, 304; achievements of, 279; and community, 215; and community organizing and development, 276; disappointments of, 282; and funding issues, 268; and leadership development, 285, 286; lessons from, 294; and management, 243; and members, 219, 220, 233; and networks of ideas, 257; and organizational development, 248–49; role in providing public goods locally, 174–77; vision of community, 223

Clearcutting, 126–27

Cloward, Richard A., 47

Coal Employment Project, 95, 199, 200, 244

Coal industry, 15–16, 148; longwall mining, 122, 162, 227

Coalition of American Electric Consumers, 91, 108, 261, 288

Coalition on Legislation for the Elderly (COLE), 108, 233–34, 249. *See also* Council of Senior West Virginians

Coalitions, 243, 259–63, 269, 289–90

Cocke County, Tenn., 189

Cocke, Dudley, 145

Cohen, Joshua, 49

Coleman, James, xiv

Coles, Robert, 309

Commission on Religion in Appalachia (CORA), 109, 162, 191, 307, 310; and coalitions, 256; and funding issues, 155, 265, 307; role as intermediary, 141, 286

Common Cause, 110

Communities of experience, 21, 209, 222

Communities of proximity, 21, 208

Community, 39–40, 45, 67–68; and class, 212–26; and democratic prospect, 210; and gender, 212–16; inclusive, 212–16; membership of, 208–12; and politics, 48, 50; and race, 212–16; and representation and participation, 211, 225; and social capital, 210, 212; vision of, 221–25. *See also names of specific groups* (e.g., Appalachian Alliance: and community)

Community-based mediating structures, 3, 71–72; achievements of, 277–81; and boards, 94, 95, 106, 187, 200, 241, 242; brokering resources, 164–65, 174, 175, 180–81, 200–201; and change, 206, 246–53, 277–78; and coalitions, 123, 191, 217, 218–19, 259–63, 290; collaboration with others, 191; and community, 206, 208–16, 219; conflicts within, 108, 119–20, 127, 188, 200, 208, 211, 212, 241–42, 246, 289; conflicts with other organizations, 127–28, 186, 201–2, 218; and continuity, 225, 233–36; and credibility, 191, 228, 240, 262, 264–67, 294; and cultural expression, 142, 143–46, 210, 222–23; and democratic prospect, 72–74, 113–14, 205, 207, 237, 271, 277–78, 279; disappointments of, 281–83; as examples for others, 120, 165, 180–81; and government, 110–11, 118, 151–53, 154, 160, 181, 191–92, 201, 287, 299, 300; and innovative leadership, 310; and issue selection, 126, 140–41, 201, 217, 225–30, 289; and leadership development, 283–86; lessons from, 288–94, 298–301; and management, 206, 239–46, 269–70; and market failures, 72, 73, 292–94; and members, 100, 106, 119–20, 127, 141, 176, 180, 187, 200, 201–2, 216–21, 230–33; and mitigating market failures, 147, 167–71, 300; and moral resources, 113, 125, 203, 207; and networks of ideas, 253–59, 277, 289–90; and networks of resources, 286–87; organizational development, 14, 155, 176, 187–89, 233, 246–53, 269–70; and political dimensions, 113–14, 146, 224, 299; and political imagination, 114–20, 146, 224; and political participation, 106–7, 108, 110, 137–38, 168; and political transcendence, 142–46, 209, 211; representation and participation in, 231; and social capital, 72, 129, 145, 147, 173, 207, 278–81; and social capital redistribution, 163, 164, 168–71, 173, 187–89, 203, 259, 293, 299; and social welfare policies, 177; and staffing, 92, 95, 109–10, 243–45; and strong democracy, 48–50, 114; sustaining, 221–25; and technical assistance and training, 150, 15, 164, 200, 216, 228, 245–46, 254–56, 260, 287; and women's leadership, 118, 193, 196–97, 200–202, 214–15, 287, 289; and women's needs, 189–93, 195, 201, 202. *See also* Free spaces; Mediating structures; Social capital; Social capital entrepreneurs; *and names of specific groups*

Community development, 78, 117, 124, 143–44, 178, 220, 222, 223, 227; defined, 272; links to community organizing, 233, 271–77

Community Development Block Grants, 77, 80

Community organizing, 88, 94, 107, 124, 139, 217, 223; contrasted with advocacy, 156, 201, 230; contrasted with social service provision, 190–91; defined, 271–72; and lawsuits, 119, 155, 229, 233. *See also* Community development

Community Work Experience Program, 136, 219

Comprehensive Employment Training Act (CETA), 164, 199, 267

Consciousness raising, 96

Cooperatives, 102, 140, 187, 197, 227, 232, 241, 275. *See also* Appalachian Center for Economic Networks

Council of Senior West Virginians, 73; achievements of, 279; and Brumley Gap Concerned Citizens, 108; and coalitions, 261, 262; and community, 209, 213, 215; and community organizing and development, 276–77; and

continuity, 233–24, 235, 236; and funding issues, 268; and issue selection, 230; and leadership development, 285; lessons from, 299; and members, 218, 231; and networks of ideas, 256; and networks of resources, 287; and organizational development, 249; role in public policy participation, 106–10, 156, 305; vision of community, 222, 224

Council of Southern Mountains, 126, 159, 228

Craft cooperatives, 104, 193–96. *See also* Marketing Appalachian Traditional Community Handcrafts

Cultural capital, 60–62, 145–46, 180, 215

Culture, 142, 145–46, 210, 222–23, 292. *See also* Roadside Theater

Cunningham, Esther, 126

Deindustrialization, 35; in Homestead, Penn., 24. *See also* Postindustrial economics

Delgado, Gary: study of training intermediaries, 254–55

Democratic promise, 2, 37, 68, 147; contrasted with democratic prospect, 167, 297–301; defined, 66–67; and policies of Reagan and Thatcher administrations, 3–4, 64; and welfare, 177. *See also* Market democracy

Democratic prospect, 1–2, 3, 6, 7, 8, 9, 13, 37–38, 68, 73, 96, 146, 147, 282; defined, 66–67, 301; and democratic promise, 167, 297–301; and expanded communal bonds, 212, 271–72; as increased and improved social capital, 71–72, 75, 171, 279, 294; lessons about, 288–94; and welfare, 177. *See also* Community-based mediating structures; Mediating structures; Social capital

Democratic wish, 8, 68; defined, 66; and public policy, 147–48, 297, 301

Dent, Tim, 106

Devolution of social services, 63–64, 73, 186–87. *See also* Kentucky Small Farms Project

Deyton, Clara, 174
Dickenson, Catherine, 90
Dickenson, Samuel, 86
Disability, 33, 99–100, 108, 211, 214,
   221, 227, 253, 286; movement, 97, 106;
   and work, 157–58. *See also* Appala-
   chian Independence Center; Virginia
   Black Lung Association
Discursive democracy, 48–49, 73, 113,
   121–29, 146
Domestic violence, xiii, 189–93, 219, 221,
   228, 255, 293
Dryzek, John, 48, 50, 59
Dunford, Calvin, 162
Dungannon, Va., 76, 140
Dungannon Depot, 77, 219–20
Dungannon Development Corporation,
   72, 98, 111, 131, 303; achievements of,
   279; and community, 208, 215; and
   community and economic development, 80; and community organizing
   and development, 276; and continuity,
   236; disappointments of, 282; and ecotourism, 83; and funding issues, 267;
   and issue selection, 227; and leadership
   development, 284; lessons from, 292;
   and members, 220; and networks of
   ideas, 254, 255–57, 258; and networks
   of resources, 287; and Phoenix Industries, 79–81, 82; role in dense horizontal networks, 76–84; and sewing factory, 79, 81–82; and social capital,
   84; vision of community, 224; and
   Women's Club, 77–78
Dungannon Historical Association, 78

Earth First! 128
Economic development, 79, 102, 128–29
Economic inequality, 7, 18–19, 24, 45, 50,
   58; and social capital, 61, 62, 96, 174,
   199
Education, 31–32, 62, 93, 167, 178, 181,
   212, 225, 272, 300; and Dungannon,
   78, 227
Employment. *See* Labor force partici-
   pation; Women and employment;
   Work
Empowerment, 272. *See also* Commu-

nity development; Community organizing; Transcendence; Transformative
politics
Environment, 62, 73, 122, 229, 253, 272,
   292, 293; and Dungannon, 83–84. *See
   also* Bumpass Cove Citizens Group;
   Western North Carolina Alliance
Environmental Support Center, 287
Equality, 40, 41, 42, 43, 46, 59, 296; and
   the nonprofit sector, 59–60, 65; and
   social capital, 60–64
Evans, Sara, 49, 96, 129, 137
Externalities, 56, 73, 153, 280; defined,
   292; and social capital, 292–93

Families, 29, 39, 45, 61
Family Resource Centers, 235
Farmers Home Administration (FmHA),
   79, 175, 176, 282
Fazzina, Catherine, 221
Federal Energy Regulatory Commission
   (FERC), 89–90, 272
Federation of Appalachian Housing
   Enterprises (FAHE), 73, 174, 176, 183,
   304; achievements of, 278; and coalitions, 260, 261, 262; and community,
   209, 213; and community organizing
   and development, 275; disappointments of, 282; and funding issues, 264,
   265, 267; as intermediary, 269; and
   issue selection, 226; and leadership
   development, 285; lessons from, 290,
   294; and management, 242; and members, 216, 217, 219; and networks of
   ideas, 254, 255, 257, 258; and organizational development, 251; role in
   reversing the flow of social capital,
   163–67; vision of community, 223–24
Female-headed households, 29–30
Ferrell, Dean, 135
Filer Commission, 41–42, 47
Financial capital, 60, 62; access to, 104,
   105, 164–65, 219; and public policy,
   148
Fisher, Stephen L., 50–51, 137, 142, 288.
   See Transformative politics
Flexible manufacturing networks, 103,
   104, 227, 241, 249, 258, 263, 273

Florence and John Schumann Foundation, 155
Ford, Carol, 92, 93, 95
Ford, Thomas, 10
Free spaces, 49, 50, 73, 96, 113, 129–37, 200, 219–20; and transformative politics, 50, 137–38, 146, 210, 284
Funding, 94, 126, 150–51, 154–55, 165, 174–75, 179, 182, 191, 200, 202, 225–26, 228, 236, 245–46, 263–67, 269–70, 286; public sources of, 265–67
Fund-raising, 80, 88, 123, 263–69, 300

Galbraith, John Kenneth, 12
Garbo, Bob, 121
Gardner, Howard, 309–10
Gaventa, John, 51
Geertz, Clifford, xv
Gilder, George, 34
Goodwin, Jackie, 168
Great Society policies and programs, 43–44, 45, 64, 106
Green Thumb, 136

Habitat for Humanity, 257
Haley, Alex, 308
Hall, Betty Jean, 200, 214, 244
Hall, Elmer, 126
Handicapped Unlimited, 97–98, 226, 243
Hansel, Pauletta, 144
Harlan County, Ky., 1–2
Harmon, Mike, 106–10
Harrison, Benjamin, 15
Head Start, 124, 227
Health and health care, 27, 33, 62, 73, 108–9, 116, 124, 129, 140, 178, 209, 216, 256, 275, 287, 292; of children, 181, 212, 227. See also West Virginia Primary Care Association
Heifer Project International, 187, 188, 257
Heilbroner, Robert, 34–35, 71
Highlander Research and Education Center, 95, 133, 159, 199, 217, 308; and Appalachian Alliance, 138, 141; and Bumpass Cove Citizens Group, 116–17, 119, 288, 291; and redbaiting, 234;

as training intermediary, 222, 254, 257, 284–85, 287
Hirschman, Albert O., 54–56, 60, 241
Hocking County, Ohio, 122
Holley, June, 105
Homestead, Penn., 24
Homophobia, 214, 290
Hontz, Ervan, 187
Housing, 32, 62, 73, 129, 138, 140, 188, 216, 230, 253, 261, 275, 287, 292, 294, 300; impact of, 164, 167, 176, 209, 212, 286. See also Clay Mountain Housing; Dungannon Development Corporation; Federation of Appalachian Housing Enterprises
Human capital, xiv, 60, 279–80
Human/Economic Appalachian Development (HEAD) Corporation, 163, 261, 263
Hutchinson, Jill, 149–50, 151–52

Ideals and values, promotion of, 102–5
Income distribution, 19–20
Intermediaries: and community-based mediating organizations, 269, 284, 291
Intermediate associations, 3, 38, 52, 84
Iron law of oligarchy, 246
Ironton, Ohio, 153
Invisible hand. See Externalities; Market capitalism; Market democracy; Smith, Adam
Ivanhoe, Virginia, 308

Jackson County, Ky., 73, 177–81, 213, 223
James C. Penney Foundation, 165
Job creation and training, 104, 129, 164, 176, 286, 292
Job Training Partnership Agency (JTPA), 104, 182
Johnson, Lyndon B., 106
Johnson City, Tenn., 114

Kentuckians For the Commonwealth (KFTC), 156, 308; and community organizing and development, 275; and networks of ideas, 254, 257, 275; and networks of resources, 286. See also Kentucky Fair Tax Coalition

Kentucky Education Reform Act
(KERA), 180, 235
Kentucky Fair Tax Coalition (KFTC),
139, 236, 279; and issue selection, 227;
and leadership development, 285
Kentucky Small Farms Project, 73, 202,
304; achievements of, 280; and community organizing and development,
276; disappointments of, 282; and
funding issues, 268; and leadership
development, 284; and management,
241; and members, 220, 230; and networks of ideas, 257, 258; and organizational development, 246; role in devolution, 186–89
Kephart, Horace, 10
King, Charlie, 17
Kuhre, Carol, 122–25

Labor force participation, 25–33; and
women, 29–30
Lad, Kathryn, 135, 136–37
Leadership, 5, 81, 83, 89, 93, 95, 99,
118, 188, 198, 206; and community,
211; and community-based mediating
structures, 237, 242, 247–48, 250, 252,
253, 280, 300; development of, 223,
224, 230, 279, 283–86; lessons from,
288–91; and organizational develop-
ment, 246–53; origins of, 107, 109,
160, 291, 300; roles, 96, 106, 202; and
social capital, 286. See also Burns,
James MacGregor; Gardner, Howard
League of Women Voters, 110
Leibig, Anne, 77–78, 241
Levy, Dianne, 189–93, 241
Lewis, John L., 67, 148
Liberty, 38, 40, 41, 42, 46, 65; American
sense of "negative liberty," 66
Liden, David, 139
Lilly, Leslie, 199–200, 202
Lilly, Madge, 90, 131
Lincoln County, W.Va., 168
Lobbying, 108, 162, 168–71, 191, 284
Lollis, David, 164–67
Louisiana Pacific, 75, 80, 83
Loury, Glenn, 60, 62, 65, 174
Luxembourg Income Study, 27

McDaniel, Lee, 86, 87, 90, 91, 242
McDowell, Peter, 156
McDowell County, W.Va., 107, 150, 213
MacIntyre, Alasdair, 309
Management Assistance Group: and
stages of organizational development,
246–53
Market capitalism, 3, 18, 33, 61–62, 129,
147; and community, 20–21, 22–25,
36, 39–40, 67; and community-based
mediating structures, 291–94, 299; and
economic inquiry, 54; and families,
29–32, 39–40; and moral resources,
55–56; and public policy, 147–48;
rehumanizing, 195–97; shortcomings
of, 2, 4, 17, 23, 53, 56–58, 62, 72, 171,
292; and unadaptive capitalism, 33–36.
See also Bourdieu, Pierre; Heilbroner,
Robert; Nisbet, Robert; Savage capitalism; Unadaptive capitalism
Market democracy, 5, 7, 13, 18, 25, 28,
33–34, 53, 58, 62, 64, 71, 75, 174, 199,
207, 283; as unadaptive capitalism, 35,
56, 58–59, 301; and welfare policies,
177
Market failures, 147–48, 171, 174; and
education, 167; and health care, 153.
See also Environment
Marketing Appalachian Traditional Community Handcrafts (MATCH), 73,
202; achievements of, 280; and coalitions, 260, 261, 263; and community,
210; and community organizing and
development, 274; and continuity, 236;
disappointments of, 282; and issue
selection, 227; and leadership development, 285; lessons from, 290, 292; and
management, 244; and members, 217–
18, 232; and organizational development, 251; role in transforming market values, 193–98; vision of community, 224. See also Churches: role in
community development
Martin, Judy, 181, 186
Massey Coal Group, 22
Maternal Infant and Health Outreach
Worker (MIHOW) program, 78, 256
Mediating structures, 2, 3, 36, and com-

munity, 208; and the democratic promise, 65–67, 110; and the democratic
prospect, 4–5, 38, 65–67, 72, 113, 173–
74, 199, 239, 270; and democratic theory, 8, 37, 38–51, 64–69, 71–72, 205;
and the democratic wish, 65–67, 68;
and economic roles, 52–53, 59, 62, 73,
173, 299; fully democratic role of,
67–69, 173, 298–301; liberal and conservative consensus on, 43–44, 64,
187; and liberation and self-actualization, 96; and management issues,
239–46, 269–70; and moral resources,
53–56, 67, 203; and political dimensions, 46–51, 73, 92, 96, 110, 113–14,
142, 299; and public policy, 3–5, 7, 8,
34, 41, 43–46, 53, 63, 64, 106–10, 177,
202–3; and role in mitigating market
failures, 8, 39, 44, 53, 56–59, 67, 73,
129, 171, 173; and social capital, 46,
51–53, 60, 62–64, 68, 71, 73, 101–5,
202–3, 298; and social dimensions, 39,
42, 72, 75, 110, 299; and social movements, 41, 42–43, 44, 47, 49, 64, 65;
and social science, 38, 40, 43, 46, 75,
80, 173–74, 205, 297–98. *See also*
Community-based mediating structures; Intermediate associations; Voluntary associations
Mediating Structures Project, 43
Meehan, Maggie, 109
Members of mediating structures: development of, 101; participation of, 108
Methodology, 307–12; and interview
protocol, 310–12
Metzenbaum, Howard, 122
Michel, Robert, 246
Midwest Academy, 255, 287
Miller, Arnold, 149
Miners for Democracy, 309
Missions of groups, 95, 98, 101, 103, 106,
137–38, 142–45, 163, 186–87, 270.
See also Community-based mediating
structures: vision of community
Mondragon, Spain, 102, 103
Moral resources, 52, 54–56, 59, 67, 68,
72, 193–94, 219; and coalitions, 262;
and community organizing and devel-

opment, 272–77; and representation
and participation, 207; and social capi-
tal, 53–56, 64, 68, 76, 291–92; and
sweat equity, 241–43, 291; as transcen-
dent communal bonds, 113–14. *See
also* Social capital
Morone, James,, 8, 65–67, 297
Morrell, Greg, 98–102, 132
Mountain Life and Work, 126
Mountain Scouts Cancer Screening pro-
gram, 181
Mount Sterling, Ky., 166, 226
Murray, Charles, 34
Myrdal, Alva, 177
Myrdal, Gunnar, 295–98

Narratives, 284, 309–10
National Council of Senior Citizens, 108
National Education Association (NEA),
167
National Endowment for the Arts, 143,
268
National Health Care Campaign, 108
Native Americans, 95
Nature Conservancy, 83
Nehemiah Project, 226
Neighborhood associations, 49
Neighborhoods, 61. *See also* Communities of proximity
Networks, 162, 190; horizontal networks,
76–84, 114, 144, 242, 258, 259, 277,
286–87, 288–90, 291; vertical net-
works, 258, 277, 286–87, 288–90. *See
also* Communities of experience; Communities of proximity
Networks of ideas, 258–59. *See also
names of specific groups* (e.g., Appalachian Alliance: and networks of ideas)
Networks of resources, 258–59. *See also
names of specific groups* (e.g., Appalachian Alliance: and networks of
resources)
Neuhaus, Richard J., 43, 53, 63, 187
New Deal, 44. *See also* Mediating structures: and public policy
Newman, Katherine S., 20
Nisbet, Robert, 38, 42, 43, 46, 52, 53,
56, 60, 62, 63, 64, 87; and the roles of

intermediate associations, 38–40, 52, 75, 84, 173; and social capital, 291
Nolichuckey River, Tenn., 114
Nonprofit sector, 3, 60. *See also* Mediating structures; Voluntary associations
Nuclear power, 140

O'Connor, James, xiv
Ohio Public Interest Campaign, 122
Ohio University, 121, 124–25
Ohio Valley Environmental Council (OVEC), 73, 304; achievements of, 278; and coalitions, 261; and community organizing and development, 272, 274; disappointments of, 281; and funding issues, 267; and issue selection, 228–29; and leadership development, 284; lessons from, 293; and members, 220, 230, 233; and networks of ideas, 254, 257; and networks of resources, 286; and organizational development, 249; role in dealing with externalities, 153–57; vision of community, 222
Older Americans Act, 106, 110
Opportunity costs, 242, 243, 262, 266
Organizational development, stages of, 246–53

Participatory democracy, 48–50, 114
Participatory research, 202
Partnership for Democracy, 156
Pauley v. Bailey, 168
Paxton, Tom, 21
Peace Development Fund, 287
Philanthropic foundations, 5, 138, 165, 202; and community-based mediating structures, 214, 270, 300; and distribution of resources, 59–60, 163, 198, 200–201, 299; list of supporting, 263–64; and networks of ideas, 256. *See also* Wolpert, Julian
Phillips, Kevin, 19
Pigeon River, N.C., 126, 127
Pittston Coal Company, 22–23, 142; strike against, 142, 210
Piven, Frances Fox, 47
Poage, Ben, 193–94, 196–98, 226

Poage, Nina, 193–94, 195–98
Points of Light Foundation, 182
Porterfield, Donna, 144–45
Postindustrial economics, 8, 9–10, 15–18, 43, 148, 197; and conflict of profits and employment, 16, 21–22; and increased economic inequality, 19–21
Poverty, 12, 27, 253, 296; interpretations of, 12–14, 296–97; and social capital, 97, 228. *See also* Economic inequality
Price, David, 45–46
Progressive Policy Institute, 44
Project READ, 78–79
Public goods, 54, 56, 57–60, 71, 114, 219; and democratic promise and prospect, 167; local public goods, 174; and social capital, 291–92
Public policy, 147–48. *See also* Community-based mediating structures: and government; Mediating structures: and public policy; Social capital: and public policy
Public Welfare Foundation, 155
Putnam, Robert, xiv, 4–5, 51, 66, 68, 84, 194, 242–43; on social capital, 51–52, 55, 56, 59, 76, 291, 297, 299

Race relations, 100, 212–14, 290, 295–98
Racism, 96, 200, 212–14 , 289
Reagan administration, 3, 8, 22, 58–59, 121, 140, 198, 201, 265, 298; and black lung policies, 159–60; and innovative leadership, 309–10; and social capital supply, 227, 283, 301
Recht, Judge Arthur, 168
Redbaiting, 119–20, 234
Reece, Florence, 1–2, 3, 5–6, 7, 9, 18, 39, 67, 120, 297, 301; and political transcendence, 142; vision of community, 222
Reece, Sam, 1
Reich, Robert, 24
Resource Mothers, 181
Roadside Theater, 73, 133; achievements of, 280; and coalitions, 261–63; and community, 210, 215; and community organizing and development, 143–45, 274; and cultural exchanges, 145; dis-

appointments of, 283; and funding issues, 267–68; and issue selection, 226; lessons from, 291, 293; and management, 245; and members, 220, 232; and networks of ideas, 257, 259; and networks of resources, 287; and organizational development, 251; role in political transcendence, 142–46; vision of community, 222–23

Robinson, Nancy, 77, 80, 81, 82, 111, 183, 242

Rogers, Joel, 49

Rogers, Mary Lee, 116, 118

Rostan, June, 95, 138, 140

"Run down" costs, 17

Rural regeneration, 123–24, 218, 227

Rutter, Paul, 136

SafeSpace, 73, 202, 304; achievements of, 278; and coalitions, 261; and community, 208, 215; and community organizing and development, 272, 273, 277; disappointments of, 282; and issue selection, 228; and leadership development, 284, 285; lessons from, 293; and management, 241; and members, 219, 220; and networks of ideas, 255, 256, 258, 259; and networks of resources, 287; and organizational development, 249; role of investment in individuals and group identity, 189–93; vision of community, 221

Salamon, Lester, 64–65, 67, 272, 298

SALT. *See* Southern Appalachian Leadership Training

Savage capitalism, 2, 71, 278. *See also* Market democracy; Unadaptive capitalism

Save Our Cumberland Mountains (SOCM), 92, 308

Save the Children Federation, 179, 182, 185, 230, 265

Schlozman, Kay Lehman, 47

Schumacher, E. F., 17, 197

Scott County, Va., 76, 85

Seitz, Jeannette, 97–99, 101–2, 132

Senior citizens, 106, 108

Serrin, William, 24

Sessions, Jim, 142, 162

Shearer, Rees, 91, 221

Sierra Club Legal Defense Fund, 257

Sills, David, 40, 42, 46, 64, 92, 95

Sizemore, Judy, 180–81

Smith, Adam, 7, 18, 25, 27, 33, 35, 39, 56, 57, 62, 153, 157

Smith, David Horton, 42, 47, 49, 96, 102, 106

Social capital, xiii–xv, 3, 5, 35, 37, 42, 51, 84, 291–94; and Appalachian migrants, 144; and class structure, 60–61, 199, 202; and coalitions, 259–63; and community, 105, 148, 173, 203, 212; and community organizing and development, 272; culture as, 142; defined, xiv, xv, 52, 61, 301; and the democratic prospect, 75, 199; and discursive democracy, 121–29; and forms of capital, 61, 199, 280; health care as, 148–53; and horizontal networks, 76–84, 114, 144, 242, 258, 259, 277, 286–87, 288, 291; housing as, 163–67, 174–77; and inequality, 60–62, 174; injury prevention as, 157–63; and labor force, 23–33, 126, 148; liberation and self-actualization, 96–102; market mitigation as, 56–59; material base of, 52, 59, 68, 72, 111, 291; and moral resources, 53–56, 64, 68, 76, 291–92; networks, 162, 190, 193–94, 200, 202, 228; and philanthropic sources, 264; and physical space, 220; and postindustrial economics, 9, 17, 22–23, 35; and public policy, 8, 9–10, 27, 33, 35, 106–10; social risk capital as, 102–5; and social science, 4–5, 60, 297–98; supply of, 199, 219; support and trust as, 84–92; and sweat equity, 241–43; training of opposition leaders as, 92–96; and value of groups and individuals, 189–93, 300; and vertical networks, 258, 277, 286–87, 288. *See also* Bourdieu, Pierre; Community-based mediating structures; Devolution of social services; Loury, Glenn; Mediating structures

Social capital entrepreneurs, xiv, 52, 72, 111, 219, 259, 264, 292, 300; and com-

munity organizing and development, 272, 275–76. *See also* Sweat equity
Social movements, 96, 97, 116, 284
Social science and social analysis, 296; and narrative, 309–10; and social capital, 4–5, 60, 297–98; supply of, 199, 219
Southeast Women's Employment Coalition (SWEC), 73–74; achievements of, 280; and coalitions, 260; and community, 210, 212, 214, 215; and community organizing and development, 274; disappointments of, 283; and funding issues, 268–69; and issue selection, 226, 230; and leadership development, 285; lessons from, 290, 292; and management, 242, 243, 244, 245; and members, 220–21; and networks of ideas, 255; role of increasing social capital, 199–202, 303; vision of community, 224
Southern Appalachian Leadership Training (SALT), 117, 159, 199, 217, 254
Southern Empowerment Project (SEP), 72, 138, 156, 305; achievements of, 280; and coalitions, 260–61; and community, 210, 214; and community organizing and development, 274, 275; disappointments of, 281; as intermediary, 269; and leadership development, 285; lessons from, 290, 292; and members, 218, 230, 231; and networks of ideas, 254, 255, 258; and networks of resources, 287; and planning, 95; and stages of organizational development, 248; role in training opposition leaders, 92–96; vision of community, 224
Sowell, Thomas, 12
Staff and staff issues, 92, 95, 100, 231, 233, 235, 236; and inclusiveness, 290; and management, 240–41, 242, 243–45; and networks of ideas, 258; and stages of organizational development, 246–48; and sweat equity, 241
Steel industry, 16, 17, 24
Story, Gail, 118–20, 133, 234
Story, Hobert J., 115
Stoughton, Pat and Bill, 188

Strong democracy, 48, 114, 120
Subsidiarity, 187. *See also* Devolution of social services; Kentucky Small Farms Project
Sweat equity, 198, 230–31, 241–43, 262, 270, 282; and psychic guarantor, 241
Szakos, Joe, 156

Talbot, Keith and Lori, 222
TEACH (Tennesseans Against Chemical Hazards), 117, 217, 261
Tennessee Environmental Council, 261
Tennessee Task Force Against Domestic Violence, 191, 255, 258, 259, 261, 262; and leadership development, 285; and networks of resources, 287
Tennessee Valley Authority (TVA), 79, 140
Tennessee Valley Energy Coalition (T-VEC), 95
"Third Sector," 41, 45
Tocqueville, Alexis de, 7, 37, 40, 52, 64, 66, 295, 298
Toffler, Alvin, 197
Town Creek Foundation, 155
Toxic waste, 126, 222, 225, 227, 229. *See also* Bumpass Cove, Tenn.; Environment
Transcendence, political, 142, 146, 255
Transformative politics, 50–51, 137–42, 146, 272, 279, 284, 288–89; and personal transformation, 272
Tri-State Environmental Council, 308
Turner, Carolene, 181

Unadaptive capitalism, 33–36, 64, 67, 71, 298
United Mine Workers of America (UMWA), 1, 2, 16, 67, 107, 276, 308–9; and health care, 148, 149
United States Environmental Protection Agency (EPA), 154
United States Forest Service, 126–27, 228, 282, 293
United States Housing and Urban Development (HUD), 174
Urban Appalachian Council, 144
U.S. Steel, 17, 21

Utilities: protest of rates and services, 122. *See also* Community-based mediating structures: and government

Vanderbilt Center for Health Services, 217, 234
Vautrin, Teri, 82
Verba, Sidney, 47
Violence, 193, 253. *See also* Domestic violence
Virginia Black Lung Association (VBLA), 73, 304; achievements of, 278, 279; and coalitions, 262; and community, 209, 213; and community organizing and development, 276; disappointments of, 282; and funding issues, 268; lessons from, 289, 291, 293; and members, 216, 231–32; and networks of ideas, 255, 257, 259; and organizational development, 249; role in protecting some from injury by others, 157–63
Virginia Department of Rehabilitative Services, 256
Virginia Polytechnic Institute and State University, 86
Virginia Water Project, 80
VISTA, 79, 176, 187, 213, 226, 249, 257
Voluntary associations, 3, 7, 37, 40, 42, 45, 46–47, 52, 65–66, 96, 102, 106, 298. *See also* Mediating structures
Voluntary sector. *See* Voluntary associations
Volunteers, 192, 240, 281

Walls, Linda, 115, 117, 119, 120, 133, 234
W. Alton Jones Foundation, 155
War on Poverty, 142. *See also* Great Society policies and programs
Washington County, Tenn., 115
Washington County, Va., 84; Board of Supervisors, 86, 89, 90
Water quality and supply, 77. *See also* Environment
Webb, Gale, 86, 87
Weiss, Chris, 244
Welfare: stages of, 177. *See also* Appalachian Communities for Children

Wellstone, Paul, 308
Western North Carolina Alliance, 73, 121, 139, 279, 304; achievements of, 278; and coalitions, 261; and community, 211, 215–16; and community organizing and development, 272, 275; disappointments of, 282; and funding issues, 265; and issue selection, 226, 228; and leadership development, 283, 285; lessons from, 289, 293; and members, 218–19, 230; and networks of ideas, 255, 258; and organizational development, 252; role in discursive democracy and dialogical communities, 126–29
West Virginia Association of Community Health Centers, 150–51, 234, 250. *See also* West Virginia Primary Care Association
West Virginia Commission on Aging, 106, 107, 109–10, 236
West Virginia Education Association, 73, 184, 303; achievements of, 278, 279; and coalitions, 262; and community, 209, 212, 213, 214; and community organizing and development, 272, 276; disappointments of, 281; and funding issues, 268; and issue selection, 230; and leadership development, 283; lessons from, 289, 292, 299; and management, 245; and members, 217, 231; and networks of ideas, 254, 256; and networks of resources, 287; and organizational development, 251, 253; role in increasing the supply of social capital, 167–71; vision of community, 222
West Virginia Primary Care Association, 73, 305; achievements of, 279; and coalitions, 261, 262; and community, 209, 210, 213; and community organizing and development, 275; and continuity, 234; disappointments of, 281; and funding issues, 266, 268; and issue selection, 228; and leadership development, 285; lessons from, 290, 292; and management, 243; and members, 216; and networks of ideas, 255, 256, 257; and networks of resources, 287; and

organizational development, 250; role in countering market forces, 148–53; vision of community, 224

West Virginia Primary Care Study Group, 150–51, 234, 250

West Virginia teachers' strike, 140, 167–71, 251, 279

"Which Side Are You On?" 1–2, 3, 6, 295, 301

Whitesburg, Ky., 142

Wierton Steel, 308

Wilson, Roxy, 133

Winkler, Peg, 135

Wise, Mike, 86, 88

Wolpert, Julian, 59, 62, 65, 163

Women and employment, 199

Woods, Cricket, 89

Work: nature and amount of, 22–23, 25, 62, 102, 148, 174; and development efforts, 79, 136; and social capital, 25–36, 126; and women, 199–202

Worker Owned Network (WON), 102

Yellow Creek Concerned Citizens, 289, 291

Youth Project, 117

Z. Smith Reynolds Foundation, 265

www.ingramcontent.com/pod-product-compliance
Lightning Source LLC
Chambersburg PA
CBHW022300280326
41932CB00010B/924